Women's Fastpitch Softball —

THE PATH TO THE GOLD

An Historical Look at Women's Fastpitch in the United States

Written by
Mary L. Littlewood

First Editon

Published by the National Fastpitch Coaches Association

Columbia, Missouri

NATIONAL FASTPITCH
COACHES ASSOCIATION
409 Vandiver Drive, Suite 5-202
Columbia, MO 65202
573/875-3033
573/875-2924 (fax)
http://www.nfca.org

Printed in the United States of America.

Designed and edited by Lacy Lee Baker.

98 99 00 01 02   10 9 8 7 6 5 4 3 2 1

Library of Congress Catalog Card Number: 98-66286

ISBN: 0-9664310-0-6

DEDICATION

To my family —

Mom and Dad – Louise E. and Thomas N. Littlewood –
　　They had 6th grade educations and raised
　　four children who became college graduates
Brother Thomas B. Littlewood –
　　The organizer in the family – a successful
　　journalist, educator and author.
Sister Ellen J. Littlewood Frahm –
　　Being idle is not something she understands.
　　After receiving a degree in nursing and
　　working in that capacity for several years,
　　she returned to college and earned a degree
　　in education.
Brother Robert C. Littlewood –
　　The "baby of the family" – a "kick back never
　　get stressed" kind of guy who successfully
　　pursued a career in the insurance business.

MY FAMILY AND I'M PROUD OF THEM!

TABLE OF CONTENTS

Appendices

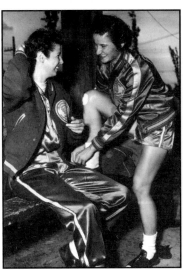

PREFACE

During my years as an assistant professor in physical education and later the head softball coach at Arizona State University, I observed many major changes not only in the acceptance and support of women's athletics, but also in the attitudes of young female athletes. As female athletes were given more opportunities in terms of scholarships, team budgets, full-time coaches, facilities, etc., they *expected* more. As a day passes and becomes part of history, there are fewer and fewer Americans, in particular those on the distaff side, who can remember there ever being a pre-Title IX era. Those opportunities afforded by the passing of Title IX in 1972 to young athletically talented girls growing up in the U.S. are now taken for granted just as the inclusion of women's fastpitch softball in the Olympics will one day be taken for granted.

For four decades prior to the passing of Title IX, strong-willed, highly skilled young women donned their uniforms and trotted out on softball diamonds all over the United States. They loved to play the game of fastpitch and they were *never* content to finish second. Time after time, teams displayed the competitive spirit, keen desire to win and sense of loyalty that were also indicative of the gold medal-winning USA Olympic team in 1996.

The pioneers of the game — the women who drove thousands of miles on two-lane highways to compete in the first world championships in the 1930's to play possibly only one game, and during World War II were paid to razzle-dazzle the crowds who came to see games in the National Girls Baseball League, and in the 1950's and '60's competed with and against some of the greatest players to ever step onto a softball field — have a story to tell. This book was written to tell that story. The hope is that the reader, after finishing the last page, feels an empathy for the players and better understands the events and happenings that were landmarks along the path to the Olympic gold medal.

First and foremost, thanks must go to the National Fastpitch Coaches Association and to their Executive Director, Lacy Lee Baker. Without Lacy Lee's belief in me and my ability to write such a book, and without the NFCA's financial backing, this book would not have been possible.

Crucial to my research for the book was the cooperation of Bill Plummer, the National Softball Hall of Fame Services Manager for the Amateur Softball Association. Bill guided my visit to the ASA archives in Oklahoma City, and he has contributed numerous photos, rule books and other information that have greatly enhanced the quality of the book. Without Bill's assistance and the cooperation of the ASA, it would not have been possible for the book to be complete or accurate.

Special thanks go to Art Cashion, historian for the International Softball Congress; Connie Claussen, University of Nebraska, Omaha; Alice Kolski, former player in the National Girls Baseball League; the National Fastpitch Coaches Association, and the NCAA, NAIA and NJCAA offices for providing the facts for the appendices; and Emily Alexander, ASA umpire, for her assistance with the rules chapter.

Since my intent was for the emphasis of the book to be on the women themselves rather than lists of dates and facts, it was important that I meet and talk with as many of the pioneer players as possible. I personally interviewed approximately 50 former players, most of whom are Hall of Famers and/or All-Americans in the ASA or the National Softball Congress, in their homes, at tournaments and at team and league reunions. In addition, I interviewed over the phone in excess of 60 former players and corresponded with many more. I was constantly amazed by the strength of character of these women, and was overwhelmed by their strong devotion to the game and their unquestioning willingness to share not only memories, but in some cases, priceless, irreplaceable memorabilia. I thank, in particular, Dot Wilkinson and Ricki Caito for the photos, articles and rule books they provided to me and for their cordial hospitality during my numerous visits.

Last but certainly not least, my heartfelt appreciation goes to Joanie Arvin for drawing the illustrations; to my brother Thomas B. Littlewood, for all of his suggestions, and to Sandra Stultz for her hours of typing and critiquing.

FOREWARD

By Bill Plummer III
National Softball Hall of Fame Services Manager
Oklahoma City, Oklahoma

One of the teams that captivated the media and the spectators at the 1996 Olympic Games was the gold medal-winning U.S. softball team. Many people had anticipated that Olympic softball would be worth waiting for and it was. The event was clearly one of the most outstanding Olympic debuts of all time.

Athletes, such as Dot Richardson, Sheila Cornell, Lisa Fernandez, Michele Granger and Michele Smith, who before had lived in the shadows were finally cast into the sunlight at Golden Park in Columbus for a glorious 10 days of competition. For years, these athletes practiced, worked and played fastpitch with untold zeal and passion, not unlike some of the outstanding athletes who are mentioned in this book. There was, however, a big difference. Olympic softball hadn't become a reality and was only a dream when Marie Wadlow, Bertha Tickey, Kay Rich, Joan Joyce, Freda Savona, Carol Spanks, Shirley Topley, Dot Wilkinson and too many others to mention played softball. These athletes had only a hope and a desire that someday softball would get its day in the sun and the long overdue recognition it had deserved for many, many years.

While Richardson and others are enjoying the fame associated with winning the gold medal, Bertha Tickey and others who helped pave the way for today's athletes are getting their just due in this book. Without these athletes and the efforts of the Amateur Softball Association, women's softball would have remained in the school yards and playgrounds and not achieved the popularity and status it enjoys today.

And if it wasn't for Mary Littlewood, a genuine devotee of fastpitch, the women's fastpitch story would have remained only a memory and locked in time forever. Through Mary's efforts, today's athletes and those of the future can read about the great athletes of the past who were the standard bearers for women's fastpitch softball.

Olympic softball was long overdue. So was this book. Now that both have been achieved, readers can feel the same frustration, disappointment, joy, sorrow and happiness experienced by the flag-bearers along the path to the 1996 Olympic Games. Women fastpitch players of the future certainly owe a debt of gratitude to those athletes of the past who believed in their sport with boundless passion. To them, and to Mary Littlewood, I say "thank you." You believed in your sport just as much as Mary believed in writing this book.

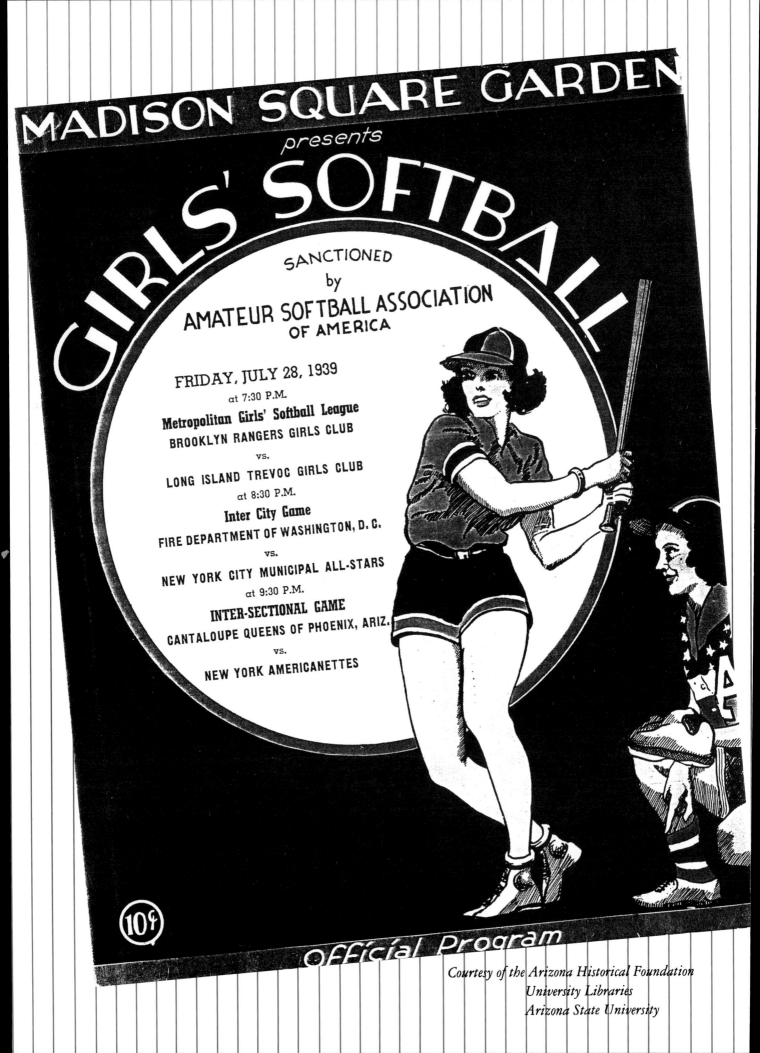

Women's fastpitch softball in the 1996 Olympics! Over a century after the suspected beginnings of softball in this country in 1887, the United States women's softball team won the gold medal in the 1996 Olympics. The path to that gold medal — a long, winding one with abrupt u-turns — was cleared and trampled down by the cleats of thousands of girls and women who played the game in the 1930's, 40's, 50's and 60's. Under the auspices of the Amateur Softball Association, National Softball Congress and the National Girls Baseball League (even though they played softball, baseball was used in the name of the league), Dots, Berthas, Dodies and Willies threw, hit, slid and ran, night after night, on softball diamonds all over the country. Their reasons for playing were simple — they played because they loved to play the game! A team's roster might include 13-year-olds or 40-year-olds, assembly workers making parts for war planes or school teachers, all with the common ability to throw and catch a ball with one fluid motion. They were strong, hard-working independent women — some married with children and some single — who were fiercely loyal to family, country and softball!

Clearing the Path — From 1887 to 1930's

1

These pioneers of women's fastpitch softball evolved from a generation of Americans who looked upon the female as the fairer and weaker sex whose main goal in life was to become engaged, marry and rear a family. Women were seen as dainty, delicate creatures who had no business working up a sweat on a playing field.

Before the Civil War, nice women exercised very infrequently; they wore skirts when they ran and to be utterly proper, they didn't run at all. Sometimes a few bold spirits would go ice-skating, although a contemporary book of etiquette urged them to hang onto the coat tails of their male partners, thus enjoying all the pleasure without incurring any of the fatigue of the exercise. (19:14)

The conflict between the fact that a woman was strong enough physically to bear children but could not safely run even short distances didn't seem to be obvious to anyone. Typical of the belief at that time was expressed in this article in the *New York Times*:

Every girl, it seems, has a large store of vital and nervous energy upon which to draw in the great crisis of motherhood. If the foolish virgin uses up this deposit in daily expenditures on the hockey field or tennis court, then she is left bankrupt in her great crisis and her children have to pay the bill. (11:124)

This negative attitude toward women participating in strenuous athletic activity was reinforced by Baron Pierre de Coubertin, the

4 THE PATH TO THE GOLD

founder of the modern Olympics, who wrote:

> *All 245 athletes from 14 nations who competed in the first Olympics in Athens in 1896 were men. Women were expected to lend their applause, not their athletic skills. Distance running by women was thought to be un-ladylike, a violation of natural law. The common wisdom held that a woman was not physiologically capable of running mile after mile; that she wouldn't be able to bear children; that her uterus would fall out; that she would grow a mustache; that she was a man, or wanted to be one."(22:46)*

In 1887, the year that it is suspected that softball got its start, President Grover Cleveland ruled over a nation that was seeing an increase in its wealth caused by trade, manufacturing, transportation and technology. The growing middle class enjoyed the good things of life to an increasing extent, living in homes crowded with weighty furniture, thick draperies and innumerable knickknacks. Just five years after the first electric generating system opened in New York City and one year before the first home camera was marketed by Kodak, the age of technology was just beginning to emerge. It was into this world — at the Farragut Boat Club in Chicago — that the game of softball was introduced. George W. Hancock, a reporter for the Chicago Board of Trade, and some of his friends were at the Farragut Boat Club waiting to hear the results of the Yale-Harvard football game.

> *But the real game was just about to begin. It might have been Tom Jenkins, a dry goods merchant; Lyman Glover, a theater manager; or Edwin Anderson, a superintendent of the Boat Club — someone got out a boxing glove, used the laces to tie it into a mushy sort of cannonball, and began tossing it around the room. Someone else picked up a broom handle and said, "Here, pitch me one." (3:5)*

The first game of indoor baseball was played. Since the base and pitching distances were shorter and the ball larger than in regulation baseball, it would seem that this was the game that eventually emerged as softball.

While it is agreed that Chicago is where the game was born, softball experienced an important part of its infancy in Minneapolis. In 1895, Lewis Rober, Sr., a lieutenant with Minneapolis' Fire Company No. 11, needed a game that would keep his men in shape and occupy their time when they weren't fighting fires. It is not clear as to whether Rober knew of the game that had been played at the Farragut Boat Club in Chicago. Chances are he didn't. He came up with the idea to adapt the game of baseball so that it could be played on the vacant lot adjacent to the firehouse. He cut the base distances in half, set the pitching distance at 35 feet and had a woodworker turn out a pile of bats two inches in diameter. The game immediately became popular among the firefighters and eventually spread throughout the Minneapolis-St. Paul area.

The name of kitten ball was given to the game in 1900 — named after Rober's first team, the Kittens. Kitten ball leagues were formed under the jurisdiction of the Minneapolis Park Board and were popular among men and women of all ages. In 1922, the park authorities changed the name of the game to diamond ball. By then, there were 64 men's teams and 25 women's teams in organized league competition.

Diamond ball remained popular in the Minneapolis area well into the 1930's. Around 1936, diamond ball merged with the newly organized game of softball. Since the game that originated at the Farragut Boat Club in Chicago was played indoors, Minneapolis laid claim to being the location where the game was created for the outdoors.

Called many things — playground ball, kitten ball and diamond ball were just a few of those first names — rules for the game varied.

As the age of technology progressed from the baby crib to the early stages of infancy, the interests of the average American family were expanding. The invention of the telephone allowed people to communicate beyond shouting distance, and the continuous improvement of the automobile contributed towards a more mobile society.

> *In 1900 there were only 8,000 autos registered in the entire country and only about 10 miles of paved roads for travel. Only 4,000 autos were produced in 1900, but 10 years later, 187,000 rolled out of the factories. (2:581)*

As the outside world entered more and more households, women were becoming interested in more vigorous pursuits and feeling the need for play. Hampering this quest was the traditional female garb of the times of long dresses and tight-fitting corsets. The creation of bloomers saved the day! A woman

Rules from Playground Ball Rulebook (1908)

1. The first batter to get on in an inning could run to either first or third base. All following batters in that inning had to run in the same direction.

2. A legal game consisted of five, seven or nine innings — at the option of the contesting teams.

3. They could play by points instead of runs, if desired. A point was scored by each and every base reached by a runner.

4. The bases were 35 feet apart, and the pitcher's box 30 feet from the homeplate. The ball could be anywhere from 12 to 14 inches in circumference. The bat was restricted to a 2-inch diameter.

5. Only three unfairly delivered balls were required for a base on balls. A baserunner couldn't leave his base until the ball crossed the homeplate. (1:30)

in bloomers and a loose-fitting blouse could now take a bike ride in relative comfort without fear of her skirts becoming entangled in the spokes of the wheels.

Even though women's participation in team sports en masse was still frowned upon, women's baseball teams sprang up all over the country. Many of these teams barnstormed throughout the country taking on any men's team that was willing to accept the challenge. *The Denver Post* on June 25, 1950, told of a women's baseball team as early as 1893 that traveled by railroad from Denver to Chicago playing "any and every men's team." L. C. Overholt was manager, coach and umpire on the trip that ended at the Chicago's World Fair. In *A Brief History of American Sports*, the authors mention other legitimate teams — the Chicago Stars of 1902, and the St. Louis Stars and the Boston Bloomer Girls of 1903 — that traveled and played male clubs. (8:199) A few cities, like St. Louis, had indoor baseball leagues for women.

Most girls who were born with a natural ability to throw and catch "like a boy," probably started their playing careers much like Marie Wadlow did.

The article to the right appeared in a St. Louis newspaper in 1932, telling of indoor baseball as played by 15-year-old Marie Wadlow, who would, in later years, become the first woman to be inducted into the ASA Hall of Fame.

Marie Wadlow Tells of Her Softball Beginnings

My softball career began on the sandlots of St. Louis at an age when other girls were still playing with dolls. Wherever a group of boys could come up with a bat and a softball (gloves were only for the rich kids), a game would quickly get started and I managed to "adopt" myself to one of the teams, at first only to "pigtail" in the outfield. Later, when I crashed the magic circle of the infield, I

thought I was really in the big time! Of course, it helped a lot that some of the times, my big brother had given me the price to buy a softball, which sometimes turned out to be the only one in the neighborhood and I was then the "Queen Bee" for the day.

Still later, at the age of 12, I started playing second base for a team in a church league (night softball and the ASA were undreamed of then). I hurt my wrist and couldn't field ground balls properly, but I could hit, so the manager made a pitcher out of me. — Marie Wadlow (24: 5)

St. Louis Globe-Democrat
The Magazine

PEOPLE

FICTION

Copyright, 1932, by The Globe-Democrat Publishing Co.   SUNDAY, AUGUST 14, 1932

These Girls Play Baseball Like Big Leaguers

Half of Them Would Be in the Majors If They Were Boys, Says the Coach of This Little Constellation of Feminine Diamond Enthusiasts Who Have Established an Enviable Record in Three Years of Play Under the Colors of the Peters Memorial Presbyterian Church.

At Cleveland High School she was voted the best all-around girl athlete last year. Her regular position is catcher, but she plays any place. Behind the bat she is a proficient backstop who can catch "Waddy's" inshoots and her throws to second are straight to the mark. At bat she, too, steps in like a veteran, takes a healthy cut and gets a lot of mileage out of her drives.

Girls Nickname First Baseman "Hack"

One might continue. Mention should be made of Mabel Haus-

Catcher Hemmann, a star athlete at Cleveland High School, is prepared to take a healthy cut at the ball. Note the stance. Nothing feminine about that.
—Globe-Democrat Staff Photograph.

Members of the Peters Memorial Presbyterian Church baseball team (left to right): Mabel Hausmann, Marge King, June Kunkel, Nellie Walsh, Willard Hemmann, Dorothy Petersen, Harriet Laubach, Dorothy Koerner, Marie Wadlow, Edith Tidrow and Lillian Dove.
—Globe-Democrat Staff Photograph.

"Waddy" Wadlow, one of the stars of the baseball team, makes a clean steal of home and is called safe by Coach Robert Arhelger.
—Globe-Democrat Staff Photograph.

By LOUIS LA COSS,
Globe-Democrat Staff Writer.

THE score book shows that during a season's play now drawing to a close, "Waddy" Wadlow has a batting average of .552 and as a pitcher has the rather astounding record of no games lost during which time seventy-four opposing batsmen have been struck out.

In view of which it would seem that some enterprising baseball scout should be getting "Waddy's" name on the dotted line. But this will never happen because this diamond phenom is a girl. Her name is Marie, she is 15 years old and the unfortunate circumstance is that she is of the sex that doesn't break into professional baseball.

"Waddy" is the scintillating star, however, in a little constellation of girl baseball enthusiasts who are just now concluding their third successful and successive season as exemplars of the national sport. They play under the colors of the Peters Memorial Presbyterian Church, and if you have a

desire to see them go through the motions of playing baseball as girls think it should be played, drop around any Monday or Friday night at one of the diamonds in Tower Grove Park, near Grand boulevard and Arsenal street. They may be identified by their blue uniforms with a nifty "P M" embroidered on the shirt front. And there will always be a crowd watching and cheering them because these girls have built up quite a reputation on the South Side for the brilliant fashion in which they hit and field and throw and run bases.

Nine of Original Players Still With Team

The team was organized three years ago when the Peters Memorial Presbyterian Church wished to enter a club in the South Side Sunday-School League. Nine of the original eleven members are still on the team and so eager have they been to learn the game and so proficient have they become afield

that the sighs of Coach Robert Arhelger may be pardoned.

"If they were only boys," he remarks, "I'd have half of them in the big leagues."

Perhaps this is optimism tinted by pardonable enthusiasm, but an examination of season's play shows that, at the time this story was written, these girls have gone through the season without a defeat which is a feat in any league. See them playing the game, watch them throw the ball with the accuracy of a Gelbert, watch them line base hits to the outfield with the agility of a Sunny Jim—and you will probably agree with the coach that it is a pity they cannot aspire to big time.

Take "Waddy," for instance. She is the youngest member of the team, yet she is a star. She's the regular pitcher and when she toes the rubber the opposition is in for a tough nine innings. Her curve ball has a Derringer hop on it. And she can slow ball the batter like Wee Willie Sherdel of the other day Cards. Her control is well-nigh perfect—one walk a game for

the season's average. And seventy-four strikeouts indicates that when she throws there is something "on" the ball. At bat, so the records show, she is good for a hit better than one out of two times. Her stance has nothing feminine to it. She crowds the plate, steps in as the ball is thrown, takes a healthy cut and the fielders had better be on their toes if they expect to do any catching from her bat.

But "Waddy" is only one of eleven—nine regulars and two substitutes. There is Willard Hemmann.

mann at first. A mite of a girl who wears spectacles afield, she has been dubbed "Hack" by her chums, for reasons they alone know. But she scoops up grounders and nabs high throws at first with the expertness of a Bottomley. "Frisch" at second is none other than Dorothy Petersen, and "Sparky" at third is Nellie Walsh. Edith Tidrow at shortstop completes the infield. The outfielders are Marge King, June Kunkel, Harriet Laubach, Dorothy Koerner

Continued on Page Fifteen

Baseball, whether on the sandlot, on a manicured field or indoors, was an outlet for girls who felt the need to match their skills against others. As games were played, individual players emerged as stars. Just as Marie Wadlow surfaced as a standout in the St. Louis area in the early 1930's, fans in northern Ohio a decade earlier were attracted to the feats of Alta Weiss of Ragersville, Ohio. Alta's pitching talent had brought her countrywide fame by the time she was 14 years old. Her father, a doctor and ballplayer, built a ball park for the town team, and the following year formed the Weiss All-Stars, a traveling semipro team featuring Alta as pitcher. Weiss was so well known in the Cleveland area that some sportswriters suggested — perhaps not entirely seriously, but in vain nevertheless — that she be given a tryout with the major league Indians. (8:200-201) Women's baseball teams continued to exist — as barnstorming teams and in some of the elite colleges — into the mid-1930's.

As the everyday world of families became larger due to technological advances, women sought equality between the sexes. The involvement of the United States in World War I caused more women to work at jobs that were normally performed by men. According to Gorton Carruth in *What Happened When — A Chronology of Life & Events in America*, in 1918, 1,000,000 more women were employed than in 1915. The realization by women that they could not only hold worthwhile jobs, but that they could be self-sufficient, fed the fuel of equal rights. Finally, after a struggle spanning 72 years, the nineteenth amendment to the U. S. Constitution — extending the vote to women — passed in 1919 and was ratified in 1920. The right to vote, though, did not necessarily reflect a true equality between the sexes.

> In 1920, the nineteenth amendment to the "Constitution" finally gave women the vote, but only after a campaign engineered by women suffragists that denied the feminist position staked out by their sisters 72 years earlier. Reflecting their own beliefs and the realities of American politics, they asked for the vote not on the basis of their equality with men but by arguing that women were different; that somehow their frailness, morality, and sentimentality would help civilize the rough male beast of American politics. (11:122-123)

The larger issues of equal rights and the changing role of the woman in American society, were paralleled by the struggle that women experienced to leave the grandstands and step out on the playing field. Morris A. Bealle's belief as stated in his book *The Softball Story*, "that girls do not naturally run, throw or hit like boys," and that "baseball was too much for girls," was not unique. Even though individual women were becoming national celebrities because of their accomplishments — Babe Didrikson in track, baseball and golf; Annie Oakley, the sharpshooter; Helen Wills Moody, the tennis champion known as "Little Miss Poker Face" for her cold precision; the aviator Amelia Earhart — the general consensus was that girls were not capable of playing boys' sports, and the rules of existing games should be investigated with the intent of arriving at appropriate rules adaptations for girls. Mrs. Herbert Hoover's help was sought and obtained in April of 1923. Mrs. Hoover instigated the creation of the Women's Division of the National Amateur Athletic Federation at a conference in Washington D.C. Three years later, in 1926, under the auspices of this organization, Mrs. Gladys Palmer of Ohio State University, compiled a set of baseball rules for women, "recognizing the fact that standard baseball is too strenuous for the weaker sex." (1:165) The principal items in the Palmer Code were smaller bats, shorter bases and pitching distance, and a larger and not-quite-so-hard ball. This is practically the softball structure of today.

After seeing her principles in practical application for six years, Mrs. Palmer wrote (in 1929):

From the educational standpoint, baseball, because of its highly organized nature, has a great deal in its favor as a game for girls and women. It teaches them what the boys have learned from time immemorial in their sandlot games — the ability to think quickly, to co-ordinate thought and action, to exercise good judgement and a certain faculty in divining in advance the thoughts of others. The development in girls and women of loyalty and self-confidence, as well as a sense of responsibility and good sportsmanship are not the least of the advantages of the game. (1:165)

While it was perfectly acceptable for men to play to win, women's motives for play were supposed to be social in nature.

Girls who play on the better teams — those which go to the state and regional tournaments year after year — have found softball the vehicle to make new friends and to renew pleasant acquaintances year after year. They have also found this travel beneficial and exhilarating. (1:166)

Acceptance of females competing in sports was fragile at best. Any negative inci-

Instruction in the early 1920's taught players to "get set for a high fly."

dence was cause to discontinue the competition. The Vassar College baseball team was disbanded after a girl fell and injured her leg, (11:123) and the 800-meter race was discontinued after six women collapsed after that race in the 1928 Amsterdam Olympics. An alarmist account in the *New York Times* said "that even this distance makes too great a call on feminine strength." Until the 1960 Olympics, 32 years later, women would run no race in the Olympics longer than 200 meters. (22)

A woman being injured or exhausted was equated with the activity being too taxing physically for "the weaker sex." The easy solution was to discontinue the activity rather than to investigate the possibility that the women who participated weren't in condition — that they needed to be educated as to proper training techniques prior to competition. Once an activity was discontinued, it

was decades later before it was reconsidered as an appropriate competitive activity for women. The women's marathon did not become a sanctioned Olympic event until 1984 in Los Angeles. Joan Benoit Samuelson, the winner, "did not grow a mustache. Her uterus did not fall out. She later gave birth, not to one child, but to two. She ran through both pregnancies and reeled off six miles the day her son, Anders, was born in 1990." (22:24) Elliott Gorn and Warren Goldstein, in their book published in 1993, made the following comments about the acceptance of women in sports:

> *Yet when they step out of circumscribed roles — cheerleaders at a football game, "bimbos" at a prizefight, household guardians of family values at baseball games — hostility toward women in sports surfaces easily.* (8:207)

Regardless of the degree of this hostility, the fact that authors recognized as late as 1993 a negativism toward women competing in sports is an example of the longevity of

Instruction in the 20's included "starting the swing" (left) and "completion of the underhand throw."

the struggle.

National economic woes in the late 1920's and early 1930's caused the issue of women's rights to be put on the back burner as American families struggled to maintain a lifestyle above poverty level. Almost overnight, the United States was submerged in the Great Depression. The big stock market crash, on October 29, 1929, and referred to as Black Tuesday, saw a record 16,410,030 shares being traded as huge blocks of stock were dumped for whatever they could bring. By December 1st, stocks on the New York Stock Exchange had dropped in value by $26,000,000,000. The national income statistics at that time showed that 60 percent of U. S. citizens had annual incomes of less than $2,000, which was the bare minimum to supply a family with the basic necessities of life. (2:708)

Even though President Herbert Hoover tried desperately to stem the Great Depression by granting generous credit to industry and ordering a stern check on government spending — he even reduced his own personal salary by 20 percent — the country seemed to be in a never-ending tailspin financially. According to Gorton Carruth in *What Happened When — A Chronology of Life & Events in America,* the number of unemployed in the U. S. in 1932 reached 13,000,000. National wages were 60 percent less than in 1929, dividends 56.5 percent less. Two and a half years after the October 1929 stock market crash, U. S. industry as a whole was operating at less than half its maximum 1929 volume.

While the majority of American families were operating on a very tight daily budget, the technological advances that blossomed early in the 20th century had already affected their lives. By 1930, one out of every 4.9 Americans owned an automobile, and speaking on a telephone was an everyday occurrence for most people.

Perishable food was cooled in an ice box — its effectiveness relying on the punctuality of an ice delivery man who roamed the streets on a daily basis. Clothes were washed in a wringer washing machine and hung out on clotheslines to dry. While attending talking motion pictures (first seen in 1929) may have been too expensive for many family budgets, listening to radio programs like "The Great Gildersleeve" and "Fibber McGee and Molly" was inexpensive and entertaining.

Taking Those First Steps Down The Path in the 1930's

Softball boomed! It was a game that could be played by many people for little expense and it was fun! In 1933, the year that Franklin Delano Roosevelt was inaugurated as President of the United States, the first national softball championships were conducted in Chicago as a feature of the Century of Progress exposition. Leo H. Fischer, a sportswriter for the *Chicago American*, and M. J. Pauley, a Chicago sports goods salesman, were asked to conduct that first championship event. Leo Fischer, in his book, *Winning Softball*, related:

> *M. J. Pauley and I were asked to conduct it, because of our success with a local tournament in Chicago in which more than 1,000 teams participated. Teams were brought in from a dozen states — and then the trouble began. Each had its own ideas on how the game should be played. Some used 40-foot baselines. Others had 70-*

foot intervals between the bags. Some permitted base-stealing. Others didn't. Three or four different sizes of balls were in use. There was only one thing to do. We wrote an arbitrary set of rules and turned the teams loose on a diamond built under one of the huge sky-ride towers which dominated the Chicago fair. (6:6)

It was because the newspaper publisher William Randolph Hearst supported the tournament financially that the event was even a possibility. Hearst newspapers spread the word about the tournament to the public, and thousands of people took advantage of the free admission. Seventy thousand spectators saw the first round of play, which included the following women's teams:

• Brazil, Indiana
• Caledonia, Ontario (Canadian women's champs)
• Chicago's Chase Park Girls (Park champs)
• Chicago's Great Northern Laundry (Independent)
• Chicago's Judge Hasten Debutantes
   (River Park champs)
• Chicago's Roby Playground (Girls' PG champs)
• Chicago's St. Bridget's (Church champs)
• Chicago's St. Romans
• Downer's Grove, Illinois
• Erie, Pennsylvania
• Fort Atkinson, Wisconsin
• Racine's Western
   Printeretts
• Rock Island, Illinois
• South Bend's Hoosier
   Beers
• South Bend's Sailorettes

The Chicago Great Northern Laundry team emerged as the victors in the women's championships. (See Appendix A for all ASA Champion-

ship Teams). They soared through the single elimination tournament defeating the Roby Playground team in the quarterfinals, 7-0; the Downer's Grove team in the semifinals, 10-1; and the Chase Park team in the finale, 18-3.

There never was any doubt about the winners' superiority as they outclassed every team they played and won by going-away scores. Ann Gindele, right fielder, holder of the world's record in the javelin, and the basketball and baseball throw records, starred abat and afield for Great Northern. (1:44)

The Depression didn't seem to influence the extent of financial backing of the tournament by William Randolph Hearst. The winner's trophy was solid gold and ebony costing $1,000, and the total cost of the tournament, paid by the *Evening American* newspaper, was $30,000.

While it was thought that this first national tournament was a success, it was also a turning point in the game of softball. It was apparent that a uniform set of rules that could be used throughout the nation was a necessity. On January 21 and 22, 1934, the first national rules committee meeting was held at the Hotel Sherman in Chicago. Nearly 200 delegates attended from 37 states. From this meeting came not only a universal set of

Leo Fischer was elected President without renumeration, and M. J. Pauley was elected executive secretary, a fulltime job paying $2,600 a year. Headquarters were established at the Morrison Hotel in Chicago.

rules for the official game of softball, but also the formation of the Amateur Softball Association. (See Rules Chapter for details on the evolution of the rules.)

William Randolph Hearst continued to promote the tournament through his newspapers and to support it financially through 1938. His total contribution over those years was $50,000 — $7,000 of which went toward the expenses of the 1934 tournament. Games were played on Chicago Park District fields with the chief one being Lincoln Park. Because of the large number of teams entered, the tournament used a single elimination format — or, in Morris Bealle's words, it was "a single knock-out affair." Two hundred thousand spectators took advantage of the free admission to witness the three-day affair from which Hart Motors of Chicago emerged as the women's champion. The first windmill pitchers appeared and, according to one source, "gave the batters much trouble with different styles of wind-ups." (18:41) The fans loved it — everyone was talking about the great game of softball!

When the game of softball was first played, because of "the beanbag type of pitching," it was thought that the batters would have a field day. (1:6) But as the game progressed and advanced, smart pitchers became very creative in devising windups and deliveries that were successful. While the first set of rules did eliminate the possibility of the pitcher using a sidearm or overhand delivery, there was little restriction on the use of fancy windups and trick pitches — utilizing multiple arm revolutions in the windmill; releasing the ball behind the back and under the leg; and using a hesitation step that involved

stepping towards the batter and then releasing the ball.

Charlotte Armstrong (above), A-1 Queens, pitching behind her back; and Margie Law, PBSW Ramblers, using fancy windup.

Nina Korgan, an ASA Hall of Famer who starred for the New Orleans Jax during the '40's and '50's, related that she "used to pitch both righthanded and lefthanded until the rules changed and it wasn't allowed."

Batters were frustrated by not knowing where and when the ball was going to be released! Some interesting and humerous situations arose in games.

A pitcher's speed sometimes gets the umpires into queer situations. In an Iowa game, a batter had two strikes on him, and the pitcher suddenly tossed one of those tantalizing slow balls. The hitter, taken by surprise, took a fast swing and then continued around, hitting the ball on the second circuit for a home run. One side argued that the batter had struck out on his first swing. The opposition claimed that the run counted. (23:135)

As these situations occurred in games, the ASA office was called to make a decision. Subsequently, the rules were changed and added to for the following season. Obviously, the early rule books were much thinner than the later ones!

The year of 1935 was a milestone in softball — it was not only the year that the Amateur Softball Association published its first set of rules, but it was also the first year that teams had to qualify for the national championships by winning either state or metro tournaments. While the Red Jackets team from Wichita Falls, Texas, was the people's choice at the 1935 women's championships — they played in their bare feet and sang Texas songs between innings — it was the National Screw and Manufacturing team from Cleveland that dominated play. The Savona sisters, who went on to star for the New Orleans Jax, were key players in the National Manufacturing team's win over the defending champions, the Cleveland Bloomer Girls — a game that took two days to play because of rain.

As our country was slowly surfacing from the depths of the Depression in the late 1930's, the overall attitude of Americans was upbeat and optimistic. They believed in President Roosevelt, re-electing him by a landslide in 1936. One of the tenets of FDR's New Deal was that public works should boost the standard of living. One of the ways to do so was through recreation; and the way to increase recreation was through the building of athletic facilities. Between 1935 and 1940, the Works Progress Administration (W. P. A.) spent a billion dollars building athletic fields — 3,026 of them to be exact — with a major emphasis on the dimensions of softball. Many of these were lighted and especially suited to softball.

The popularity of softball, the game that had become a national pastime because it was a fun, inexpensive game to play during the depression years, continued to escalate.

The Pauley Report, an annual report published by the ASA secretary, stated that, in 1936, there were 92,545 softball teams in this country, which played 1,850,900 games before 185,090,000 spectators. (1:51)

Opening ceremonies of 1937 ASA Championships at Soldier Field in Chicago.

The mid-1930's was the beginning of the legacy-building era. Born in the early 1920's, the oldest of our modern-day pioneers was reaching the age of "I can run — I can throw and catch — I can hit the heck out of the ball — I am good and I want to prove it and prove it NOW" attitude! Depending on where she lived in the United States, the opportunities for a girl to compete in softball varied from none whatsoever to league, state, regional and national competition. Among those states that provided opportunities for girls' softball play in the 1930's were Alabama, Arizona, California, District of Columbia, Illinois, Indiana, Iowa, Louisiana, Maryland, Missouri, Nebraska, New Jersey, Ohio, Texas, Utah, Washington and Wisconsin. From the 1940's on, softball was played in every state.

Softball in the States in the 1930's

Alabama — In 1936, there were 24 women's teams playing under Birmingham's Recreation Department but nothing was done about deciding the state champion. There were 25 men's leagues and six women's leagues operating in the state by 1937. Lighted fields sprang up all over the commonwealth, resulting in increased interest in softball. (1:78)

Arizona — The first women's softball league in Arizona — a four-team league consisting of the Ramblers, Tovera Packing Co., South Phoenix Boosters, and the Phoenix Reds — was organized in 1932 by Laura Herron who worked for the Phoenix Recreation Department. She was assisted in her efforts to develop a softball program by Arlie Gailbraith (city recreation), Ford Hoffman (public schools) and Ben Spaulding (promoter). One of the longest sponsorships of any women's fastpitch team in the country was the PBSW School Supply Company's sponsorship of the Ramblers from 1933 to 1965. When Larry Walker organized the Queens in 1937, one of the most intense rivalries that women's fastpitch softball has ever seen was started.

Pictured here are the PBSW Ramblers, as they appeared in 1935, three years after the team was organized. Back row, left to right, are Mickey Sullivan, Norma McCabe, June McCabe, Fay Harris, Velma Grubbs, Maureen Curlee. Front row, left to right, are Flora Walker, Esther Lockway, Peggy Hoffman, Louise Curtis, Margaret Mills, Katharine Moore and Jean Dalmolin. Dot Wilkinson is kneeling.

Arizona Continued — Both the Ramblers and the Queens had established themselves as nationally dominant teams by the late 1930's. Traveling by automobile, both teams made a cross-country trek to New York to play in Madison Square Garden — the Ramblers in 1938 and the Queens in 1939. The rules were adapted to play indoors — they had nine players on a team, used 55-foot bases and the players had to wear sneakers, "as the game was played on a terrazzo floor." The 20 games played by the Queens on this 6,500-mile trip through 14 states were played in front of a total of 60,000 spectators. Madison Square Garden itself drew from 18,000 to 21,000 fans each night.

INTER-SECTIONAL GAME
NINE INNING GAME

CANTALOUPE QUEENS OF PHOENIX, ARIZONA

#	Player	Position
28	Eleanor Firpo	shortstop
67	Flora Bell Walker	center field
13	Catherine Mann	third base
40	Doris Lynd	catcher
44	Nina Stockton	right field
15	Dottie Dominick	second base
20	Rose Perica	first base
38	Anita Mixon	left field
~~30 Lorraine Croswell~~		pitcher
94	Virginia Gillen	pitcher

UTILITY PLAYERS:
11 Roma Gentry   59 Edna Gillen   51 Margaret Vance
77 Alita Beauchamp   87 Charlotte Armstrong   99 Fay Harris
MANAGER: Chas. Fowler, Jr.   COACH: Lawrence Walker

NEW YORK AMERICANETTES

#	Player	Position
14	Rose DeRosa	first base
18	Hattie Michaels	left field
4	Helen Mack (Capt.)	third base
5	Millie Deegan	second base
1	~~Betty Gallagher~~ CRUGNALE RF	~~short stop~~
2	Anna Killip CF	~~right field~~
11	Sis Sargent SS	~~center field~~
9	Ruth Murdock	catcher
6	May Jardan	pitcher
~~2 Mary Ragut~~		pitcher

UTILITY PLAYERS:
3 Claire Isaicson   8 Ann Crugnale   10 Muriel Guest
12 Betty De Rocco   16 Vera McLaughlin
PLAYING MANAGER: Rose DeRosa   MASCOT: 0 Eleanor Lockhart

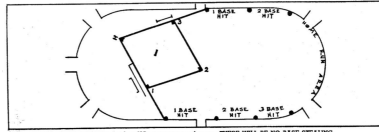

On a passed ball from pitcher to catcher, NO runner may advance. THERE WILL BE NO BASE STEALING. No base runner will be permitted to take a lead off the base. A base runner's foot should not leave the base until the girl at bat hits the ball.
A wild throw entitles the runner to advance one base provided she can make it safely.
NO BUNTING WILL BE ALLOWED.
Ogden Printing Co., Inc., N. Y. C.

California — The San Gabriel Valley Girls' Softball League and the Fiedler Field League, both organized in the early 1930's in the Los Angeles area, provided the learning ground for many female players who later starred for major fastpitch ASA teams as well as the All-American Girls' Professional Baseball League and the National Girls' Baseball League — the two professional leagues that played in the Chicago area during World War II. Marty Fiedler not only organized the Fiedler Field League but also built the field where the games were played.

According to Teddy Hamilton — she played on the Young's Market team in the Fiedler Field League and later on the Orange Lionettes and in the National Girls' Baseball League — the caliber of play in

Teddy Miner Hamilton in Young's Market uniform, 1939

Excerpts of a Phoenix Rambler Daily Log to New York, 1938

Sept. 1, 1938 — We left Phoenix this morning at 5:00 a.m. We are in Prescott now and will be leaving for Flagstaff in about 15 minutes. It's raining cats and dogs. We expect to work out in Gallup, N.M. tonight but if it is raining like it is here, we won't be able to. It is now 12:15 p.m. and our next stop is Winslow. We ate dinner at Winslow, supper at Gallup, NM. We are now in Albuquerque staying at a nice auto court. We will start out again at 7:00 in the morning. Left Albuquerque at 8:30 and ate dinner at Amarillo and are eating supper at Shamrock, Texas. We will spend the night at Oklahoma City. We worked out at Amarillo and I mean we really had a work out.

Sept. 3, 1938 — We stayed all night in Oklahoma City and what a place we stayed in. We worked out early this morning and are on our way now to Tulsa where we have a game.

Sept. 4, 1938 — We won our game last night 6-4. We left Tulsa at 8:00 a.m. this morning. We passed through small part of Kansas and we are now at Cuba, Missouri, which is about 80 miles from St. Louis. We now have only about 380 miles to go to Chicago so that means that we'll be there tomorrow night some time.

Sept. 5, 1938 — We didn't go on to Chicago tonight as we were all very tired. We will leave early tomorrow morning and then eat breakfast in Chicago. It is only about 30 miles. We are staying in a hotel in Joliet, Illinois.

Sept. 6, 1938 — We arrived here in Chicago at 11:30 this morning. It is sure a big place but it is also the dirtiest place I've ever seen. We are staying at the Allerton Hotel, located corner of Michigan Drive and work out every evening so as to keep in good shape.

Sept. 7, 1938 — It is raining hard this morning so I don't know whether we'll work out or not. We went to the show to see "My Lucky Star" with Sonja Henie last night and it cost us 90 cents. It was a good show but not worth 90 cents. Well, we just got through working out at Grant Park. It was sure muddy and hard to work out in.

Sept. 8, 1938 — We went to the big parade last night that they had celebrating the opening of the World Tournament. All the teams were supposed to march in it but we didn't get in until they were at the park because Mr. Hoffman thought it would make us

Typical of the cars driven on the trip (1937 Pontiac)

too tired to walk such a long distance. Our first game is scheduled tonight with Missouri.

Sept. 9, 1938 — Our game was postponed last night on account of rain. It is raining again today so we don't know when we'll play. We are still working out every day though — rain or not rain.

Sept. 10, 1938 — We played Oklahoma tonight. We beat 8-6.

Sept. 11, 1938 — Didn't do much. Played Nebraska at 7:00 — won 8-0. Had to wait 4 1/2 hrs. to play Calif. They got breaks and beat 3-2. That put us out. Tough luck. We all felt pretty badly about it. We went back to the hotel after the game, packed, left Chicago at 5:00 Monday morning.

Sept. 12, 1938 — Drove all day; saw beautiful country. Stayed somewhere in Penna. Don't know just where. We were all dead tired. We have had 3 hrs. sleep in 3 days.

Sept. 13, 1938 — Drove all day, arrived in N. Y. 7:00 p.m. Played ball at Madison Square Garden and beat 4-1. Sure thrilled — had 10,000 spectators. We play the team again Thurs. night.

Sept. 14, 1938 — Had a swell time today. Jack Dempsey had us at his place for lunch. He ate with us. Sure nice. All the girls were so stuffed with souvenirs from his place that they could hardly walk. We were then taken to Radio City where we went through it. Sure interesting. Went to Coney Island at night and sure did have fun. Went to bed very tired.

Sept. 15, 1938 — Played N. Y. Roverettes at Garden — played 18 innings. Finally won 2-0.

Sept. 16, 1938 — Left N. Y. at 8:00 a.m. Traveled all day and night. Sure tired out.

Sept. 17, 1938 — Been traveling all day. I am sure tired. We arrived in Cuba, Mo at 11:00 p.m.

California Continued — that early league was as good as any she saw at any time during her playing career!

Among the players who started their playing careers in the Los Angeles area leagues and who later starred for various major fastpitch teams were: Kay Rich; Bertha Petinak Ragan Tickey, Gwen Decker, Joan Alsup, Kay Rohrer, Teddie Miner Hamilton, Snookie Doyle and Louise Embree.

Competition was conducted in two divisions — the American League and the National League. Two All-Star teams — the International Stars from the National League and the American Stars from the American League — sailed to Japan in October of 1938 for a goodwill tour. There was not much leisure time aboard ship with school lessons taught by a teacher who boarded with the teams and practice. Many softballs were lost at sea!

Somewhere on the Pacific Ocean in October, 1938

Top row, left to right, are Ruth Salisbury, Lila Racey, Louise Embree, Marie Robinson, Gwen Decker, Mable Sparlin, Kay Shinen, Norma Stonebraker, Dorothy Shinen, Dorothy Harrell, Dot Israel, Virginia Alford. Next to top row, left to right: June Young, Jeane Fuller, Louise Robinson, Melita Forrester, Lois Terry, Edith Richards, Kay Rohrer, Genevieve Beck, Virginia Gillen. Second row from bottom, left to right, Lois Roberts, Wanda Macha, Jerry Cox, Noma Sugioka, Kazui Oshiki, Martha Cooper, Bobbie Borchers, Louise Hunt, Anita Carlucci, Esther Halapoff. Bottom row, left to right, unknown, Spencer Kona (coach), Freddie Pfahler (manager), unknown, Mr. Kono (Spencer's Father), Marty Fiedler (founder of league), unknown, Joe Farber (coach), Daddy Rohrer (manager & Kay's Father).

California Continued — The team to beat in northern California was the team from Alameda. Among the players who, in later years, achieved All-American status and started their playing careers with Alameda were Willie Turner, Kay Rich and Rickie Caito. J.J. Kreigs from Alameda won the ASA world tournament in 1938 and 1939.

District of Columbia — Women's softball was launched in 1936 by James Hitchens of the Agriculture Department. He organized his own Aggiettes and then the Girls Government League. In 1937, he turned over those coaching duties to Joseph Bertolini and organized the United Typewriter girls, an "outside" team. To give them a civilian league to play

in, he formed the National City Girls' League. The Typewriter team won that league and then defeated Hitchens proteges, the Aggiettes, to qualify for the world tournament in Chicago that year.(1:90)

Illinois — The Dieselettes, Sunnyland-Lettes and the Pekin-Lettes (all the same team with different sponsors) and based in Peoria, Illinois, dominated softball in Illinois from the 1940's on. Prior to that, a team called the Farrow Chix — founded in 1931 by Roy Farrow and also based in Peoria — was the team to see. Roy Farrow not only sponsored the Chix and provided the field, but also organized farm teams — elementary school girls played on the Baby Chix and from there they advanced to the Middle Road Coalettes before moving on to the senior team. The Farrow Chix, a barnstorming team that traveled to play the major teams in New Orleans, Houston, Tulsa, Cleveland, Chicago and St. Louis, won the Illinois state ASA tournament in 1939. Their games consistently drew up to 6,000 fans a night.

1941 Farrow Chix on Farrow Field
(Field Roy Farrow built on his property)
Back row, left to right are Roy Farrow (mgr.), Steve Cravens (coach), Joe Claus (coach). Front row, left to right, are Robbie Mae Price, Mickey Koepell, Mabel Ryner, Ann Ross, Irene "Pep" Kerwin, Marie Mueller, Helen Fehl, Monya Renner, Saralea Storts, Liz Farrow, Marian Kneer, June Gilmore.

Illinois Continued — The Chix and the Caterpillar Dieselettes battled for supremacy in the state for several years until, finally, in the mid 1940's, the Dieselettes surged ahead. Caterpillar offered players jobs, salaries and benefits that the Chix couldn't match. This exodus of players from the Chix to the Dieselettes depleted the ranks of Roy Farrow's team to the point that the Chix finally disbanded.

*1944 **Caterpillar Dieselettes** — First row, left to right, Minnie Pyell (chaperone), Marie Wadlow, Charlotte Daniels, Pepper Kerwin, Jess Crowel, Dutch Leonard (coaches). Second row, left to right, Maxine Crump, Norma Humphrey Natzke, Sid Eslinger, Whitey, Betty Wanless, Virgi Luciano, Anne Elliott, Gabby Kneer, unknown.*

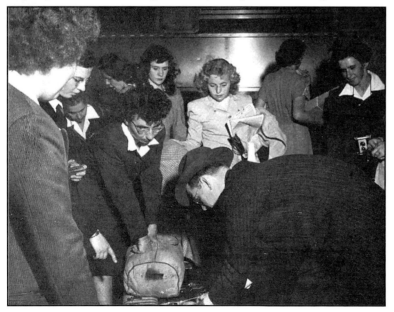

The Caterpillar Dieselette team boarding its own private railroad car enroute to the 1949 ASA World Tourney.

Indiana — A lot of softball was played in Indiana as far back as 1932, particularly in the cities of South Bend, Brazil and Indianapolis. A state tournament in 1932 reported the Hoosier Beers of South Bend winning the women's championship.

Iowa — Girls' softball had its beginnings in Iowa in 1931. The Des Moines' Greenwood Electric Company sponsored a team that dominated state competition during those early years. Among Greenwood's top players were: Eleanor Anderson, Luree Kisor, Delores Hohl and Coleen Summy. (1:105)

Louisiana — The team to put Louisiana on the softball map was the Jax Brewers. Sponsored by the Jackson Brewing Company of New Orleans, this high class women's team won five ASA world championships.

Pictured above, top row, left to right, are Buck Brehm, Freda Savona, Lillian Theard, Nina Korgan, Mary Pembo, Blache Soniat, Heard Ragas. Middle row, left to right, Olympia Savona, June Bradley, Bertha Hebert, Selma Meinecke. Bottom row, left to right, Edith Doul, Hazel Mermilliod, Dottie Pitts, Dorothy Walker. Missing from picture: Lottie Jackson.

Louisiana Continued — From 1939 to 1941, the Jax played an average of 100 games a season, and were selected as one of the few teams ever to play in Madison Square Garden and the Canadian Exposition in Toronto. Their strength can be attributed to the dedication and hard work of their founder, Heard Ragas, who convinced the Jackson Brewing Company of New Orleans that backing this team would be a feather in its cap. Thanks to the support, the elite of the women's fastpitch softball world — such as Freda and Olympia Savona, Nina Korgan, and Lottie Jackson — were enticed into moving to New Orleans to join the Jax organization.

Maryland — The Motley Girls Club won the state title in 1936, and the Crown, Cork & Seal team took the title the next three years. Perhaps the strongest team in Maryland during the late 1930's and 1940's, though, was the Cummings Construction Co. team from Baltimore. Standout players at that time were Flo Blanck, Mary Walter, Bertha Kelly, Bess Price and Dot Vinzant. (1:111)

Missouri — One of the first records of a ball and bat game played by girls in Missouri was in the *St. Louis Globe-Democrat* newspaper dated August 14, 1932. The article tells about Marie Wadlow, a future ASA Hall of Famer, playing on a girls' indoor baseball team in a league in south St. Louis called the South Side Sunday-School League. Games were played every Monday and Friday nights at Tower Grove Park, near Grand Boulevard and Arsenal Street in St. Louis. One of the requirements to be a team member was that the girl attend Sunday School on the four Sundays prior to the opening of the season, and throughout the summer they had to be present at least two out of every four Sundays.

ST. LOUIS CHURCH ATHLETIC ASSOCIATION

This certifies that........Marie Wadlow.................... has agreed to uphold the rules of the Association and has paid his registration fee for the year ending October 1, 1931 and is entitled to represent....Tabernacle Baptist....... ....Church during that year.

Registration No. ....578........

....
Executive Secretary.
(Over)

ST. LOUIS CHURCH ATHLETIC ASSOCIATION

This certifies that........Marie Wadlow.................... has agreed to uphold the rules of the Association and has paid his registration fee for the year ending October 1, 19.32 and is entitled to represent....Peters Memorial......... ....Presbyterian.........Church during that year.

Registration No. ......1106........

....
Executive Secretary.
(Over)

Peters Girls' Baseball Nine Defeats Grace, 26-4

The Peters Memorial Presbyterian Church nine, South Side champions, romped over Grace Presbyterian, West End title holders, 26 to 4, in the first game of the city championship series of the St. Louis Church Girls' Indoor League. Wadlow hurled a fine contest for the winner, striking out nine batters in the seven-inning tilt. She also led her teammates with the willow, collecting six hits in a like number of tries. Among the half dozen blows were two doubles.

Peter's Nine Clinches Girls' Church Loop Title

The Peter's Memorial Presbyterian nine, South Side titleholders, clinched the St. Louis Church Girl's Indoor League pennant by trouncing the Grace Presbyterian team, West End champions, 17 to 2, for their second straight victory over the West End club. The South Siders won the first game by a score of 26 to 4.

Wadlow, star hurler for the Memorial aggregation, allowed only three hits and struck out seven batters in the seven-inning contest. She again led her teammates with the willow, getting three hits out of five trips to the plate.

Missouri Continued — From 1933 into the early 1940's, girls softball teams had the opportunity to play games sanctioned by an organization founded by George Sisler, the baseball immortal. Sisler and his financial backers built four night softball parks and orga-

The Curlee Clothing Company team dominated play in the 1930's.

nized the American Softball Association — a group primarily composed of softball teams in the St. Louis area. The American Softball Association functioned until 1945 at which time the Amateur Softball Association became the major organizer of softball in the country.

The top women's team when softball competition first started in St. Louis was the Curlee Clothing Co. team.

The Curlee Clothing Company even chartered a train to take fans to their men's and women's games in Mayfield, Kentucky.

Nebraska — Women's softball started in 1936 with the Syracuse Bluebirds annexing the state title. (1:128)

New Jersey — Five years after the Great Depression rocked the nation, 17-year-old Margaret "Toots" Nusse organized a girls softball team in the city of Linden, New Jersey — the Linden Arians. For seven consecutive years — 1935 to 1942 — they reigned as champions of the Union County League. They annexed their first state title in 1936 and successfully defended their laurels during their next eight campaigns. Nusse led the team to 18 state championships and five regional titles. The Arians — with Toots

The Original Arians
Front row, left to right, Coach Julius Rosenberg, Marion Pyner, Margaret "Toots" Nusse, Helen Derrig, Anna Masnick, Coach Lloyd Kingsley. Second row, left to right, Ruth Cushing, Emily Pecina, Betty Kingsley, Adelaide Falkenberg, Vera Glowa, Julie Horhota, Lillian Frey. Third row, left to right, Kay Iwanyshyn, Fritz Walck, Ellen Jolly, Blanche Kontour, Ann Marhan, Gee Payson.

Nusse being the key to their spirit and success — dominated play in New Jersey for several decades. (25:4)

Ohio — Teams from the Cleveland area dominated play, winning the world championships in 1935, 1936 and 1937. Outstanding players for the Bloomer Girls and the National Manufacturing team were Freda and Olympia Savona, Dora Underwood, Vera Vining and Marjorie Wood. (1:137)

Texas — Austin, the Texas capital, was the first city in the Lone Star State to go in for softball in a big way. By 1934, the league in Austin had grown into a well knit organization of 68 men's and 16 women's teams. In 1934, the Amateur Athletic Federation conducted a state tournament for girls in Texas, held in Beaumont, and won by the Red-and-White Girls. The women's all-time team (up to 1957) consisted of Puddin Steck and Candy Cadelari, catchers; Billy Smith, Tommie Russum, Doris McRay and Sissie Mackey, pitchers; Louise Walla, first base; Petie Barbier, second base; Ann Varner, third base; Annabelle Willy, shortstop; Winnie Chase, Reds Mahoney and Frenchy Kiber, outfielders; and Annia Starukstka, utility. (1:149-150)

The American National Insurance Company Girls softball team won the state tournaments in 1937 and 1938 and was one of the top contenders in 1939. The team traveled to St. Louis to play that city's top teams.

Utah — Dennis Murphy, of the city recreation board, promoted, financed and developed women's softball in the state. The first league was formed in 1933 and consisted of Kolub Lumber, Lucky 13, Copperettes, American Linen, Salt Lake Shamrocks and Dupler Fur. Some of the finest female players in the early years were Ruth Hobbs, Lenore Weight, Kay Dehart, Pat Baxter, Shirley Turpin, Bonnie Heusser, Wilma Freston, Jerry Smith, Emma Ullock and Ann Lamb. (1:150)

Virginia — Richmond's Lucky Strike team won the first women's state title in 1937.

Washington — They became affiliated with the ASA in 1938. The first women champs were Wright & Grady of Vancouver, BC, in 1940. (1:157)

Wisconsin — The women organized the Milwaukee Women's Municipal Athletic Association in 1933 and launched the first girls' softball league-the Schuster circuit. (1:159)

Canada — Women's softball started in Canada in 1920. Toronto was its hotbed. It had its own organization within the Canadian Amateur Softball Association — the Provincial Women's Softball Union. Its first President was Ann Spalding of Preston. The greatest interest in softball was during World War II. Canadian teams participated in most of the early world championships held in the United States. Among their strongest teams have been the Crofton Athletic Club and the Kalyx Cups of Toronto. (1:163)

To say that those women who were the first to compete in fastpitch softball were tough is an understatement. They drove sometimes thousands of miles in standard shift, non-air-conditioned automobiles on two-lane highways just to play one game. (The early ASA world tournaments were single elimination.) With little or no sleep, they jogged out on the playing field — warmed up — and played inning after inning of "do or die" softball. They loved to play the game and they loved to win! Many played without gloves, mitts or the catcher's protective equipment. "Toots" Nusse, the founder and mainstay of the Linden Arians from 1934 to 1958, never used a glove. She claimed "I just couldn't get used to it." Among others who shunned the use of a glove were Marion Fox, an ASA All-American who pitched for Toronto, Canada, in the '50's, and Monia Wieskowski, a strong armed, tough-skinned first baseman for the Farrow Chix in Illinois in the 1930's.

Marion Fox, a pitcher for Toronto, Canada, did not wear a glove.

Bruised bodies, jammed fingers and skinned knees were considered to be inevitable bi-products for a catcher in those days. Not realizing that they were "the weaker sex," those first women catchers wore only what was required in the way of protective equipment. According to Dot Wilkinson, a catcher for the PBSW Ramblers and an ASA Hall of Famer, she wore only a mask (because it was required) during the first years that she caught and when the chest protector became mandatory, she took out all of the padding so that it wouldn't be so bulky.

This first decade of competitive women's fastpitch softball saw the beginning of a legacy that would continue to get stronger and stronger. Even though the struggle of an American woman to be completely accepted as an athlete would continue for years, women all over the country were putting on their cleats and gloves and battling it out on the softball field. Nothing and no one would deter them!

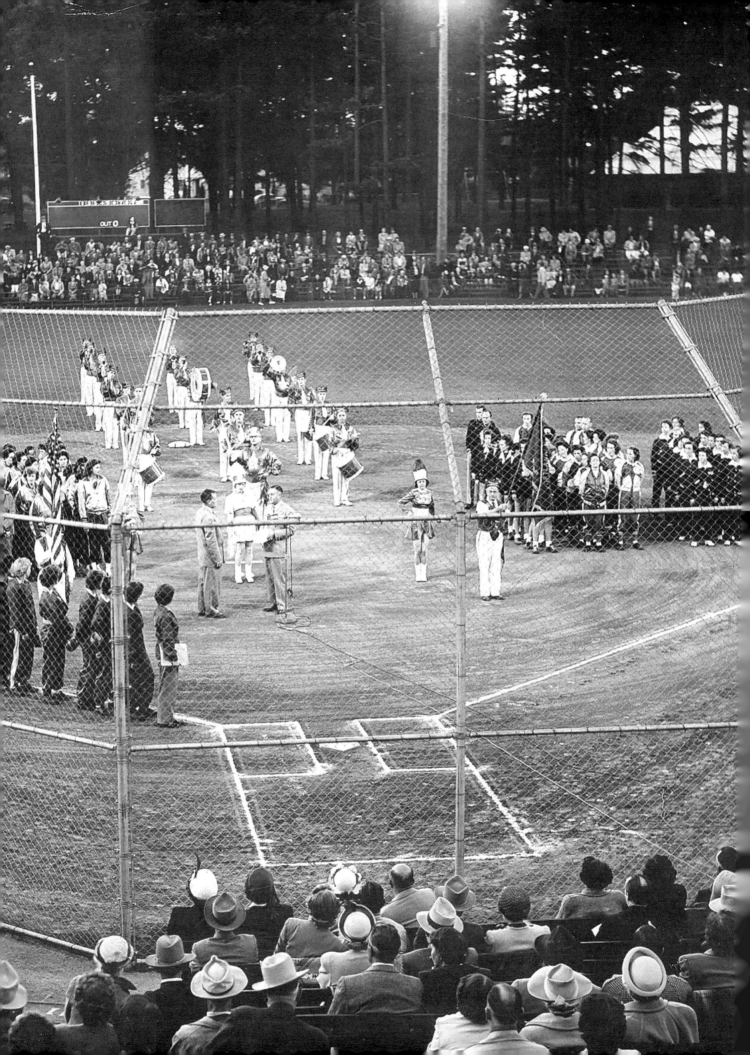

The outbreak of war in Europe in September of 1939 created international unrest and concern. The United States Congress, led by President Roosevelt, who was re-elected for an unprecedented third term, wanted the United States to support democracy but, if possible, to stay out of the conflict. American industry increased production of military supplies, which were shipped to our allies. This accelerated industrial production, lowered the unemployment rate and bolstered our economy.

The average American was living longer — 64 years in 1940 as compared to 49 years in 1900 — and, even though family budgets were still tight, life was wholesome and comfortable. Families ate at home — the first McDonalds didn't open until 1948 in California — went to the movies, played games and listened to the radio for entertainment. Teenagers and retirees alike listened and danced to the tunes of Tommy Dorsey, Glenn Miller and other big-name bands. The place to be on a Saturday night was a dance hall, such as the Riverside Ballroom in Phoenix, where one could tip a beer and dance until the wee hours of the morning.

Even though the sale of automobiles in America decreased considerably during the depression years — 25 million cars in the U.S. in 1940 as compared to 50 million in 1931 — most American families owned one. The news of the war was worrisome, but most Americans felt that FDR would steer the country clear of direct involvement in it. Congress, more tuned to the realism of the situation than the general public, passed the Selective Service Act, the first peacetime draft in the United States, in 1940. This law provided for 900,000 men between the ages of 20 and 36 to be taken each year.

While the coming of war in Europe caused the cancellation of many international sports contests — the 1940 Olympic Games; the Davis Cup and Wimbledon tennis championships — fastpitch softball in the U. S. continued to grow in popularity. As more and more women donned a glove and joined the ranks of fastpitch softball teams, the question of "could the woman who was a fierce competitor on the softball diamond still be feminine," became a major issue. It had taken so long for our society to accept the idea of a woman merely stepping out on the playing field that it should have been expected that the idea of a woman playing a game that involved getting dirty sliding into base, chewing gum and arguing with umpires would be difficult to accept. Those were activities that were in conflict with "being a lady."

For generations, the role of the female in American society had been clearly defined — to be ladylike at all times with one's hands folded in one's lap, and to be supportive and subservient to the male. Changing that attitude would not — *and did not* — happen overnight.

Opening ceremonies prior to the 1949 ASA World Championships at Normandale Field in Portland, Oregon.

The Feminine Issue

An outgrowth of this issue and one that created a great ugliness over a period of decades was the belief that any woman playing fastpitch softball was a lesbian. It would seem that our society has not only been guilty of being judgmental and stereotyping, but it has also been reluctant to change. As late as 1978, Edward Claflin said in his book, *The Irresistible American Softball Book*:

> *As for the stereotype of the woman softball player as a big, brawny, unfeminine Amazon — forget it. Female players come in all shapes and sizes, and besides, you shouldn't indulge in stereotypes. (3:4)*

The avid fan who attended fastpitch softball games for the excitement of watching highly skilled women turning a double play or snagging an over-the-shoulder fly ball in the outfield wasn't disappointed. He saw a diversity of women out on the field — tall, short, shapely, stocky, cute, not so cute. All played hard with a keen dedication to the game. The lifestyle of these women should have been incidental, but instead it became a major issue that caused many problems for a lot of people.

It was not uncommon during the 1940's, 50's and 60's for a woman attending college to be told that if she wanted to continue as a student in good standing at that institution, she must discontinue playing ASA softball. Kay Rich, an ASA Hall of Famer, attended a school that was part of the state university system in California in the mid-1940's. She had been asked to play on one of the major ASA teams in northern California while she attended college. Knowing that she could

handle both and anxious to pit her skills against others, Kay decided to join the softball team. An instructor at her college discovered that she was a member of that team, called her in and told her that by playing softball, she was mingling with the "undesirables" and that she should quit the team immediately. Kay had observed that women were participating in tennis, golf, swimming and basketball so why couldn't she play softball?! She refused to quit the softball team. As a consequence, a national basketball rating in officiating that she had just earned was taken away from her. The bitterness that she felt from that action continues to this day.

This was not an isolated case that happened in only that particular time period. Other women faced this same problem in Ohio, Arizona, Illinois, Connecticut — in states all over the country — in the 40's, 50's and 60's. In one instance, a coed who refused to quit playing softball was kicked out of school; and in another, a female student was so intimidated — staying in college was crucial to her future — that she quit playing ball.

College instructors, in particular those in physical education departments, seemed to wage the nastiest and most heated battles against coeds in their departments playing ball outside the college setting. The department chair of a college in central California made it extremely difficult for physical education major students who continued to play ball to enter the college's teacher training program. This female chair believed "that highly competitive team sport experiences were antithetical to the aura of demure femininity she strove to instill." (26:14)

The problem didn't disappear upon the

coed's graduation from college. Many women who chose a teaching career had to face the same decision again. If they wanted to keep their teaching positions, they had to quit playing ASA softball. Some chose to play ball anonymously — under a fake name — so that their jobs wouldn't be jeopardized, and others quit playing ball. The obstacles that were placed in front of women at that time caused many talented athletes to shorten their playing careers.

The Amateur Softball Association of America, the major governing body of softball, and the news media consistently promoted the idea that the playing ability of these women did not detract from their femininity. The ASA, for a period of time starting in 1942, held Miss Softball of America selections in conjunction with the ASA world championships.

Among the award winners for Miss Softball of America were Bertha Ragan, Orange (top left); Carolyn Broady, Buena Park (top right); Margie Law, Phoenix (bottom, left), and Patty Wilkes, Monrovia, CA (bottom right).

Newspaper accounts of women's games included comments and adjectives that reinforced the fact that these were women playing the game.

- *The <u>beautiful</u> Kay hit a home run, a single and a double and started out a dazzling double play to nip a Pomona rally.*

- *The pitching genius of <u>lovely</u> Margie Law.*

- *Dot Wilkinson, talented and <u>pulchritudinous</u> (endowed with physical beauty) catcher for the Ramblers.*

- *Even the locker room scene cannot take away from the <u>loveliness</u> of the A-1 Queens.*

- *The <u>attractive young lady</u> is Jean Hutsell, Rambler fielder.*

- *<u>Blonde bombshell</u> Teddy Hamilton.*

- *<u>Pretty</u> Flavilla Hagen will pitch for Karl's Shoes, facing Genevieve Beck. In the second game, <u>glamorous, blonde-haired</u> Jenny Guido hurls for Mansfield's against Virginia Gillen.*

- *Swinging <u>smart lipsticks</u> as well as sturdy bats, female softballers play like men but don't look like them.*

- *Followers of the sport say there may be no Miss Universe among the 300 players but that there are many girls on the club rosters, such as the youthful Carol Spanks of Buena Park, who are <u>attractive enough to be worthy competitors in most beauty contests</u>.*

The name of a team could indicate whether the team was a men's team or a women's team. Many women's softball teams selected names that included the name of the sponsor or the home city of that team, and a feminine nickname. Adding "ette" to the end of a name denoted that the team was female in gender.

- Orange Lionettes (Orange, CA)
- West Allis Bankettes (West Allis, WI)
- Raybestos Brakettes (Stratford, CT)
- Crystal-ettes (Reading, PA)
- Anchorettes (Indianapolis, IN)
- Caterpillar Dieselettes (Peoria, IL)
- Pekin-Lettes (Pekin, IL)

Teams such as the Lady Pride (Decatur, IL); Sterling Belles (NJ); Lorelei Ladies (Atlanta, GA); and A-1 Queens from Phoenix left no doubt that they were women's teams.

Selecting uniforms that were feminine looking was not easy. Ready-made uniforms for women didn't exist. The only uniforms available to purchase were men's baseball uniforms with baggy, knicker-length pants made out of heavy material in men's sizes and patterned to conform to a male body. While these uniforms did protect the body when sliding, diving, etc., they were not very attractive on women and they were extremely hot in summer temperature.

Some women's teams, refusing to accept the fact that men's baseball uniforms were all that was available for them to wear, designed and made their own. Teams from the west coast and Arizona were the first to appear in attractive, custom-designed short shorts and short skirts. According to Virginia Dobson Bickle, a Phoenix Rambler during the 1940's and early 50's, they shocked the crowds when they appeared for the first time in their shorts.

Charlotte Armstong, a six-time NSC All-American, designed the uniforms worn by the Phoenix A-1 Queens, a national NSC power.

Red Satin Shorts

Our team dressed in short red satin shorts. Nearly all west coast teams dressed in this fashion. I remember playing in the national tournament in Cleveland against the New Orleans Jax. When we took off our satin sweats revealing much leg as opposed to the Jax in their baseball uniforms, the large crowd did not think that we could play — we were only girls. We did lose a hard fought final game 1-0, but the crowd would have given us all the trophies! We found this kind of response everywhere we traveled east of Arizona. They loved us! — Virginia Dobson Bickle, a Phoenix Rambler

Dot Dobie, Erv Lind Florists, and Bev Cox, PBSW Ramblers, wore the short-shorts style of uniform.

Some teams continued wearing baseball style uniforms for several years. Uniforms were made from a material that varied from a satin-type such as the Indianapolis Anchorettes have on (right), to the heavy, flannel-type cotton material of the Pekin-Lettes of Illinois. These two teams, by the way, were two of the strongest teams coming out of the midwestern states during the 1950's and 1960's. Their coaches, Maxine Thayer of the Anchorettes, and Chuck McCord of the Pekin-Lettes, were both fierce competitors, dedicated not only to their teams, but to the promotion of women's fastpitch softball.

*1956 **Indianapolis Anchorettes***
First row, left to right, are Judy Waggoner, Elsie Wulf, Betty Nissley, Janice Eck, Janet Waggoner. Second row, left to right, Mary Bauer, Carole Woodruff, Helen Campbell (Stegemoller), Joann Anderson, and Joyce Anderson. Third row, left to right, John Gorman (coach), JoAnn Hooper, Mary Ann Mase, Katie Gorman, Pat Tatum, Mae Tatum, and Maxine Thayer (manager).

Maxine Thayer, Indianapolis Anchorettes

Maxine started her career in softball in the early 1940's as a player, playing with the Pepsi-Cola team in Indianapolis as the short fielder — the tenth player on teams in those

Maxine Thayer

days. Her fame, though, was achieved through her coaching and dedicated efforts promoting softball in the Indianapolis area. Maxine coached for 28 years — first with the Indianapolis Anchorettes, and later with the M.K. Peppers. Her first year of coaching, in 1956, Maxine led the Anchorettes to the ASA world championships in Clearwater, Florida. That was the first time in history that an Indiana team had qualified for a major championship. Over her 28-year career, Maxine's teams amassed an overall record of 1,118 wins and 475 losses.

Known as an intense and outspoken person, Maxine was very protective of her players on and off the field. If a player gave 100 percent, Maxine gave 150 percent. Maxine was inducted into the ASA Hall of Honor in 1988.

Chuck McCord, Pekin-Lettes

Chuck McCord managed the Peoria Dieselettes from 1947 to 1955, at which time the team moved to Sunnyland and became the Sunnyland-Lettes. They remained there for three good seasons after which they moved to Pekin to be known since then as the Pekin-Lettes. During Chuck's 25-year reign as manager, his teams compiled an impressive 808-177 won-loss record. They competed in 16 national tournaments with their best finish being third in 1950, 1951 and 1965.

Chuck had great pride in his teams, not only for their success on the field, but for their behavior off the field. Among his former players are ASA Hall of Famers Marie Wadlow, Carolyn Thome Hart, Lou Albrecht, Lorene Ramsey and Marlys Taber.

McCord served as State ASA Commissioner in Illinois and Chairman of the ASA Hall of Fame selection committee for several decades. He was inducted into the ASA Hall of Honor in 1977.

Chuck McCord with ASA Hall of Famers Carolyn Thome Hart (left) and Marie Wadlow.

Pictured left to right are Carolyn Thome Hart, Pauline Schlicher, Eleanor Rudolph, Manager Chuck McCord of the Pekin-Lettes, Pekin, Illinois.

By the time the 1950's and 1960's arrived, teams wore a variety of uniforms.

Pictured at left are three styles of uniforms, modeled by Pepper Kerwin, Pekin-Lettes (far left); Jean Dallinga, Utah Spudnuts (middle); and Pat Richmond, Fresno Rockets.

World War II — Men Are Gone and the Women Take Over

The 1940 ASA World Championships were held in Detroit — the first time they had ever been held out of Chicago. The game at that time was played with 10 players on a team, women's pitching distance was 38 feet and the "undertaker rule" was in effect — the pitcher had to dress completely in dark blue or black with no lettering or numbers on the front. (See Rules Chapter for details.)

From the 52 women's teams entered in the world championships, the PBSW Phoenix Ramblers emerged as the champions. According to Morris A. Bealle:

A new star arose in the women's tournament in the Phoenix Ramblers. After knocking at the door for several years in a row, these comely misses from the Southwest finally made it and have been a power in American women's softball ever since ...

Amy Peralta set the style for women windmillers. Her blinding speed baffled all of the opposition batters. Starring abat and afield for the Ramblers was catcher Dot Wilkinson. (1:56)

While every year there were more and more skilled female players all over the country, the Los Angeles area continued to be a hotbed for softball talent. One of the strongest leagues there at that time was the San Gabriel Valley Girls' Niteball League.

Kay Rich, later to become an ASA Hall of Famer, finished the season with a .505 batting average and led her Glendora nine — they used the official softball rules of that time except that they played with nine players on a team instead of 10 — to the 1941 league championships. The Glendora team had hoped to represent California in Detroit at the ASA world championships, but couldn't raise the necessary $1,000 to make the trip.

Kay Rich in Glendora uniform, 1941

On December 7, 1941, the Japanese launched a surprise attack on the United States base at Pearl Harbor. In all, about 19 ships were sunk or badly damaged, and 3,000 Americans lost their lives. The next day, on December 8th, a declaration of war against Japan was passed by Congress. We were no longer a neutral power pouring money and materials into the war effort. We were in the war at last.

Immediately the nation's industry tooled up for full-scale war production. The efforts of the entire nation were directed to winning this war. Rationing and controls were placed on public use of products that were needed in the war effort. For the most part, the civilian population took this in stride. Auto production was cut by 20 percent, a gasoline curfew closed filling stations from 7 p.m. to 7 a.m., and civilian consumption of rubber was decreased by 80 percent.

As most of our able-bodied men went off to fight in the war, the women of the nation replaced them in the work force. Between the years 1942 to 1945, five million women went to work in the defense industry alone. Women who played softball continued to play the game, but many of them now also worked in war-related jobs.

Balancing a job, family and softball proved to be a challenge.

Flossie Ballard (A-1 Queens) and Margie Law (Phoenix Ramblers) commuted to the Goodyear plant during the war to make parts for war planes; the car is Margie's "Lulu Bell." Margie is on far right; Flossie is taking the picture (doors wouldn't open so passengers had to crawl through windows!).

The decade of the 1940's saw primarily two teams dominate the ASA national scene — the Phoenix Ramblers and the New Orleans Jax. The Ramblers took the championship in 1940, 1948 and 1949; and the Jax in 1942, 1943, 1945, 1946 and 1947. Games between these two teams were always hotly contested with rhubarbs and protests being common.

The PBSW Ramblers

The Ramblers, organized in 1933 by Ford Hoffman and sponsored by the PBSW (Peterson-Brooke-Steiner-Wist) School Supply Company of Phoenix, was a solid team from top to bottom. All-Americans Dot Wilkinson, Amy Peralta, Margie Law and Virginia Dobson were referred to often as offensive and defensive stalwarts of this completely Arizona-bred team. Ford and the Rambler team were quite proud that they were consistently successful without having to import players from other teams across the country.

1948 Phoenix Ramblers
Pictured left to right are Ford Hoffman, Dot Wilkinson, Jean Hutsell, Marie Rogers, Betty Harris, Nadine Moody, Margie Law, Virginia Dobson, Jessie Glasscock, Delores Low, Amy Peralta, Luella Reese, Mary Irwin and Zada Boles.

Ford Hoffman, PBSW Ramblers

Ford was coaching football at Arizona State College (now Arizona State University) when his wife, Peggy, and some of her friends called upon him to help coach their newly formed girls softball team. Ford not only coached that team in 1933, but he loved it so much that he continued working with them in some capacity until the team's demise in 1965. Peterson-Brooke-Steiner-Wist Supply & Equipment Company agreed to be their sponsor, and thus was born the PBSW Ramblers, a team that would prove to be dominant nationally for three decades.

Ford, a father-figure to his players, encouraged them to get an education, helping more than one financially through college. His players liked and respected him, giving him all they could on the field. Ford served as president of the ASA in 1958, and was inducted into the ASA's Hall of Honor in 1980.

1946 New Orleans Jax

Pictured on top: Nina Korgan. Back row, left to right, Buck Brehm, Freda Savona, Selma Meinicke, Skipper Dahl, unknown. Front row, left to right, Mary Pembo, unknown, Hazel Gill.

New Orleans Jax

In 1938, Heard Ragas conceived the idea of forming a New Orleans major girls softball team. With the backing of the Jackson Brewing Co. of New Orleans, the New Orleans Jax Brewers team was formed. National dominance by the Jax team was not achieved until Freda and Olympia Savona from Cleveland, Ohio, and Nina Korgan from Tulsa, Oklahoma, were added to the roster. The team was referred to in 1947 as "being destined to become the greatest champion the game has ever known."

The Higgins Midgets, from Tulsa, led by Nina Korgan who later starred for the Jax and was inducted into the ASA Hall of Fame, won the championship in 1941. In one tournament game, Nina Korgan, using what she calls the "rocking chair" style of pitching delivery, struck out 20 of 21 batters. That was one of the highlights of her career.

The 1944 ASA Championship was won for the first time ever by a team from the northwest — the Lind and Pomeroy team from Portland, Oregon. A contingent of 17 players, coaches, and family drove in two station wagons from Portland to Cleveland for the tournament. They played a total of 10 games — five enroute and five in the tournament — didn't give up a single run and scored 16 against the opponents. In the final game against the Phoenix Ramblers, the Lind and Pomeroy team finally scored a run in the 11th inning to win 1-0. The distaff battery of Betty Evans, 18-year-old ace pitcher, and Dottie Moore, the sparkplug of the team who scored the winning run in the finals, led this Port-

1944 *Lind and Pomeroy ASA World Championship Team*

Pictured, back row, left to right: Ray Brooks, state softball commissioner; Nina Deputy; Dotty Moore; Nadine Hoard; Erv Lind, coach and sponsor; Alyce Johnson; Irene Maas; Pat Carson; Glenn Gianini, Coach. Front row, left to right, Kay Gianini; Vivian Bonner; Norma Eby; Betty Evans; Martha Howell; Jerry Burroughs.

land team to its first national title. There could have been another record broken on this 2,000 mile cross country trip — they had a total of 27 flat tires! Obviously, they were happy to get home!

Wartime travel restrictions made it necessary for the ASA to cut down drastically on the number of teams participating in the 1942 world tournament. It was accomplished by dividing the nation into 15 regions and holding regional tournaments with only one winner qualifying to go on to the world tournament. That format worked well and continues to this day. Because of the reduced number of teams in the world tournament, it was possible for the event to be a double-

elimination affair for the first time. Prior to 1942, the ASA tournaments were single elimination, which meant that a team could drive thousands of miles to play only one game. The "double knockout tournament," as Morris A. Bealle called it, was much more desirable.

While men's civilian teams were reduced greatly in number, the number of men's military teams soared. Women's teams maintained their status quo for the most part although traveling great distances was curtailed. Some women's teams, such as the New Orleans Jax, traveled to military bases and played exhibition games against the troops. Nina Korgan said that she could always tell when the troops were about to be shipped overseas because there were a lot of MP's around. One memorable experience stands out in Nina's mind. After playing a game on an army base, Nina went into a grocery store there to buy some sandwich materials before driving home. The butcher wrapped up some ham and cheese, laid the packages on the counter and marked three x's on them. He said "that's for striking me out" and gave me the packages free! Nina was touched by that gesture and remembers it to this day.

1949 ASA Championship Was One to Remember

A play that could go down in the history books as one of the longest in a game — and also one of Marie Wadlow's most memorable moments — occurred in a game between the Phoenix Ramblers and the Caterpillar Dieselettes from Illinois. Marie (or Waddy as she was called) was one of the first two women to be inducted into the ASA Hall of Fame and related the story in an article in the *ASA Balls and Strikes* in March of 1957.

Marie Wadlow of the Caterpillar Dieselettes lies unconscious after a play at home between her and Margie Law of the Phoenix Ramblers.

At Portland, the Dieselettes finished fourth, beating Orange, 2-0, then being knocked into the loser's bracket by Phoenix, 1-0. I guess that was the wildest and most heartbreaking loss of my career. Pitching a two-hitter against the Ramblers, with 11 strikeouts (the Dieselettes had four hits off Amy Peralta and eight strikeouts), the score was 0-0 going into the last of the 7th inning.

There was one out with Margie Law on third base for the Ramblers.

A fly ball was hit to left field. Margie tagged up and headed for home. The throw from Dieselette leftfielder Carolyn Thome was well ahead of Margie, so Margie turned around and headed back to third. However, the throw from Carolyn went over the head of the catcher, so the third base coach waved Margie back to home. There was a short backstop, though, so

the Dieselette first baseman, Lillian Goll, who was backing up the play, picked up the ball and started chasing Margie back to third. Lillian's throw to third was high and sailed into left field. Margie turned once again and headed back to home. Carolyn's throw again was ahead of Margie — Margie headed back to third.

The throw went over the catcher's head again! The Dieselette catcher, Marian Kneer, shagged the ball and flipped it to me on homeplate. I guess I REALLY had the plate blocked, because just as I caught the ball and turned to tag Margie — POWIE!!

Margie hit me like a ton of bricks, I dropped the ball, and Margie scored the winning run! It took several minutes to revive me, and after I found out what had happened, I wished that they had left me in the blissful state of unconsciousness!! — Marie Wadlow

Western States Major Girls Softball League Formed

The formation of one of the strongest women's fastpitch leagues in the country occurred in 1946 when Ford Hoffman, Erv Lind, Dennis Murphy and Shorty Hill met to discuss that possibility. The league was formed with the original members being Phoenix, Salt Lake City, Buena Park and Portland. The name of the league changed to the Pacific Coast League in 1951. Among other teams that joined the league later were the Orange Lionettes, Fresno Rockets, Hun-

Pictured on back row, left to right, Ginny Lindorff (Utah), Margaret Dobson (Portland), Dot Wilkinson (Phoenix), Virginia Dobson (Phoenix), Joan Alsup (Buena Park). Front row, left to right, Dennis Murphy (Utah), Utah coach, Erv Lind (Portland), Ford Hoffman (Phoenix), Shorty Hill (Buena Park).

tington Park Blues, Whittier Gold Sox, Portland Pennants, San Diego, Seattle, Vancouver, A-1 Queens and the Sun City Saints.

A Redhot Rivalry — The A-1 Queens and the Phoenix Ramblers

It was during the 1940's that the Phoenix A-1 Queens and the Phoenix Ramblers began a rivalry comparable to none — one that established Phoenix as the "Softball Capital of the World." Larry Walker organized the Queens in 1935, although from then until 1947 they had several different sponsors — Coggins Sporting Goods, Allen Furniture Queens, Denton Tire Queens, and Cantaloupe Queens. The A-1 Brewing Company took over permanent sponsorship of the Queens in 1947. The Queens, led by trick pitcher Charlotte Armstrong, speedballer Carolyn Morris, captain and catcher Lois Williams, and speedy, hard-hitting Dodie Nelson in centerfield proved to be a national power in the National Softball Congress for most of a decade. The Queens were known not only for their playing ability but for their beauty. The *Arizona Highways* magazine in its August 1949 issue labeled them as "the most beautiful softball team in the world." Their manager, Larry Walker, placed great value on beauty and attractiveness. He said that newcomers to the team were screened on the basis of character first, feminine charm second and ability to play ball third. He also would not allow a player to wear a bandage or a brace — anything that would detract from the attractiveness of the uniform. Those players who were unfortunate enough to get a strawberry from sliding hoped and prayed that they wouldn't have to slide again soon!

Arizona Brewing Company A-1 Queens of Phoenix, Arizona
Left to right: Louise Curtis, Billie Vandeventer, Frances Tolmachoff, Betty Fernstrom, Charlotte Armstrong, Dodie Nelson, Joyce Nelson, Ethel Fuller, Betty Giertz, Lois Williams and Margie Yetman.

The Queens and the Ramblers were about as evenly matched as any two teams could be. Many of their games ended in a tie or with a one-run difference. During the 1948 season, each of the teams won 13 games and there were three ties. Their games were not only heated contests on the field but also in the stands. A Rambler fan was a Rambler fan to death!! And the same was true of Queens' fans. Neither would ever think of sitting on "the other side." That would be disloyal. Skirmishes in the stands were common — a woman swinging her purse at a Rambler heckler or two men arguing over who was the most attractive femme on the field.

If there wasn't a whole lot of action on the field, players created it. They would often get into arguments leading to knock-down drag-out fights which was, according to Dot Wilkinson, "what the fans came to see." Dot was referred to in one article as "the lady lippy Durocher" of softball! It wasn't unusual to see a player ejected from the game, and on occasion a game had to be forfeited. A turn of events, how-

Larry Walker, NSC

Even though Larry Walker's beliefs may not have been popular with everyone — his National Softball Congress clashed with the ASA for several years — he was successful. His success was evident not only in wins vs. losses, but also in providing opportunities for girls to play softball.

Walker coached like he played. An aggressive base-runner himself, Larry believed in his players running whenever the opportunity presented itself. His gambling on the bases forced defensive errors and scored runs. He liked to win, and he wouldn't hesitate getting in the face of the umpire if there was a questionable call.

Known to be a shrewd businessman, Larry Walker was a promoter and a good softball coach. He knew the game, and he passed that knowledge along to his players.

ever, occurred in the 1947 ASA World Championships.

> *In the 1947 World Championships between Tony Piet's Pontiac Queens and the Jax Brewers, a robust Jax player, Freda Savona, protested strenuously about an umpire's call. The umpire was thrown out of the tournament (3:120).*

Umpires definitely earned their pay. They had their hands full not only calling the game, but also handling a multitude of disturbances on and off the field. Games between the Ramblers and the Queens would draw from 2,000 to 5,000 very vocal spectators who loved to watch these fiery women play the game of softball.

Many of the major softball teams aided charitable organizations by donating some or all of the gate receipts to that organization. While the rivalry between the Ramblers and the A-1 Queens was intense at times, much good also came from their competition.

The Phoenix Maids, another strong team from Arizona during the 1940's, joined the Queens in a benefit game at Tucson to help rehabilitate a five-year old girl hurt critically in a train-truck accident. The Maids, a team formed in 1946, were coached by Walt Ruth, a prominent Arizona athlete. With a roster bolstered by ex-Ramblers and ex-Queens, the Maids at times pushed the Ramblers, Queens, and even the powerful New Orleans Jax to the limit. In the 1948 ASA World Championships, it took the strong Jax to oust the Maids from the tournament. Originally called the Park-N-Shop Maids and then the Holsum Maids, they played some years with no sponsor and were simply the Phoenix Maids.

Typical crowd hollering for the Ramblers and the A-1 Queens.

Dodie Nelson, A-1 Queens, hitting, with Dot Wilkinson, Ramblers, catching.

The Holsum Maids, pictured above left to right, are Tinsie Clow, Margie Lang, Mildred Dixon, Flossie Ballard, Bonnie Coylier, Sis King, Kay Sopharie, Louis Curtis, Eleanor Clow, Maria Burris, Katie Jones, Wanda Fields, Patsy Smith.

Formation of the National Softball Congress

Unhappy with the Amateur Softball Association of America, Larry Walker, founder and manager of the A-1 Queens, organized his own softball group in 1947 called the National Softball Congress. The main selling point of the NSC was its offer to return half of its tournament gate receipts as expenses for the competing teams. From 1947 to 1954, the NSC held its own world championships. (See the NSC Championship Teams and All-Americans appendix.) Participating teams were given a share of the gate receipts depending on their finish in the championship. Many teams that had been affiliated with the ASA jumped ship and joined the NSC — the New Orleans Jax, Lorelei Ladies from Atlanta, Salt Lake City Shamrocks, and Portland's Erv Lind Florists were among them.

There was much debate during the years of the NSC as to whether their teams were professional in nature. The ASA maintained that players in the NSC were getting paid to play, therefore they were professionals. In a feature article in the August 1949 issue of the *Arizona Highways* magazine, it said, "Manager Walker of the Queens scoffs at the idea salaries are paid and says the girls are entitled only to expenses. But expenses, 'tis said, can cover a multitude of things, especially when it comes to rigging out the stylish Queens." In fact, one pitcher said that she received $500 a month during the playing season and was paid a bonus when they played men's teams, and another player said that she was paid an inflated salary for working as an usherette at the softball park.

The ASA's stand on professionalism was very firm. Only amateur teams could be affiliated with its organization, and if an ASA team played a professional team, that made the ASA team also professional and ineligible for ASA competition. The New Orleans Jax suffered from an ASA decision concerning professionalism — a decision that is questioned to this day. The Jax won the 1948 ASA Championship and, after the tournament, scheduled a series of games against the NSC A-1 Queens. The ASA promptly declared the Jax professionals and forfeited its championship to the Ramblers. The Jax immediately switched their allegiance to the NSC. In their eyes, the Jax were amateurs when they won the championship, and the title was rightfully theirs to keep.

The riff between the ASA and the NSC was so heated during the 1947 season that all requests by the Ramblers to play exhibition games with the Queens were denied by the ASA. The ASA's statement was:

> *Ramblers are world champs and should rest on their laurels for the balance of the season. Arizona should appreciate the international recognition received. Don't by any means play NSC champs or title will be revoked and given to Toronto. (20:38)*

By the following season, however, the ASA re-evaluated the situation and revamped their rules to allow competition between amateurs and professionals within a closed league. The Ramblers, the ASA world champion, and the A-1 Queens, the NSC world champion, could now battle it out to see who was the best. Wouldn't you know it — they split!

The NSC folded its tent in 1954 with the men's teams joining the International Softball Congress and the women's teams returning to the ASA.

All-American Girls Professional Baseball League
(Played Softball 1943 to 1945; Baseball 1946 to 1954)

Many major and minor league baseball teams disbanded in the early 1940's because of a shortage of manpower. Owners of the ball parks that had housed these now non-existent teams were left with weed-filled fields and empty stands. P. K. Wrigley, the chewing gum magnate who had inherited the Chicago Cubs, convened a meeting at the Wrigley Building in Chicago in 1942 to discuss possible uses of these ball parks. The idea was conceived at that meeting of organizing the All-American Girls Professional Baseball League. It was determined that players would be recruited on the basis of not only playing ability but also moral character and femininity. Strong players from the dominant women's fastpitch softball teams were among those recruited.

The first spring training was held on May 17, 1943. Four teams of 15 players each were selected — the Racine Belles, Kenosha Comets, Rockford Peaches and South Bend Blue Sox. To assure that all four teams would be equal in strength, managers weren't told until after the final selections were made which team they would be assigned. One of the features of the spring training camp was a visit to Helena Rubenstein's beauty salon where the girls were given suggestions on proper make-up, how to dress, etc. Among those issues discussed during the camp were the league's rigid rules of conduct both on and off the field. All teams would wear the same uniform but in different colors.

Players made from $65 to $150 a week playing an 108-game, six-to-seven nights a week schedule. During the first two years, the game resembled softball rather than

Baseball Cards of AAGPBL Players

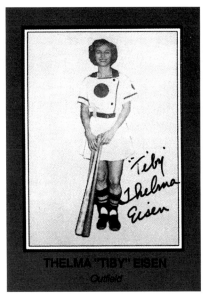

Snookie Doyle, Rockford Peaches   *Nickie Fox, Rockford Peaches*   *Tiby Eisen, Fort Wayne Daisies*

baseball. Pitching was underhand from 40', the ball was 12", bases were extended from softball, and runners could lead-off and steal. During the first year or so, the name of the league was All-American Girls Softball League. Gradually, though, the rules changed to resemble more closely baseball and, by 1950, pitching was overhand from 50', bases were 72' and the ball size was 10".

The championship team in that first inaugural season was the Racine Belles. Teams that played in the league at various times were:

Racine Belles	1943-1950
Moved to Battlecreek, MI	1951-1952
Moved to Muskegon, MI	1953
Kenosha Comets	1943-1952
Rockford Peaches	1943-1954
South Bend Blue Sox	1943-1954
Milwaukee Chicks	1944
Moved to Grand Rapids, MI	1945-1954
Minneapolis Millerettes	1944
Moved to Ft. Wayne Daisies	1945-1954
Muskegon Lassies	1946-1950
Moved to Kalamazoo, MI	1950-1954
Peoria Redwings	1946-1951
Chicago Colleens	1948
Springfield Sallies (IL)	1948

The size of the ball used in the All-American Girls Baseball League decreased every year. Left to right: 12 inch ball (1943-44); 11 1/2 inch (1945); 11 inch (1946-47); 10 3/8 inch (1948-49); 10 inch (1950); and 9 1/4 inch - men's major league ball.

National Girls Baseball League
(Played Softball 1944 to 1954)

The words "baseball" and "softball" seemed to be used synonomously in those days. Although during the first few years of the existence of the All-American Girls Baseball League softball was played (1943 through 1945), a form of baseball was played from 1946 to 1954. Therefore, labeling that league a "baseball" league seemed correct. However, in the case of the National Girls Baseball League — a virtually unheard of league that existed in the Chicago area from 1944 to 1954 — softball was played. Why the league was labeled a baseball league, no one seems to know.

The National Girls Baseball League was started in 1944 by Charley Bidwill, the owner of the Chicago Cardinals football team, and Emery Parichy, a women's team sponsor who built a softball stadium in Forest Park. Teams that played in the league at one time or another were the Queens, Bloomer Girls, Music Maids, Bluebirds, Checashers, Cardinals, Belles, and the Rockolas. Just as in the All-American Girls Baseball League, the coaches and/or managers of the teams were predominantly former major league baseball players. All of the teams were based in the Chicago area and drew from 4,000 to 13,000 fans a night.

Players were paid from $50 to $300 a week to play softball games six out of seven nights. Pitching was underhand from 40', bases were 60', bunting and base stealing were both permitted and there were nine players on a team.

1952 Match Queens
Bat boy (front).
Front row, left to right, Ginny Hanselman, Lou Fiski, Alice Kolski, Pinky Pirok, Jane McCawley, and Puddin Steck. Back row, left to right, Freda Savona, Babe Massa, Ginny Busick, Tom Fatovich (owner), Ann Knezich, Dottie Hane, Jean Conklin.

Leadership of the league passed to Red Grange in 1947. Grange, well-known football star for the University of Illinois and the Chicago Bears, was elected commissioner of the league and was optimistic about its future. The league had attracted 400,000 spectators during the 1946 season and the expectations were that the number would be increased in 1947.

Many of the top women fastpitch players in the country had been recruited to "play for money," so the caliber of play was high. Among them were Freda and Olympia Savona, Lottie Jackson, Ricki Caito, Irene Kerwin, Mary Pembo, Nancy Ito, Betty Evans, Norma Eby and Ginny Busick. They had already established themselves as existing or up-and-coming stars through their amateur softball exploits, and many of them returned to amateur softball after the professional league folded in 1954. There were many other players, however, whose total softball identity rested with the National Girls Baseball League.

*1954 **Parichy Bloomer Girls***
Front row, left to right, Fran Morlock, June Borowy, Ginny Hanselman, Maddy English, Bea Sanderson, Shirley Crites, Corky Brunky. Back row, left to right, Dot Whalen, Audrey Wagnier, O'Doud, Manager, Joanne Winters, Sophie Kurys, JoDe Rose.

Their achievements — though accomplished over a shorter time span — were no less remarkable than those of amateur players so well heard of. These women who devoted in some cases a decade of their lives to the success of the league have been relatively anonymous over the years. They were a part of the women's fastpitch legacy, however, and deserve recognition. (See Appendix G for championship teams and record holders.)

Wilda Mae (Willie) Turner, one of the most outstanding pitchers in the National Girls Baseball League, played with the Parichy Bloomer Girls from 1945 to 1952. During her first year in the league in 1945, she pitched the first perfect game in the history of the league, facing 27 batters in nine innings. Her earned run average that season was .014 and in her second season (1946) was .022. When recruiting her, Emery Parichy, the owner of the team, commented that "she had a fast ball that would drop suddenly at homeplate. No one could touch her!"

Alice Kolski not only led the league several seasons in batting but also played all positions. Her ability to pitch, catch, play infield and outfield earned Alice the league's MVP award several seasons.

Willie Turner

Alice Kolski

1944 *National Girls Baseball League Awards*

Pictured, left to right, Arch Wolfe, league president; Lonnie Stark, lead pitcher; Alice Kolski, MVP; Marge Smith, lead hitter; Commissioner.

The United States was recovering from a decade of international turmoil. The direct involvement of the United States in World War II, the explosion of the first atomic bomb on July 16, 1945, and the escalating spread of communism in the world were events that would send America in a direction that would never be reversed. Our role changed from one of political isolation to that of a world peacemaker.

In addition to world problems, spiraling inflation, acute shortage of housing and bitter labor disputes were facing Americans. President Harry S. Truman, who took over the leadership of the country when President Roosevelt died on April 12, 1945, had his hands full. As a result of the international need for world peace, the United Nations was formed in 1945. The first major challenge for the United Nations was to decide on a plan of action to combat the attempt of the North Koreans, supported by Chinese Communists, to take over the control of Korea. Since no other nation could afford to enter Korea in force, the success of the effort relied on the involvement of the United States. Hence America embarked on a costly, unpopular war — the Korean War (1950-1953).

In 1950 on the homefront, illiteracy reached a new low of 3.2 percent of the population. Although wages were up 139 percent from 1939, buying power was up only 35 percent due to inflation. The most popular modes of travel were still the automobile and railroad, however the airplane was being developed rapidly as an affordable means of travel. Passengers carried by U. S. airlines in 1948 totaled almost 13 million, over 10 times the number of a decade before.

The inauguration in the United States of transcontinental television broadcasts in 1951 caused a decline in motion picture attendance. The televising of sporting events became popular immediately with the first national telecast of a college football game occurring in 1952.

To combat the increase in television popularity, the movie industry introduced wide-screen projection (CinemaScope) and 3-D movies in 1953. Within the next decade, television viewing, due to the development of color television and more sophisticated telecasting techniques, would take over the entertainment industry as the most popular pastime of Americans.

1949 Admiral 12" Table Top TV

Orange and Portland shake hands after a game.

While Senator Joseph R. McCarthy from Wisconsin was creating havoc by verbally attacking suspected communists in various organizations in America, the civil rights movement was beginning to simmer. Even though President Harry S. Truman had established a Committee on Civil Rights in 1946, no action was taken on the committee's recommendations. President Truman took the initiative himself in 1948 and desegregated the armed forces by executive order. The rumbling became a roar on May 17, 1954, when racial segregation in public schools was declared unconstitutional by the U. S. Supreme Court. It had taken almost a century from the thirteenth amendment to the U. S. Constitution (abolishing slavery in this country) being ratified in 1865 to desegregating the public schools in 1954.

Breaking the Color Barrier

The breaking of the color barrier in baseball occurred on April 15, 1947, when Jackie Robinson became the first black player to appear in the modern major leagues. According to an article in the *Arizona Republic* on March 30, 1997, Robinson had promised Branch Rickey that he would not respond to any of the abuse and ridicule that he would undoubtedly encounter.

Despite a season-long torrent of the most vivid, demeaning and degrading abuse human ears could receive, Robinson, as per instructions from Dodgers General Manager Branch Rickey, said and did nothing except play with a unique brand of ferocity and, sometimes, rage.

To become the first black in an all-white league required courage and fortitude. Even though his career was not a long one — he retired from baseball in 1955 — Jackie made a major impact in the sports world. Others who would become the first blacks to play on major sports teams in this country were: Fritz Pollard, who played with the Akron Pros in the NFL in 1920; Earl Lloyd who played with the Washington Capitols in the NBA in 1950; and Willie O'Ree with the Boston Bruins in the NHL in 1958.

As Jackie Robinson was making history in baseball, Billie Harris, the first African-American woman to be inducted into the ASA Hall of Fame, was beginning her playing career in fastpitch softball. Billie was 14 years old, a high school student in Tucson, Arizona, with a burning desire to play sports. Even though there were some girls sports in her school, Billie wasn't allowed to play. She was told that "she threw the ball too hard" in softball! Since softball was about the only team sport being played outside of school and it was inexpensive to play, Billie decided to try playing recreational softball. If she was going to be playing the game, why not learn to be a pitcher?

So Billie practiced for hours either throwing a ball against a wall or pitching to her friend, Charles Dickson, out on the street. She ran miles every day shagging wild pitches that eluded Charles' glove. She joined a Tucson Recreation Department team called the Sunshine Girls in 1948. They traveled to Phoenix to play a game, and the coaches of the PBSW Ramblers noticed this young black gal who could not only pitch with accuracy and speed, but could hit and run like a deer. Even though there were some all-black women's

Billie Harris, the first African-American woman to be inducted into the ASA Hall of Fame, played for the PBSW Ramblers.

softball teams in the country — the Ebonettes from Los Angeles was one — there were few if any black women playing on a predominantly white team. No one really knew how Billie would be accepted by the Phoenix crowds, so both she and Ford Hoffman agreed that she should be introduced to the Rambler fans gradually. During the first few years, Billie continued to live in Tucson and commuted via the bus or car from Tucson to Phoenix for select games. As it turned out, Phoenix crowds were receptive of Billie and she eventually moved to Phoenix and was a regular on the Ramblers' roster.

Ford Hoffman and Billie's Rambler teammates accepted her as the athlete that she was and suffered right along with her as she was discriminated against. While the climate in Phoenix was somewhat predictable in terms of the public's reaction to a black woman playing on a predominantly white team, problems could not always be anticipated when the team traveled. On one road trip, the entire team poured out of the cars to eat dinner in a restaurant. Billie walked directly to the restroom while the rest of the team and Ford sat at tables and ordered steak dinners. Billie emerged from the restroom and sat down with the team. The owner of the restaurant promptly approached Ford and informed him that Billie would have to exit the establishment. Blacks were not allowed to eat inside! So Ford, after finding out that their steaks were already cooked, told the team that they weren't going to eat there after all, and the entire group left the premises.

There were occasions when Billie was the target of jeers and boos from crowds, and Billie and her Rambler teammates can relate many stories of discrimination in restaurants,

motels and other public places. There was concern when it was announced that the 1956 ASA World Championships would be held in Clearwater, Florida. The Ramblers management, anticipating problems enroute to and during the tournament, did not take Billie with them. They wanted to avoid any kind of a problem that would embarrass Billie or be a danger to her. That decision proved to be a wise one. There were numerous incidences of racial discrimination and some violence. Jeanne Contel, an ASA Hall of Famer playing with the Fresno Rockets, related that she and her teammates were naive and ignorant about racial discrimination in the south. She drank out of a fountain that was labeled "for blacks only," and she and her teammates rebelliously sat in the section of the outfield bleachers that was designated for blacks.

Almost two decades later, in 1975, Billie toured South Africa with the Sun City Saints. She was overwhelmed by the South African whites' acceptance of her. According to Billie, "I was not allowed to associate with black people, and they were not allowed to watch me play. I was an honorary white. The whites had never seen a black person perform. I was the belle of the ball." Billie was probably the first black lady that went inside the assembly building in South Africa, according to A. C. Williams, the coach of the team. This experience was to the opposite extreme for Billie from the acts of discrimination she had experienced in the United States — in particular in the southern states.

Throughout the 1950's and 1960's, the civil rights issue of equal opportunity and rights for American blacks continued to be a timebomb. Riots occurred throughout the country — in the Watts section of Los Angeles, in Chicago, Detroit and other major cities. Having the opportunity to watch athletes like Jackie Robinson, Billie Harris and, eventually, thousands of other blacks perform on the playing field, helped Anglo-Americans accept people for who they were. Dedicated, highly skilled, fiercely competitive black athletes helped to defuse the timebomb.

Orange and Fresno Lead the Way

The Orange Lionettes won the ASA world championships a total of five times in this decade — in 1950, 1951, 1952, and 1955 behind the stalwart pitching of Bertha Ragan; and in 1956 (Ragan joined the Raybestos team in 1956) due to a heroic effort by pitchers Teddy Hamilton and Nonie Hoehn. The Fresno and Phoenix teams battled each other and Orange mightily year after year with the Leach Motor Rockets (Fresno) taking home the championship trophy in 1953 and 1954, and the Hacienda Rockets (Fresno) — same team with different name — going home with the title in 1957. The Phoenix Ramblers, although they were not successful in dethroning either the Lionettes or Rockets, were consistently in the running right up until the final tournament games. It was common to see a newspaper heading that read "Fresno, Orange and Phoenix in Finals."

Orange Lionettes

In 1935, several girls living in the Orange area got together with hopes of forming a softball team. They were interested in occupying their summers, and softball seemed to be a pleasant way to accomplish that. They had decided that if they were going to have a team, they wanted it to be a first-class one with sharp uniforms and appropriate equipment. With that in mind, Elsie Kokx and Betty Bergen started talking to interested girls in that area. Among those first players were Melba Estes and Ruth Lee (later became Ruth Sears, an ASA Hall of Famer).

*1952 **World Softball Champions** — Orange Lionettes*
World champions for the third consecutive year, Orange, Calif., Lionettes with Coca-Cola Bottler Award. Standing, left to right, are Girlie Morner, Bobbie Allen, Elaine Harris, Ruth Sears, Bertha Ragan, Anne Babashoff, Shirley Stayton, Carol Ingersoll. Kneeling, left to right, are Manager Elwood Case, Lefty Bennett, Bobbie Jordan, JoAnn McLachlin, Bev Connors, Coach Chub Sears.

Orange Lionettes Continued

They now had the talent, so the next task was to find a sponsor for the team. The local Lions Club of Orange, a very civic minded group that worked closely with numerous youth groups, seemed to be a likely prospect. Plans were presented and the Lions Club liked the idea. Thus, the Orange Lionettes softball team was formed.

Their first coach, Carl Schroeder, organized practices and established a playing schedule. They primarily played teams in the Los Angeles area, winning the state championships in 1937 and 1938 behind the pitching of Lois Terry, considered then to be one of the premier pitchers in the game.

Lois Terry suffered a severe shoulder injury late in the 1930's, so Elwood Case, the Lionettes' new business manager, searched the southern California area for a replacement. He learned of a 13-year old sensation from Dinuba, California — Bertha Petinak — but, because of her youth, was not successful in recruiting her. When she was 14 years old, Bertha did move to the Orange area during the summer months and would prove to be one of the best woman fastpitch pitchers of all time — Bertha Petinak Ragan Tickey.

The Orange Lionettes, from 1935 to 1975 (when the team went pro), won the ASA national championship a total of nine times — second only to the Raybestos Brakettes. ASA Hall of Famers who played on the Lionettes were Rosie Adams, Lou Albrecht, Sharron Backus, Ricki Caito, Mickey Davis, Nancy Ito, Joan Joyce, Ruth Sears, Carol Spanks, Bertha Tickey, Shirley Topley and Nancy Welborn.

The 1951 tournament was held in Detroit, Michigan, with most teams housed in the Hotel Fort Shelby. Traveling by automobile was still the most common mode of transportation used by teams, although by the mid to late 1950's, airline travel was becoming more affordable.

Fort Shelby Hotel, Detroit (right) and Orange Lionettes boarding plane for Florida, 1956 (below)

Some members of the Fresno team leaving for Detroit, 1951 (right).

Fresno Rockets

Charles G. "Dutch" Chandler and Kermit Lynch, both Army Air Corps soldiers stationed in 1942 at Hammer Field in Fresno, played for the Hammer Field team — Kermit as the pitcher and Dutch the catcher. While playing a game in Phoenix, they noticed that the women's game which preceded theirs was extremely popular, drawing a total of 8,000 screaming fans (most of whom did not stay for the men's game!). They were intrigued by the interest in women's softball and were determined, upon returning home, to form a team in Fresno. They advertised in the newspaper for interested women, had exhaustive tryouts, and made final selections. This first team, taking the field in 1946, was called the San Joaquin Maids. The original team roster included: Bernie Amaral, Yvonne Clausen Andersen, Ginny Busick, Jean Everest, Lois Ingram, Dolores Douglas Littlefield, Betty Schuler Maim, Eleanor Huber Miller, Vera "Granny" Miller, Nadine Nickols, Ellyn Palici, Kay Rich, Bette Miller Tietgens, Irene Huber Vaughn, Doris Vickers, and Etta Weaver. Ed Ormen, sports editor for *The Fresno Bee*, gave the team the new name of Fresno Rockets in 1947. The team sponsors changed over the years, which changed the first part of the name, but the "Rockets" stuck.

Charles "Dutch" Chandler and Kay Rich

The highlights that appear in the ASA rule books of the world championships, indicate how closely matched the teams in the final games were and, in particular, the pitchers.

1951 World Championship Highlights

Just as they predicted, the Orange, Calif., Lionettes successfully defended their crown in the women's division of the ASA World Tournament, staged as a climax to Detroit's 250th anniversary celebration. The Lionettes won five consecutive games, but it wasn't all peaches and cream. They had to battle 20 innings in the final before subduing their neighborhood rivals, the Fresno Rockets, by a 2-1 score in an all-California showdown. Bertha Ragan, regarded as softball's leading woman pitcher, worked every inning for the Lionettes in the championship battles. In the finale, she fanned 22, scattered seven hits and walked only three. It was a bitter struggle from start to finish as Fresno tried mightily to snap Orange's domination. The Lionettes grabbed a second-inning run which Fresno equalized in the fourth and after that, Ragan and her pitching rivals reeled off inning after inning in almost flawless fashion. Ginny Busick battled Bertha virtually on even terms until the 15th when she was forced to retire following an injury in a collision. The payoff run, the marker which enabled Orange to hang up its second World's championship, came when Marilyn Jensen walked JoAnn McLachlan and a wild pitch followed. A moment later, Pat Collins lashed a single to right which broke up the thriller. (ASA 1952 Rule Book)

Bertha Ragan was the workhorse for the Lionettes, striking out 65 batters in 51 innings in 1952, and 29 batters in 24 innings on the final day of the 1953 tournament. The following comments appeared in the newspaper prior to one of the games between Fresno and Orange.

Fresno will face the woman generally regarded as the best pitcher in the business. She is Bertha Petinak Ragan, formerly of Dinuba. In addition to leading her team to three consecutive championships the last three years, Mrs. Ragan was named the most valuable player in last year's tournament. Her specialty is a rising floater, which has baffled the Rockets for years.

However, Fresno, behind the steady pitching of rookie Carol Nelson, and thanks to the bat of Betty Schlegal, turned five hits into two big runs in the final game of the 1953 tournament to beat Orange, 2-0.

Fresno, sparked by Kay Rich, named most valuable player of the tournament, defended its national title in 1954 by once again defeating the Orange Lionettes in the finals 2-0. Fresno's 19-year-old Carol Nelson pitched superbly against Orange, holding the Lionettes to two hits.

Pitcher Bertha Ragan

1954 World Championship Highlights —
Two Perfect No-Hit No-Run Games

Among the highlights of the 1954 tournament were two perfect games — one thrown by Bertha Ragan against R. H. Hall of St. Petersburg, Florida, and the other pitched by Phoenix's Margie Law against the Kutis team from St. Louis.

Kay Rich, Fresno Rockets, trying to beat out a hit against the PBSW Ramblers from Phoenix in Game 16 of 1954 ASA Championships. Kay Rohrer of the Ramblers takes the throw. Fresno won the game 5-1.

Law's Perfect Game

Phoenix's Law saved her best-pitched game for the standoff battle with the rampaging St. Louis as she uncorked a perfect performance, second of the tournament, to guide the Ramblers to a 3-0 victory over Kutis and into the finals of the loser's bracket against Orange.

Margie faced the regulation 21 batters as her teammates came through with flawless support to enable her to match Ragan's perfect game earlier in the tournament.

									R	H	E
Phoenix......	2	0	0	0	1	0	0	—	3	7	0
St. Louis.....	0	0	0	0	0	0	0	—	0	0	2

Ragan's Perfect Game

Bertha Ragan stole the spotlight in the second round action by registering a perfect game to the expense of R.H. Hall of St. Petersburg, Fla.

In pacing the Lionettes to their second victory by 3-0, blazin' Bertha struck out 19, just one short of the tournament record she established last year in Toronto when she fanned 20 members of Greenwood Electric of Des Moines, Iowa.

Ragan enjoyed fine fielding support as she downed the Southern champions who put up a commendable battle in the face of her sterling pitching. The Lionettes had to fight all the way to secure the victory. (1955 ASA Rule Book)

ORANGE	AB	R	H	E	FLORIDA	AB	R	H	E
Sears, 1b	4	0	2	0	Palmer, 3b	3	0	0	0
Jordan, 3b	4	0	1	0	Riggs, lf	3	0	0	0
Ragan, p	4	0	0	0	Giese, p	3	0	0	0
Kamm'r, rf	4	0	1	0	Ferrell, 3b	2	0	0	1
Morner, c	3	1	0	0	Poston, 1b	2	0	0	1
Slappey, cf	3	1	1	0	Brearly, ss	2	0	0	2
Connors, ss	2	0	0	0	Browden, rf	2	0	0	0
Dixon, 2b	3	1	2	0	Milliken, c	2	0	0	0
Misko, lf	1	0	0	0	Carpenter, cf	1	0	0	0
					#McKenzie	1	0	0	0
TOTALS:	28	3	7	0		21	0	0	4

#Batted for Carpenter in the 6th.

1954 ASA World Championship Team — The Leach Motor Rockets, Fresno
Bat Girl - Jo Ellen Chandler. Front row, left to right, Kay Rich, Irene Huber, Rose Williamson, Terry Urrutia,
Betty Schlegal, Rita Rameriz, Pat Richmond. Top row, left to right, Bernice Amaral (coach), Gloria May, Jeanne
Contel, Carol Nelson, Yvonne Anderson, Barbara Prather, Vera Miller, Joan Alsup, Dutch Chandler (team founder).

Bernice Amaral, Fresno Rockets

Bernice Amaral was the first woman to manage a world championship team! She took over as manager of the Fresno Rockets in 1951, and, during her nine-year reign, she directed the team to three world championships (1953, 1954, 1957), three second-place finishes (1951, 1952, 1958), a third-place finish in 1956 and a fourth-place finish in 1955. According to one player, "Bernie's ability to condition the players and get the best from each individual really made our clubs. She never allowed a player to be bigger than the team, and she had the ability to time our team's peaking for late in the season."

The Orange Lionettes, without the services of ace pitcher Bertha Ragan (she joined the Raybestos Brakettes in 1956), surprised some by successfully defending their title in 1956.

1956 World Championship Highlights — Orange's Fifth World Title Aided by Two Perfect Games

Everybody wrote off the Lionettes, it appeared, except the Lionettes themselves. Despite the blow which would have rocked the morale of most teams, the girls from Orange resolved they would do their best to defend their championship when the time arrived. Before then they'd prepared for the battle by tackling the strongest teams available.

DEFENSE TIME finally rolled around and by this time the Lionettes, demonstrating in league competition they had lost little of their all-around class when Ragan left, surprised very few people by successfully defending their world championship in a thrill-packed tournament which left all Florida buzzing about the high caliber of women's competition.

The Lionettes, registering six victories without a defeat, had to topple their neighbors, the Buena Park Lynx, 1-0, to seal the championship. The manner in which they accomplished the trick left a large, rain-spattered crowd limp from tension and excitement.

Teddy Hamilton made it just as official as possible that Orange is the best in the country by uncorking a perfect no-hitter against the Lynx to match teammate Nonie Hoehn's perfect game against Indianapolis.

The triumph gave the Lionettes their fifth world championship (1950-51-52-55 were the other title years) and enabled them to tie the new Orleans Jax Maids for most world trophies. The Jax Maids scored in 1942-43-45-46-47.

The victory, achieved shortly past the stroke of midnight after rain marred the program for the third time during the week of play, was stashed away in the first inning when Snookie Doyle doubled home Thelma Eisen, who got on via a single and advanced on Estelle Caito's sacrifice.

Pat Snellings, Buena's 200-pound pitching star, then held the Lionettes at bay but with Hamilton churning a no-hitter, the jig was up for the team that had fought valiantly through the loser's bracket.

The game was played under harrowing conditions. The Buena Park-Kansas City afternoon contest was rained out after four and two-thirds innings and resumed again at 10 p.m. after several truckloads of Mexico Gulf beach sand were dumped all over the diamond.

Both the Lionettes and Lynx insisted on playing the final at the appointed time because of plane reservations and the game did not get started until 11 o'clock. Buena would have had to beat Orange twice to take the championship.

The victory for pig-tailed Hamilton, who was added to the Orange roster for the tournament, was her third of the meet, matching Hoehn's three victories.

Between them, Hamilton and Hoehn allowed only eight hits and one run as the Lionettes marched through six rivals to the championship. The victory juggernaut moved in this manner 4-0 over Indianapolis, 2-0 over Fresno, 4-0 over Phoenix, 7-1 over Portland, 1-0 over Kansas City and 1-0 over Buena Park. Thus, Orange beat teams that finished second, third, fifth, sixth, seventh and tenth. (1957 ASA Rule Book)

Above, opening ceremonies of the 1956 ASA World Championships. To the right, Snookie Doyle, Orange Lionettes, attempts to score against catcher Dot Wilkinson of the Phoenix Ramblers.

Left, Helen Campbell, pitcher for Indianapolis Anchorettes, puts tag on Nonie Hoehn, Orange Lionettes, with Betty Nissley, Anchorettes catcher, blocking the plate in 1956 ASA Championships. Above, Liz Locke, Portland Florists, rounds the bases against the Raybestos Brakettes.

Due to the brilliant pitching of Ginny Busick, Fresno came back in 1957 to capture the championship trophy.

1957 World Championship Highlights —
Fresno Wins World Title on Busick 5-0 Record, Derails Phoenix Drive

BUENA PARK, Calif. — As has been the case since 1948, the Pacific Coast remains in possession of the Amateur Softball Association Women's World Championship for 1957.

But there is one change in the script.

The title now belongs to the Fresno Hacienda Rockets who won five straight on veteran Ginny Busick's spectacular pitching. The defending champion Orange Lionettes, seeking their third successive crown and sixth since 1950, were unequal to the task and finished fourth with a 5-2 record.

TO CLINCH THE championship, the Rockets, skippered by Bernice Amaral, throttled a courageous comeback by the Phoenix, Ariz., Ramblers in the final by a 1-0 score. The Ramblers, losing to Orange in the opening game of the tournament, launched an amazing seven-game win skein in the loser's bracket to reach the showdown game. But that's when they ran out of petrol in the face of Busick's classy pitching.

Ginny, standout all year for the Rockets, turned in a brilliant tournament performance. She pitched all five victories and allowed a total of only 10 hits and one run. She had a no-hitter (against St. Louis Setlich Sign), a one-hitter and a pair of two-hitters.

Despite her one-woman pitching show, Ginny had to share mound laurels in the tournament with Bertha Ragan of the Stratford, Conn., Raybestos Brakettes, who pitched successive no-hitters on the same day; Margie Law of the Ramblers, who chalked up the only perfect game of the tournament; and Alma Wilson, also of the Ramblers, and Buena Park's Eloise Bielefeld, who joined the top-drawer pitchers with no-hit performances.

Ragan zipped her successive no-hitters — a la Johnny Vander Meer — against the Indianapolis Anchor Tool Anchorettes and Houston's La Rosettes. Law's "perfecto" was at the expense of St. Louis; Bielefeld no-hit the Asheboro, N. C. Bardin Rockets, and Wilson turned in her hitless job against the Minneapolis Comets.

For Fresno, the championship was the third in ASA history, the Rockets having won previously in '53 and '54. Last year the Rockets had to settle for a sixth-place tie with Lancaster, Pa., Girls on a 2-2 record. (1958 ASA Rule Book)

Pitcher Ginny Busick

1958 —The Raybestos Brakettes Dynasty Begins

The feature article in the ASA's *Balls and Strikes* newspaper dated September, 1958, described the beginning of a dynasty that would continue through two decades. The Raybestos Brakettes, behind the combined no-hit pitching of veteran Bertha Ragan and 17-year old rookie, Joan Joyce, defeated the Fresno Rockets 1-0 in a seven-inning pitching duel.

Brakettes Bring First World Title to East;
Ragan, Joyce Spin 1-0 No-Hit Final at Rockets

For the first time in the Amateur Softball Association's 26-year history, the Women's World championship belongs to an eastern team. This distinction was achieved by the Raybestos Brakettes of Stratford, who swept past six opponents in brilliant fashion (five via shutouts) and thus shattered a 10-year grip on the World title held by western clubs. It was the 13th time the Brakettes had competed in a World Tournament.

The Brakettes defeated the defending Fresno, Calif., Rockets, 1-0, in the final behind combined sensational no-hit pitching by the veteran Bertha Ragan and rookie Joan Joyce. Their all-important run was a round-tripper by Mary Hartman, the only homer of the drama-packed tournament.

A standing-room only crowd numbering more than 15,000 was treated to a real championship battle as the Rockets, bidding for their fourth world championship, fought bitterly to the finish but to no avail in the face of the Brakettes dead-end pitching.

Ragan, who allowed no earned runs in 43 innings over four previous games (three of them going overtime), started the no-hitter but had to leave with one out in the third when she suffered a severely strained hip muscle fielding a bunt and was removed to a hospital.

With the chips down, Joyce came through with a gilt-edged performance. She retired the first 10 Rockets to face her before walking Terry Urrutia with two out in the sixth and registered eight strikeouts in her 4 2/3 innings of relief duty.

Urrutia was the only Rocket to get on base against Joyce. Thus Joan, 17, a raw rookie in world tournament competition, pitched a total of 11 2/3 hitless innings and had 19 strikeouts while walking only two to help Ragan lead the Brakettes to the championship.

Ragan herself did almost as well, so well in fact that she was named the tournament's most valuable player without dissent. In the 45 1/3 innings she pitched, the opposition gathered only 14 hits, one unearned run and Bertha claimed 55 on strikeouts. . . . . .

Hartman's homer came in the seventh inning and while it clinched the championship, it in no way detracted from a splendid pitching job by Fresno's Ginny Busick, who pitched every one of the 61 innings played by the Rockets.

Joan Joyce related that her first exposure to world tournament competition and this first championship won by the Brakettes were among the most memorable moments of her playing career. The title contest was a springboard for Joyce into prominence as one of the game's all-time greats.

Mary Hartman crosses the plate following her dramatic seventh-inning inside-the-park home run against the Fresno Rockets that gave the Brakettes the 1958 crown.

The Brakettes surround sponsor William S. Simpson following the first national title in 1958.

To the right, Brakette pitcher Joan Joyce became one of the all-time greats.

The Raybestos Brakettes

The beginning of the remarkable Brakettes story centers on a trio of individuals: William S. Simpson, president of the Raybestos-Manhattan Corporation, who organized the team in 1947 and has maintained sponsorship during the majority of years of its existence, and a pair of mound stars, Bertha Ragan Tickey and Joan Joyce. National recognition for the Brakettes wasn't easily attained, however. The club, an offspring of an informal industrial league unit, struggled for seasons before copping its first national tournament victory — a 2-1 decision over San Antonio, Texas, in the 1950 championships.

The first sign that the Brakettes were to become a national title contender came in the 1953 tourney in Toronto, Canada, when the club finished as quarterfinalists and outfielder Dena Kuczo was chosen to the All-America team, the first time such an honor had come to a Raybestos player. The success was short-lived, however, as the club dropped its first two

Raybestos Brakettes, Stratford, Connecticut
Front row, left to right, batboy Mickey Macchietto; Beverly Mulonet; Louise Schippani; Sara Lou Beebe; Janice Ragan, daughter of Bertha Ragan; Edna Fraser; Frances Spellman; Ann DeLuca; Manager Vince Cullen. Back row, left to right, Joe Barber, Connecticut commissioner; William S. Simpson, general manager Raybestos Division; Coach Al Martin; Barbara Abernethy; Marie Ottavicno; Joan Wallace; Joan Kammeyer; Joan Joyce; Mary Hartman; Brenda Reilly; and James Carbone and Ray Iwanicki, tournament committeemen.

Raybestos Continued

assignments in the 1954 classic at Orange, California, to the defending champion, Fresno Rockets, and Vancouver, Canada. The following year, although qualifying for title play, the team did not make the trip to the national event in Portland, Oregon.

But Brakette fortunes took a sharp and upward swing in 1956 when the incredible Ragan came to Stratford, and 16-year old Joan Joyce joined the club as an inexperienced but highly-promising first-year player. The Brakettes, with the help of a multitude of superb players imported from all areas of the country, have won the ASA Championships a total of 24 times in the 63 years of its existence — a record far surpassing any others.

Bertha Ragan, Raybestos Brakettes

The Brakettes successfully defended their title in 1959 by defeating the Erv Lind Florists in nine innings, 1-0. The world championships were, once again, played at Memorial Field in Stratford, Connecticut. Leading up to the game-winning play in the final game, Louise Mazzuca was instructed by her manager, Harvey Oberg, to intentionally walk Brakette catcher, Mickey Macchietto — the big hitter for the Brakettes at that time — which loaded the bases. The next batter, Edna Fraser, then rapped a single to right center field which drove in Mary Hartman for the winning run.

Bertha Ragan held the Portland team to one hit — by Margaret Dobson — and Louise Mazzuca gave up four hits to the "big bats" of Connecticut. Enroute to the finals, Mazzuca threw two no-hit games and three shutouts to share the spotlight with Ragan as the tournament's top pitchers.

Louise Mazzuca, Erv Lind Florists. In six games, Mazzuca had a total of 91 strikeouts.

1997 ASA WOMEN'S MAJOR FAST PITCH NATIONAL CHAMPIONSHIP

Legends who attended the 1997 ASA Women's Major Fastpitch National Championship in Phoenix grouped around Rose Mofford, a former Phoenix A-1 Queen and governor of Arizona. She's seated in the second row from the front, sixth from the left.

While this was a decade that saw tremendous accomplishments by man, it was also an era of much bloodshed — both internationally and domestically. We progressed from sending our first man, Alan Shepard, into space in 1961, to landing the spacecraft Apollo 11 on the moon in 1969. The harnessing of atomic energy was channeled into a multitude of uses. The artificial kidney was developed and the laser beam discovered in 1960, and the first VCR was demonstrated in 1963. The invention, in 1969, of a bubble memory system for use in computers, which allowed for data to be retained in the computer even after it was turned off, was the beginning of the age of the computer for both business and home use.

In one of the closest political races in the history of our country, Americans elected John F. Kennedy as the President of the United States in November of 1960. JFK's youth — he was the second-youngest man ever to win the nation's highest office — and his charisma won the hearts of the American masses. The reminder that evil does exist in mankind was hurled into the faces of young and old alike throughout the world when the news media announced, in very somber voices, the assassination of John F. Kennedy on November 22, 1963. Vice President Lyndon B. Johnson took over the reins of the country that same afternoon.

The role of the United States as an international peacemaker plunged the country into constant worldwide vigilance and, in some cases, direct involvement in foreign strife. The attempt by communist forces to take over the control of Vietnam forced us into becoming enmeshed in a long, extremely bloody and unpopular war. Under the leadership of JFK and then President Lyndon Johnson, our country had sent by April of 1969 a total of 543,000 U.S. troops to fight in the jungles of Vietnam. President Richard M. Nixon re-evaluated the situation after he took office in 1969, and, by the end of that year, had ordered the withdrawal of 110,000 U. S. troops from Vietnam. That began our exodus from a war that would end in 1975 with South Vietnam surrendering to communist-ruled North Vietnam.

In the meantime on the homefront, the world of the typical American family was expanding. With the consistent improvement of the automobile and the development of the Boeing 707, the first American-made jet airliner, interstate travel was becoming more common. Watching television was becoming more popular every year and, by 1964, color television set sales had outstripped those of black-and-white receivers. ABC TV taped coverage of the 1961 Amateur Softball Association World Championships. The first coast-to-coast color telecast of a college football game occurred in 1962, and the first satellite television coverage to Europe of a bowl game was in 1968. The introduction in this decade of the instant-replay feature, playing back magnetic videotape recorded simultaneously with the live broadcast, greatly enhanced the quality of televised sports events.

American women athletes continued the struggle of being accepted. While women were successful in invading some previously male-dominated sports — the first women jockeys appeared in February, 1969 — the belief persisted that women should not be allowed to run long-distance races or participate in sports that involved physical contact.

> *One of the first women to run the Boston Marathon was the world-class distance runner Kathrine Switzer, in 1967. Denied official entrance in the all-male race, she signed up as K. V. Switzer and ran alongside the men for the length of the race even after officials tried to tear her number from her back. In 1972, she was one of the first nine women to officially run the Boston Marathon. (22:46)*

Girls were still playing the six player, two-court game of basketball (the rules changed to a five-player, full-court game in 1971), and coeds and beginning teachers were still, in some cases, being forced to play ASA softball under anonymous names for fear of jeopardizing their school or job status. The "man's world" was well-defined with little flexibility. In 1962, Dot Wilkinson of the Phoenix Ramblers received a merit award from the Phoenix Press Club for her accomplishments in softball. The award was to be presented to Dot at a special banquet. While it appeared to be a step forward that the Press Club recognized Dot's accomplishments, the banquet room itself was evidently off limits to women during mealtime so Dot had to eat dinner upstairs! She was allowed inside the all-male banquet room only briefly to receive her award. It wasn't until 1976 that the banquet itself was opened to women. Dot was the first woman to be inducted into the Arizona Sports Hall of Fame — an event that was again sponsored by the Phoenix Press Club. This time she sat at the head table with the other honorees and received a standing ovation when her award was presented. While there were a few boos cast her direction, the thrill of finally being accepted for her achievements and the opportunity to rub shoulders and be recognized with the great male athletes of that time was one that Dot will never forget.

Women were not to be discouraged, though, from playing the game they loved — fastpitch softball! They put on their cleats, grabbed their gloves and sprinted out on the field to the cheers of thousands of loyal fans. Newspaper accounts of crowds from 5,000 to 15,000 watching a women's fastpitch game were common. The Pekin-Lettes from Pekin, Illinois, claim to hold the record for attendance during a season. In 1964, 110,000 fans attended their home games. For a two-game series with a Japanese team in 1962, the Pekin-Lettes drew 20,000 people.

It didn't matter what jurisdiction the teams were playing under as to whether people came to watch. National Softball Congress games played in the 1940's and 1950's drew large crowds, as did National Girls' Baseball League games during that same time period. The record shows that in 1948, the A-1 Queens played before 279,000 fans in their 153 games. Watching women play fastpitch softball was the place to be!

Stratford crowd watches an ASA world championship game.

While the schools were doing everything within their power to prohibit girls from playing competitive softball, those same girls were playing their hearts out on after-school teams. Women were performing on the softball diamond in the heat of battle as few realized they could. While college officials were lecturing that a girl couldn't pitch more than one seven-inning game in a day, Joan Joyce was pitching 32 consecutive innings in a world championship — the last 19 innings of which were in a marathon that finally ended at 2:30 a.m. During her last season with the Orange Lionettes in 1955, Bertha Ragan pitched 69 games. The A-1 Queens had only two pitchers in 1948 to throw a total of 153 games — that's 76 games apiece! And how many could catch in a squat position 43 innings in one day as Dot Wilkinson did in 1950 — and still be able to walk the next day?!

The only injury that would keep one of these gals from playing had to be serious enough for her to go to a hospital — it was an ambulance that carried Bertha Ragan off the field in the final game in 1958. Nina Korgan, ace pitcher for the New Orleans Jax in the 1940's, told about an arm injury that necessitated her arm being put in a sling. The doctor had instructed her to definitely not play for at least a week. Nina dressed in uniform for a game that they were playing that night. Her intent was to follow the doctor's orders and watch the game from the bench. The Jax got behind, though, early in the game, so Nina commenced to take off the sling and go out and pitch. They won the game. According to Nina, "losing was just not something you accepted, no matter what!"

The effect that child-bearing would have on a woman's athletic career was not well known or tested until the late 1940's. When the sprinter Fanny Blankers-Koen, a mother of two, won four gold medals at the 1948 Olympics, it was clear that going through labor did not hinder a woman's athletic abilities. Then, in 1952, Juno Irwin, an American diver, earned a bronze medal while three and a half months pregnant with her second child.

Phoenix Rambler Margie Law, then a mother of a three-year-old son, pitched the final game for her team in the ASA world championships in Portland, Oregon, while she was six months pregnant. She said that after the final game, the Lind and Pomeroy team jokingly threatened to protest the game because the Ramblers had too many players on the field! Margie commented that the birth of her second son, Bobby, was a breeze compared to that of her first son, Stan. Margie did not play softball at all during her pregnancy with Stan.

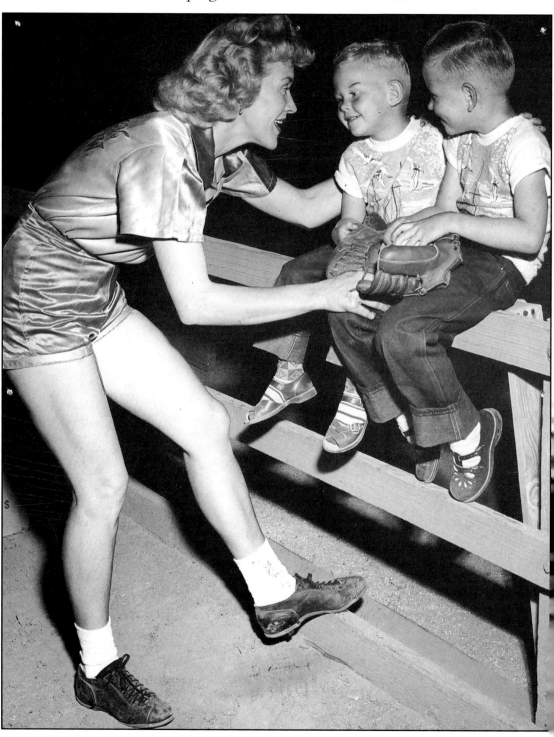

Margie Law with sons Bobby and Stan

Title Alternates Between Raybestos and Orange; Whittier Gold Sox, Erv Lind Florists Sneak Through

Once again, it was Bertha Ragan pitching against Louise Mazzuca in the title game of an ASA world championship — this time before 18,000 fans at Memorial Field in Stratford in 1960. Once again, the Raybestos Brakettes came away with the victory. Bertha Ragan, pitching four scoreless games leading up to the finals, and a two-hit shutout in the final game, came away as co-winner of the most valuable player award, sharing that honor with Louise Mazzuca. Even though Mazzuca's efforts fell short in the final game, she pitched superbly throughout the tournament, throwing three no-hitters and striking out 75 batters in 45 innings. The Brakettes joined the Orange Lionettes and the New Orleans Jax as the only teams in the history of the ASA to have won three consecutive world championships.

The 1961 World Championships proved to be one of the most exciting tournaments in the history of the ASA. The Whittier Gold Sox, after a lackluster season, surprised many by defeating the powerful Orange Lionettes in regional competition to qualify for the world championships. Their confidence bolstered by ousting the Lionettes in regionals, the Gold Sox commenced to move right through the world championship bracket. They bested the Phoenix Ramblers 3-1, Reading, Pa., 2-1, the Pekin-Lettes in nine innings 3-0, and the Toronto team 2-1. This placed them in the first final game against the Brakettes. The Brakettes' route to that spot was, sur-

prisingly, through the loser's bracket, having been upset in their first tournament game by the Reading, Pa., team, 2-1. Even though every team that they faced was out for blood, the Brakettes hung tough and won eight straight games to work their way back to the first final game against Whittier. The Brakettes came away with that first game, winning 2-0, which forced a second game since both the Brakettes and the Gold Sox now each had one loss. This final game turned into a marathon — tied 1-1 going into the 19th inning. Joan Joyce had pitched 31 innings that day going into the Whittier half of the inning. Colleen Riley reached first on a single with two outs. She brazenly stole second and third. A bold move with two outs, Coach Margo Davis gave Sherry Noland the signal for a squeeze bunt. Riley was off with the pitch, steaming towards home. It worked! At 2:30 a.m. in fog that was settling slowly onto the field, Whittier had won the 1961 ASA Championships! Joan Joyce's heroic efforts — she pitched 32 consecutive innings and struck out 40 batters in the title contest — won her the most valuable player award.

SECOND GAME

STRATFORD	ab	r	h	WHITTIER	ab	r	h
Maci'eto, c	8	0	2	Riley, rf	8	1	2
Mulonet, s	9	0	2	J'reguy, lf	5	0	0
Dixon, 2	9	0	1	May, cf	6	0	0
Joyce, p	8	1	2	Aybretch, p	7	0	1
D;wling, fr	8	0	1	Backus, s	7	0	2
Otavi'no, 3	7	0	0	Lee, c	7	0	0
D'Luea, lf	7	0	0	Ambord, 2	6	0	0
Fraser, cf	6	0	1	Donham, 3	6	0	0
Reilly, 1	8	0	1	Noland, lf	2	1	0
TOTALS	70	1	9	TOTALS	54	1	5

Noland walked for Jaureguy in 15th. Two out when winning run scored.
Stratford 000 000 000 000 001 000—1
Whittier 000 000 000 000 001 001—2

E—Backus 5, Barmore, Macchetto, Reilly, PO-A — Stratford 56-9, Whittier 57-28. L—Stratford 18. Whittier 7. 2B—Dowling, Backus. SB—Riley 4. SAC Fraser. RBI—Dowling, Backus, Noland.

Whittier Gold Sox, Whittier, California
Lower row, left to right: Coach Johnny Brooks, Kathy Donham, Chris Ambord, Adele Jareguy, Sanni Barmore, Sharron Backus, Sherry Nolan, Manager Margo Davis. Top row, from left to right: Colleen Riley, Carol Lee, Salli Russell, Pat Smith, Darlene May, Lou Albrecht, Sharon Fry, bat girl Dalene. Missing from photo: Bill Adair, sponsor.

The Whittier Gold Sox

The Gold Sox originated in 1954, joined the San Gabriel Valley double A league and won that league in 1954-55-56. They became associate members of the Pacific Coast Women's Softball League in 1956. Winning the Southern California State Tournament, the South Pacific Regional Tournament and the ASA World Tournament in 1961 was the culmination of several years of hard work.

Margo Davis, the manager and coach, organized the team in 1954 and stayed with them throughout the years. Margo was known by teammates and opponents alike for her aggressive play-calling offensively. Her call for a squeeze bunt with two outs in the final game against Raybestos in 1961 was an example of the gambles that she was willing to take. Her assistant coach and business manager, Johnnie Brooks, was a "jack of all trades" to the team and proved to be irreplacable.

Margo Davis

It's Orange Lionettes Again in 1962

After losing to Stratford in their second game of the 1962 ASA World Championships, the Orange Lionettes marched through the loser's bracket and became only the second team in the history of the ASA to capture the title via that route. The highlights tell the story.

1962 Women's World Tournament Highlights

The Orange Lionettes, carving one of the most sensational comebacks in the three-decade history of the ASA Women's World Tournament, swooped to a record sixth championship in the manner expected of conquerors.

They defeated the defending titlists, the Whittier Gold Sox, 3-2, then 1-0 in 13 innings in a double final to a tournament that packaged every imaginable thrill and then some.

The dramatic all-California showdown, staged 3,000 miles across continent from the home base of both principals, climaxed Orange's spectacular march through the loser's bracket to the throne.

The Lionettes, shaded in their second outing by the former champion Raybestos Brakettes, 2-1, had to win seven consecutive matches against rugged opposition to bag the title.

It was only the second time in history that a team came out of the loser's bracket in women's competition to capture the championship. Previously the feat had been accomplished by the Phoenix Arizona Ramblers in 1949.

By virtue of their sixth world triumph, the Lionettes became the ASA's winningest women's team in history. After taking all the marbles in 1956, the Lionettes then shared the distinction of most championships, five, with the New Orleans Jax Maids. Orange also won in 1950, '51 and '52. The Lionettes, Jax Maids and the Brakettes are the only clubs ever to win three consecutive championships.

In the same ring with the defending Whittier champions for the first final meeting, the Lionettes did their best to stash a quick victory and survival by scoring thrice in the first inning. They needed all this margin to secure the 3-2 victory that forced the showdown. Ginny Hanselman meanwhile held the Gold Sox to runs in the second and sixth although yielding six safeties.

Then in the game that counted for everything, the sudden death situation developed as Carol Gilmore and Lou Albrecht, outstanding pitchers of the tournament, locked in a tense scoreless battle through the regular distance. They battled for 12 innings before the Lionettes put across the clincher in the 13th.

In this round, Ricki Caito tripled to left field with one down. Johanna Moore and Sally Carmen were intentionally walked to load the bases. Gilmore then grounded to first and Jan Threadgold threw home to force Caito but when the return throw to first attempting to double the slow-moving Gilmore was late, Moore flashed home with the game's only run, while Threadgold momentarily hesitated.

Whittier moved through five games without a loss before colliding with the Orange juggernaut. In those five games, Albrecht had pitched shutout ball, one a perfect game against the Takashimaya Department store team of Osaka, Japan, that nation's first representative in the ASA world competition. The Osaka entry, incidentally, gave a surprisingly strong accounting of itself, with a 2-2 record. Back to Albrecht. Her runless string was halted after five games, then

1962 Highlights Continued

carried for 18 more innings before Moore came dashing home with the run that clinched the championship. Lou was named the most valuable player of the tournament, a distinction she would have traded in gladly to keep Moore on third, and along with Gilmore and Joan Joyce, she was named to the tournaments's all-star pitching staff. All this is not to imply that Gilmore was any less brilliant in her pitching, which carried Orange to the title. Albrecht fashioned a string of 39 scoreless innings before yielding a cluster of three in the first final. Gilmore, doubtless benefitting by Hanselman's alternating, nevertheless accounted for 43 consecutive scoreless innings and didn't give up a single run in the tournament. (ASA 1963 Rule Book)

What wasn't mentioned in the highlights, though, was the role that the Lionettes' dirty uniforms played in their victories! The Lionettes changed uniforms for the second game — the one they eventually lost. As the team was preparing for the third game, they decided that, to give themselves the best possible chance of winning, they'd better wear the uniforms from the first game that they had won. They did — and they won! Since laundering might change the "karma," the

Above, Cotton Williamson of Orange scores in the first final game vs. the Whittier Gold Sox. The Whittier catcher is Carol Lee. To the right, Orange catcher Nancy Ito and pitcher Ginny Hanselman wait for a pop fly.

Lionettes continued wearing the same dirty uniforms (even socks) right through to the end. As Ginny Hanselman described, "We just stood them up in a corner at night!" Winning that

The Lionettes' Carol Spanks scores on the Pekin-Lettes' catcher Rudy Rudolph.

tournament was, to Ginny, one of the most memorable experiences of her playing career. She said, "We had a very large following from the Orange area. During the tourney, so many people were calling the local paper that they had to hire extra people and add six extra phone lines. We got home on a week night, landed at the Orange County airport just before midnight, and as we got off the plane, hundreds of fans yelled for us. What a year that was!"

Raybestos Regains Title

Stormy Irwin's account, in her publication *Women in Softball*, of the 1963 ASA Championships tells the story.

1963 saw Raybestos Brakettes return the women's championship to Connecticut when Mickey Stratton sliced a line drive in the eighth inning which rolled to the left field barricade for an inside-the-park homer and a rousing 1-0 victory over Portland's Erv Lind Florists before a turnaway crowd of 15,000 in Stratford. Joan Joyce pitched a one-hitter, and struck out 14, giving her four wins in tournament play. Jackie Rice was the losing pitcher. The big bats of Raybestos were only able to tag Rice for six hits, which was a huge accomplishment since the Brakettes have the most fearsome batting lineup in the nation, from lead-off batter all the way to number nine!

The defending national champs, Orange Lionettes, had a rough time, losing their opening game to Phoenix, 1-0, then winning three before losing again to Fresno, 3-0. Gloria May gathered three hits in the win, one a triple, helping Fresno knock the Lionettes out of tourney play. Gerry Murphy, Gloria May and Sheila Patterson scored the three runs for the Rockets.

BALLS and STRIKES

MARIE WADLOW
1621 E. CRESTWOOD DR.
PEORIA, ILL.

OFFICIAL NEWSPAPER OF THE
AMATEUR SOFTBALL ASSOCIATION

Circulated in Every State and in 104 Foreign Countries

VOL. 31, No. 9   Second Class Postage at Newark, N.J.   SEPTEMBER, 1963   PRICE 15 CENTS Per Copy $1.75 per Year CANADA AND FOREIGN $2. per Year

Brakettes Recapture World Title
★ ★ ★   ★ ★ ★   ★ ★ ★
Joyce, Ragan Sparkle; Stratton Homer Clinches

WORLD CHAMPIONS FOR THE FOURTH TIME, the Raybestos Brakettes pose for this scrapbook prize minutes after defeating Lind Florists of Portland for the title. Front, from left: Laura Malesh, Ann DeLuca, Marie Ottaviano, Joan Joyce, Mickey Stratton, Bertha Ragan, Edna Fraser and batgirl Rudy Nemergut. Second row, from left: Ray Iwanicki, Bob Gann, co-sponsors of awards; Tom Ashcroft, scorer; Barbara Stawski, Millie Dubord, Beverly Danaher, Carol LaRose, Frances Spellman, Donna LoPiano, Manager Vin Devitt, Shirley Topley, Karen Hovan, Stephanie Tenney, William S. Simpson, general manager of Raybestos Division, Don Porter, executive secretary of ASA, and Bernard Iassogna, Connecticut State Softball Commissioner.

Portland's Rice Falls To Joan's One-Hitter In Wrapup
★ ★ ★

Final Standings

TEAM	WON	LOST	PCT.
1 STRATFORD, CONNECTICUT - RAYBESTOS BRAKETTES	6	0	1.000
2 PORTLAND, OREGON - ERV LIND FLORISTS	6	2	.750
3 WHITTIER, CALIFORNIA - GOLD SOX	3	2	.600
4 PHOENIX, ARIZONA -PBSW RAMBLERS	4	2	.667
5. MINNEAPOLIS, MINNESOTA -COMETS	2	2	.500
6 FRESNO, CALIFORNIA - ROCKETS	3	2	.600
7 HOUSTON, TEXAS - BLUES	2	2	.500
8 ORANGE CALIFORNIA -LIONETTES	3	2	.600
9 TOPEKA, KANSAS -OHSE MEATS	1	2	.333
10 DETROIT, MICHIGAN - BUDDY'S PIZZA	2	2	.500
11 INDIANAPOLIS, INDIANA - SOUTH-EASTERN SUPPLY CO., INC.	1	2	.333
12 SALT LAKE CITY, UTAH- SPUD-NUT SHAMROCKS	1	2	.333
13 NASHVILLE, TENNESSEE -BELLES	1	2	.333
14 ELIZABETH, NEW JERSEY - MARAUDERS	1	2	.333
15 TORONTO, CANADA - NATIONAL TORCHES	0	2	.000
16 ORLANDO, FLORIDA -REBELS	0	2	.000
17 COCHITUATE, MASSACHUSETTS - COCHITUATE MOTORS CORVETTES	0	2	.000
18 OKLAHOMA CITY, OKLAHOMA- RUF-NEX	0	2	.000
19 RICHMOND, VIRGINIA-POLLYANNAS	0	2	.000

BY EMMETT SPILLANE
STRATFORD, Conn.-- The Raybestos Brakettes returned the Women's World Softball championship to Stratford after a two-year absence in a sensational windup to a tournament that was packed with every imaginable thrill and chill.

The Brakettes, winning their fourth World title, became the 1963 rulers when Mickey Stratton sliced a line drive in the overtime eighth which rolled to the left field barrifade for an inside-the-park homer and a 1-0 victory over Portland's scrappy Erv Lind Florists before a turnaway crowd of 15,000.

★ ★ ★

THE CLIMATE clout enabled Joan Joyce to gain the nod over Portland's Jackie Rice, as Joyce pitched a one-hitter and struck out 14 in chalking up her fourth straight success of the tourney.

In winning the title for the fourth time, the Brakettes rolled to six consecutive victories. Joyce hurled a 1-0 win over Nashville; Bertha Ragan tossed a no-hitter to subdue Topeka, 11-0; Joyce tamed the Fresno Rockets, 2-0, in 12 innings; Ragan blanked Minneapolis, 4-0; Joyce downed Whittier, 5-0; and Joan again came through with the big win in the finale.

★ ★ ★

FOR POSTING her four con-

secutive wins, allowing only one earned run in 34 innings, striking out 66 and yielding just eleven hits, Joyce was named the tournament's Most Valuable Player. She was also selected on the World All Star team as a pitcher, along with Rice and Babel Bennett of Fresno.

The crowd was estimated by Amateur Softball Association officials as the largest ever to attend a tournament game, men's or women's and ticket sales were stopped well before the game began.

★ ★ ★

THE TURNOUT WAS treated to an exciting ball game, with both teams making scoring threats without success, and then,

THE BIG GAME

STRATFORD	ab	r	h	rbi	PORTLAND	ab	r	h	rbi
Stratton rf	3	1	1	1	Piper rf	3	0	1	0
Malesh c	4	0	1	0	Pettina cf	3	0	0	0
Topley 1b	3	0	1	0	Fitzwater ss	3	0	0	0
Joyce p	3	0	0	0	Doble 3b	3	0	0	0
Lopiano 2b	3	0	1	0	Rice p	3	0	0	0
Oknaher ss	3	0	0	0	Harrison lf	3	0	0	0
DeLuca cf	3	0	0	0	Spady 1b	3	0	0	0
LaRose 3b	2	0	0	0	Menold 2b	3	0	0	0
Fraser lf	3	0	2	0	Bredeen c	3	0	0	0
	27	1	6	1		27	0	1	0

Stratford .... 000 000 01—1
Portland .... 000 000 00—0
E—Joyce 2, Danaher, LaRose. PO-A—Stratford 24-4, Portland 24-14. LOB—Stratford 7, Portland 3. 3B—LoPiano. HR—Stratton. SB—Topley, S—Stratton. LoPiano, Topley.

	IP	H	R	ER	BB	SO
Joyce (W)	8	1	0	0	0	14
Rice (L)	8	1	1	2	4	

WP—Joyce. PB—Malesh. U—Susor, O. Restaino, N. S. Mayhew. Ind. Paing. Tex. Lee. N. Y., Wilkman, Mass., Brown. Wash. SCORER—Laudenslager.

suddenly, the break which ended the nine-day softball marathon.

Stratton's round-tripper was similar to an opposite-field homer down the right field foulline by Mary Hartman which enabled the Brakettes to nip Fresno in 1958 and give Raybestos its first of three consecutive World Tournament championships at Memorial field.

Raybestos repeated before the home crowd in 1959 and 1960, but Whittier dethroned the Brakettes in 1961 at Portland. Last year, again at Memorial field, Raybestos came in third as Orange battled out of the losers' bracket to sweep a doubleheader from Whittier on the final night.

★ ★ ★

THE DEFENDING Orange Lionettes had a rough time. They lost their opening game to Phoenix, 1-0, then won three before losing again to Fresno in the 28th game of the bracket.

★ ★ ★

RICE, NOT NORMALLY a strike-out pitcher, started strongly, fanning three of the first four Brakettes to face her. The Portland pitcher retired the first seven Raybestos batters before walking Carol LaRose on four straight pitches.

Edna Fraser followed the walk

Continued on Page 2

Portland's Erv Lind Florists Win Title in 1964

After finishing as runners-up in three of the last five championships, the Erv Lind Florists team from Portland, Oregon, took home the title for the second time in the history of the team. In a year that saw some switching of teams by major players — Joan Joyce pitched for the Orange Lionettes in '64, '65 and '66; and Shirley Topley joined the Raybestos Brakettes for the 1964 season — the Portland team sailed through the tournament to meet the Brakettes in the finals. The title game was a tight pitching duel between the Florists' Jackie Rice and the Brakettes' Bertha Tickey. Rice, the tournament MVP, pitched one of her finest games, giving up four scattered hits. The Florists scored the only run needed for their first world championship in 20 years, when Hap Piper singled home Marlene Piper from second base in the bottom of the fourth inning.

Chris Pettina, one of the Florists' leading hitters, scores.

1964 Women's World Championship Tournament

Game 1	Orange	2	Stratford	0
Game 2	Atlanta	9	Elizabeth	4
Game 3	Bye			
Game 4	Orlando	2	Cochituate	0
Game 5	Orange	1	St. Petersburg	0
Game 6	Portland	4	Topeka	0
Game 7	Adrian	10	Shakopee	0
Game 8	Atlanta	1	Baltimore	0
Game 9	Phoenix	5	Pekin	0
Game 10	Salt Lake City	4	Toronto	3
Game 11	Houston	7	Enid	1
Game 12	Orlando	2	Fresno	1
Game 13	Portland	1	Orange	0
Game 14	Adrian	4	Atlanta	2
Game 15	Phoenix	3	Salt Lake City	2
Game 16	Orlando	7	Houston	3
Game 17	Portland	4	Adrian	0
Game 18	Orlando	1	Phoenix	0
Game 19	Portland	3	Orlando	0
Game 20	Stratford	8	Shakopee (E)	0
Game 21	Elizabeth	9	Enid (E)	0
Game 22	Bye			
Game 23	St. Petersburg	3	Cochituate (E)	0
Game 24	Stratford	1	Pekin (E)	0
Game 26	Baltimore	3	St. Petersburg (E)	1
Game 27	Topeka	4	Fresno (E)	0
Game 28	Stratford	3	Salt Lake City (E)	0
Game 29	Houston	1	Toronto (E)	0
Game 30	Orange	8	Baltimore (E)	0
Game 31	Topeka	1	Atlanta (E)	0
Game 32	Stratford	1	Houston (E)	0
Game 33	Orange	4	Topeka (E)	0
Game 34	Stratford	4	Elizabeth (E)	0

Game 35	Orange	1	Phoenix (E)	0
Game 36	Stratford	2	Orange (E)	0
Game 37	Stratford	1	Orlando (E)	0
Game 38	Portland	1	Stratford (E)	0

E-Eliminated from tournament

1964 Women's Fast Pitch World Championship
(Box Score of Final Game)

Stratford	ab	r	h	Portland	ab	r	h
Harrison, rf	3	0	1	Pettina, cf	3	0	2
Stratton, c	2	0	0	Menold, 2b	3	0	0
LaRose, 3b	3	0	0	M.Piper, rf	3	1	1
Topley, 1b	3	0	1	Fitzwater, ss	2	0	1
Lopiano, 2b	3	0	1	B. Piper, 1b	2	0	1
Tickey, p	2	0	0	Dobie, 3b	1	0	0
Deluca, cf	2	0	0	Rice, p	2	0	0
Danaher, ss	2	0	1	Bredeen, c	2	0	0
Fraser, lf	2	0	0	Sisley, lf	2	0	0
TOTALS:	22	0	4	TOTALS:	20	1	5

Score by innings:

Stratford...................	000	000	0	—	0
Portland......................	000	100	x	—	1

DP-Portland 1. LOB-Stratford2, Portand 3. 2B-Danaher. SB-Pettina, Dobie, Fitzwater.

	IP	H	R	ER	BB	SO
Tickey (L)...........	6	5	1	1	0	5
Rice (W)..............	7	4	0	0	0	1

T-1:05. A-4,927.

Erv Lind Florists

The Erv Lind Florists team, originally the Lind and Pomeroy team, was founded by Erv Lind in 1937. For 28 years, Portland softball fans cheered 1,012 victories and suffered through 324 losses as the purple-clad Florists rolled up a .774 winning percentage on their way to a pair of Amateur Softball Association championships in 1944 and 1964, and a National Softball Congress title in 1954. From 1959 on, the Florists finished no lower than fourth in world competition. From 1937 through 1965, there were a total of six Florists inducted into the ASA Hall of Fame — Betty Evans Grayson, Margaret Dobson, Jackie Rice, Chris Miner, Carolyn Fitzwater and Dot Dobie.

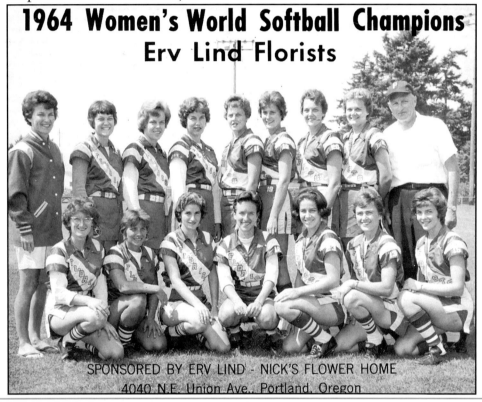

1964 Women's World Softball Champions Erv Lind Florists

SPONSORED BY ERV LIND - NICK'S FLOWER HOME
4040 N.E. Union Ave., Portland, Oregon

Pictured on the front row, left to right, are S. Bredeen, M. Wallis, B. Sisley, M. Shaffer, S. Seamon, D. Dobie, R. Menold. Back row, left to right, are Lois Williams (coach), C. Miner, M. Piper, J. Rice, C. Fitzwater, S. McNeeny, H. Piper, T. Penwell, and Erv Lind (manager).

Erv Lind, Erv Lind Florists

Erv Lind not only built one of the finest women's softball teams to ever come out of the northwest, but he was a truly devoted man whose time was constantly spent helping others. He gave of himself with boundless energy and dedicated his efforts to both youth and softball. He was, according to one player, "a father image who treated us more as family than as players." He was known as "the big Swede who had only one speed — fast." Erv was inducted into the ASA Hall of Honor in 1985.

Orange and Raybestos Battle It Out for Rest of Decade

The Lionettes and Brakettes were evenly matched throughout the 1965 and 1966 seasons. Joan Joyce pitched for Orange through 1966, rejoining the Brakettes for the 1967 season, and even though Bertha Ragan Tickey was winding down her career — she retired at the conclusion of the 1968 ASA Championships — she still had some no-hitters left in her.

The championship trophy was won by the Lionettes in 1965, and the Brakettes in 1966, 1967 and 1968. At the conclusion of the 1966 season, Orange lost five of its starting players, including outstanding pitchers Joan Joyce and Lou Albrecht. In an unprecedented move, Carol Spanks, the new franchise holder, and Shirley Topley, the new coach, brought up eight players from their farm team, the Cubettes. The youth and inexperience took its toll early on, but by the end of the season, Orange had won 52, lost 10 and finished fifth in the national tournament. The Raybestos Brakettes, on the other hand, were as strong as they had ever been, and their 1967 and 1968 teams were labeled by some as being the strongest teams ever in the history of the game. By tournament time in 1968, the Lionettes were playing as if they had played together for years and were runners-up, once again, to the Brakettes.

Orange's Impossible Dream Comes True

1969 was a year that no Lionette player or fan will ever forget! It was, according to Carol Spanks, a Lionette star for two decades and the franchise holder at that time, one of the most amazing team efforts that she had ever experienced.

A few of us went back to play in the All-Star series of 1967. At the banquet, Don Porter announced that the winner of the 1969 nationals would represent the U.S. in Osaka, Japan, at the world championships.

We decided that we would set that as a team goal — making the trip to Japan as representatives of the U. S. It was the first time as a team that I can remember setting an obvious goal. We had lost a lot of experienced players and had brought up some from our farm team. We struggled some in 1967, but by the end of that season and the following one, we were playing well as a team. We had contacted Nancy Welborn previously and asked her if she wanted to come down and pitch for us, but, because of other commitments, she couldn't. We were pleasantly surprised during the winter of '68-'69 when we received a letter from Nancy saying that she would like to come to play with us that summer. She was exactly what we needed — a really good pitcher.

We were off to Tucson for nationals! Our farm team, the Cubettes, and lots of fans also made the trip. We got to Tucson and I don't think that there was a player on our team who didn't believe that we were going to win the tournament! Our team had adopted the song, "The Impossible Dream," as our song. We had a song — we had a crowd! In the meantime, Stratford had sailed through their season and came into the tournament as heavy favorites. They had already planned to go to Las Vegas after the tournament to celebrate! We played them in the finals of the winner's bracket — Nancy pitched a perfect game — and we won it 1-0 in 14 innings. Stratford came through the loser's bracket to face us again. As we were taking infield practice, a member of our farm team went to the announcer and asked if they would play "The Impossible Dream" on the PA. They did — then, just before the game started, the moon came up and it was ORANGE! WE WON!! We heard later that Stratford still went to Vegas — they went to a show and, wouldn't you know, the singer sang "The Impossible Dream." We loved it! — Carol Spanks

The End of an Era

Many of the teams that had dominated play over the years — among them the Phoenix Ramblers, Erv Lind Florists and Fresno Rockets — were winding down during the 1960's. The Dot Wilkinson's, Kay Rich's and Bertha Tickey's of the softball world had competed as fiercely as an athlete can for 20 to 30 years, and their bodies were telling them that enough

Reunion of former pro and amateur players in Palm Springs, California.

was enough. The numerous bumps and bruises, jammed fingers, pulled muscles and broken bones had taken their toll. But, even though their playing careers were drawing to a close, they would continue to enjoy friendships with not only their teammates, but also their opponents, for many years to come. Just as Wilt Chamberlain and Bill Russell expressed in a television interview during the 1997 NCAA basketball championships, these pioneers of women's fastpitch softball were "arch-rivals during play, but had the deep-

est respect for each other now"! A camaraderie was established that only grew richer with age.

Reunions are held all over the country of former teammates and opponents from past years. A group of 150 to 200 former players — of ASA ball as well as the AAGPBL and the National Girls Baseball League — get together annually just prior to the Dinah Shore LPGA Golf Tournament in Palm Springs to play a game and enjoy a potluck.

Rose Mofford, former governor of Arizona who played with the Phoenix A-1 Queens in the 1930's, organizes an annual reunion of former players that is held in Phoenix. The Pekin-Lettes, Erv Lind Florists and Fresno Rockets are among those teams that get together on a regular basis.

The attitude of these pioneers of the game is more than adequately reflected in these comments made by Dot Dobie Buckley, an ASA Hall of Famer who played from 1944 to 1974 in the northwest (see next page).

Above, some of the Queens and Ramblers get toget... in Phoenix. They are, front row, left to right, Do... Wilkinson, Delores Low, Ricki Caito, Kay Eldr... and Billie Harris; and back row, left to right, Charlotte Armstrong, Virginia Bickle, Eleanor McLeod, Margie Law and Flossie Ballard.

Looking Back

I am so proud to have been a part of that era because I believe it was the BEST! Yes, I would have liked to have had a try for the Olympics, but to have gone through what we did was a far greater thrill. We demonstrated and proved that women could participate in sports — be good — and that it didn't detract from their femininity.

I dearly loved the game — it was always a challenge to improve skills and game knowledge. In 30 years, I never stopped learning. To have accomplished what we did was every bit as great an accomplishment as going to the Olympics. We just didn't get a medal around our necks for it. — Dot Dobie Buckley

If it's possible to relate the quality of those playing experiences in six words, then Pat Carson Durkee succeeded. Pat played from 1937 to 1952 — first with ASA teams and then in the National Girls Baseball League in Chicago. When asked for her comments on those days of playing softball, Pat simply said, "It has been one great life"!

Above, Fresno Rockets meet for a reunion. They are, back row, left to right, Betty Schlegal, Evonne Anderson, Jeanne Contel, Andie Ervin, Carol (Nelson) Cammarota and Jamie May. Center row, left to right: Vera Miller, Joan Alsup Galloway, Lee Sylvester, Pat Richmond. Front row, left to right, Terry Urrutia, Marlene Donahue, Connie Kennedy, Gloria May, Gerry Murphy.

Midwestern softball players reunite after 40 years. Pictured, back row, left to right, Mary Miller, Pat Schultz, Amy Irene Applegren, Joan Nelson, Lorene Ramsey, Madeline Dotta, Irene (Pepper) Kerwin, Becky Beckmann, Dorothy Peel, Beverly Brown, Ann Mullins Tendel, Barb Waddell. Front row, left to right, Amy Jane Applegren, Marie Nelson, Ester Torry, Joy Belsley, Barb Fuller, Norma Harden, Eleanor (Rudy) Rudolph.

A faltering economy, concern over racial injustice and student opposition to U. S. military activities caused a general dissatisfaction with American life throughout the country. The unemployment rate by December 4, 1970, had risen to 5.8 percent — a result of an economy that had been moving in a downward spiral for three years. Perhaps the most volatile situation confronting President Nixon, though, was the explosive unrest evident on college campuses. The President's announcement on April 30th that the U. S. would invade Cambodia, sparked a fury among college students that resulted in demonstrations that caused deaths on two college campuses. U. S. troops were still in Vietnam with the death toll in excess of 44,000 by the end of 1970, and the youth of America were tired of being forced into a situation that jeopardized their lives for causes that were completely alien to them.

Using violence as a means of fulfilling demands and proving a point politically, was escalating on an international basis. As flying became more common as a means of travel — the first jumbo jet, a 747, was put into service in 1970 — the hijacking of commercial airliners became more prevalent. In an attempt to combat this, security measures at all of the major airports were beefed up. Even the sacred Olympic Games were touched by violence. For the first time in their history, the Games were suspended on September 5, 1972, after Arab terrorists entered the Olympic Village, took two Israeli coaches and nine Israeli athletes hostage and later killed them.

Unrest existed, too, in the American sports world. Professional male athletes were demanding more and more money and benefits, and threatened to strike or sue if their demands were not met. There was still a major inequity between salaries of men and women in professional athletics. In 1971, the top money winners in golf were Jack Nicklaus, who had earned $244,490 during the year, and Kathy Whitworth, who had earned only $41,182. It was during this same year, 1971, when Billie Jean King became the first woman athlete in history to win more than $100,000 in a year.

Women long distance runners were still fighting the battle of being allowed to run marathons. After they were, once again, not permitted to compete officially in distance races, Kathrine Switzer, Nina Kuscik and others created their own women's-only race.

The race was called the Mini Marathon (after the miniskirt) and it drew 78 women. At a news conference, some of the organizers were asked by reporters to pose with their dresses pulled up over their knees. They refused! (22:46) The struggle continued for women who excelled in athletics to be recognized, first and foremost, as athletes.

In 1972, six women competing in the regular New York City Marathon, including

Pre-game ceremonies between Santa Ana and the Sunbirds of the International Women's Professional Softball Association.

Nina Kuscik, staged a protest of the ruling that they must start the race 10 minutes ahead of the men. When the time elapsed, the women got up and ran with the men. The Amateur Athletic Union added 10 minutes to their finishing times. Kuscik sued and simultaneous start times soon became legal. (22:47)

Title IX

The act that has affected the future of female athletes in the United States more than any other in the history of this country was the passing of Title IX on June 23, 1972. Title IX of the Education Amendments to the Civil Rights Act of 1964 is a federal law that states: No person . . . shall, on the basis of sex, be excluded from participation in, be denied the benefits of, or be subjected to discrimination under any educational programs or activities receiving federal financial assistance. While this law, in essence, affects all students, male and female, in all subject areas, the greatest impact has been on girls and women's sports — possibly because that is where the greatest inequities existed. The significance of Title IX in American society is that culturally, women athletes and girls are accepted, empowered, esteemed and idolized now as compared to their being ridiculed and criticized in 1972. Members of the U. S. gold-medal winning soccer, basketball and softball teams in the 1996 Olympics were beneficiaries of Title IX. From birth to winning the gold medal, these superb athletes grew up with a love for sports that was not questioned.

How has ASA softball been affected by the passing of Title IX? Colleges and universities receiving federal funds must provide equity regardless of sex in athletic scholarships, budgets, practice times, equipment, coaching and recruitment. While it has taken years for some schools to reach complete compliance (and many are still not there), improvements in the opportunities for female athletes were visible almost immediately. Athletic scholarships, though limited by the Association for Intercollegiate Athletics for Women (AIAW), were offered to female athletes by the mid-1970's. After women's collegiate athletic programs were taken over by the NCAA in 1982, the number of athletic scholarships given to women increased dramatically. Accepting an athletic scholarship meant committing oneself to that program and agreeing to comply with the requirements of that program. This meant that a collegiate softball player's life was controlled by her college coach from the beginning of the school year, which in most cases is sometime around September 1st, through post-season play, which could go through May. In some cases, an athlete might be required to attend summer school in order to maintain eligibility, and oftentimes players are asked to participate in off-season conditioning and weight-training programs. What has happened is that college players who choose to play ASA ball during their limited free time in the summer, practice minimally, and, in some cases, play few games with the team of their choice prior to the qualifying tournaments in August. These players are trained and developed in school programs and get together just for tournaments. The leagues and teams that were so strong during the 1940's, '50's and '60's couldn't continue to exist under these circumstances. One of the few exceptions to this is the Raybestos Brakettes. The Brakettes, probably because they consistently recruit strong players from all over the country, have continued as a national power longer than any other team.

While the passing of Title IX certainly was a plus for women's athletics in most respects, it also caused a change in the scope of ASA women's fastpitch softball. The ASA player of today is a college player first who chooses to play ASA ball during a few months in the summer, rather than a Pekin-Lette or a Florist first who just happens to also go to college. (See History of College Softball chapter for more details on Title IX.)

ASA Youth Programs Changed Character of Women's Major Teams

The Amateur Softball Association, realizing the importance of providing softball instructional programs as well as organized competition to the youth of the nation, started such a program in 1974. Each year, the ASA national office invests nearly a quarter of a million dollars on coaching and skill schools, teaching videos, literature and incalculable hours of staff personnel time to provide the best possible playing experience for the nation's youth. The number of youth teams has grown from 6,207 teams in 1974 to 78,600 teams in 1996. (USA Softball printout)

National championships in fastpitch softball are held annually for boys and girls in the following divisions: 18 & under, 16 & under, 14 & under, 12 & under, and 10 & under. Prior to 1974, girls of any age could play on women's major fastpitch teams — and they did! Players like Rosie Adams, Betty Evans, Chris Miner and Dot Wilkinson began playing as young as 11 years old. Playing with and against older, experienced players provided to the youngsters the opportunity to learn from the veterans. Sometimes it seemed to be a crash course in learning! When 15-year-old Chris Miner batted against Joan Joyce in the 1962 ASA Championships, Chris struck out. She said that she didn't even see the ball but she "heard it go by"! Also, the veterans on the team, in some cases, became role models for the younger players to admire and imitate.

Fifteen-year-old Chris Miner, Erv Lind Florists, bats against Joan Joyce, saying later of the exerience, "It helps if you see the ball."

Dot Wilkinson, far right, began playing for the Phoenix Ramblers when she was 11 years old. In this 1933 photo, she's 13 and pictured here with teammates (left to right) Esther Holton, Mickey Sullivan, Jan Dalmolin and Katie Gould.

Betty Evans of the Erv Lind Florists shows her pitching motion at 15 years of age.

The ASA Junior Olympic program has obviously been a successful program. Thousands and thousands of young players throughout the country are given the opportunity to learn and play the wonderful game of fastpitch softball. But, even though the advantages of such a program far outweigh the disadvantages, the "old-timers" say that something was lost along the way!

Rosie Adams, on the front row far right, was 13 years old in this team picture of the Orange Lionettes' 1965 world championship team. Pictured with her are front row, left to right, Sue "Dusty" Dustin Loversky, Sally Palmer, Shirley Smith, Sharron Backus, Sharon Iriye, Cec Ponce, and Adams. Standing, left to right, are Frank Cirelli, Odette Griffin, Nancy Ito, Lou Albrecht, Joan Joyce, Shirley Topley, Carol Spanks, Johnna Moore and Carl Cowles.

1970 Orange Lionettes Upset Dominant Brakettes

The momentum that the Lionettes had generated by upsetting the Brakettes in the 1969 ASA Championships, unbeknownst to the Orange players, carried over to the tournament in 1970. As Carol Spanks said, "We went back to the 1970 tourney in Stratford not thinking that we had much of a chance of winning it. It was held just prior to the world championships in Japan. Going to Japan had been our goal, so we just didn't know what would happen in Stratford." As it turned out, after an early loss to Stratford, Nancy Welborn pitched magnificently. The Lionettes worked their way through the loser's bracket to the finals to face the Brakettes once again. Welborn outdueled Joan Joyce in a 20-inning marathon to give the Brakettes their first loss, not only in the tournament but in the season. Then, after a brief rest, Nancy won a seven-inning 1-0 game from Donna Lopiano, which gave the Lionettes the title and Welborn the most valuable player award.

The confidence that the Raybestos players and fans felt going into that tournament was cause for an interesting story that was a sidelight to the play itself. Prior to the Orange team leaving its hotel for the field to play the finals, the players noticed a sign in the lobby announcing a victory dinner that would be held at 9 p.m. The first final game was scheduled to begin at 7 p.m! The Orange players were somewhat surprised that it was assumed that there would be only one game that night — that the Lionettes would lose the 7:00 game, which would put them out of the tournament. Orange commenced to win not only the first game but also the succeeding one! They returned to the hotel at 1 a.m. in the morning and went to the victory dinner. The room was filled with Stratford people. As Orange entered the room, you could hear a pin drop! The players went through the buffet line, sat down and ate. As they were finishing their meals, Joe Barber asked that someone from the Lionettes come up to the front to receive a cake. Carol

went up to get the cake — a flat cake that obviously had been decorated to celebrate the Raybestos Brakettes winning the tournament! The name "Raybestos" had been scraped off, and the "Lionettes" written in! And the flying R's, one of the symbols of the Brakettes team, were still on the cake! The Orange players obviously delighted in forcing a change in plans!

Brakettes Win Eight Consecutive Titles Despite IWPSA

After the disappointments in 1969 and 1970, the Brakettes commenced to reel off an incredible streak of eight consecutive ASA national championships — 1971, 1972, 1973, 1974, 1975, 1976, 1977, 1978. Never before in the history of the ASA had a team dominated like the Brakettes. By the end of the decade, they had won a total of 15 national championships, with eight of them won in consecutive years. Had the International Women's Professional Softball Association not intervened and enticed almost the entire Brakettes team, including their mound ace, Joan Joyce, into their folds, winning eight consecutive titles wouldn't have been surprising. But the pro league was formed in 1976, with the Connecticut Falcons (almost entirely made up of Brakettes) being the dominant team. The general consensus was that this exodus of players to the new pro league would result in a shift of power in amateur softball from the east coast back to the west coast, but that didn't happen. Ralph Raymond and his assistant, John Stratton, recruited strong players from around the country to form a team that was referred to as the "Miracle Team of '76." Among those recruited was pitcher Barbara Reinalda, who would prove to be extremely worthy of carrying the victory torch for the Brakettes. Between the years 1976 and 1991, Barbara's overall ERA was 0.31, with a 309-31 win-loss record.

1976 ASA Champions — Raybestos Brakettes

Standing, left to right, are Bill Simpson, sponsor; Joanne Burruano; ASA Executive Director Don Porter; Barb Clark; Lynn Spagnesi; Lisa Brummel; Sue Enquist; John Stratton, coach; Tom Ashcroft, scorekeeper; Pat Harrison; Sue Mochrie; Bertha Tickey; Sue Paylor; Andy Van Etten, coach; Connie Clabby; unknown; Ralph Raymond, manager. Middle row, left to right, Diane Schumacher; Barbara Reinalda. Front row, left to right (kneeling) are Cheryl Caouette; Elaine Marcil; Laura Rubino; Lisa Dennis; Diane Seery; Beth Quesnel; Mary Lou Tomasiewicz, bat girl.

International Women's Professional Softball Association

In 1974, tennis great Billie Jean King, golf star Jane Blalock and softball's outstanding Joan Joyce were in Rotunda, Florida, for the women's Superstar competition. During breaks between events and in other conversations among the trio, discussions led to the decision that a women's professional softball league was long overdue and should be attempted. Billie Jean King contacted Dennis Murphy, the man who had helped organize and founded World Team Tennis, the World Hockey Association and the American Basketball Association. When King, in conversation with Murphy, realized that he had also had a founding hand in the Little League for girls, Bobby Sox Softball in the early 1960's and therefore had a background in softball, she invited Murphy to join her in founding a women's professional league.

Murphy immediately contacted Fullerton, Calif., sports editor and longtime friend Bob Lenard, who had been a supporter of women's softball, for his advice and opinion relative to the project. After a period of months of discussions, research and background information with Lenard and others oriented in the softball world, Murphy and King moved forward on the project.

The first women's professional draft, with 10 memberships that produced a combined $250,000 performance bond, was held in Chicago in January. The 10 memberships — Buffalo, Connecticut, Chicago, Michigan, Pennsylvania, Phoenix, San Diego, San Jose, Santa Ana and Southern California — then met in Phoenix in February and settled on a 120-game schedule for each team and then went to work to place their teams on the field. (WPS Media/Rule Guide, 1976)

Even as early as 1976, the first year of the league, it became evident that the International Women's Professional Softball Association would face controversies that would plague it throughout its ex-

Donna Lopiano, Chicago Ravens pitcher

IWPSA Continued

istence. Among the biggest problems were: the polarity of talent among players; lack of fastpitch experience or knowledge by some managers and owners; apparent inappropriate distribution and lack of money; and unsuitability of "stadiums" and playing fields. Many complained that an amateur team should not be allowed to enter the league as a team, as the Raybestos Brakettes did. Just as Joan Joyce and the Brakettes team dominated amateur play, they, as the Connecticut Falcons, dominated the pro league. The Falcons were so dominant that other teams were always fighting for second or third place.

Many amateur players who went into the league thinking that eventually salaries would be high enough that they could make a living playing professional softball were disgruntled with the $1,200 to $3,000 that they actually saw that first year. In some cases, players were not paid at all after that first season. Financial difficulties caused four of the original 10 teams to fold at the end of the first season, and another two teams dropped out after the 1977 season. Playing to empty bleachers and having to travel from the east coast to the west coast more than once during a season created a financial situation that was disastrous.

The younger gals who had given up their amateur status to play professional softball could still return to ASA softball with some longevity left to their playing careers. For the older players, though, their last professional game played was probably the last game played in their careers. College players wanting to return to college ball had to appeal to the AIAW prior to 1982, and NCAA from 1982 on, to get any college eligibility back. In many cases, one year of eligibility was lost.

Runner Joyce Compton, Connecticut Falcons, slides into home.

1976 All-Star Team

Western All-Stars
Mary Lou Pennington - San Jose - C
Nancy Ito - San Diego - C
Cheryl Stice - Phoenix - 1B
Adele Johnson - San Diego - 2B
Brenda Gamblin - San Jose - 3B
Mary Flint - San Jose - SS
Shirley Topley - Santa Ana - Ut
Debbie Bevers - So. Calif. - LF
Diane Kalliam - San Jose - CF
Debbie Ricketts - Santa Ana - RF
Carol Spanks - Santa Ana - Ut. OF
Bonnie Johnson - San Jose - P
Charlotte Graham - San Jose - P
Cathy Benedetto - Santa Ana - P
Nancy Welborn - San Diego - P
Laura Malesh - Manager
Topley and Welborn - Coaches

Eastern All-Stars
Carole Myers - Michigan - C
Judy Martino - Connecticut - C
Joyce Compton - Connecticut - 1B
Willie Roze - Connecticut - 2B
Toni Swarthout - Connecticut - 3B
Sharron Backus - Connecticut- SS
Karen Gallagher - Chicago - Ut
Mary Ann Cardillo - Buffalo- LF
Pat Guenzler - Chicago - CF
Kathy Krygier - Connecticut - RF
Cathy Irvine - Michigan - Ut OF
Joan Joyce - Connecticut - P
Donna Lopiano - Chicago - P
Cindy Henderson - Michigan - P
Kathy Neal - Connecticut - P
Joan Joyce - Manager

Stepheny Tenney, Santa Ana, covers the base as Nancy Plantz, Sunbirds, slides.

1976 Western All-Stars
Front row, left to right: bat girl, Charlotte Graham, Diane Kalliam, Mary Flint, Debbie Ricketts, Adele Johnson, Debbie Bevers. Back row, left to right: Mary Lou Pennington, Bonnie Johnson, Brenda Gamblin, Cathy Benedetto, Carol Spanks, Nancy Ito, Nancy Welborn, Cheryl Stice, Shirley Topley, Laura Malesh.

1979 *Sun City Saints*

Pictured, bottom row, left to right, are bat girl, Shawn Ritchey, Lisa Clinchy, Karen Fellenz, Paula Stufflebeam; second row, left to right, Michele Thomas, Deanne Clark, Marilyn Rau, Terri Smith, Suzie Gaw, Rockie LaRose; top row, left to right, Garald Stapley (coach), Thelma Keith (coach), Paula Noel, Lynn Mooney, Lisa Stuck, Gail Davenport, Katie Nielsen, unknown.

Sun City Stadium — Home of the Sun City Saints

Sun City Saints Win ASA Title in 1979

After years of being strong contenders for the national title, the Sun City Saints from Arizona came away victorious in the 1979 ASA National Championships held in Springfield, Missouri. The streak of winning eight consecutive national titles established by the Raybestos Brakettes was snapped when the favored Brakettes lost two consecutive games and were eliminated from the tournament. The Saints defense, behind the strong pitching of Michelle Thomas, didn't allow a run to be scored against them during the entire tournament. In the final contest, the Saints defeated the Glendale Blazers, 2-0. ASA All-American catcher, Marilyn Rau, led the Saints with a .500 batting average, and was named most valuable player for the tournament.

The Sun City Saints

The story of the Sun City Saints began in 1965 when the Phoenix Ramblers team (a national power during the 1940's and '50's) decided to hang up their cleats. Some of the players, determined not to let the team die, started searching the Phoenix area for a new home. Bev Dryer, one of the younger players with the Ramblers at the time, led the search that found its way to Sun City, Arizona, a booming retirement community northwest of Phoenix. Bev's persistence and charm won over the management of the Del E. Webb Development Company, the builder of Sun City, and a ballpark was built. Through a community-wide contest, the team was named the "Saints" and all systems were go for the 1966 season.

Sun Citians fell in love with the team quickly and supported the team 100 percent. Much to the delight of the team, thousands of geriatric Sun City residents became their loyal fans. A concentrated effort on the part of the team members to participate in Sun City activities, and the eagerness of Sun Citians to "have their own team" made for a wonderfully successful relationship.

ASA Hall of Famer Marilyn Rau led the Saints to the 1979 ASA title.

The technological age had boomed to the point that gadgets and devices that at one time were thought to be science fiction in nature were taken for granted. Every American family owned, not just one, but several color television sets and automobiles. Children from birth on were as familiar with computers and computerized games as they were with blocks. The development of pagers and mobile phones made it possible to communicate with anyone, anywhere, anytime.

While many Americans were enjoying the conveniences of modern technology, the unemployment rate and the number of homeless people in this country were rising. A long standing challenge for an American president was to attempt to maintain some kind of equilibrium domestically while continuing in the role as international peacemaker.

Radical policy changes were instituted in the Soviet Union. The tearing down of the Berlin Wall in 1989, which since August 31, 1961, had divided East and West Berlin, was the first step on the path to German reunification. In 1990, the Soviet Congress enacted sweeping changes in Soviet communist government, which included the end to one-party government, legalization of private ownership of factories, and the creation of a strong presidency. Similar moves toward democracy were taken throughout Eastern Bloc nations.

Space travel had become almost as humdrum as riding the bus. Those people who were on the edge of their seats in 1969 listening to reports of Apollo 11's landing the first man on the moon were rarely even aware of spacecraft flights in the 1980's and '90's.

In the softball world, the overall structure of ASA women's fastpitch softball competition and the character of teams had changed. There were still a few of the old teams competing — the Brakettes, the Pekin-Lettes and the Orlando Rebels were among them — but for the most part, summer teams were composed of college players, or former college players, who got together for the purpose of competing in qualifying tournaments with the hopes of going on to nationals. The team roster, and sometimes even the team name, could easily change from year to year. The large, rowdy, loyal local crowds who had cheered their "girls" on in the earlier years, had retired with their teams. Thanks to the marvels of world-wide television coverage, the sportsminded person now had a multitude of viewing options at any given time during the day or night. The avid Rambler fan who, in years gone by, had only one or two choices of what to do with her leisure time, now had lots of choices.

From the first world championships in 1965 in Melbourne, Australia, through the 1995 Pan American Games, the United States national team dominated international play, winning nine gold and three silver medals in a total of 13 competitions. The announcement that every softball enthusiast in the country was waiting for finally came on June 13, 1991 — women's fastpitch softball would be included in the 1996 Olympic Games! After three decades of false alarms, the International Olympic Committee finally approved softball as an Olympic sport.

The Brakettes' Dynasty Begins to Crumble — Orlando Rebels and California Teams Knock Them Off

The decade of the 1980's began with a familiar note — the Raybestos Brakettes won the 1980 ASA National Championships. That dominance, though, would soon change. The Orlando Rebels, a team founded in 1954 by Marge Ricker and frequently a strong contender for the national title, finally won the big one in 1981! After so many years of coming close but not quite making it, Marge Ricker could hardly believe that they had done

it. An article in the April 1982 *Woman's Softball* magazine relates how she felt.

Years from now, Marge will still relive every pitch of the Rebels' 2-1 triumph over the Raybestos Brakettes. She will savor every hit, every strike, every slide. Particularly that magic moment shortly after midnight when Patty Pyle slid into home plate with the winning run.

Fireworks didn't explode in Marge's brain at that exact moment. Victory didn't sink in until later. After too many years of too close, her mind refused to accept reality. The tragedy of a 1-0 deficit had become the triumph of a 2-1 victory.

She said "This team was a coach's dream. It was the extra little ingredients that put us there." Pandemonium broke out after the Rebels' victory. The place went wild with Rebel fans and former players congratulating Marge and her players.

1981 ASA National Champions — Orlando Rebels
Pictured, back row, left to right, are Snooki Mulder, Joan Ackerman, Darlene Lowry, Lou Piel, Sandy Loveless, Marcia Newsome, Patty Pyle, Joan Blackford, Marge Ricker (manager). Kneeling, left to right, Jae Butera, Dot Richardson, Lindi James, Sonya Smith, Shirley Burton.

Marge Ricker, Orlando Rebels

Marge Ricker, the Orlando Rebels manager from 1954 to 1985, put softball first, last and always! During her 32 years with the Rebels, her teams amassed a record of 1,470 wins and 476 losses. The highlight of her career was defeating the Raybestos Brakettes in the final game of the 1981 ASA National Championships, 2-1, to win the title.

Ricker always demanded a lot from her players but no more than she did from herself. She was the first to arrive at the park and the last to leave. One of her players said, "She's very human, very dedicated. She puts softball in front of everything." Marge believed that to win a tournament you had to get a good break and then have the knowledge to take advantage of it. She was inducted into the ASA Hall of Honor in 1980.

Marge Ricker

Both the Bertha Tickey award and the Erv Lind award went to Orlando Rebels' players. Dot Richardson won the Erv Lind award, depicting her as the best defensive player of the tournament, and the Bertha Tickey award designating the most valuable pitcher of the tournament went to Rebels' pitcher, Lou Piel.

Power Shifts to the West Coast

During the next two years, 1982 and 1983, the Raybestos Brakettes fought gallantly to regain their dominance. They successfully regained the title in 1982, and then had to stage an incredible march through the loser's bracket, winning nine games in a row, to win the championship again in 1983 in Salt Lake City. California teams were beginning to emerge as title contenders. The strong Junior Olympic program in California fed into the college programs, which, in turn, fed into the ASA Women's Major program. It was a California team, the California Diamond Blaz-

ers, who defeated the Brakettes 1-0 to win the 1984 ASA National Championships. The Blazers were led by Sue Lewis, their power-hitting first baseman, who led the tournament in batting with a .421 average, including three home runs. Tracy Compton, a college pitcher from Southern California, held the Brakettes to five hits and no runs. Five of the top eight finishers were from California — the Orange County Majestics were third; Long Beach Renegades were fifth; Computerland Hustle sixth; and Bettencourt Blast seventh.

The remaining championships in the 1980's were a ping pong battle between the Brakettes, and various teams from Southern California. The Brakettes regained the title in 1985, only to be dethroned in 1986 by the Southern California Invasion. The Orange County Majestics, coached by ASA Hall of Famers Shirley Topley and Carol Spanks, were victorious in 1987, before the honors went back once again to Stratford and the Brakettes in 1988. In 1989, the ball bounced back to California, with the Whittier Raiders victorious.

Brakettes Recruiting Pays Off — Win 1990, 1991 and 1992 Titles

With a team roster bolstered by some of the strongest college and ex-college players in the country, the Raybestos Brakettes snatched the national title back and successfully held onto it for three consecutive years — 1990, 1991 and 1992. The title game in the 1991 ASA National Championships was one that will be remembered forever by all in attendance that day, August 24, in Decatur, Illinois. With the 1990 title already under their belts, the Brakettes went into the 1991 tournament sporting an impressive 64-1 record. The October 1991 issue of *Women's Fastpitch World* related the drama that unfolded on August 24, 1991.

Barbara Reinalda (left) and Kathy Arendsen, two links in a great Brakettes pitching chain, with 760 career wins between them.

Faced with elimination and down to their last strike, the Brakettes refused to settle for second best as they rallied to defeat the surprising California Knights of Burbank 2-1 in 10 innings and 8-0 in the final to successfully defend their championship before a crowd of 5,500. The 2-1 win over the Knights was one of the most remarkable softball wins in the Brakettes' 45-year history. Facing the team that had sent them into the loser's bracket (a 1-0 loss in the semifinals), the Brakettes trailed 1-0 with two out when No. 9 Doreen Denmon walked up to the plate in the bottom of the seventh.

With the trophy table already being put into position in anticipation of a Knights win, Denmon, a .206 hitter, gallantly fought off several Lori Harrigan offerings, fouling off four pitches before lining a double to right field. When the count reached 0-2, even the most loyal Raybestos fans had to be wondering "what if we had . . . ."

Those doubts were erased when leadoff Dot Richardson smacked an 0-2 pitch to left center to deliver pinch-runner Michelle Palmer with the tying run. Raybestos won the game in the bottom of the 10th as Jill Justin's gapper to right center scored Dionna Harris, who had singled with two out.

The Brakettes fielded the strongest pitching corps in the U. S. with ASA All-Americans Kathy Arendsen, Barbara Reinalda, Cheri Kempf and Lisa Fernandez. Their team ERA for the 1991 season was 0.25. Offensively, future Olympians Dot Richardson and Sheila Cornell, and ASA All-American Pat Dufficy, led the way.

Returning for the 1992 season for the Brakettes was almost the complete roster that had successfully won the title the two previous years. For the 23rd time in the 59-year history of the ASA championships, the Raybestos Brakettes were victorious.

Dot Richardson (left) and Lisa Fernandez display some of the awards won by the Raybestos Brakettes and themselves.

1991 ASA National Champions — Raybestos Brakettes

Pictured here, front row, left to right, are Jill (Justin) Coffel, Lelie Adams, Pat Dufficy, Barb Reinalda, Kathy Arendsen, Cheri Kempf, Sheila (Cornell) Douty and Kris Schmidt. Back row, left to right, Ralph Raymond (head coach), unknown, Doreen Denmon, Julie Standering, Dot Richardson, Lisa Fernandez, Karen (Walker) Deegen, Mary Jo Firnbach, Dionna Harris, Michelle Parker, Bob Baird (assistant coach), John Stratton (assistant coach).

Redding Rebels Establish Themselves as National Power — Win Titles in 1993, 1994 and 1995

For years, the Redding Rebels from California had ranked as one of the true powerhouses of women's fastpitch softball. They won the Class A national championship in 1985, and had never finished lower than ninth since moving up to the major division in 1987. The Rebels placed third in 1989 and 1991, and second in 1990 and 1992. Even though they had never won a national championship, the Rebels enjoyed perhaps more success against the Raybestos Brakettes than any

team in the country. Yet one hurdle remained for Roger Dawes, the Rebels' coach, manager and sponsor, and that was to beat the Brakettes when it mattered the most. As Dawes said prior to the 1993 tournament, "Until we find a way to beat Lisa Fernandez, we won't beat the Brakettes." With a team stacked with ASA All-Americans, the Redding Rebels found a way to beat Fernandez and the Brakettes to not only win the 1993 ASA Championships, but to successfully defend their title the next two years. The Rebels in 1993 fielded perhaps the best corner combination in the country with Cindy

Cooper at third base and Kelly Jackson at first base, and were led by All-Americans Julie Smith (.354) and Barbara Jordan (.340) at the plate. All-American and future Olympian, Michele Smith, the Rebels' ace pitcher, performed brilliantly on the mound, winning the Bertha Tickey award in 1993, 1994 and 1995.

The Redding Rebels

Roger Dawes founded the Rebels in 1977 as an 18 & under team. His motive was simple — he had three daughters with whom he wanted to spend more time. From that first team to the present one, Roger's philosophy of coaching hasn't changed. He strives to instill self-discipline in his players and involve them in the planning of the team. The Rebels went to their first nationals in 1981, won the A Division nationals in 1985 and moved up to the major division in 1986. Since 1988, Roger's teams have never finished lower than third. From 1986 to 1996, 12 Redding Rebels have been chosen as ASA First Team All-Americans. One of them, Michele Smith, has been selected as an All-American eight consecutive years — 1990 through 1997.

1993 ASA National Champions — Redding Rebels
Pictured, top row, left to right, are Ken Dedontney (assistant coach), Kelly Jackson, Tami Brown, Barbara Jordan, Dee Dee Weiman, Roger Dawes (head coach), Denise Day, Chris Parris, Lori Sippel, Jennifer Brundage, Cindy Cooper, Art Martineau (assistant coach), Michelle Gromacki, Susie Lady, Vicky Dawes (scorekeeper). Bottom row, left to right, Julie Smith, Angie Jacobs, Michele Smith.

In the 1992 nationals, the Brakettes' Lisa Fernandez pitches to the Rebels' Kelly Jackson.

1996 ASA National Champions — California Commotion
Picture above, front row, left to right, are bat girl, Gillian Boxx, Kristy Howard, Jenny Condon and Karen (Walker) Deegen. Back row, left to right, Stacey Nuveman, Christa Williams, Jill (Justin) Coffel, Sheila (Cornell) Douty, Jennifer Brundage, Amy Chellevold, Lisa Fernandez and Lydia Stiglich.

California Teams Dominate — Commotion Wins in 1996

The California Commotion from Woodland Hills, California, won its first title in 1996 with a roster that boasted six Olympians and two alternates. The Commotion posted a 6-1 record, rolling over the Topton VIPs of Pennsylvania, 3-0; the Thunderbolts from Keene, New Hampshire, 5-0; the St. Louis Classics of St. Louis 8-0; the Redding Rebels from Redding, California; and the California Jazz of Bellflower, California, 10-0. The California Jazz turned out to be the surprise team in the tournament, collecting wins over the defending champion Redding Rebels to advance to the finals. In the finals, the Jazz beat the Commotion 2-1 before falling in the "if" game.

Lisa Fernandez of the Commotion was named MVP, and fellow Olympian, Kim Maher of the Redding Rebels, won the batting title with a .500 average. Gillian Boxx of the Commotion won the Erv Lind award, and Desarie Knipfer of the California Jazz won the Bertha Tickey award. Fifteen of the 16 first team All-Americans were from California teams.

Women's Professional Fastpitch

The newest women's professional fastpitch softball league, Women's Professional Fastpitch, made its debut in June 1997. The result of an idea hatched in 1989 by former Utah State University player, Jane Cowles, and former Utah State University head softball coach, John Horan, the league's inaugural season consisted of a 72-game schedule played by six teams — Atlanta; Charlotte, North Carolina; Tampa; Orlando; Raleigh/Durham, North Carolina; and Hampton/Newport News, Virginia. Based on several years of research and experimentation of the game rules, it was determined that the league's rules would include using a 12-inch optic yellow ball, 46-foot pitching distance and 65-foot base distances. Baserunners were permitted to leave the base once the pitcher's hands separated, and the outfield fences were 220-230 feet in left and right field, and 240-250 feet in center field.

The 15 players on each team's roster were primarily former college players from NCAA Divisions I, II and III schools, and NAIA institutions. The average player's salary was $2,000 a month.

The Orlando Wahoos won the 1997 title by defeating the Virginia Roadsters in a best-of-five-game series. Debbie Doom, former UCLA star, won the MVP award by pitching the Wahoos to three championship victories by scores of 3-1, 10-3 and 11-1.

Doom's comments on the altered rules of softball that were used in the league appeared in the September 10, 1997, issue of the *Arizona Republic*.

It's hard to be a super-successful pitcher in this league, because you're pitching from 46 feet. My whole career, from high school to college to ASA ball to international play, involved pitching from 40 feet. It's a very big change.

It's a lot harder on your body, and probably every pitcher in the league was hurting at the end of the season. The hitters used lively bats and the balls had a very hard core inside. They wanted more offense in the league and they got it.

1997 WPF Award Winners

Most Valuable Player
Sarah Dawson, Orlando Wahoos
Hitter of the Year
Liz Mazera, Orlando Wahoos
Pitcher of the Year
Sarah Dawson, Orlando Wahoos
Defensive Player of the Year
Rashunda Taylor, Orlando Wahoos
Coach of the Year
Lu Harris, Orlando Wahoos
Home Run Champions
Sue Lewis-Newton, Orlando Wahoos
Liz Mazera, Orlando Wahoos
Trisha Reinhardt, Durham Dragons

For the 1998 season, the rules were changed to reduce the length of the basepaths from 65 to 60 feet, and the pitching distance from 46 to 43 feet. League officials, optimistic about the future, were planning to expand the league to more teams in 1999.

The Legacy Turned to Gold

From a hot dog and a coke to an Olympic Gold Medal — from the batter having the option of running to either first base or third base to running to first base only — from using "pancake" gloves (or no gloves), wooden bats and no catcher's equipment to using sliding pads, batting gloves and pitching machines — from the pitcher using a windmill

Nera White

Elsie Wulf

delivery with multiple arm revolutions and releasing the ball who knows when from 35 feet to very specific pitching rules that take up pages in the rule book — from 10,000 screaming loyal fans cheering their "girls" on to a few hundred who may not even know the names of the teams — from driving 3,000 miles in a stick shift car and having 27 flat tires to play possibly one game in a national championship to boarding an airplane and reaching the destination three hours later — from being ridiculed and criticized to being empowered, esteemed and idolized — THAT is the path that we've traveled en route to winning the gold medal in 1996!

From 1930 on, thousands of women got the clutch hit to win the game, made the spectacular catch for the third out and out-hustled the defense to beat out a bunt. For every well-known name, there were a multitude of others who were solid, highly competitive ball players who displayed a fierce determination to win. Players like Robbie Mulkey, who played for the Orange Lionettes and later with the Erv Lind Florists; Nera White, a basketball hall-of-famer who also starred on the softball diamond for the Nashville Mustangs; Dot Elliot, pitching ace for the Atlanta Lorelei Ladies; and Elsie Wulf, who was not a flashy player but "always got the job done" at third base for the Indianapolis Anchorettes, were typical of the thousands of fine women athletes who excelled "between the lines." It was the legacy of each and every player who ever donned a uniform and questioned an umpire's call that turned to gold in the 1996 Olympic Games!

Dot Elliot

Robbie Mulkey

A packed house watched the 1996 Olympic softball competition in Columbus, Georgia.

Even though the first official international competition wasn't held until 1965 — the world championships in Melbourne, Australia — women's fastpitch softball teams from the United States traveled abroad as early as 1938 on goodwill tours. Two teams from the Fiedler Field League in Los Angeles departed from San Pedro, California, in early September, 1938, on the Japanese ship Chichibu Maru enroute to Hawaii, Japan and the Philippines. The Orange Lionettes were invited by the U. S. government to tour the far east in 1960, and the Sun City Saints traveled to South Africa in 1975. There were others. While the intent of these goodwill trips was just that — to establish goodwill between our country and the countries visited — the first international competition that involved teams from several countries in a tournament format with one team emerging as champion was held in Melbourne, Australia, in 1965.

Since the 1965 Women's World Championships, the United States women's fastpitch teams have dominated international play like few teams have in the history of sport. In the eight world championships that

the United States has participated in, the Americans have come home with five gold and two silver medals; and in five Pan American Games, the U.S. has won four gold medals and one silver. America has amassed a lifetime record of 74-9 in world championships and 51-3 in the Pan American Games — a combined win-loss record of 125-12. U. S. teams have outscored their opponents 806-85 in the process. Winning the gold medal at the 1996 Olympic Games was a continuation of a dynasty established by women's fastpitch softball teams from the United States for three decades.

Prior to 1990, the team that won the ASA championships the preceding season earned the right to represent the U.S. in the world championships. From 1990 on, the U.S. national team became the official representative to the world championships. A selection process determined which players would participate on the U.S. Pan American Games teams. The teams and the results of that international competition follow.

1978 World Champions — Raybestos Brakettes

Back row, left to right, unknown, Ralph Raymond (coach), Frank Taylor, (ASA commissioner-Virginia), John Stratton (coach), unknown, Marilyn Rau, Diane Schumacher, Gina Vecchione, Barbara Reinalda, Kathy Strahan, Joan Van Ness, Connie Clabby, Sue Enquist, Doreen Denmon, Beth Quesnel. Front row, left to right, Pat Dufficy, Kathy Arendsen, Lana Svec, Pat Fernandes, Barb Clark.

1965 World Championships *Melbourne, Australia*	1970 World Championships *Osaka, Japan*	1974 World Championships *Stratford, CT, USA*	1978 World Championships *San Salvador, El Salvador*
Silver Medalists (8-3) (Raybestos Brakettes)	**Silver Medalists (8-3) (Orange Lionettes)**	**Gold Medalists (9-0) (Raybestos Brakettes)**	**Gold Medalists (9-0) (Raybestos Brakettes)**
Vin Devitt-Coach	Shirley Topley-Coach	Ralph Raymond-Coach	Ralph Raymond-Coach
Kathryn "Sis" King	Carol Spanks	Rose Marie Adams	Barbara Reinalda
Bertha Tickey	Cecilia Ponce	Sharron Backus	Joan Van Ness
Donna Lopiano	Nancy Ito	Joann Cackowski	Gina Vecchione
Carol La Rose	Mickey Davis	Barbara Clark	Sue Enquist
Pat Harrison	Susan Kay Sims	Joyce Compton	Kathy Strahan
Rosemary Stratton	Mary Lou Adams	Kathy Elliott	Marilyn Rau
Laura Malesh	Nancy Welborn	Joan Joyce	Pat Fernandes
Bev Danaher	Jacqueline Lee Rice	Peggy Kellers	Doreen Denmon
Edna Fraser	Roxanne Marie Zavala	Joan Moser	Barbara Clark
Ann DeLuca	Karel Deette Graham	Cecilia Ponce	Kathy Arendsen
Millie Dubord	Patricia Jane Schnell	Willie Roze	Diane Schumacher
Mary Bennett	Sherron Marie Bredeen	Irene Shea	Constance Clabby
Brenda Reilly	Rose Marie Adams	Clair Beth Tomasiewicz	Lana Svec
		Susan Tomko	Beth Quesnel
		Pat Whitman	

1982 World Championship
Taipei, Taiwan

(Orlando Rebels)
Fourth (7-3)

Marge Ricker-Coach
Marcia Newsome
Darlene Lowery
Melissa Coulter
Patty Pyle
Snooki Mulder
Lindy James
Lou Piel
Sandra Loveless
Shirley Burton
Kathy Stilwell
Tracy Compton
Jae Butera
Dot Richardson
Amy Lyons
Joanne Blackford
Debbie Doom

1986 World Championship
Auckland, New Zealand

(Raybestos Brakettes)
Gold Medalists (13-0)

Ralph Raymond-Coach
Dot Richardson
Jackie Gaw
Kristen Peterson
Lisa Ishikawa
Allyson Rioux
Elizabeth O'Connor
Michele Granger
Deanne Moore
Lea Ann Jarvis
Trish Mang
Chris Dinoto
Jennae Lambdin
Gretchen Larson
Kathy Arendsen
Doreen Denmon
Pat Dufficy
Barbara Reinalda

1990 World Championship
Normal, IL, USA

U. S. Team
Gold Medalists (10-0)

Ralph Raymond-Coach
Lisa Fernandez
Mary Lou Flippen
Tammy Holloway
Sheila Cornell
Pam Newton
Dot Richardson
Karen Sanchelli
Lea Ann Jarvis
Jill Justin
Kris Peterson
Xan Silva
Denise Eckert
Suzy Brazney
Lisa Longaker
Debbie Doom
Becky Duffin
Kathy Arendsen

1994 World Championship
Newfoundland, Canada

U. S. Team
Gold Medalists (10-0)

Ralph Raymond-Coach
Laura Berg
Gillian Boxx
Jenny Condon
Sheila Cornell
Pat Dufficy
Lisa Fernandez
Michele Granger
Michelle Gromacki
Lori Harrigan
Barbara Jordan
Jill Justin
Martha O'Kelley
Susie Parra
Dot Richardson
Karen Sanchelli
Julie Smith
Michele Smith

1979 Pan American Games
San Juan, Puerto Rico

Gold Medalists (9-0)

Ralph Raymond-Coach
Marilyn Rau
Julie Winklepleck
Kathy Arendsen
Melannie Kyler
Paula Noel
Diane Schumacher
Dot Richardson
Joan Van Ness
Kathy Strahan
Gwen Berner
Shirley Mapes
Sue Enquist
Sylvia Ortiz
Brenda Marshall
Paula Stufflebeam
Suzie Gaw
Barbara Reinalda
Linda Spagnola

1983 Pan American Games
Caracas, Venezuela

Silver Medalists (9-2)

Ralph Raymond-Coach
Kathy Arendsen
Suzie Brazney
Sheila Cornell
Pat Dufficy
Suzie Gaw
Venus Jennings
Darlene Lowery
Missy Mapes
Deanne Moore
Starleen Orullian
Barbara Reinalda
Dot Richardson
Allyson Rioux
Diane Schumacher
Wendy Smith
Lori Stoll
Gina Vecchione
Pam Warner

1987 Pan American Games
Indianapolis, IN, USA

Gold Medalists (9-0)

Carol Spanks-Coach
Annette Ausseresses
Lisa Baker
Denise Carter
Kathy Escarcega
JoAnn Ferrieri
Suzie Gaw
Suzy Brazney
Mary Mizera
Vicki Morrow
Donna McElrea
Elizabeth O'Connor
Catharine Stedman
Alison Stowell
Dot Richardson
Ella Vilche
Rhonda Wheatley
Michele Granger
Sheila Cornell

1991 Pan American Games
Santiago de Cuba, Cuba

Gold Medalists (9-0)

Shirley Topley-Coach
Barb Booth
Suzie Brazney
Sheila Cornell
Denise Day
Brenda Dobbelaar
Debbie Doom
Lisa Fernandez
Suzie Gaw
Michele Granger
Debbie Hoddevik
Mindy Jenkins
Tricia Johnson
Jill Justin
Ann Rowan
Kris Schmidt
Julie Smith
Camille Spitaleri
Julie Standering

1995 Pan American Games
Parana, Argentina

Gold Medalists (12-0)

Ralph Raymond-Coach
Patti Benedict
Jenny Condon
Sheila Cornell
Debbie Doom
Pat Dufficy
Michele Granger
Lori Harrigan
Barbara Jordan
Jill Justin
Kim Maher
Martha O'Kelley
Susie Parra
Dot Richardson
Ann Rowan
Karen Sanchelli
Julie Smith
Michele Smith
Shelly Stokes

History of the International Softball Federation and the First World Championships

Since its inception in 1965 as a full-fledged active international federation, the International Softball Federation (ISF) has promoted and developed softball throughout the world to where today the sport is on the verge of becoming one of the truly great international global sports. The growth of the ISF in recent years has been nothing but spectacular. By 1996, there were 100 federations/associations that were members of the ISF. The growth reflects the hard work and effort of such people as Don E. Porter, current ISF president, and former ISF president W. W. (Bill) Kethan who, among others, has led the ISF to its pres-

1979 USA Gold Medalists in Pan American Games
Back row, left to right, Lorene Ramsey (coach), Julie Winklepleck, Shirley Mapes, Kathy Strahan, Paula Noel, Melannie Kyler, Suzie Gaw, Marilyn Rau, Ralph Raymond (manager). Middle row, left to right, Gail Weldon (trainer), Sue Enquist, Lynn Spagnola, Brenda Marshall, Gwen Berner, Sylvia Ortiz, Paula Stufflebeam, Connie Claussen (team leader). Front row, left to right, Joan Van Ness, Barb Reinalda, Kathy Arendsen, Diane Schumacher, Dot Richardson.

tigious standing among the international sports community.

Besides the world championships, softball is played internationally in various world competitions including the Pan American Games, Central American-Caribbean and Central American games. Dozens of regional and continental championships and numerous team exchanges and technical support began to unfold from continent to continent, thus bolstering the overall development of the sport. (From ISF Publication)

What started out as a dream became a reality in February, 1965, when Melbourne, Australia, hosted the first International Softball Women's World Fast Pitch Championship. The idea of hosting a world championship came about during an overseas trip in August of 1962 when three members of the Australia Women's Softball Council, Esther Deason, Merle Short and Marjorie Dwyer, changed their plans and attended the ASA Women's Major Fast Pitch National Championship in Stratford, Connecticut. Nineteen teams competed in the championship, 17 from the USA and one each from Canada and Japan.

The three met with Don E. Porter, ISF president, to discuss the possibility of holding an international softball series with each country sending a team. The Australian women returned home and sent out invitations to the 22 affiliated countries listed in the ASA rule book and recommended that each country finance its team's air travel to the world championship. The Australia Softball Federation would be responsible for accommodations, entertainment and transportation once each team arrived in Australia.

Ironically, host Australia won that first

ISF Women's World Championship in 1965, defeating the USA, represented by the Raybestos Brakettes, in the title game, 1-0. Other countries competing were Japan, New Zealand and New Guinea.

The ISF met during that championship and mapped out plans for future expansion and development. W.W. (Bill) Kethan, the first ISF president, was optimistic about the future growth of the sport internationally and felt events such as the world championship would go a long ways to help develop better understanding between nations. As history has shown, Kethan was correct. Since the first world championship, the sport has developed internationally to where today it is played in more than 100 countries by more than 40 million people. It made its debut as

an Olympic sport in 1996, and was also approved to be in the Olympic Games to be held in 2000 in Sydney, Australia. (From ISF publication)

Don Porter, president of the International Softball Federation and former executive director of the ASA, was the driving force in getting softball approved for the Olympic Games. His quest took almost 30 years, with the official announcement coming after the 1991 International Olympic Committee meeting in Birmingham, England.

Gold Medal Coaches

Ralph Raymond, 1996 Olympic Coach

Under Ralph Raymond's tutelage, the Raybestos Brakettes compiled an awesome record of 1,992 wins and 162 losses, which established them as one of the all-time great and enduring sports dynasties. His Brakette teams won 17 national titles and finished as runners-up seven times. Equally imposing is Raymond's international record. As head coach of the USA national team, he has produced five gold medals in ISF world championship play, and 12 other gold medals in competitions including the Pan American Games, World Games, Intercontinental Cup, World Cup, Challenger Cup, South Pacific Classic and Superball Classic. The highlight of his coaching career was guiding the USA national team to the gold medal at the 1996 Olympic Games in Columbus, Georgia. Raymond was inducted into the ASA Hall of Honor in 1993.

Shirley Topley, 1991 Pan American Coach

This 11-time ASA All-American and Hall of Famer either played or acted as player/coach in British Columbia, with the Orange Lionettes and the Raybestos Brakettes. She coached the Lionettes to two national championships and to league titles every year she was with them. Shirley's career win-loss record is an outstanding 389 wins and 67 losses.

After retiring as an amateur player in 1975, Shirley played one year in the pro league, and then was the head coach of the Orange County Desperados and the Majestics, leading the Majestics to the national title in 1987. She was the assistant coach to the U.S. team in the world championships in 1990, and the head coach of the U.S. Pan American Games team in 1991. Shirley also worked with the U.S. teams that competed in the 1993 Intercontinental Cup, the 1994 South Pacific Classic, the 1995 Pan American Games and the 1996 Olympic Games. Very competitive as a player, Shirley is highly respected as a coach.

Carol Spanks, 1987 Pan American Coach

From 1951 through 1975, Carol played ASA softball with the Buena Park Kittens, the Buena Park Lynx and the Orange Lionettes. A 13-time ASA All-American and member of the ASA Hall of Fame, Spanks loved to play the game and never wanted to quit. After playing one year in the pro league in 1976, Carol retired as a player and concentrated on coaching.

She was the head softball coach at Cal Poly Pomona for several years, and also worked with the Orange County Desperados and the Majestics. Carol was the head coach to the U.S. team that won the gold medal in the South Pacific Classic in 1985, and to the U.S. Pan American Games team in 1987. In addition, Carol worked with the U.S. team that competed in the Tri-Nations Championships in 1988, the South Pacific Classic in 1993 and the world championships in 1994. As a player and as a coach, Spanks has been known for her "never quit no matter what the score is" attitude.

Women's Fastpitch Softball in the 1996 Olympic Games

Softball May Be Olympic Sport In '68

After almost three decades of false alarms, women's fastpitch softball finally made it into the Olympic Games in the summer of 1996. As early as 1965, newspaper articles carried hopeful predictions that softball would be included in the Olympics.

Softball was approved by the International Olympic Committee for the 1996 Games and announced on June 13, 1991. Softball enthusiasts all over the world were elated that, after such a long struggle, it was finally going to happen. It was a dream come true.

Olympic Possibility For Softball In '76

A total of 20 players — 15 players and five alternates — were selected on September 4, 1995, at the Olympic Team Trials in Oklahoma City, Oklahoma. The coaching staff was

U.S. OLYMPIC SOFTBALL TEAM
Games of the XXVIth Olympiad
July 19 - August 4, 1996

Atlanta 1996

Members of America's first Olympic softball team were, pictured on the front row, left to right, Julie Smith, Dot Richardson, Laura Berg, Dani Tyler, Shelly Stokes, Kim Maher. Middle row, left to right, Michele Smith, Leah O'Brien, Christa Williams, Dionna Harris, Lisa Fernandez, Gillian Boxx, Michelle Granger, Lori Harrigan. Back row, left to right, Ronnie Isham (team leader), Ralph Raymond (head coach), Sheila Cornell, Margie Wright (assistant coach) and Ralph Weekly (assistant coach).

comprised of Ralph Raymond, head coach, and assistant coaches, Ralph Weekly and Margie Wright.

Prior to the beginning of the Olympics, the team toured the country playing exhibition games in 21 cities. The tour began in Sacramento, California, on April 26-27 and ended in Atlanta, Georgia, on July 4th.

Despite the fact that *Sports Illustrated* picked Canada and Australia to win the gold and silver medals and the United States to

finish third in the 1996 Olympic Games, the U. S. team was heavily favored to win the gold by softball enthusiasts throughout the world. Since 1986, the USA team posted an impressive 110-1 record in international play and won three consecutive world championships.

The U. S. team knew going into the Olympics that the path to the gold medal would not be an easy one. Teams from China, Australia, Japan and Canada traditionally were strong international contenders.

Round-robin competition saw the United States team win easily over Puerto Rico, 10-0; the Netherlands, 9-0; Japan, 4-1; and Chinese Taipei, 4-0, before facing a talented Canadian squad. Led by world class pitchers Karen Snelgrove and Lori Sippel, both of whom played their college ball in the U. S., the Canadian team battled gallantly before bowing to the Americans 4-2.

The USA met its match in the sixth game against Australia, a pitching duel between aces Lisa Fernandez from the U. S. and Australian Tanya Harding. Had it not been for a mental error by American Dani Tyler in the fifth inning — she failed to touch home plate after driving the ball into the centerfield bleachers and was called out on an appeal — the game would have been over in seven innings and Fernandez would have recorded the first perfect game in Olympic history. As it was, the U.S. scored a run in the top of the tenth inning to give the Americans an apparent victory. The Australians, however, weren't to be denied. U.S. pitching ace Lisa Fernandez, with her perfect game still intact, retired the first two batters and had two strikes on Australia's Joanne Brown. Fernandez threw a rise ball which she later admitted "flattened out over the plate," which resulted in a home run to center field, which also scored a teammate who had reached second base by gratis of the tie-breaker rule. The final score was Australia 2 - USA 1.

While the dramatic defeat to Australia may have deflated lesser teams, the U. S. team, whose roster was loaded with world-class competitors, bounced back. Behind the stellar pitching of Michele Smith and led by Sheila Cornell at the plate, the United States defeated China 3-2 to finish first in round robin play.

In the first of two semifinal games, the U. S. made it two-in-a-row against China, defeating them 1-0 in 10 innings. That victory placed the Americans in the finals which, once again, pitted them against the Chinese team. The drama of the gold medal game was recounted by Ronald A. Babb in his article "USA Strikes Gold in Atlanta," which appeared in the August/September 1996 issue of *USA Softball Magazine*.

It was the shot heard around the world.

In the bottom of the third inning, Laura Berg was on. Her gaze focused intently on teammate Dot Richardson who was bouncing and stretching before stepping into the box to take her swings against Chinese pitcher Yaju Liu.

And then it came, a jolting right field rope that sent Chinese outfielder Ziang Wei scurrying to the fence in time to witness the ball slicing past her as it completed its destination into the stands and into history.

Berg and Richardson rounded the bases as the sound of a deafening chorus of "USA . . . USA" resonated from a raucous crowd of supporters who had waited hours, days, and for some, decades to live this moment.

With arms raised in triumph they crossed the plate, Berg first, then Richardson. They were greeted by a swarming host of teammates who in an instant must have realized that their dreams too had been realized.

The Chinese never recovered and the USA went on to win the most important softball game of all time, 3-1, and permanently etched their names in history as the first to ever win an Olympic gold medal.

While researching the history of women's fastpitch softball and the success of certain teams, it became obvious that a team's success was directly dependent upon the effectiveness of its pitching staff. Pitching in fastpitch softball has always dominated the game — especially during the years when the women's pitching distance was less than 40 feet, prior to 1965. It can be noted that in many of the semifinal and final games played in the ASA world championships during the 1950's, the games went extra innings and the final score was 1-0, or 2-1 — low scoring pitcher's duels.

Some of the names of the great pitchers have been well known over the years — Bertha Ragan Tickey, Margie Law, Amy Peralta, Ginny Busick, Nina Korgan, Betty Evans, Joan Joyce are among them — and are emblazoned on Hall of Fame plaques in the Amateur Softball Association of America headquarters in Oklahoma City. There are others, however, who, for one reason or another, have remained virtually anonymous to the general public. Their teams may not have made it to the world championships consistently, or their playing careers were not very long, or perhaps that pitcher's stardom was achieved in either the National Softball Congress or one of the professional leagues. Among those names are Charlotte "Skippy" Armstrong, Carolyn Morris, Willie Turner, Louise Mazzucca, Teddy Hamilton, Lois Terry,

Ann Kmezich, Joanne Winter, Alma Wilson, Lottie Jackson and Alice Jorgensen.

How did they pitch? What made them so good? Were pitching deliveries the same from 35 feet as they are from 40 feet? The one factor that has determined the delivery used by a pitcher more than any other has been the rules. In the early days, the rules were not only few in number, but they were also loose and fairly non-restrictive. The pioneers of the mound quickly became very creative in devising fancy wind-ups and trick pitches. Two of the most ingenious pitchers in the early years were Charlotte "Skippy" Armstrong, a six-time All-American in the National Softball Congress who pitched for the A-1 Queens, and "Bullet Betty" Evans, labeled one of the greatest pitchers of her time who pitched for the Erv Lind Florists of Portland. Skippy Armstrong used eight different trick pitches — releasing the ball from behind her back and under her leg were just two of them.

Charlotte "Skippy" Armstrong

Obviously in the early days, batters became extremely frustrated and were made to look very foolish at the plate. Skippy told of a game that the Queens played against the New Orleans Jax, a nationally dominant team in the 1940's. Skippy was pitching against Freda Savona, a legend in her time who was perhaps one of the strongest hitters in the history of the game. Since it was an exhibition game, Skippy could pull out all stops from her arsenal of pitches — and she did! Freda was left standing at the plate in a daze after the third strike was called. She quickly snapped out of it and commenced to march directly to the pitcher's mound with bat in hand. In a quiet and con-trolled voice, Freda informed Skippy that she never wanted to repeat that experience again!

"Bullet Betty" Evans was referred to as a "pure stylist" who used a variety of trick pitches very effectively. A batter facing Betty when she was using a windmill delivery would see Betty, without a glove, alternating between cir-cling her left arm and then her right arm and switching the ball from hand to hand depend-ing on which arm was moving at the time. The ball might be released at any time from either hand. Betty also was a master at using "the slip pitch" — the ball was released during the windmill arm action with the arm continuing to circle after the release.

Betty Evans, Erv Lind Florists

Betty Evans and Margie Law were among those pitchers who threw a "submarine pitch" — the ball was released very close to the ground with the rear knee and knuckles of the pitcher's throwing hand almost touching the ground.

Two other pitching styles that have fallen by the wayside over the years were the "rock-ing chair" and the "wrist ball." The rocking chair, used by Nina Korgan, ASA Hall of Famer with the New Orleans Jax, was a fairly simple-looking delivery that involved the pitcher taking the ball straight back and then coming straight through towards the plate. A view of the pitcher from the throwing arm side would show that the pitching hand traced a pattern in the air that resembled the rocker on a rocking chair, hence the name.

Rocking chair pitching motion

Wilda Mae Turner
1939 - 1946 — ASA ball in Alameda, California
1946 - 1954 — National Girls Baseball (Softball) League

Windmill delivery in the 1940's.

One of the first pitchers to use the "wrist ball" in this country was Nickie Fox, a pitcher in the All-American Girls Professional Baseball League (AA GPBL). Nickie, who learned to pitch in Canada, pitched underhand during the first few years of the AAGPBL when the size of the ball and the game played more closely resembled softball than baseball. When throwing a wrist ball, the ball was gripped with the fingers going across the seams. The backswing resembled that used in a figure eight. As the throwing arm came forward, the knuckles were facing out. Using a lot of wrist action, the ball came off the fingers with a rise ball spin and the arm followed through towards either an inside or an outside target.

Changes in the rules — in particular, the pitching rules — during those early years were crucial to making the total game more equitable in terms of offense versus defense. (See Rules Chapter for details.) Trick pitches, in particular the slip pitch which allowed the pitcher to use multiple revolutions of the throwing arm, were very deceptive and unfair to the batter. After multiple arm revolutions were made illegal in 1952, the windmill delivery became much the same as it is used today.

Windmill delivery in the 1970's.

Figure Eight

A style of pitching that was one of the most popular in the early years was the figure eight. Bertha Ragan Tickey, an ASA Hall of Famer and 18-time All-American, used a figure eight delivery. The term "figure eight" was given to this delivery because the horizontal pattern traced in the air by the pitcher's throwing arm resembled an eight.

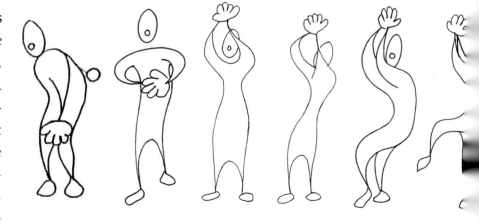

Figure eight pitching motion

*Nancy Welborn —
Member of ASA
Hall of Fame;
played with
McCullough Chain
Saws, Eugene,
Oregon, and Orange
Lionettes.*

Slingshot

Perhaps the greatest pitcher in the history of the game to use the slingshot delivery was Joan Joyce. Even though Joan as a teenager was taught to use the windmill delivery, an astute observer suggested to her that she switch to the slingshot, and she was never sorry. The slingshot was the ideal style for Joan's long levers and tremendous strength.

Joan Joyce pitching for the Connecticut Falcons in 1976.

Various newspaper articles have referred to a particular pitcher as having been the best ever in the history of the game — other articles have described a certain pitcher's fast ball as having been clocked at over 100 mph — and other pitchers have been described as being so deceptive that the batter was left standing with her bat on her shoulder completely mesmerized! Comparing pitchers from different eras is like comparing apples to oranges. If the rules of the game had always been the same; and if there existed an octogenarian who was also an expert on fastpitch pitching; and if there were available statistics on all pitchers that were consistently the same, then it might be possible. But why is it important to have one best anyway?! If longevity of success can be used as an indicator of the best ever, then that pitcher would have to be Bertha Ragan Tickey. Bertha was first selected as an ASA First Team All-

American in 1949 and her last selection was in 1968 — a span of 19 years during which Bertha was selected first team ASA All-American a total of 18 times.

On the other hand, supporters of Joan Joyce's would point out that no other pitcher in the history of the game has totally dominated the opposition like she did. Then there are the staunch fans of the 1930's and 1940's who, without hesitation, would argue that their hometown heroine — Marie Wadlow, or Margie Law, or Amy Peralta, or Ginny Busick, or "Bullet Betty" Evans, or Charlotte Armstrong, or windmiller Willie Turner or Nina Korgan — was the best. However, since there were few valid records or statistics kept prior to 1948, how could it be proven? Fact: There have been many excellent (and, in the early years, creative) women fastpitch softball pitchers during the history of the game!

Most will agree that Kathy Arendsen, a windmill pitcher, was one of the most dominant pitchers of the 1980's. In her career, she went 334-25.

OFFICIAL SOFTBALL

RULES ◆ 1945

Scene of World Softball Championships, Lakewood Elks Stadium — Lakewood, Ohio

LOUISVILLE SLUGGER
- - -
HILLERICH & BRADSBY CO
LOUISVILLE. KY.

10¢

Kitten-ball, diamond-ball, playground baseball, mush-ball, indoor-outdoor — these were the games from which our modern day game of softball evolved. Those first games were played using rules that were drastically different from those used in the game today. Some games were played indoors and some were played outdoors. In playground ball, the first batter getting on base could choose to run to either first base or third base. All following batters in that same inning had to run in the same direction. Even during the first few years of softball competition, from 1934 to 1938, the game could be played on either a 45' base diamond or a 60' base diamond.

As a result of the chaos caused by as many different sets of rules used as the number of teams entered in the 1933 national championships in Chicago, it was evident that it was imperative that one set of rules for use throughout the nation be developed. Consequently, a national rules committee was formed and met for the first time January 21-22, 1934, at the Hotel Sherman in Chicago. Delegates from 37 states attended, representing the following organizations:

> National Softball Association
> Amateur Softball Association of America
> National Collegiate Athletic Association
> National Recreation Association
> National Federation of State High School
>   Athletic Associations
> Central Association of the Amateur

> Athletic Union
> Young Men's Christian Association
> Young Men's Hebrew Association
> American Legion
> National A.Z.A. Organization
> Catholic Youth Organization
> Parks and Playgrounds
> Industrial Organizations

This group agreed on a common set of rules and the first "Official Softball Rules" were published that year, 1934, by the Spalding Athletic Library. In the event that a necessary rule was overlooked by the committee, they indicated in the book that if a situation occurred in the game that was not included in the softball rulebook, that "the rules of baseball shall apply."

The first Amateur Softball Association Rule Book was published the following year in 1935. By then, the Joint Rules Committee had been streamlined down to the following members:

> C.E. Brewer, Commissioner of Recreation,
>   Detroit, Michigan
> Arthur T. Noren, Secretary, New York City
> A. O. Anderson, American Physical Education
>   Association
> H. Ross Bunce, Young Men's Christian
>   Association
> K. Mark Cowen, Director of Recreation,
>   Roanoke, Virginia
> Charles W. Davis, Director of Recreation and
>   Physical Education, Berkeley, CA
> Leo H. Fischer, Amateur Softball Association
>   of America, Chicago, IL
> Major John L. Griffith, Chicago, Illinois

Ernest W. Johnson, Superintendent of Playgrounds, St. Paul, Minnesota
R. C. Miller, Director of Recreation, Oshkosh, Wisconsin
Arthur Williams, National Recreation Association
Jack Elder, Catholic Youth Organization, Chicago, Illinois
Philip Rosier, National Softball Association, Chicago, Illinois
Samuel Rothenfeld, Young Men's Hebrew Association, New York City

From 1935 on, the Amateur Softball Association has been the major governing body for softball in the country, and is recognized as such by the United States Olympic Committee. With the assistance of committees, the rules are determined by the ASA and published in a rule book annually.

A chart illustrating the major rules changes from 1934 to 1996 is included later in this chapter. A more vivid and complete picture can be painted, though, of the evolution of the rules if a comparison is made of the actual wording and length of some of the rules in the 1935 and the 1997 rule books — in particular, those rules that have had a major influence on the way the game is played. The rules that have affected the game perhaps more than any others are the pitching rules, and the rules dealing with equipment.

The pitching rules as they appeared in the 1935 ASA Rule Book on pages 15 & 16:

Amateur Softball Association of America
OFFICIAL RULES OF SOFTBALL (1935)

Pitching Rule (Rule 8) —- Preliminary to pitching, the pitcher shall take his position facing the batsman, with both feet squarely on the ground and both feet on top of the pitcher's plate. The ball shall be held in both hands, in front of the body.

In the act of delivering the ball to the batsman, he must keep one foot in contact with the pitcher's plate, and shall not take more than one step forward until the ball has actually left his hand.

In the forward swing of the arm, the hand shall be below the hip and the ball not more than six inches from the body (leg). A snap or jerky release of the ball at the hip is prohibited.

The ball shall be delivered with a full arm swing following through and at no time in the forward swing shall the arm cross the front of the body.

At no time during the progress of the game shall the pitcher be allowed to use tape, or other substance, upon the pitching hand or fingers, nor shall any foreign substance be applied to the ball, provided that, under the supervision and control of the umpire, powdered rosin may be used to dry the hands.

That was the complete rule — a total of 202 words taking up one-third of a page.

These pictures were used in the 1934 rule book to illustrate illegal pitching deliveries and correct pitching form. These were the official rules of softball even though they were published by the Spalding Athletic Library.

Common Forms of Illegal Delivery

Three common violations of the official softball pitching rules: (1) the pitcher is in position, facing the batter, but does not have both feet on the pitching slab; (2) the ball is more than six inches from the body and is being delivered from above the hip; (3) the ball is being delivered across the front of the body.

Correct Softball Pitching Form

Here is a pitcher following the rules: (1) He has taken his position facing the batter, with both feet on the slab, before delivering the ball; (2) the pitch is being made from below the hip, with the ball not more than six inches from the body; (3)the follow-through, with the arm parallel to the body and one foot still in contact with the slab until after delivering the ball.

There is quite a difference between the details and completeness of the pitching regulations as they appear in the 1997 rule book and the brief rules section in the 1935 book.

Amateur Softball Association of America
1997 OFFICIAL RULES OF SOFTBALL

Rule 6 — PITCHING REGULATIONS
Section 1. PRELIMINARIES.
Before starting the delivery (pitch), the pitcher shall comply with the following:
A. Both feet must be on the ground within the 24-inch length of the pitcher' plate. The shoulders shall be in line with first and third bases.
   1. (Male Only)
   2. (Female Only) She shall take a position with both feet in contact with the pitcher's plate.
B. The pitcher shall take the signal from the catcher with the hands separated. The ball must remain in either the glove or pitching hand.
C. The pitcher shall hold the ball in both hands for not less than one second and not more than 10 seconds before releasing it.
   1. (Male Only)
   2. (Female Only) Both feet must remain in contact with the pitching plate at all times prior to the forward step.
D. The pitcher shall not be considered in the pitching position unless the catcher is in position to receive the pitch.
E. The pitcher may not take the pitching position on or near the pitcher's plate without having the ball in his possession.

Section 2. STARTING THE PITCH.
The pitch starts when one hand is taken off the ball after the hands have been placed together.

Section 3. LEGAL DELIVERY.
A. The pitcher must not make any motion to pitch without immediately delivering the ball to the batter.
B. The pitcher must not use a pitching motion in which, after having the ball in both hands in the pitching position, the pitcher removes one hand from the ball, and returns the ball to both hands in front of the body.
C. The pitcher must not make a stop or reversal of the forward motion after separating the hands.
D. The pitcher must not make two revolutions of the arm on the windmill pitch. A pitcher may drop the arm to the side and to the rear before starting the windmill motion.
E. The delivery must be an underhanded motion with the hand below the hip and the wrist not farther from the body than the elbow.
F. The release of the ball and follow through of the hand and wrist must be forward and past the straight line of the body.
G. In the act of delivering the ball, the pitcher must take one step with the non-pivot foot simultaneous with the release of the ball. The step must be forward and toward the batter within the 24-inch length of the pitcher's plate.
    NOTE: It is not a step if the pitcher slides the pivot foot across the pitcher's plate, provided contact is maintained with the plate. Raising the foot off the pitching plate and returning it to the plate creates a rocking motion and is an illegal act.

H. Pushing off with the pivot foot from a place other than the pitcher's plate is illegal. This includes a "crow hop" as defined under Rule 1.

I. (Female Only) The pivot foot must remain in contact with or push off and drag away from the pitching plate prior to the front foot touching the ground, as long as the pivot foot remains in contact with the ground.

J. (Male Only)

K. The pitcher must not make another revolution after releasing the ball.

L. The pitcher shall not deliberately drop, roll or bounce the ball in order to prevent the batter from hitting it.

M. The pitcher has 20 seconds to release the next pitch after receiving the ball or after the umpire indicates "play ball."

Section 4. INTENTIONAL WALK. (For details, refer to the rule book)

Section 5. DEFENSIVE POSITIONING. (For details, refer to the rule book)

Section 6. FOREIGN SUBSTANCE. (For details, refer to the rule book)

Section 7. CATCHER. (For details, refer to the rule book)

Section 8. THROWING TO A BASE. (For details, refer to the rule book)

Section 9. WARM-UP PITCHES. (For details, refer to the rule book)

Section 10. NO PITCH. (For details, refer to the rule book)

Section 11. DROPPED BALL. (For details, refer to the rule book)

These pitching regulations fill four full pages in the book. It would appear that every situation that could possibly arise in a game has been covered in the rules.

The rule pertaining to bats, balls, gloves and shoes as it appeared in the 1935 rule book on page 13:

Amateur Softball Association of America
OFFICIAL RULES OF SOFTBALL (1935)

Rule 3 — Equipment

<u>Section 1.</u> The bat shall be made of wood, not more than 34 inches in length and not more than 2 1/8 inches in diameter at its largest part. Willow or fungo bats are prohibited. The bats shall have a safety grip of cork, tape or composition material. Such safety grip shall not be less than 10 inches in length and shall not extend more than 15 inches from the small end of the bat.

<u>Section 2.</u> The official ball shall be the regular or smooth seam (not out seam) softball. The regulation size of the ball for both the 45 and 60 foot diamonds shall be 12 inches in circumference and it shall weigh not less than 6 and not more than 6 1/2 ounces.

(Balls will be accepted as official if they measure between 12 and 12 1/2 inches in circumference.)

<u>Section 6.</u> Gloves may be worn by any or all players if desired.

<u>Section 7.</u> Rubber soled shoes, or shoes with rubber or leather cleats are recommended. Shoes with metal spikes are prohibited.

These advertisements that appeared in ASA rule books from different years illustrate examples of the bats and balls that were used in that time period.

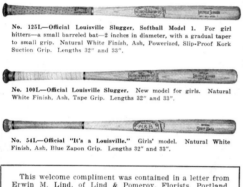

1945 ASA Rule Book   *1944 ASA Rule Book*

Notice the uniforms, "pancake" gloves and footwear used during the late 1930's and early 1940's.

Dorothy "Snookie" Harrell Doyle, pictured here in 1937 at age 13 while playing in Fiedler Field League in California, later played in the AAGPBL and with the Orange Lionettes.

Members of the Sunday Morning Class team from Toronto, Canada, as pictured in the 1945 ASA Rule Book. They are, left to right, Verne McCormick, Kelly Parkhouse, Tinny Morrison, Kay Doughty and Marie Kirkpatrick.

Shirley Topley and one of the first pitching machines (above, left), and Shirley feeding a Hummer in 1976.

Bases changed from a thin, reversible quilted one that was staked down on two sides — to a slightly padded one with straps, staked down in the center — to a firm, thick base anchored into a secure foundation in the ground, the Hollywood base.

THE HOLLYWOOD IMPACT® BASE

THE LOW PROFILE BASE

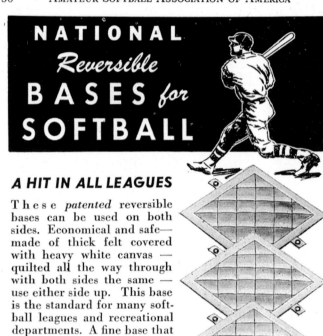
Bases, too, have changed through the years. The advertisement at the top right appeared in the 1944 ASA Rule Book, while Hollybwood Bases, now owned by Schutt Sports, advertised their bases in the 1997 ASA Rule Book (top left). Immediate top, Carolyn Fitzwater rounds the bases in the 1956 nationals. At right, action in 1976 in the pro league.

The rule in the 1997 rule book pertaining to equipment is extremely detailed. It seems obvious that, as the game has been played over the years, players have been somewhat creative in selecting the bats that work best for them! As problems have surfaced because of these "creative selections" — not just with bats but with all pieces of equipment used in the game — the rules committee has added more subheadings in order to clarify legal vs. illegal. The following rule will illustrate this point rather vividly.

Amateur Softball Association of America
1997 OFFICIAL RULES OF SOFTBALL

Rule 3 — EQUIPMENT
Section 1. THE OFFICIAL BAT.

A. Shall be made of one piece of hardwood, or formed from a block of wood consisting of two or more pieces of wood bonded together with an adhesive in such a way that the grain direction of all pieces is essentially parallel to the length of the bat.

B. Shall be metal, plastic, graphite, carbon, magnesium, fiberglass, ceramic or any other composite material approved by the ASA. Any new composite construction bat must be reviewed and approved by the ASA.

C. May be laminated but must contain only wood or adhesive and have a clear finish (if finished).

D. Shall be round or three-sided and shall be smooth. If the barrel end has a knurled finish the maximum surface roughness is no more than 250 if measured by a profilometer or 4/1000 if measured by a spectrograph.

E. Shall not be more than 34 inches long, nor exceed 38 ounces in weight.

F. If round, shall not be more than 2 1/4 inches in diameter at its largest part; and if three-sided, shall not exceed 2 1/4 inches on the hitting surface. A tolerance of 1/32 inch is permitted to allow for expansion on the round bat. NOTE: if the bat ring goes over the bat it should be considered a legal bat.

G. If metal, may be angular.

H. Shall not have exposed rivets, pins, rough or sharp edges or any form of exterior fastener that would present a hazard. A metal bat shall be free of burrs.

I. If metal, shall not have a wooden handle.

J. Shall have a safety grip of cork, tape (no smooth, plastic tape) or composition material. The safety grip shall not be less than 10 inches long and shall not extend more than 15 inches from the small end of the bat. Any molded finger-formed grip made by the bat manufacturer, if used must be permanently attached to the bat or attached to the bat with safety tape and must be approved by the Equipment Standards Committee. Resin, pine tar or spray substances placed on the safety grip to enhance the grip are permissible on the grip only. Tape applied to any bat must be continuously spiral. It does not have to be a solid layer of tape. It may not exceed two layers. Taping of a bat less than the required length is considered illegal.

K. If metal, and not made of one-piece construction with the barrel end closed, shall have a rubber or vinyl plastic or other approved material insert firmly secured at the large end of the bat.

L. Shall have a safety knob of a minimum of 1/4 inch protruding at a 90-degree angle from the handle. It may be molded, lathed, welded or permanently fastened. A "flare" or "cone" grip attached to the bat will be considered altered. The knob may be taped as long as there is no violation of this section.

M. Shall be marked OFFICIAL SOFTBALL by the manufacturer. If the words OFFICIAL SOFTBALL cannot be read due to wear and tear on the bat, the bat should be declared legal if it is legal in all other aspects.

Section 2. WARM-UP BATS. Has 4 subheadings and fills 1/3 of a page.

Section 3. THE OFFICIAL SOFTBALL. Has 13 subheadings pertaining to fastpitch — fills two full pages. (Size — From 11 7/8 inches to 12 1/8 inches in circumference. Weight — From 6 1/4 ounces to 7 ounces.)

Section 4. Gloves may be worn by any player, but mitts may be used only by the catcher and first baseman. No top lacing, webbing or other device between the thumb and body of the glove or mitt worn by a first baseman or catcher, or a glove worn by any fielder, shall be more than five inches in length. The pitcher's glove shall not be partially or one solid color of white or gray.

Section 5. MASKS, BODY PROTECTORS, SHIN GUARDS AND HELMETS. (For details, refer to the rule book)

Section 6. UNIFORM.

A. Headwear. (For details, refer to the rule book)

B. Pants/Sliding Pants. (For details, refer to the rule book)

C. Undershirts. (For details, refer to the rule book)

D. Numbers. (For details, refer to the rule book)

E. Casts/Prostheses. (For details, refer to the rule book)

F. Jewelry. (For details, refer to the rule book)

G. Shoes. Must be worn by all players. A shoe shall be considered official if it is made with either canvas or leather uppers or similar material(s). The soles may be either smooth or have soft or hard rubber cleats. Ordinary metal sole or heel plates may be used if the spikes on the plates do not extend more than 3/4 of an inch from the sole or the heel of the shoe. Shoes with round metal spikes are illegal. No shoes with detachable cleats that screw ON are allowed; however, shoes with detachable cleats that screw INTO the shoe are allowed.

Just as the rules of the game have changed considerably over the years, so has the terminology used to explain the rules. A "fairly delivered ball" in 1935 is now called a strike; an "unfairly delivered ball" is a ball; the "batsman" has become known as the batter; the "coacher" is either the first base coach or the third base coach; and what was then called a "bunt hit ball" is now called a bunt.

It didn't matter what terminology was used in the early days of competition, the game then was dominated by pitching and defense, and it still is. It's no wonder during those first years that the defense had an advantage! The pitcher was not only closer to homeplate than now — 35' from 1937 to 1951 and 38' from 1952 to 1965 — but there were also few restrictions on what kind of a delivery was legal. It didn't take long before the truly competitive pitcher devised some very deceptive moves. One of the most difficult types of pitchers to hit was the windmill pitcher who used what was called a "slip" pitch. A "slip" pitch was thrown by a pitcher who used multiple arm revolutions in a windmill delivery with the ball being released at any point during those revolutions. The batter obviously had trouble knowing just when the ball was actually going to be propelled in her direction! To back up this devious pitcher were not only four infielders but also four outfielders — the fourth was called the short fielder who roved behind second base.

No game is much fun to play unless both teams at least have a chance! Carol Spanks, an ASA Hall of Famer who played for many years with the Orange Lionettes, said that it was much more fun for her as a shortstop when Joan Joyce, also a Hall of Famer, pitched for the opposing team rather than for her team! The infield saw more action. Many of the rules changes have been made with one purpose in mind — to make the battle on the field between the offense and the defense more equitable.

The pitching distance was gradually increased, the bunt was made legal in 1938 and the 10th player was removed from the field in 1947. It took seven years of using the "undertaker" rule, which required the pitcher to wear either black or dark blue with no lettering or trim on the front, before it was decided that it wasn't necessary.

The "undertaker" rule was eliminated in 1948 — the same year that the pitching distance was increased to 38 feet from 35 feet. Giving the batter that much more time to see the ball coming into the plate may have contributed to the decision to take the pitchers out of their drab apparel and allow them to dress like the rest of the team. As more rules were added to restrict the pitcher to "fairly deliver the ball," and aluminum bats and a livelier ball became part of the game, the offensive side of the battle on the field became more aggressive and successful.

The rules changes that have been made over the years were made with one objective in mind — to make the game of women's fastpitch softball an exciting, safe contest between the offense and defense. Thanks should go to not only the many people who have served on the ASA Rules Committees, but also to the men and women "in blue" who have so cheerfully enforced the rules!

ASA Hall of Famer Nina Korgan decked out in all-black uniform when the "undertaker" rule was in effect.

Changes in uniforms and equipment.

Ginny Hanselman, a pitcher for the I.M.A. team from Flint, Michigan, is shown here in a one-piece red-satin uniform in 1950.

Michele Smith led her team, the Redding Rebels, to three consecutive national titles from 1993 to 1995. Here, she's shown pitching for the U.S. Olympic team in 1996.

Joan Joyce, perhaps the most dominant player of her time, pitches for the Orange Lionettes in 1965. Ironically, she was pitching at her old field, the Raybestos Memorial Field in Stratford, Connecticut.

ASA Hall of Famer Nancy Ito catches for the Orange Lionettes in 1970.

May Dockerty, at four-feet tall, caught for Ginny Hanselman on the Flint, Michigan, team in 1950.

Michelle Gromacki, a catcher for the U.S. national team that competed in the world championships in 1994, wears the catcher's equipment of the 1990's.

AMATEUR SOFTBALL ASSOCIATION
Major Rule Changes from 1934 to 1997

Year	Pitching/Bases	Equipment	General
1934	37'/60' Multi-arm revolutions legal. Ball cannot be more than 6" from body & pitcher cannot deliver ball across in front of body. Pitcher must pause at least one second before delivery.	Wooden bats Rubber cleats Catcher's mask recommended	10 players No bunting Baserunner can't leave until ball reaches batter. Rule book published by Spalding Athletic Library.
1935	37' 8 1/2"/60'		First year of ASA rule book
1936	40'/60'	Metal cleats legal	No third strike rule
1937	35'/60'	Mitts worn by 1B & C only	Baserunner can leave as ball is pitched.
1938	35'/60' Pitcher must have a follow through with the hand and wrist passing the straight line of the body before the ball is released.	Pitchers can't wear white or light gray uniforms.	Bunt is legal
1939	35'/60' Illegal pitch if pitcher continues to wind-up after taking a step towards the batter.	Masks and chest protectors must be worn by female catcher.	
1940	35'/60'		Third strike rule
1941	35'/60'	All visible parts of the pitcher's uniform must be black or dark blue with no lettering or trim on front.	
1946	35'/55'		Nine players
1947	35'/60'		

Year	Pitching/Bases	Equipment	General
1948	35'/60'	Pitcher no longer has to wear dark uniform.	
1952	38'/60' Bars multiple windmill		Appeal play defined
1953	38'/60'	Ball marked "Official Softball"	
1958	38'/60'		Softball Recodification Committee changed format of rule book.
1962	38'/60'		Duty of pitcher to play runner back to base to allow him sufficient time to return.
1965	40'/60'		Obvious interference rule — breaking up double play.
1967	40'/60'		Pitcher must play runner back to base from within radius of 8' from pitcher's plate.
1970	40'/60'	Aluminum bats	
1971	40'/60'		Play back action by pitcher compels runner to either go forward or back.
1973	40'/60'	Defines a legal uniform. Illegal for pitcher to wear multi-colored glove.	
1975	40'/60'		Circle marked on field 8' radius from pitcher's plate.
1977	40'/60' Pitcher must pause minimum of 2 seconds before delivery		

Year	Pitching/Bases	Equipment	General
1979	40'/60' Starting pitcher cannot re-enter as a pitcher. Pitcher must pause minimum of one second before delivery.		Designated hitter (DH). Starting line-up may re-enter one time.
1981	40'/60' Pitcher must take signal with hands separated. Pitcher no longer has to come to a complete stop after bringing hands together. Starting pitcher may re-enter as a pitcher.	Caps, visors & headbands are optional for females but may not be mixed. If one is worn, all must wear.	
1983	40'/60'	Caps, visors & headbands still optional & cannot be mixed. If one wears, others do not have to. Those worn must be alike. Adult female catcher not required to wear body protector. Catcher's mask must have throat protector.	Disclaimer put in
1985	40'/60' Pitcher can step back with the non pivot foot before hands are brought together. The leap is legal.		
1986	40'/60'		DH can re-enter
1987	40'/60' 43'/60' NCAA;NAIA		DH changed to DP Slap bunt defined
1988	40'/60'	Female offensive players must wear double ear flap helmets.	
1989	40'/60'	Sliding pants defined	Sacrifice fly defined for stat purposes.
1991	40'/60' Female pitcher must start with both feet on pitcher's plate. Female pitcher cannot leap.		

Year	Pitching/Bases	Equipment	General
1992	40'/60' Crow hop and leaping defined		
1994	40'/60'		Blood rule Run rule used after 5 innings (8 runs) Tie breaker rule

1995	40'/60'		Short handed rule -
			  can play with fewer
			  than 9 players if
			  necessary

1996	40'/60' The pitch starts when hand is taken off the ball.	Ball caps, visors, headbands are optional for players and, if worn, can be mixed.	

1997	40'/60'	Players' pants can be long or
		  short as long as they are like
		  in color.
			Interference rule — If
			on a foul fly and ball
			is not caught, runner
			is out, ball dead,
			strike called and
			batter remains at bat.

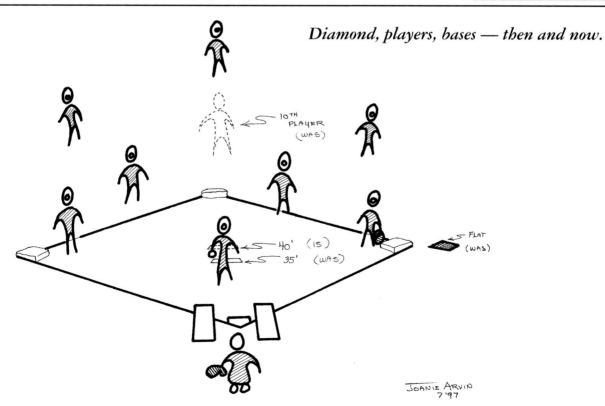

Diamond, players, bases — then and now.

A high school or college girl in the 1940's, 50's and 60's who had an interest in playing sports, in particular team sports, had to be satisfied with playing in sports days and play days. In some of these, girls weren't even allowed to play with others from her own school. Slips of paper were drawn to determine which girls would play together. The objective of the day was for girls from one school to meet those from other schools in a fun setting. Even if the play day allowed for girls from one school to play together, winning was not emphasized nor were wins tallied. After a few hours of playing games, all of the participants chitchatted over punch and cookies. Needless to say, the girl who was a natural athlete and had a keen desire to match her skills against others, was totally frustrated.

If a group of girls got together and requested that a team in a particular sport be organized, some colleges and universities may have allowed for that to happen, but the students themselves, in most cases, had to arrange for the games, coaches, transportation, etc. The competition was never labeled as an "intercollegiate athletic event"; it was referred to as "extramurals." To a female athlete then, any competition was better than none and it didn't matter what it was called — an eight-game schedule was as exciting as an eighty-game schedule is now.

It appeared that the majority of faculty members at colleges and universities through-

out the country were of the belief that a female coed should conform to the stereotyped image of feminism that had prevailed in this country for centuries, and that image did not include battling it out on a dirty softball field. Collegiate physical education department faculty, in particular, resisted the female athlete's quest for competition at a higher level. One department chair in a college in central California stated, "that highly competitive team sport experiences were antithetical to the aura of demure femininity she strove to instill." (26:14)

The chapter on the 1940's relates several tales of coed softball players being confronted with major problems at college because they chose to play ASA softball. Female students at colleges all over the country during the 1940's, 50's and 60's were faced with those problems — remain as a physical education major at college and quit playing ASA ball; continue playing ball and jeopardize their status in college; or continue as a student and play ball under a false name.

During this pre-Title IX period of time, any women's athletics that did exist were organized and governed by that school's physical education department. On a national scope, the American Association of Health, Physical Education and Recreation (AAHPER), and the National Association for Girls and Women in Sport (NAGWS), provided services in which physical educators

The University of Washington celebrates a big hit in the 1996 NCAA Women's College World Series.

could take advantage. The first national organization to be formed that dealt strictly with extramural collegiate competition for women was the National Joint Committee for Extramural Sports for College Women (NJCESCW), which was formed in 1957. This committee was comprised of two representatives from the National Association of Physical Education for College Women (NAPECW), the Athletic and Recreation Federation of College Women (ARFCW), and the Division for Girls and Women's Sports (DGWS).

As the leadership of the NJCESCW and DGWS passed from the older women whose ideas were embedded in the 19th century to younger women who themselves were victims of the "you can't play ASA softball and still be feminine" regime, the policies and practices of those organizations became more liberal.

As the DGWS became more involved in the competitive arena, and as attitudes toward competition for women changed, it became clear that DGWS should control collegiate athletics for women. The young women leaders of DGWS envisioned a new model of intercollegiate athletics. They accepted the desirability of organized competition, but rejected the commercialization rampant in men's athletics (NCAA).(10:282)

One of the outcomes of this more liberal philosophy was the formation of the Commission on Intercollegiate Athletics for Women (CIAW), the foremother of the Association for Intercollegiate Athletics for Women (AIAW). In March of 1966, the DGWS approved the CIAW and it began to function in the fall of 1967. Their basic functions were to establish standards and control

competition through sanctioning regional tournaments, to encourage the formation of local or regional governing bodies of women physical educators, and to sponsor national championships.

First Women's College World Series Held in Omaha in 1969

John F. Kennedy College in Wahoo, Nebraska, was a small private college that recognized and promoted athletic excellence among its coeds. They not only awarded scholarships in women's basketball and softball, but they allocated budgets that were adequate enough to provide coaches, equipment and travel. Since there weren't many women's collegiate softball programs at that time that were comparable to theirs, the JFK team had to travel a lot to find competition.

Don Joe, the JFK College manager, approached Carl P. Kelley, Omaha Metro Softball commissioner and the president of the Omaha Softball Association, and suggested to him that Omaha sponsor a College World Series in softball for women. Connie Claussen, then the chairperson for the physical education department at the University of Nebraska at Omaha, was asked if she would represent the colleges in this effort and become a member of the tournament committee. Connie readily agreed. This committee of Carl Kelley, Lola Kelley (Carl's wife), O.W. Smith (state ASA commissioner for Nebraska), Don Joe, Kay Werner (Secretary of the Omaha Softball Association) and Connie Claussen planned the first Women's College World Series, held May 16-18, 1969, at the George W. Dill Softball Complex in Omaha and in Fremont, Nebraska.

Kay Werner

Carl P. Kelley

Connie Claussen

This first tournament, as well as those held in 1970, 1971 and 1972, were sanctioned by the Nebraska State Softball Association, the Omaha Metro Softball Association, the ASA and the CIAW (representing DGWS). The number of entries in the tournament went from nine in 1969 to 28 teams in 1971. The initial nine teams entered were: John F. Kennedy College; Illinois State University; St. Petersburg Junior College, Florida; Southwest Missouri State College; Colorado State University; Kearney State College; Creighton University; Black Hills State College; and University of Nebraska at Omaha.

John F. Kennedy College won the first three tournaments, 1969-1971, but every year the competition got tougher. In 1970, Southwest Missouri State College defeated JFK in the first final game, 2-0, and, in 1971, the keenest competition came from Iowa State. (See Appendix C for all WCWS results.)

The Women's College World Series during those first three years was open to any school that wanted to enter. There was no qualifying process and only a minimum of eligibility requirements for the student-athletes. In many cases, a team budget was virtually nonexistent. Arizona State

First Women's College World Series Champs — John F. Kennedy College
Pictured on the top row, left to right, are Coach Ken Christensen, Sandy Messerich, Adrienne Perrino, Karen Hughs, Cindy Thompson, Kay Sharr, Coach Don Joe. Center row, left to right, Charlene Thompson, Ginny Nelson, Judy Lloyd, Linda Manning and Sandy Konrad. Bottom row, left to right, Karen Peitz, Cathy Buell, Jeanna Schliffke, Lois Stuflick and Beth Richards.

University's softball budget during the 1970-71 year, the first year its softball team entered the WCWS, was one-third of $500! The team sports budget of $500 and uniforms were shared by volleyball, basketball and softball. Needless to say, it was necessary for the ASU team to raise money any way they could in order to fund the trip to Omaha. While the team did fly to Omaha, the 12 players and one coach stayed in the basement of a friend of one of the players. The entire team shared one bathroom, the players slept on the floor in sleeping bags, and the friend, who happened to be a school principal, arranged for everyone to use the showers at his school. That is an example of how much these talented athletes wanted to not only play the game of softball, but to pit their skills against others.

AIAW Formed in 1971-1972

In 1971-72, the CIAW became the AIAW, an affiliate organization of AAHPER and a substructure of the DGWS. CIAW still conducted the national championships for the

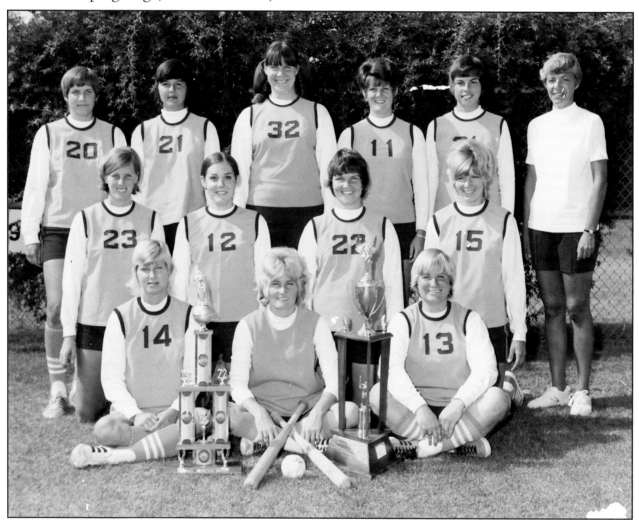

1972 WCWS Championship Arizona State University Softball Team
(Note the generic uniforms shared by three teams) Top row, left to right, Marilyn Rau, Susan Halter, Betty Barr, Patty McKee, Cassie Hayes, Coach Mary Littlewood. Middle row, left to right, Lynn Mooney, Mary Evans, Paula Miller, Georgia Buelow. Bottom row, left to right, Leanne Easley, Ginger Kurtz, Judy Hoke.

1971-72 academic year with the AIAW taking over complete control on women's intercollegiate athletics in the summer of 1972.

The first Delegate Assembly of the AIAW met in November 1973 and approved the following purposes and functions:

1. Hold national championships;
2. Conduct athletics within the "spirit of the game" for achieving educational values from sport;
3. Increase public understanding and appreciation of the importance and value of athletics in contributing to enrichment of life;
4. Encourage and facilitate research in athletics;
5. Offer assistance in development of and improvement of intercollegiate programs;
6. Sponsor conferences, institutes, and meetings for member schools;
7. Cooperate with other professional groups interested in sports programs and opportunities for women;
8. Provide direction and maintain a relationship with AIAW regional organizations.

AIAW's initial stance concerning scholarships for female athletes was that they were not allowed, therefore any school awarding scholarships was not eligible to become a member of AIAW. Only schools that were members of AIAW could send softball teams to the WCWS.

Since John F. Kennedy College awarded scholarships to their student-athletes, they were not eligible to become members of AIAW and therefore were not eligible to enter the 1972 Women's College World Series. The 1972 WCWS was a first in many respects. It was the first WCWS that JFK College was not in, it was the first that required teams to qualify by winning a DGWS-sanctioned state tournament, and it was the first tournament that was truly a "World Series." The field of 28 teams in the 1971 tournament was so large that it was difficult to conduct the competition within the guidelines of DGWS so it was decided that the number of entries had to be limited, hence the state qualifying requirement. Tournament officials were delighted to hear that the University of Tokyo would enter the 1972 tournament, making it a true "World Series."

The University of Tokyo team proved to be a crowd-pleaser as it battled to the final game against Arizona State University. ASU emerged the winner in an extra-inning pitching duel between ASU's Paula Miller and Tokyo's Yruiko Tagashira. The Japanese players — small and quick with few English-speaking skills — and their coaches, who led each team huddle with a formal bow, were a total delight on and off the field. ASU's bare-bones roster of 12 was definitely outnumbered by the 25 Japanese players — 10 of whom were paired-off pitchers and catchers.

Title IX Passed in 1972

The passing of Title IX, federal legislation whose purpose was to give equal opportunities to all American youth regardless of sex, on June 23, 1972, was monumental in determining the future of women athletes in the United States. Title IX of the Education Amendments to the Civil Rights Act of 1964 is a federal law that states:

No person . . . shall, on the basis of sex, be excluded from participation in, be denied the benefits of, or be subjected to discrimination under any educational programs or activities receiving federal financial assistance. It was realized that schools would have to be given some time to make changes, therefore Title IX demanded complete compliance for secondary schools and colleges by July 21, 1978. While it has taken many schools decades to comply with the law (and many are still not there), positive changes in the girls athletic programs in high schools and colleges were visible immediately. (Note: It wasn't until 1977-78, that the Arizona State University softball team's budget allowed them to purchase "real" softball uniforms!)

No longer could college administrators stick their heads in the sand and ignore the inequities between the men's and the women's athletic programs. Attention was given to providing full-time head coaches, equitable budgets and adequate playing facilities. The professional woman physical educator who initially "fell" into coaching because of her interest in athletics, could now devote all of her energies and time to accepting the challenge of coaching. Those terms that for decades were unacceptable labels to attach to the "feminine" half of the school, were now not only acceptable but were badges of honor. A girl was proud to tell others that she was a member of the softball "team," as was the coach proud to be referred to as "coach."

Omaha's WCWS and AIAW Continued Through the 1970's

Under the threat of a class action suit filed in January 1973 against the NEA, AAHPER, DGWS, and AIAW, the AIAW Delegate Assembly reversed its stand on scholarships for women athletes. While the AIAW leaders wanted to fight the suit in court, AAHPER and DGWS leaders did not, so the group as a whole decided to change its stance concerning scholarships. Schools that awarded scholarships, from then on, could become members of the AIAW, and their teams could compete in AIAW-sanctioned events.

For its entire life span, the AIAW endured a series of threats to its existence and its educational athletic model. The most significant of these was a life threatening struggle with the NCAA. It became apparent to the male-controlled members of the NCAA, after Title IX was passed and upheld in the courts, that women's athletics were here to stay and that they would be in a stronger position to protect their men's programs if they also controlled women's athletics. While the final battle for control was still years away, the constant threat affected the future operations and actions of both the AIAW and the NCAA.

In the meantime, Connie Claussen and Carl Kelley, with the help of a multitude of Omaha personnel, continued to run the Women's College World Series at the George Dill Softball Complex in Omaha. From 1973 to 1976, the qualifying procedures and format remained the same — the tournament was double-elimination and teams qualified through state tournaments. The 1977 WCWS was, for the first time, cosponsored by the AIAW and the ASA, and teams qualified through regional tournaments instead of state tournaments. The AIAW also decided that for more exposure throughout the country a different region should host the WCWS every three years starting in 1980.

The strength of UCLA as a national

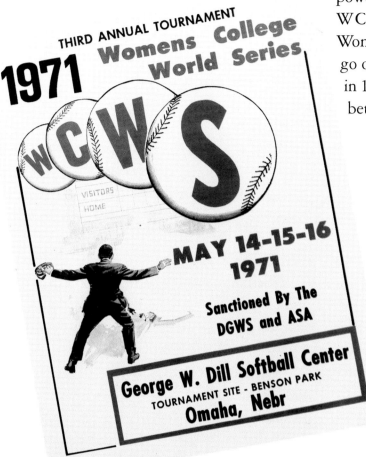

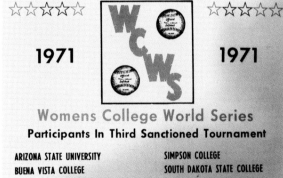

Womens College World Series
Participants In Third Sanctioned Tournament

ARIZONA STATE UNIVERSITY	SIMPSON COLLEGE
BUENA VISTA COLLEGE	SOUTH DAKOTA STATE COLLEGE
CENTRAL MISSOURI STATE COLLEGE	SOUTHERN ILLINOIS UNIVERSITY
CONCORDIA TEACHERS COLLEGE	SOUTHWEST BAPTIST COLLEGE
EASTERN ILLINOIS UNIVERSITY	SOUTHWEST MISSOURI STATE COLLEGE
ILLINOIS STATE UNIVERSITY	UNIVERSITY OF MINNESOTA AT DULUTH
IOWA STATE UNIVERSITY	UNIVERSITY OF NEBRASKA AT LINCOLN
JOHN F. KENNEDY COLLEGE	UNIVERSITY OF NEBRASKA AT OMAHA
KANSAS STATE TEACHERS COLLEGE	UNIVERSITY OF NORTHERN COLORADO
KEARNEY STATE COLLEGE	UNIVERSITY OF SOUTH DAKOTA
LUTHER COLLEGE	UPPER IOWA UNIVERSITY
MIDLAND COLLEGE	WARTBURG COLLEGE
MINOT STATE COLLEGE	WAYNE STATE COLLEGE
PARSONS COLLEGE	WISCONSIN STATE UNIVERSITY

power was first evident as it won the 1978 WCWS and were runners-up to Texas Woman's University in 1979. UCLA would go on to win the first NCAA championship in 1982, as well as seven other national titles between 1982 and 1997.

WCWS Became AIAW Championship in 1980

For the first time, in 1980, the Women's College World Series became the AIAW National Championship, sponsored by the AIAW only. While the blessing of the Amateur Softball Association was appreciated, the ASA was no longer a cosponsor of the event. Another major change in the setup of the tournament was that AIAW teams were placed into two divisions — Divisions I and II — dependent upon the size of the school, budget, etc. Each division held its own tournament at separate locations. The Division I tournament was held at the University of Oklahoma, and the Division II tournament was at California State College at Sacramento.

AIAW and NCAA Battle Over Women's Championships

After several years of an ongoing struggle between the AIAW and the NCAA, and unsuccessful attempts by the NCAA to reduce the authority of Title IX, the NCAA decided to offer championships in women's sports. Walter Byers, the NCAA's executive director at that time and their first full-time director, later wrote in his book, *Unsportsmanlike Conduct:*

Despite all the meetings, the NCAA and the AIAW were on a collision course. By 1975, 331 NCAA member schools, or 46 percent of the total, were not members of the AIAW. Most of those schools, plus other NCAA colleges served by the AIAW, preferred that the NCAA enter women's athletics.

At the 1980 NCAA Convention, delegates approved women's championships for Divisions II and III basketball, field hockey, swimming, tennis and volleyball. That set the stage for the ultimate debate at the 1981 NCAA Convention about a new governance structure, which included women's athletics, and sponsorship of Division I women's championships.

A record number of delegates and visitors attended that convention, which also happened to be the 75th annual meeting of the NCAA. A total of 1,300 people packed the convention center at the Fontainebleau Hilton Hotel in Miami Beach. After much debate and some attempts at parliamentary reshuffling, the historic governance structure that made women's athletics a part of the NCAA received the two-thirds approval necessary for passage. The vote for Division I women's championships followed shortly, with the original vote deadlocked at 124-124. The motion was defeated, 127 for and 128 against, in a recount. Later brought back to the floor after delegates voted 141-105 to reconsider, the motion was finally approved 137-117. A total of 19 Division I women's sports, including softball, were now under the governance of the NCAA. The next morning, delegates returned to approve additional women's championships for Divisions II and III, softball among them.

Judith R. Holland, a former AIAW president and women's athletic director at UCLA at the time, was an outspoken advocate for the NCAA. She commented to the *Miami Herald:*

"What we're asking for is simply a choice. We are trying to allow more options for women, the same type of opportunities men have."

Holland was referring to the fact that men's athletics could compete in either the NCAA or the NAIA, and that now women's programs would be given the choice of the AIAW or the NCAA.

For one year (1981), both the AIAW and the NCAA offered some women's championships, forcing colleges to choose between them for each sport. However, the first NCAA softball championships were not held until the spring of 1982.

The rate of defection from the AIAW by larger institutions and the loss of TV contracts made it clear which organization would prevail. The NCAA had far greater resources.

An event that sparked much unrest among AIAW softball teams in 1981 was a colossal foul-up in the selection of teams that would participate in that championship. Both Indiana University and Arizona State University were invited to participate as at-large teams. A protest, filed over the AIAW selection process, triggered a reconsideration by the softball committee as to which teams would be the at-large teams. The next morning, both Indiana and Arizona State were notified that "it was a mistake. You're not invited after all"! Needless to say, this action caused much dissatisfaction with the AIAW, not just by Indiana and ASU, but by everyone familiar with the situation. Schools that may have been undecided up to that point about whether to go with the NCAA or the AIAW, were given a strong shove in the direction of the NCAA.

Later that year, the AIAW canceled its 1982-83 championships and went to court against the NCAA in an antitrust lawsuit. The AIAW's main points in the case were that (1) the AIAW championships looked less appealing since the organization would not be able to pay competitors' expenses, which the NCAA had done for men's championships and would do for the women as well, and (2) because of the NCAA's contacts with the networks to gain TV exposure for NCAA women's championships, it would block the AIAW from a network TV contract. In Byers' book, he contended that while the first point was true, the second was not. The loss of that lawsuit to the NCAA was the finishing blow to the AIAW.

The AIAW, even though they were forced to relinquish their control of women's collegiate athletic programs, had a major impact on the future of women's athletics. That impact is best described in the following comments:

The AIAW's legacy to the sports world is monumental. The association was successful for a decade at offering an alternative model on intercollegiate athletics for female athletes. The women created a highly effective governance structure and won the Title IX "war." But AIAW's very success led to its demise as, beyond the wildest dreams of its creators, it fulfilled its mission of providing opportunity for female athletes ...

The struggle for survival of a women's athletic model of intercollegiate athletics failed. The opportunity for the female collegiate athletes, however, succeeded. (10:302)

NCAA Championships Begin in 1982

The first task of the NCAA was to name a committee to administer the championships. Committee members were: Sharron Backus, UCLA; Connie Claussen, University of Nebraska, Omaha; Mary Higgins, Creighton University (chair); June Walker, Trenton State College; Joan Howard, Fitchburg State College; Gayle Blevins, Indiana University; Susan Craig, University of New Mexico; Sally Guerette, University of Vermont; Gary Boeyink, Central College (Iowa); Beverly Downing, St. Augustine's College; Judy Martino, University of South Carolina, and Jane Scheper, Northern Kentucky University.

The first NCAA championships provided for fields of 16 teams in Division I, 10 teams in Division II and 16 teams in Division III. The Diamond D-100 softball was chosen to be the official ball for the championships. The Division I championship was hosted by Creighton University, again in Omaha; Sacred Heart was the site for the Division II championships; and Trenton State hosted the first of many Division III championships. *The NCAA News* printed the following recap of the Division I championships in its June 1982 paper:

If a single athlete can be responsible for a team's success, UCLA's Debbie Doom should qualify. Doom, a freshman pitcher, won all five of UCLA's games as the Bruins earned the title in the 1982 NCAA Division I Women's Softball Championship, played May 27-31 at Omaha, Nebraska. Doom pitched a two-hit shutout for a 2-0 decision (in eight innings) in the final game over Fresno State.

UCLA scored the two winning runs in the top of the eighth without the benefit of a hit. Two walks, a double steal, a sacrifice fly and an error produced the runs.

The rally was characteristic of UCLA's victories throughout the tournament. The Bruins scored just seven runs to win the five games but did not allow a run in their last 43 innings of play.

Doom allowed 21 hits and one run in 41 2/3 innings during her five wins; she struck out 62 batters. Doom and Tracy Compton combined for a perfect game in UCLA's 10-0 second-round win over Western Michigan.

Western Michigan suffered a second no-hit loss later, as Fullerton State's Kathy Van Wyk (33-0 entering the tournament) bested the Broncos, 2-0. Van Wyk's unbeaten season earlier had been ended by Arizona State, 2-0.

UCLA finished the season with a record of 33-7-2; Fresno State was 43-11.

UCLA, coached by ASA Hall of Famer Sharron Backus, had many outstanding players on its roster. Among them were future Olympians Dot Richardson and Sheila Cornell.

Through 1997, UCLA won the NCAA title eight times. The 1995 crown, however, had to be returned because of NCAA violations. According to the NCAA Committee on Infractions, UCLA had awarded soccer scholarships to some of its softball players. This was an infraction of the rules

UCLA's Dot Richardson was the NCAA's Player of the Decade in the 1980's and later achieved Olympic fame.

*1990 **National Champion UCLA Bruins***

Winners of a third consecutive NCAA title, the 1990 Bruins were back row, left to right, Kirk Walker (assistant coach), Missy Phillips, Kristy Howard, Karla Parrent, Kerry Dienelt, Yvonne Gutierrez and Sue Enquist (assistant coach). Middle row, left to right, Kelly Inouye, Valerie Girard (trainer), Shauna Flynn, Bea Chiaravanont, Sharron Backus (head coach) with trophy, Erica Viencina and Lisa Fernandez. Kneeling on the front row, left to right, Heather Compton, Shelly Montgomery, Lisa Longaker, Maria Rodriguez and Dee Dee Weiman.

and required the Bruins to vacate their 1995 championship title and be put on probation. Even though originally banned from the 1997 championship, UCLA appealed and won the right to delay the probation until the 1998 season. The Bruins finished second in 1997.

While UCLA dominated in the 1980's, the team to beat in the 1990's was the University of Arizona, coached by Mike Candrea. The first sign of Arizona's dominance was in the 1991 championships. The Wildcats defeated UCLA, stopping the Bruins' attempt to be the first institution to win four consecutive NCAA championships, and went on to win the 1991 title. Bill Redmer recapped the action in his July 1991 issue of *Women's Fastpitch World:*

Debbie Day had her day and it was May 26th, 1991, as she hurled the University of Arizona to the 1991 College Softball World Series Championship and destiny ... The Wildcats dropped defending champion UCLA, 5-1, for the crown. Earlier they defeated the Bruins 1-0 to drop them into the loser's bracket. UCLA didn't dominate as it has in the past, they struggled throughout the tournament and its fabled pitching staff ran out of gas at the end. Early on it looked as if a new champion was possible for the first time in a long time. Speculation was rampant.

Arizona finished that season with a 56-15 record, and went on to finish either first or second for the next six years. They won the title in 1993, 1994, 1996 and 1997.

By the 1998 season, NCAA championship brackets had expanded to 32 teams for Division I, 32 for Division II and 40 for Division III. It was anticipated that, in 1999, the Division I bracket would be further expanded to 48 teams.

Increased Growth, Major Rule Changes and Continued Compliance with Title IX

In 1982, the year of the first NCAA championships, 409 NCAA schools and 243 junior colleges fielded women's fastpitch softball teams. Since then, those numbers have increased with 779 NCAA schools playing fastpitch in 1998. In addition, 249 NAIA and 384 junior college teams would take the field in 1998. That's a 117 percent increase in 16 years.

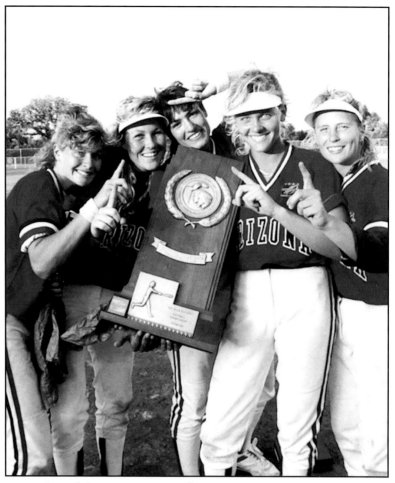

Members of the 1991 NCAA Champion Arizona Wildcat team show off the hardware. From left to right are Julie Standering, Julie Jones, Marcie Aguilar, Suzy Lady and Kristin Gauthier.

As the total number of teams increased, collegiate coaches felt the need to make their own alterations to the rules of the game. The ASA rules were used until 1997, with collegiate coaches making exceptions to those rules as early as 1983. The first change was the designated hitter entry rule and others included:

- 1987 — Pitching distance moved from 40 to 43 feet.
- 1994 — Development and use of an optic yellow ball with raised red seams and a COR of .50.
- 1996 — Banning of titanium bats from championship play.
- 1997 — Development of NCAA Softball Rule Book.

The key factor at work during the seventies, eighties and nineties was compliance with Title IX. Many men's athletic groups tried to get the government to dilute the effect of Title IX, mainly because they felt the law was causing many colleges and universities to drop men's sports to increase women's sports offerings and funding. The football coaches had the most organized attack as they lobbied Congress to exempt football participant numbers when applying Title IX regulations. They felt there was no comparable women's sport in terms of numbers and by taking football out of the mix, the numbers for the remaining men's sports and women's sports would be comparable. Although Congress enjoyed mingling with the most notable football coaches of the day, the Department of Education did not agree that football should be exempted. As the 25th anniversary of Title IX neared in 1997, the long-standing Title IX interpretation was reaffirmed.

For softball, like most of the other women's sports, the journey toward compliance with the law resulted in more scholarship dollars, school-purchased equipment, upgraded travel means and accommodations, and nicer facilities. Softball coaching job descriptions, in Division I especially, changed to resemble their male counterparts, as softball coaching was con-

Fastpitch Softball Sponsorship Numbers For Educational Institutions
(1983-1998)

	NCAA I	NCAA II	NCAA III	NAIA	NJCAA I	NJCAA 3	NWAACC	Cal JC	HS
1982	143	106	160	——	243	——		——	7,569
1983	136	119	186	——	251	——		——	7,528
1984	140	113	198	——	211	——		74	7,831
1985	152	128	213	——	207	——		75	8,507
1986	165	139	223	——	215	——		76	8,945
1987	175	138	230	——	195	——		70	8,271
1988	172	139	232	229	203	——		78	8,314
1989	172	145	233	235	198	——		78	8,474
1990	171	150	235	248	238	——		76	8,688
1991	174	162	245	242	207	——		80	8,867
1992	182	171	252	235	199	——		80	9,015
1993	186	172	260	240	212	——		72	9,157
1994	192	190	264	241	207	——		71	10,243
1995	196	194	291	239	262	——		71	10,708
1996	205	222	312	209	195	90		74	11,452
1997	221	226	320	238	184	72	19	73	11,895
1998	226	228	325	249	204	86	19	75	Not avail.

sidered a full-time job. Coaches at most large institutions were no longer required to coach several different sports and teach.

Recruiting became the name of the game, as more and more high school and travel-ball team players looked for scholarship dollars. From 1982 to 1997, high schools sponsoring fastpitch softball rose from 7,569 to 11,895. ASA reports indicate that the 16,000 ASA youth teams in 1980 grew to almost 65,000 teams by 1994. Most of the larger institutions hired at least one full-time assistant, while some hired two.

As the next century approached, colleges focused on building stadium facilities designed specifically for the collegiate fastpitch game. No longer were fans sentenced to the use of port-a-potties or bringing lawn chairs and their own refreshments. College softball was hitting the big time.

The U.S. athletes who won the gold medal in the 1996 Olympic Games were the benefactors of the Title IX battle, begun decades before by the DGWS and AIAW leaders. Those women administrators had the foresight to recognize that women's athletics could be a healthy part of the school program and possessed the fortitude to do something about it. For softball, however, the journey began years before when players of the past began the march along the path to the gold.

Fresno State's new softball stadium, the "New" Bulldog diamond, was christened February 24, 1996, against UCLA. The crowd, which swelled to 5,427 strong, set a new all-time NCAA attendance record.

Appendices

NATIONAL CHAMPIONSHIP TEAMS

1933 Great Northerns, Chicago, IL	1966 Raybestos Brakettes, Stratford, CT
1934 Hart Motors, Chicago, IL	1967 Raybestos Brakettes, Stratford, CT
1935 Bloomer Girls, Cleveland, OH	1968 Raybestos Brakettes, Stratford, CT
1936 National Manufacturing, Cleveland, OH	1969 Orange Lionettes, Orange, CA
1937 National Manufacturing, Cleveland, OH	1970 Orange Lionettes, Orange, CA
1938 J.J. Kreigs, Alameda, CA	1971 Raybestos Brakettes, Stratford, CT
1939 J.J. Kreigs, Alameda, CA	1972 Raybestos Brakettes, Stratford, CT
1940 Arizona Ramblers, Phoenix, AZ	1973 Raybestos Brakettes, Stratford, CT
1941 Higgins Midgets, Tulsa, OK	1974 Raybestos Brakettes, Stratford, CT
1942 Jax Maids, New Orleans, LA	1975 Raybestos Brakettes, Stratford, CT
1943 Jax Maids, New Orleans, LA	1976 Raybestos Brakettes, Stratford, CT
1944 Lind and Pomeroy, Portland, OR	1977 Raybestos Brakettes, Stratford, CT
1945 Jax Maids, New Orleans, LA	1978 Raybestos Brakettes, Stratford, CT
1946 Jax Maids, New Orleans, LA	1979 Sun City Saints, Sun City, AZ
1947 Jax Maids, New Orleans, LA	1980 Raybestos Brakettes, Stratford, CT
1948 Arizona Ramblers, Phoenix, AZ	1981 Rebels, Orlando, FL
1949 Arizona Ramblers, Phoenix, AZ	1982 Raybestos Brakettes, Stratford, CT
1950 Orange Lionettes, Orange, CA	1983 Raybestos Brakettes, Stratford, CT
1951 Orange Lionettes, Orange, CA	1984 Los Angeles Diamonds, Los Angeles, CA
1952 Orange Lionettes, Orange, CA	1985 Hi-Ho Brakettes, Stratford, CT
1953 Betsy Ross Motor Rockets, Fresno, CA	1986 Southern Calif. Invasion, Los Angeles, CA
1954 Leach Motor Rockets, Fresno, CA	1987 Majestics, Orange County, CA
1955 Orange Lionettes, Orange, CA	1988 Hi-Ho Brakettes, Stratford, CT
1956 Orange Lionettes, Orange, CA	1989 Whittier Raiders, Whittier, CA
1957 Hacienda Rockets, Fresno, CA	1990 Raybestos Brakettes, Stratford, CT
1958 Raybestos Brakettes, Stratford, CT	1991 Raybestos Brakettes, Stratford, CT
1959 Raybestos Brakettes, Stratford, CT	1992 Raybestos Brakettes, Stratford, CT
1960 Raybestos Brakettes, Stratford, CT	1993 Rebels, Redding, CA
1961 Gold Sox, Whittier, CA	1994 Rebels, Redding, CA
1962 Orange Lionettes, Orange, CA	1995 Rebels, Redding, CA
1963 Raybestos Brakettes, Stratford, CT	1996 Calif. Commotion, Woodland Hills, CA
1964 Erv Lind Florists, Portland, OR	1997 Calif. Commotion, Woodland Hills, CA
1965 Orange Lionettes, Orange, CA	

TEAM RECORD HOLDERS

FIELDING

Highest Fielding Percentage — .996%; Stratford, CT, 1965

Most Errors in a Game — 11; Houston, TX, 1947

Most Errors in a Tournament — 18; Pekin, IL, 1965

Most Putouts in a Game — 81; Calif. Raiders and Jefferson City, MO; 1981

Most Putouts in a Tournament — 277; Stratford, CT, 1961

Most Assists in a Tournament — 124; Stratford, CT, 1983

Most Games in a Tournament — 11; Stratford, CT, 1983

FIELDING CONTINUED ...

Most Double Plays in a Tournament — 7; Portland, OR, 1949

Most Consecutive Wins Out of a Loser's Bracket — 9; Stratford, CT, 1983

Most Stolen Bases in a Tournament — 14; Portland, OR, 1962

Most RBI's in a Game — 26; Stratford, CT, 1992

Most Consecutive National Championships — 8; Stratford, CT

Most Total National Championships — 23; Stratford, CT

BATTING

Highest Batting Average — .358; Stratford, CT, 1983

Most Hits in a Game — 27; Stratford, CT, 1992

Most Hits in a Tournament — 10; Stratford, CT, 1992

Most Home Runs in a Tournament — 10; Stratford, CT, 1992

Most Triples in a Tournament — 7; Phoenix, AZ, 1955, and Ashland, OH, 1977

Most Doubles in a Tournament — 12; Stratford, CT, 1968 and 1983

Most Runs in a Game — 30; Stratford, CT, 1992

Most Runs in an Inning — 12; Stratford, CT, 1992

Most Runs in a Tournament — 58; Stratford, CT, 1992

INDIVIDUAL RECORD HOLDERS

BATTING

Most Runs Scored in a Tournament — 9;
Irene Shea, Stratford, CT, 1975
Pat Dufficy, Stratford, CT, 1983
Kris Peterson, Stratford, CT, 1987

Most Hits in a Tournament — 16; Pat Guenzler, Stratford, CT, 1983

Most Hits in a Game — 5; Kay Rich, Fresno, CA, 1955, and Tricia Popowski, Stratford, CT, 1992

Most Consecutive Hits — 9; Kris Peterson, Stratford, CT, 1987

Most Doubles in a National Championship — 6; Dot Richardson, Stratford, CT, 1989

Most Triples in a National Championship — 3; Irene Huber, Fresno, CA, 1949; Lu Flanagan, Seattle, WA, 1971; Lana Svec, Ashland, OH, 1977; Marilyn Rau, Sun City, AZ, 1978/1981

Highest Batting Average — .632; Diane Kalliam, Santa Clara, CA, 1975

Most Home Runs —
5; Kim Maher, Fresno, CA, 1994
4; Robbie Mulkey, Portland, OR, 1949

Most RBI's in a National Championship — 12; Kim Maher, Fresno, CA, 1994

Most RBI's in a Game — 7; Dionna Harris, Stratford, CT, 1992

Most At Bats in a National Championship — 41; Jackie Gaw, Stratford, CT, 1983, and Irene Shea, Stratford, CT, 1974

PITCHING

Most Innings Pitched in a Tournament —
70; Joan Joyce, Stratford, CT, 1973
69 2/3; Joan Joyce, Stratford, CT, 1974

Most Strikeouts in a Game — 40 (19 innings); Joan Joyce, Stratford, CT, 1961

Most Strikeouts in a Tournament — 134; Joan Joyce, Stratford, CT, 1973

Most Strikeouts in a Seven Inning Game —
20; Bertha Tickey, Orange, CA, 1953
19; Bertha Tickey, Orange, CA, 1954

Most Strikeouts by Two Pitchers in One Game — 65; Becky Duffin, Jefferson City, MO, and Tiffany Boyd, California Raiders, 1987

Most Consecutive Strikeouts in a Game — 18; Michele Granger, Orange County, CA, 1988

Most No-Hitters in a National Championship — 3; Louise Mazzuca, Portland, OR, 1960

Most Perfect Games in a National Championship — 2; Bertha Tickey - Stratford, CT, 1950/54, and Margie Law, Phoenix, AZ, 1954/57

Most Wins in a National Championship — 8; Joan Joyce, Stratford, CT, 1973

BERTHA TICKEY AND ERV LIND AWARD WINNERS

BERTHA TICKEY AWARD

1968	Bertha Tickey, Stratford, CT
1969	Nancy Welborn, Orange, CA
1970	Nancy Welborn, Orange, CA
1971	Nancy Welborn, Orange, CA
1972	Nancy Welborn, Orange, CA
1973	Joan Joyce, Stratford, CT
1974	Joan Joyce, Stratford, CT
1975	Joan Joyce, Stratford, CT
1976	Barb Reinalda, Stratford, CT
1977	Barb Reinalda, Stratford, CT
1978	Kathy Arendsen, Stratford, CT
1979	Michelle Thomas, Sun City, AZ
1980	Kathy Arendsen, Stratford, CT
1981	Mary Lou Piel, Orlando, FL
1982	Kathy Arendsen, Stratford, CT
1983	Barb Reinalda, Stratford, CT
1984	Kathy Van Wyk, Los Angeles, CA
1985	Susan Lefebvre, Long Beach, CA
1986	Michele Granger, Orange County, CA
1987	Michele Granger, Orange County, CA
1988	Michele Granger, Orange County, CA
1989	Lisa Longaker, Whittier, CA
1990	Michele Smith, Redding, CA
1991	Kathy Arendsen, Stratford, CT
1992	Lisa Fernandez, Stratford, CT
1993	Michele Smith, Redding, CA
1994	Michele Smith, Redding, CA
1995	Michele Smith, Redding, CA
1996	Desarie Knipfer, Bellflower, CA
1997	Lisa Fernandez, Lakewood, CA

Bertha Tickey Award — *Presented to the outstanding pitcher in the Women's Major Fast Pitch National Championship.*

ERV LIND AWARD

1965	Nera White, Nashville, TN
1966	Gladys Crespo, Stratford, CT
1967	Margaret Propst, Topeka, KS
1968	Carol Spanks, Orange, CA
1969	Carol Spanks, Orange, CA
1970	Carol Spanks, Orange, CA
1971	No Award Given
1972	Chris Miner, Fresno, CA
1973	Kathy Fraser, Bloomington, MN
1974	Jamie Smith, Lansing, MI
1975	Bethel Stout, St. Louis, MO
1976	Dori Anderson, Orlando, FL
1977	Kathy Strahan, Stratford, CT
1978	Mary Faure, Greeley, CO
1979	Dot Richardson, Orlando, FL
1980	Suzy Brazney, Long Beach, CA
1981	Dot Richardson, Orlando, FL
1982	Helen Andrade, Sun City, AZ
1983	Jonelle Johnson, Sacramento, CA
1984	Dot Richardson, Stratford, CT
1985	Allyson Rioux, Stratford, CT
1986	Dot Richardson, Stratford, CT
1987	Dot Richardson, Stratford, CT
1988	Julie Standering, Los Angeles, CA
1989	Kris Peterson, Stratford, CT
1990	Dot Richardson, Stratford, CT
1991	Julie Smith, Redding, CA
1992	Ann Rowan, Phoenix, AZ
1993	Julie Smith, Redding, CA
1994	Martha O'Kelley, San Gabriel, CA
1995	Dot Richardson, Woodland, CA
1996	Gillian Boxx, Woodland, CA
1997	Jennifer McFalls, Redding, CA

Erv Lind Award — *Presented to the outstanding defensive player in the Women's Major Fast Pitch National Championship.*

ASA WOMEN'S FASTPITCH FIRST TEAM ALL-AMERICANS

NAME	YEARS	TEAM	POSITION
	— A —		
Ackers, Judy	1967	OSHE Meats, Topeka	C
Adams, Mary	1972	Orange Lionettes	OF
Adams, Pat	1970	Lorelei Ladies, Atlanta	2B
Adams, Rosie	1971, 72, 73	Raybestos Brakettes	2B
Ahern, Maureen	1976	Shamrocks-Tonawanda, NY	3B
Albrecht, Lou	1961, 62	Whittier Gold Sox	P
	1965	Orange Lionettes	OF
Alsup, Joan	1953	Fresno Rockets	P
Anderson, Cindy	1979	West Allis Bankettes	DP
Anderson, Dori	1976	Orlando Rebels	UT
Anderson, Yvonne	1954	Fresno Rockets	OF
Andrade, Helen	1982	Sun City Saints	UT
Archer, Mary	1953	Toronto, Canada	UT
Arendsen, Kathy	1978, 80, 81 1982, 83, 86, 91	Raybestos Brakettes	P
Arvizu, Yo	1985	Long Beach Renegades	1B
	— B —		
Bachman, Susan	1976, 79	Orlando Rebels	OF/2B
Backus, Sharron	1962	Whittier Gold Sox	UT
	1964	Orange Lionettes	OF
	1971, 74	Raybestos Brakettes	OF/SS
Bade, Leslie	1978, 79	West Allis Bankettes	OF
Baker, Lisa	1986	California Invasion	OF
	1988	Los Angeles Diamonds	3B
Barnes, Gloria	1953	Denver, CO	OF
Beadlescomb, Tracy	1984	LaPalma Restrauant-Flint, MI	OF
Benedetto, Cathy	1969	Yakima Webb Cats	1B
	1970	Dr. Bernard's-Portland	UT
Bennett, Mabel	1963	Fresno Rockets	P
Berg, Laura	1994	"A's"- Newport Beach	OF
Bergstrom, Kris	1984	Bettencourt Blast-Hayward	OF
Betz, Audrey	1958	Lancaster, CA	OF
	1962	Crystal-ettes Reading, PA	OF
Blasse, Angela	1961	Burry Biscuit-Elizabeth, NJ	UT
Boles, Zada	1955	Phoenix Ramblers	OF
Bonelli, Gloria	1950	Pekin-Lettes	UT
Bonham, Jean	1960	Phoenix Ramblers	1B
Bonifas, Leanne	1987	Pekin-Lettes	DP
Bonovito, Rose	1965	New Haven, CT	OF
Boulette, Paula	1972	Drifters-Waltham, MA	C
Boyd, Mary	1971	Telford, PA	C
Boxx, Gillian	1996, 97	California Commotion	C

NAME	YEARS	TEAM	POSITION
Brazney, Suzy	1980	Long Beach Renegades	UT
	1982	California Blazers	C
	1983	Sepulveda Blazers	UT
	1984	CA Diamond Blazers	C
	1986, 89, 1991, 92	Orange County Majestics	C
	1995	Phoenix Sunbirds	C
Breski, Cindy	1975	Buffalo, NY	1B
Brown, Carolyn	1954	Buena Park Lynx	2B
Brown, Rachel	1992	Phoenix Sunbirds	OF
Brundage, Jennifer	1993	Redding Rebels	OF
	1997	California Commotion	3B
Bryan, Edwina	1966	Lorelei Ladies, Atlanta	SS
Buchanan, Denny	1974	Sun City Saints	OF
Burke, Kandi	1985	Orange Cty Majestics	DH
Burns, Lela	1977	Burbank Royals	P
Busick, Ginny	1951, 57, 58	Fresno Rockets	P
	— C —		
Caito, Ricki	1956, 57, 60	Orange Lionettes	2B
Carlson, Thelma	1958	Forest Grove, OR	OF
Carter, Josie	1986	Classic, OK	OF
Chellevold, Amy	1996, 97	Calif. Commotion	UT/OF
Clarke, Rhonda	1980	Long Beach Renegades	P
Clinchy, Lisa	1981	Sun City Saints	1B
Cline, Jen	1997	California Jazz	DP
Coats, Linda	1976	Sun City Saints	OF
Coleman, Gail	1980	Magic-Macomb, IL	1B
Collict, Joy	1956, 61	Filters Electric Perks-Toronto, Canada	C
Collins, Michelle	1993	VIP's-Topton, PA	P
Compton, Heather	1994, 95	California Jazz	P
Compton, Tracy	1983	California Blazers	P
	1984, 85	Los Angeles Diamonds	P
Condon, Jenny	1996	California Commotion	OF
Coney, Shirley	1950, 51	Pekin-Lettes	2B
Contel, Jeanne	1953, 55, 57, 1958, 63	Fresno Rockets	3B
Cooper, Cindy	1990	Redding Rebels	3B
Cornell, Sheila (Douty)	1982	California Blazers	3B
	1983	Sepulveda Blazers	1B
	1985, 86	LA Diamonds	3B/1B
	1988	Raybestos Brakettes	1B
	1989	Hi-Ho Brakettes	1B
	1991, 92 1993, 95	Raybestos Brakettes	1B
	1997	California Commotion	1B
Cox, Beverly	1955	Erv Lind Florists	2B
Crespo, Gladys	1966	Raybestos Brakettes	UT
Cutright, Pat	1981	Magic-Macomb, IL	OF

ASA ALL-AMERICANS CONTINUED ...

NAME	YEARS	TEAM	POSITION
— D —			
Davenport, Gail	1979	Sun City Saints	OF
Daves, Jean	1964, 70, 71	Orlando Rebels	P
Davidson, Dottie	1976	Orlando Rebels	P
Davis, Denise	1993	VIP's-Topton, PA	DP
Davis, Mickey	1968	Orlando Rebels	OF
DeLuca, Ann	1960	Raybestos Brakettes	OF
Denmon, Doreen	1980, 85	Raybestos Brakettes	C
Diamond, Sherry	1975	Sexton Ford-Moline, IL	2B
Dicks, Janet	1962	Crystal-ettes Reading, PA	OF
Dixon, Millie	1953	Orange Lionettes	2B
	1961	Raybestos Brakettes	2B
Dobson, Margaret	1949, 50	Erv Lind Florists	3B
Doom, Debbie	1980,	Sun City Saints	P
	1987, 89, 92	Orange County Majestics	P
Doyle, Snookie	1956	Orange Lionettes	SS
Drew, Marge	1972	Drifters-Waltham, MA	1B
Drikow, Phyllis	1954	Kutis Funeral Home St. Louis	3B
Dufficy, Pat	1983, 84, 86,	Raybestos Brakettes	SS/3B
	1988, 93, 94	Raybestos Brakettes	UT/OF
Duffin, Becky	1989	Classics-St. Louis, MO	P
Duncan, Jake	1952	Kansas City Dons	2B
— E —			
Easley, Lee Ann	1977	Sun City Saints	2B
Eckert, Denise	1989	Whittier Raiders	OF
Edde, Pam	1980	Long Beach Renegades	OF
Eischens, Arlene	1962	Minneapolis Comets	C
Eisen, Thelma (Tiby)	1955, 57, 58	Orange Lionettes	OF/UT
Enquist, Sue	1976, 78, 81	Raybestos Brakettes	OF
Erickson, Lisa	1991	Burbank Knights	OF
Estes, Lydia	1975	Plain American-Washington, D.C.	2B
Evans, (Grayson) Betty	1948	Erv Lind Florists	P
— F —			
Faure, Mary	1978,	Greeley, CO	UT
	1982	Sun City Saints	1B
Fernandez, Lisa	1990, 91,		
	1992, 93	Raybestos Brakettes	P
	1995, 96, 97	California Commotion	P
Findley, Jeri	1977, 78	West Allis Bankettes	OF
Fitzwater, Carolyn	1962, 63, 64	Erv Lind Florists	SS
Flippen, Mary Lou	1989	Redding Rebels	OF
Fluellen, Monique	1994	Majestics-Montclair, NJ	P
Ford, Francis	1949	Boise, ID	OF
Foster, Rina	1991	Redding Rebels	OF
Fox, Marion	1953, 56	Toronto, Canada	P
Fraser, Kathy	1973	Benjos-Bloomington, MN	UT

NAME	YEARS	TEAM	POSITION
— G —			
Gabel, Lynda	1966	Orlando Rebels	OF
Garcia, Barbara	1981, 82	Sun City Saints	OF
Gaw, Suzie	1978, 82, 1993, 95	Sun City Saints	UT
Genz, Paulette	1979	Shimers-Bloomington, MN	P
Gilmore, Carol	1962	Orange Lionettes	P
Gilpen, Mary	1951	Schrader-Cleveland, OH	OF
Glasscock, Jessie	1948	Phoenix Ramblers	SS
Glomboske, Kristen	1987	California Raiders	C
Graham, Charlotte	1973, 79	Santa Clara Laurels	P
Granger, Michele	1986, 87,88	Orange Cty Majestics	P
Greene, Carol	1972	Drifters-Waltham, MA	OF
Greer, Nelwyn	1952	Baton Rouge, LA	1B
Griffin, Odette	1960, 66	Orange Lionettes	OF
Gromacki, Michelle	1990	Redding Rebels	C
Guenzler, Pat	1975	Kutis Funeral Home-St. Louis	OF
	1983	Raybestos Brakettes	OF
Guiterrez, Yvonne	1990, 92, 1995, 96	California Commotion	OF
Gunter, Sue	1967	Nashville TN	2B
— H —			
Hall, Cathie	1988	Redding Rebels	DP
Hamilton, Gail	1980	Glendale, CA	2B
Harrigan, Lori	1991	Burbank Knights	P
Harris, Betty	1949	Phoenix Ramblers	2B
Harris, Billie	1958, 59	Phoenix Ramblers	P
	1969	Yakima Webb Cats	P
Harris, Dionna	1995, 96	California Jazz	OF
Harris, Elaine	1952, 57	Orange Lionettes	OF
Harrison, Pat	1966, 68, 70	Raybestos Brakettes	OF
Hedberg, Wendy	1982	Magic-Macomb, IL	UT
Hiltz, Terry	1952	Nortowns-Toronto, Can.	P
Hoehn, Nonie	1956, 59	Orange Lionettes	P
Hoke, Judy	1975, 76	Sun City Saints	OF
Holloway, Tammy	1989	St. Louis Classics	C
Horky, Rita	1964	Orlando Rebels	OF
Huber, Alberta	1949	Boise, ID	OF
Huber, Irene	1949, 52	Fresno Rockets	OF
Hyde, Barbara	1979	Hill Nautilus-Adelphia, MD	1B
— I —			
Ito, Nancy	1964, 65, 68, 1969, 70, 72	Orange Lionettes	C
— J —			
Jackson, Kelly	1990, 92	Redding Rebels	1B/UT
Jarvis, Leanne	1985	New Jersey Belles	C
	1986, 87, 88, 1989, 90	Raybestos Brakettes	C/DP
Jenkins, Mindy	1995	Lady Pride-Decatur, IL	OF
Jennings, Venus	1978	Law Equipment Greeley, CO	OF
Jerry, Nedra	1982	California Blazers	OF

ASA ALL-AMERICANS CONTINUED ...

NAME	YEARS	TEAM	POSITION
Johnson, Eva	1970	San Antonio, TX	3B
Johnson, Jonelle	1983	Sports Time Express-Sacramento	C
Johnson, Kari	1987	Redding Rebels	2B
Johnson, Stacey	1986	OKC Classics	UT
Johnson, Trinity	1997	California Jazz	UT
Johnson, Trish	1994	Michigan Cruise	1B
Jordan, Barbara	1987, 88	California Invasion	OF
Joyce, Joan	1959, 60, 61, 1962, 63	Raybestos Brakettes	1B/UT/P
	1964, 65, 66	Orange Lionettes	UT/P
	1967, 68, 69, 70, 71, 72, 1973, 74, 75	Raybestos Brakettes	P
Jungwirth, Judy	1973	Benjos-Bloomington, MN	UT
Justin, Jill	1989, 1990, 92, 93	Hi Ho Brakettes-Stratford Raybestos Brakettes	OF OF

— K —

NAME	YEARS	TEAM	POSITION
Kaiser, Lorraine	1951	American Lithofold-Detroit, MI	UT
Kalliam, Diane	1971, 73, 1974, 75	Santa Clara Laurels	OF/SS
Kammeyer, Joan	1954	Orange Lionettes	OF
Keeney, Phyllis	1957	Huntington Park Blues	OF
Kellers, Peggy	1968, 71, 1973, 74	Raybestos Brakettes	C
King, Elise	1985	Long Beach Renegades	OF
King, Kathryn (Sis)	1959, 63, 64	Phoenix Ramblers	OF
	1965	Raybestos Brakettes	OF
Klement, Teri	1996	California Jazz	OF
Kluge, Mary Ann	1974	Shamrocks-Tonawanda, NY	UT
Knipfer, Desarie	1996	California Jazz	P
Kragseth, Sue	1981	Bloomington, MN	3B
Kuczo, Dena	1953	Raybestos Brakettes	OF
Kurrell, Pam	1961	Lock Drug Jets-Redwood City	OF

— L —

NAME	YEARS	TEAM	POSITION
Lambdin, Jennae	1991	Orange County Majestics	OF
Langevain, Debbie	1976, 77	Burbank Royals	SS/UT
	1987	California Invasion	1B
LaRose, Carol	1964, 65	Raybestos Brakettes	3B
Law, Margie	1948, 49, 1950, 51,	Phoenix Ramblers	OF/P
	1952	Phoenix Ramblers	C
	1953, 54, 1955, 57	Phoenix Ramblers	P
Lee, Carol	1962, 63	Whittier Gold Sox	C
Leeke, Harriet	1955	Phoenix Ramblers	UT
LeFebvre, Susan	1985, 1986, 87	Long Beach Renegades California Invasion	P P

NAME	YEARS	TEAM	POSITION
Leising, Janet	1977	Shamrocks-Tonawanda, NY	C
Lewis, Sue	1984	Los Angeles Diamonds	1B
Lichtenbergen, Carol	1969, 71	Schaeferettes-Plainfield, NJ	OF
Lillock, Cyndi	1971	Santa Clara Laurels	OF
Lindenberg, Nina	1996	California Jazz	3B
Litherland, Martha	1977	Sarver Paving-Ashland, OH	OF
Lockabey, Annabell	1956	Orange Lionettes	OF
Long, Chick	1956	Lancaster, PA	UT
Longaker, Lisa	1989	Whittier Raiders	P
	1990	California Raiders	P
Lopiano, Donna	1963, 65, 1966, 67, 68	Raybestos Brakettes	2B/1B
	1970, 71, 72	Raybestos Brakettes	P/UT

— M —

NAME	YEARS	TEAM	POSITION
Macchietto (Stratton) M.	1958, 59, 61, 1964, 65	Raybestos Brakettes	C/UT
Maher, Kim	1994, 96, 97	Redding Rebels	OF
Mahoney, Lu	1952	Lynx Buena Park, CA	3B
Malesh, Laura	1953	Regina, Canada	OF
	1963	Raybestos Brakettes	C
Mapes, Missy	1979	Orlando Rebels	3B
	1983	Raybestos Brakettes	3B
Maumausolo, Scia	1996	California A's	C
Maurek, Veronica	1968	Perkasie, PA	2B
May, Darlene	1961, 62	Whittier Gold Sox	OF
	1969	Orlando Rebels	OF
May, Gloria	1955, 57, 63	Fresno Rockets	1B
Mazzucca, Louise	1959, 60, 61	Erv Lind Florists	P
McCarger, Wanda	1969	Yakima Webb Cats	2B
McDaniel, Norma Jean	1955	Kansas City Dons	P
McFalls, Jennifer	1995, 97	Redding Rebels	DH/SS
McGuinn, Mary	1967	Raybestos Brakettes	C
McLachlan, JoAnn	1951	Orange Lionettes	OF
Michal, Donna	1985	New Jersey Belles	UT
Miller, Mary	1967	OSHE Meats, Topeka	P
Miller, Rainey	1986	Utah Bees	OF
Miner (Pettina), Chris	1962, 63	Erv Lind Florists	OF/SS
	1970	Dr. Bernard's-Portland	SS
	1972	Fresno Rockets	UT
Mizera, Liz	1986	California Invasion	SS
	1987	Orange County Majestics	SS
Mooney, Lynn	1977	Sun City Saints	3B
Moore, Billie	1967	OSHE Meats, Topeka	3B
	1971	Raybestos Brakettes	3B
Moore, Joanna	1954	Buena Park Lynx	OF
Moser, Joan	1980	Allentown, PA	OF
Mosteller, Cindy	1987	Lone Star Lady Majestics	3B
Motal, Peanut	1983	Natural Light Comets	OF
Moxley, Joyce	1961	Filter Electric Perks-Toronto, CAN	OF

ASA ALL-AMERICANS CONTINUED ...

NAME	YEARS	TEAM	POSITION
Mulkey, Robbie	1949	Erv Lind Florists	1B
	1956, 58	Orange Lionettes	1B
Mullins, Ann	1965, 70	Pekin-Lettes	C
Mulonet, Beverly	1958, 59, 61	Raybestos Brakettes	SS
Murphy, Gerry	1966	Fresno Rockets	2B

— N —

Naples, Dorothy	1951	Schrader-Cleveland, OH	3B
Naze, Nancy	1976	West Allis Bankettes	UT
Nelson, Carol	1954	Fresno Rockets	P
Newton, Pam	1988, 87, 1989, 90	California Invasion	UT/2B
Noel, Paula	1974, 75, 77	Sun City Saints	P
Nutter, Kim	1985,	Orange County Majestics	OF
	1987	California Invasion	OF
Nutter, Mary	1974, 75	Laurel-Lansing, MI	OF

— O —

Oberg, Terry	1984	Bettencourt Blast-Hayward	3B
O'Connor, Liz	1987	Raybestos Brakettes	1B
O'Kelly , Martha	1994	San Grabriel, CA	UT
Olsen, Suzie	1983	Utah Bees	DH
Orullian, Starleen	1981	Utah Bees	C
Ottaviano, Marie	1961	Raybestos Brakettes	3B
Owen, Mary	1981	Bloomington, MN	UT

— P —

Pagette, Linda	1982	Wyoming Royals	P
Palmer, Sally	1964	Orange Lionettes	2B
Parks, Janice	1992	California Commotion	3B
Parris, Chris	1994, 95	Redding Rebels	3B
Parrish, Thelma	1949, 50	Erv Lind Florists	OF
Patterson, Sheila	1972	Fresno Rockets	OF
Paulson, Joane	1962	Comets-Minneapolis, MN	3B
Peralta, Amy	1948, 49	Phoenix Ramblers	P
Peterson, Joy	1967, 69	Utah Bees	UT
Peterson, Kristen	1985, 87,	Raybestos Brakettes	OF/3B
	1989	Raybestos Brakettes	UT
Phillips, Bess	1976	Plain America-Wash., D.C.	P
Pickering, Sara	1994	California Jazz	2B
Piel, Mary Lou	1978	Law Equipment-Greeley, CO	P
	1981	Orlando Rebels	P
Piper, Hap	1956, 59, 60	Erv Lind Florists	OF/3B
Piper, Marlene	1963, 64, 65, 1968, 70, 74	Dr. Bernard's-Portland	OF
Pleu, Christina	1996	California Jazz	UT
Pollard, Jerry	1955	Kansas City Dons	OF
Ponce, Cecelia	1967, 70	Orange Lionettes	OF
	1973	Raybestos Brakettes	OF
Popowski, Trish	1992	Raybestos Brakettes	2B
Prather, Barbara	1954	Fresno Rockets	UT
Propst, Margaret	1967	OSHE Meats, Topeka	P
Purvis, Kay	1975	Laurels-Lansing, MI	C

NAME	YEARS	TEAM	POSITION
Pyle, Patty	1979, 81	Orlando Rebels	OF/2B

— Q —

Quintana, Gloria	1957	Huntington Park Blues	SS

— R —

Ramsey, Lorene	1960, 65	Pekin-Lettes	P
Rathbun, Jodi	1988,	Avanti's-Peoria, IL	UT
	1995	St. Louis Classics	UT
Rau, Marilyn	1973, 75, 76, 78, 79, 80, 81, 1982, 84	Sun City Saints	C
Rebenar, Margaret	1982	Sundowners, OK	DH
Ragan (Tickey), Bertha	1949, 50, 51, 52, 53, 1954, 55, 1956, 57, 58, 59, 60, 64, 65,	Orange Lionettes	P
	1966, 67, 68	Raybestos Brakettes	P
Reinalda, Barbara	1976, 77, 78, 1981, 83, 84	Raybestos Brakettes	P
Reinoehl, Pam	1984	Computerland Blast-Hayward	2B
Reudrich, Mary	1973	Santa Clara Laurels	OF
Rice, Jackie	1963, 64	Erv Lind Florists	P
Rich, Kay	1949, 51, 52, 1953, 54, 55	Fresno Rockets	SS
Richards, Maridee	1983	Beach City Desperados	C
Richardson, Dot	1979, 81 1984, 86, 87, 88, 89, 90, 1991, 93, 95	Orlando Rebels Raybestos Brakettes	SS SS
Ricks, Mary	1985	Long Beach Renegades	OF
Rioux, Allyson	1982, 83	Raybestos Brakettes	2B
	1985	Raybestos Brakettes	UT
Robinson, Robbie	1966	Orlando Rebels	C
Rodebush, Louise	1980	Utah Bees	OF
Rodina, Kim	1994	Newport Beach, CA.	SS
Rogers, Chenita	1988, 90	California Invasion	OF
Rouse, Priscilla	1992, 95	California Commotion	OF/UT
Rowan, Ann	1992	Phoenix Sunbirds	UT
Roze, Willie	1967, 69, 71, 1972, 74	Raybestos Brakettes	OF
Russell, Skig	1975	Laurels-Lansing, MI	OF

— S —

Salsbury, Carol	1974	Santa Clara Laurels	1B
Sanchelli, Karen	1989, 90	Hi Ho Brakettes-Raybestos	C
Sanderson, Bea	1952	Nortowns-Toronto, CAN	UT
Schlegel, Betty	1951	Fresno Rockets	C
Schmidt, Eileen	1993	VIP's-Topton, PA	C
Schmidt, Kris	1991	Raybestos Brakettes	OF
Schneider, Debbie	1990	California Invasion	UT
Schumacher, Diane	1976, 77, 1978, 84	Raybestos Brakettes	1B
Schwenk, Donna	1974	Anchorettes-IN	P
Sears, Ruth	1950, 51, 1953, 54	Orange Lionettes	1B
Seery, Diane	1976	Raybestos Brakettes	C
Seritella, Christy	1992	Phoenix Sunbirds	C
Shea, Irene	1973, 74, 75	Raybestos Brakettes	3B

ASA ALL-AMERICANS CONTINUED ...

NAME	YEARS	TEAM	POSITION
Sims, Sue	1972	Orange Lionettes	3B
Sijats, Eva	1969	Anchorettes-IN	C
Silva, Xan	1989, 90	California Invasion	OF
Simmons, Brenda	1983	Natural Light Comets-TX	OF
Sinovich, Sue	1975	St. Louis, MO	P
Sippel, Lori	1992, 93	Redding Rebels	P
Slappey, Tommie	1958	Fresno Rockets	OF
Smith, Cindy	1997	Phoenix Sunbirds	OF
Smith, Jamie	1974	Lansing, MI	UT
Smith, Julie	1991, 93	Redding Rebels	UT
	1996, 97	Redding Rebels	2B
Smith, Michelle	1990, 91, 92, 93, 94, 95,		
	1996, 97	Redding Rebels	P
Smith, Wendy	1986	Pekin-Lettes	OF
Snelling, Pat	1956	Buena Park Lynx	P
Sodano, Sharon	1991,	Burbank Knights	3B
	1993	Phoenix Sunbirds	3B
Spanks, Carol	1956	Buena Park Lynx	3B
	1959, 60, 62,		
	1963, 67	Orange Lionettes	3B/SS
	1967, 68, 69	Orange Lionettes	SS
	1970, 72, 73	Orange Lionettes	SS
Spradley, Linda	1974	Sun City Saints	C
Stahl, Kathy	1997	Redding Rebels	UT
Steamer, Dorsey	1994	New Jersey Majestics	OF
Stiglich, Lidia	1994	California Jazz	C
Stockman, Patty	1980	Marion, IA	UT
Stokes, Shelly	1993	Fresno Rockets	C
Stottlemyre, Denette	1981	Bears-Hamilton, MO	OF
Stracham, Val	1975	Precision Plating-MN	UT
Strahan, Kathleen	1977	Raybestos Brakettes	SS
Standering, Julie	1988	California Invasion	UT
Stout, Bethel	1975	Kutis Funeral Home-St. Louis	UT
Summers, Jerry	1956	Kansas City Dons	OF
Svec, Lana	1977, 78, 79	Saving Paving-Ashland, OH	C
Swartout, Toni	1966, 68, 69	Orlando Rebels	3B

— T —

NAME	YEARS	TEAM	POSITION
Taber, Marlys	1978, 80	West Allis Bankettes	SS
Taylor, Mary	1969	Yakima Webb Cats	OF
Tenney, Stephany	1971	Orlando Rebels	UT
Thaler, Linda	1984	LaPalma Restaurant-Flint, MI	OF
Thomas, Barbara	1973	Sun City Saints	OF
Thomas, Michelle	1979, 82	Sun City Saints	P
Thomas, Sunne Bea	1960	Pekin-Lettes	OF
Thome (Hart), Carolyn	1950, 51, 1952, 59	Pekin-Lettes	OF
Thompson, Charlene	1977	Lorelei Ladies-Atlanta	OF
Tomasiewicz, Ellen	1978	Raybestos Brakettes	2B

NAME	YEARS	TEAM	POSITION
Topley, Shirley	1961	Queens-Vancouver, CAN	1B
	1962, 65, 68	Orange Lionettes	1B
	1964	Raybestos Brakettes	1B
Toppi, Catherine	1977	Coed-Bridgeport, CT	OF
Townsend, Carol	1979	West Allis Bankettes	P

— U —

NAME	YEARS	TEAM	POSITION
Ugo, Gina	1996	Michigan Cruise	P
Urrutia, Terry	1958	Fresno Rockets	2B

— V —

NAME	YEARS	TEAM	POSITION
VanKirk, Leslie	1986	Los Angeles Diamonds	2B
VanNess, Joan	1978	Raybestos Brakettes	3B
VanWyk, Kathy	1984, 85, 86	Los Angeles Diamonds	P
Vecchione, Gina	1980, 82, 1983, 88	Raybestos Brakettes	OF
Viola, Alia	1996	California Jazz	SS
Vogel, Lori	1988	Dolls-Downers Grove, IL	P

— W —

NAME	YEARS	TEAM	POSITION
Wadlow, Marie	1950	Dieselettes-Peoria, IL	P
Waldrup, Kelly	1986	Pekin-Lettes	DH
Walker, Karen	1987	Raybestos Brakettes	OF
	1992	California Commotion	SS
Walker, Pat	1966, 67, 68	Orlando Rebels	OF
Walsh, Ginny	1982	Raybestos Brakettes	SS
Ward, Kim	1994	A's-Newport Beach, CA	DP
Washington, Katherine	1967	Nashville, TN	OF
Welborn, Nancy	1969, 70, 71, 1972, 73	Orange Lionettes	P
Wells, Linda	1988	Pekin-Lettes	C
Wells, Sandra	1970	Lorelei Ladies, Atlanta	OF
Wernonen, Elsa	1961	Erv Lind Florists	UT
White, Janice	1966	Atlanta, GA	C
White, Nera	1959, 65	Sterling Belles-Nashville, TN	OF/SS
Whitley, Donna	1985	Long Beach Renegades	SS
Whitmann, Pat	1968	Perkasie, PA	P
Wilkinson, Dot	1948, 49, 50, 52, 53, 54, 1955, 57, 60	Phoenix Ramblers	C
Williams, Christa	1997	California Jazz	P
Williamson, Kay	1963	Orange Lionettes	OF
Wilson, Alma	1957	Phoenix Ramblers	P
Wiley, Charlotte	1991	Knights-Burbank, CA	DP
Wisniewski, Mary	1984	Shamrocks-Buffalo, NY	OF
Wright, Margie	1988	Pekin-Lettes	P
Wuest, Kim	1996	California Jazz	1B
Wylie, Cathy	1994	Redding Rebels	UT

— Y —

NAME	YEARS	TEAM	POSITION
Yori, Mary	1979	Langhurst Motors-Marion, IA	UT

— Z —

NAME	YEARS	TEAM	POSITION
Zobril, Chris	1995	California Jazz	2B
Zollinger, Sis	1973	Orlando Rebels	1B

ASA NATIONAL FASTPITCH SOFTBALL HALL OF FAME

PURPOSE

* To honor those men and women who have played a major role in the growth and development of softball — one of the great sports of the United States.
* To help bring to the attention of the American public the widespread value of and interest in the game of softball by honoring those who have made outstanding contributions to its success. The National Softball Hall of Fame was established in 1957.

ELIGIBILITY

Hall of Fame Nomination Requirements (Players). To be selected for the ASA Hall of Fame, a person must have been an active player in ASA whose active playing days have been terminated for a minimum of three years. If a candidate has been accepted by the ASA for his or her championship play, he or she will be eligible for selection.

1. **Evaluation of Candidates.** The length of playing time is to be considered as a factor in the evaluation of candidates. No minimum playing time is required. Fame of national level shall be used as a gauge for candidacy, and it shall be national fame at a national championship level. Factual and detailed information must be presented to the committee before a candidate can be accepted. Scrapbooks and newspaper clippings are acceptable, also letters from competent references. To be eligible for selection to the Hall of Fame, only participation at the super and major diivision levels will be considered.

2. **Prerequisites.** A player must have been selected to the first-team All-America twice and the second team All-America at least one time to be considered.
    a. *Fast Pitch*
        1. **Old Timers.** If a player competed from 1933 through 1950 or when there was no second-team All-Americans, he or she shall be considered on the material available. Since records are not complete prior to this time and there was no second-team All-America, all available material shall be considered.
        2. 1951 - 1985. To be considered, a player must have been selected as an All-American a minimum of three times (first team twice, second team once). NOTE: If a player has any combination of five all-star teams, he or she would be eligible for consideration. National tournament averages and statistics and number of times competing in the national tournament will be considered, such as leading hitter, defensive leader, stolen bases leader, etc.
        3. After 1985. To be considered, a player must have been selected to at least five All-America teams or a combination of seven all-star/All-America teams.

GENERAL PROVISIONS

1. **Submission Deadline.** Candidates must be submitted by September 1 of each year.
2. **Nomination Forms.** Each commissioner shall be sent nomination blanks and each commissioner shall have the opportunity to nominate no more than two from his area each year.
    Nominations will close on and must be received in the ASA National Office by September 1.
3. **May Not Compete.** A player who has been named to the National Softball Hall of Fame may not compete in any future ASA tournaments leading to national or international championship play except Masters and Seniors divisions.
4. **Selection.** The names of candidates proposed for selection to the Hall of Fame and Hall of Honor shall remain confidential and released only to the Hall of Fame Selection Committee. Voting shall be done by a written ballot.
5. **Removal From Hall of Fame.** The Hall of Fame Selection Committee by a three-fourths vote may, with just cause, recommend removal of an individual elected to the Hall of Fame or Honor. Such recommendation, when approved by a two-thirds vote of the Council, shall remove said individual from Hall of Fame or Honor.

    Hall of Fame Awards — A specially designed plaque shall be given those elected to the Hall of Fame.

    In addition, each shall receive a Hall of Fame or Honor "bronze metallic" identification card which shall permit the selectee and spouse to attend all ASA tournaments.

    Presentation — Announcement of the year's selections shall be made at the ASA Council Meeting with special stories sent to the home area of the selectees, as directed by the commissioner from the area.

    Induction — Formal induction ceremonies and presentation of awards will be made during the annual Hall of Fame Softball Classic in Oklahoma City.

ASA HALL OF FAME INDUCTEES

1957	Amy Peralta Shelton*	Pitcher
1957	Marie Wadlow*	Pitcher
1959	Betty Evans Grayson*	Pitcher
1960	Nina Korgan	Pitcher
1960	Ruth Sears	First Base
1963	Kay Rich	Shortstop
1964	Margaret Dobson	Third Base
1965	Marjorie Law	Pitcher/Infielder/Outfielder
1966	Carolyn Thome Hart*	Outfielder
1969	Jeanne Contel	Infielder
1969	Mickey Stratton	Catcher
1970	Dot Wilkinson	Catcher
1971	Virginia Busick*	Pitcher
1972	Bertha Ragan Tickey	Pitcher
1973	Estelle (Ricki) Caito	Second Base
1973	Gloria May	First Base
1975	Kathryn (Sis) King	Catcher
1976	Pat Harrison	Outfielder
1976	Pat Walker	Outfielder
1980	Jean Daves	Pitcher
1981	Carol Spanks	Infielder/Pitcher
1981	Shirley Topley	First Base
1982	Nancy Welborn	Pitcher
1982	Nancy Ito*	Catcher
1982	Billie Harris	Pitcher
1983	Donna Lopiano	Infielder/Pitcher
1983	Joan Joyce	Pitcher
1984	Mickey Davis	Outfielder
1984	Jackie Rice	Pitcher
1984	Diane Kalliam	Outfielder/Shortstop
1985	Sharron Backus	Shortstop
1985	Willie Roze	Outfielder
1985	E. Louise Albrecht	Pitcher
1986	Chris Pettina Miner	Infielder
1986	Peggy Kellers	Catcher
1987	Lorene Ramsey	Pitcher
1987	Rose Marie Adams	Infielder
1991	Marilyn Rau	Catcher
1991	Marlys Taber	Shortstop
1992	Diane Schumacher	First Base
1992	Carolyn Fitzwater	Second Base
1995	Dorothy Dobie	Infielder
1996	Kathy Arendsen	Pitcher
1996	Gina Vecchione	Outfielder
1998	Freda Savona*	Shortstop

* Deceased

Rosie Adams, Second Base
Inducted 1987

As you might expect, when Hall of Famer Rosie Adams turned 14 years of age August 22, 1965, she wasn't attending a birthday party. She was participating in the ASA Women's Major Fast Pitch National Championships, playing second base for the Orange Lionettes. The youngest player to play in an ASA national championship, Adams played seven years for the Lionettes and four years for the Raybestos Brakettes.

After serving as a back-up infielder in 1965 and 1966, Rosie became the starting second baseman in 1967 and continued as the starter through the 1970 season. In 1971, she joined the Raybestos Brakettes of Stratford, Connecticut, and earned first team All-American honors in 1971, 1972 and 1973. In 1969, Rosie was named a second team All-American as the Lionettes repeated as the national champion and earned a berth in the 1970 Women's World Fast Pitch Championships in Osaka, Japan. Rosie's bases-loaded double off Hall of Fame pitcher Joan Joyce gave the Lionettes the national title and sent them to Japan for the world championships. Japan won the world championships, beating the USA (Lionettes) 1-0.

Rosie joined the Brakettes in 1971 and was a member of four consecutive national championship teams. In 1974, she competed in her second ISF world championship as the Brakettes, representing the USA, won the gold medal. Rosie left the Brakettes after that season to return to Orange to play the 1975 season, her last as an active amateur player. She played two years of professional softball for Santa Ana, California, and Buffalo, New York, before retiring.

In four years with the Brakettes, Rosie batted .279 in national championship play, having 19 hits in 68 at bats. Overall, she batted .187 in 11 national championships with 29 hits in 155 at bats. Although all of her defensive statistics are not available, she did have a .959 fielding percentage in six years with the Lionettes, with 802 putouts, 520 assists and only 56 errors. She had a .209 batting average during her 11-year career with 340 hits in 1,624 at bats and 133 runs batted in (RBI).

Named scholar-athlete at Mater Dei Catholic High School in 1968 and 1969, Rosie graduated from California State University, Fullerton, in 1970. While at Fullerton, she was a three-time All-American point guard and was a member of a national championship team in 1969 and 1970. She later obtained a master's degree in education and training integrated with physical fitness from Memphis State University in 1985 in her off-duty time while serving in the United States Navy. After spending 12 1/2 years in the Navy, Rosie was pursuing a career in television sports broadcasting for the NBC affiliate in San Diego, California, in 1998.

Louise Albrecht, Pitcher
Inducted 1985

Starring as a pitcher and outfielder during a 24-year career, Louise Albrecht played for some of the nation's top women's teams in compiling a record of 304 wins and 83 losses for a winning percentage of .785. Among the teams were Whittier, California (Gold Sox); Orange, California (Lionettes); California Chaparrels; Dieselettes; Sunnyland Lettes; and Raybestos Brakettes. A native of Illmo, Missouri, Albrecht had her best season in 1952 when she won 56 of 58 games and batted .300. She had a lifetime batting average of .258. In

LOUISE ALBRECHT CONTINUED ...

eight national championships, she won 17 games and lost seven, allowing 77 hits in 160 1/3rd innings while striking out 82 batters. She allowed only 16 earned runs for an earned run average of 0.70.

Her six All-American team selections were evenly divided between first and second teams with first team honors in 1961, 1962 and 1965. Second team selections were in 1963, 1964 and 1969. In addition in 1962, she also won the tournament's most valuable player award as she compiled a 5-2 pitching record, allowing only four earned runs in 59 innings. During the regular season, Lou had a 16-7 record and a 1.04 earned run average.

She was a member of national championship teams in 1961 and 1965 and three runners-up in 1966, 1969 and 1972. Winning the 1961 national championship was, according to Louise, her "greatest thrill in softball." Albrecht was undefeated in the tournament (4-0) and her earned run average was 0.36, allowing only two earned runs in 38 2/3rd innings. Lou beat Hall of Famer Joan Joyce 2-1 in an epic 19-inning struggle for the national title, giving up nine hits and striking out four. Joyce fanned 40 batters and allowed five hits in the "if" game of the championship. Stratford won the first game of the championship round, 2-0, to force the "if" game.

At the regional level, she compiled a 27-9 win-loss record and was named to the all-regional team in 12 of the 13 regionals she played in. She retired as an active player in 1969. In March, 1992, she retired as associate director of athletics from Southern Connecticut State University where she served more than 20 years. She went to Southern in 1970 after coaching previously at Western Connecticut State University and California State University, Fullerton. Albrecht coached volleyball and was named to head the school's softball program in 1971. She guided the softball program until 1985, and her teams compiled a 125-111-1 win-loss-tie record. Albrecht was appointed assistant director of athletics and primary administrator in 1980 and assumed her role as associate director in 1984. She was a member of the NCAA Women's Basketball Rules Committee and the NCAA Council. Albrecht has been active as a national rules interpreter for women's basketball.

She received an Associate of Arts degree from Chaffey College, and a Bachelor of Arts and Master's of Arts from Whittier College. She also has a sixth-year professional certificate from Southern Connecticut.

Kathy Arendsen, Pitcher
Inducted 1996

Growing up in Zealand, Michigan, Kathy Arendsen dreamed of becoming the first woman major leaguer. That all changed when she first saw Hall of Famer Joan Joyce pitch for the legendary Raybestos Brakettes of Stratford, Connecticut. Joan Joyce became Kathy's role model. As we know, success does not come overnight or in a year, but Kathy was determined to be the best she could be ... maybe even one of the sport's all-time greats.

Ultimately, through hard work and determination, Kathy succeeded in becoming the best she could be and certainly one of the sport's all-time great pitchers. Her induction in 1996 was a testimony of her overpow-

ering career.

It is unlikely the Raybestos Brakettes would have experienced their great success between 1978-1993 without Kathy on the mound. During that period, they won nine ASA national championships, three ISF world championships and five United States Olympic Festivals. Kathy also was a member of two USA Pan American teams.

Arendsen was a dominant force in the sport on and off the field. She won 334 games, lost only 25, hurled 79 no-hitters, 42 perfect games and 265 shutouts. In 2,362 innings, Arendsen struck out 4,308 batters and had a lifetime earned run average of 0.15. Her accomplishments on the field brought her and women's fastpitch untold media coverage in national publications and on television. The coverage put Kathy into a role she didn't seek but it was one that she handled very well when fastpitch needed a boost to move it forward.

In 1981, Kathy was named a finalist for the James E. Sullivan Award, which is awarded annually to the nation's outstanding amateur athlete. It was the first time a softball player has been a finalist for this award. By 1998, the only other player to be a finalist was Dot Richardson in 1996.

In 1983, Arendsen was one of the torch bearers for the opening ceremonies of the United States Olympic Festival in Colorado Springs, Colorado. Thirteen times she was named as ASA All-American and four times was named the winner of the Bertha Tickey Award as the outstanding pitcher in the ASA Women's Major Fast Pitch National Championship. The last time was in 1991, two years before she retired.

While Arendsen had more than her share of highlights during her career, she said the biggest thrill was being invited to play for the Brakettes, which was her childhood dream. Other thrills included beating UCLA for the Women's College World Series title in 1979 while playing for Texas Woman's University, and the Brakettes' winning the 1991 ASA national title. If there was a disappointment, Kathy said it was "not getting a chance to play in the Olympics. Everything else was great."

Since her retirement, she has remained active in the sport, serving on the first-ever USA Softball Olympic Selection Committee in addition to her college coaching duties at Mississippi State University. Joan Joyce would be proud. She was an inspiration to a young lady from Zealand, Michigan, who in 1996 joined her in the National Softball Hall of Fame.

Sharron Backus, Shortstop
Inducted 1985

Some players, after an outstanding career, turn to coaching softball. One of them was Hall of Famer Sharron Backus, who was inducted in 1985.

Backus, who started playing softball at eight, played amateur softball from 1961 to 1975 before playing pro softball for two seasons for the Connecticut Falcons. She compiled a .251 batting average. She started her amateur career with the Whittier Gold Sox in 1961 and played for them until 1964 when she joined the Orange Lionettes. With the Gold Sox, Backus batted .268, .298 and .301 and earned ASA second team All-American honors in 1962 (age 16) and 1963 at shortstop. In 1961, the Gold Sox won the ASA Women's Major Fast Pitch National Championship and were runners-up in 1962 and 1963. Backus said winning that first national cham-

SHARRON BACKUS CONTINUED ...

pionship was the greatest thrill of her career.

In three years with the Lionettes, one of women's fastpitch all-time outstanding teams, Backus batted .285 (1964), .293 (1965) and .263 (1966) and was a first-team All-American short-stop in 1964 and 1966. The remainder of Sharron's amateur career was spent with the Raybestos Brakettes (1969-1975).

With the Brakettes, Backus was a member of five national championship teams (1971-1975) and earned ASA All-American honors three times (1970, 1971, and 1974). In all, she partici-pated in 13 ASA national championships. Backus had a seven-year .292 batting average with the Brakettes and played on seven ASA national championship teams.

Her highest average was .361 in 1971, the same year Raybestos avenged two straight losses to the Orange Lionettes by capturing the championship and becoming the first ASA team to compile an unbeaten record (57-0). She was a seven-time All-American. In 1974, Raybestos represented the USA in the ISF Women's World Fast Pitch Championship and won. Backus was the seventh leading hitter on the team with a .296 batting average and finished the season batting .318.

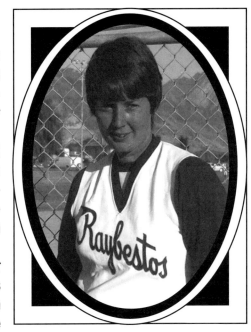

In 1975, Backus was named head softball coach at UCLA and coached the Lady Bruins for 21 years before retiring in June, 1997. During her 21 years as head coach, Backus compiled a record of 847-167-3. She led the Bruins to eight national championships, compiling a postseason record of 118-32. Since the NCAA started holding women's softball championships in 1982, UCLA reached the Women's College World Series 14 of 15 seasons and won seven NCAA crowns, including three straight (1988-1990).

She also coached five players who received the Honda Broderick Award, presented to the sport's top player, a total of eight times in 12 years. No less than 29 of her players earned All-American acclaim a total of 53 times. She also is a member of the NFCA Hall of Fame and the Women's Sports Foundation Hall of Fame. She coached Olympic gold medalists Dot Richardson, Lisa Fernandez and Sheila Cornell.

A 1969 graduate of California State University, Fullerton, Backus did post graduate work at Pepperdine University and California State University, Fullerton. Before being named head coach at UCLA, she taught and coached at Western High School in Anaheim, California. She was born February 12, 1946, in Anaheim.

Virginia Busick, Pitcher
Inducted 1971

Virginia Busick's father has to share some of the credit for his daughter developing into one of the top pitchers in the 1940's and 1950's. In 1946, after the wartime blackout of games had been lifted, Ginny's father encouraged her to try out for a new team that was forming in Fresno, California, called the Rockets.

"Believe it or not, I was bashful, so my father put me in the car and took me," recalled Ginny. "I'll never forget that day! We walked onto the field and two men came out to meet me. They asked what position I played and my father said 'she pitches.' They gave me a glove and said, 'Let's see you pitch!'"

Ginny got the position and, in the years that followed, thousands of people saw Busick pitch for the Rockets, one of the all time top teams in women's fastpitch history. She started playing organized softball at 11 with the Selma Goble Discers in Selma, California.

GINNY BUSICK CONTINUED ...

Fresno won ASA national titles in 1953, 1954 and 1957 with Ginny compiling a 5-0 record and allowing one run and 10 hits in the latter tournament. She finished the season with a 32-4 record and allowed only 10 earned runs.

She repeated as an All-American in 1958, compiling a 5-2 record with a 0.35 earned run average in the national championship. Ginny played for the Rockets from 1946-1951, was out of California for three years, then played in Los Angeles in 1955 and 1956 before rejoining the Rockets in 1957. In 11 years playing in the Pacific Coast Women's League, she was one of the top pitchers. In 1951, she compiled a 20-10 record with 251 strikeouts and earned her first ASA All-American honor with a 4-1 record in the national tournament, including 55 strikeouts. She also won the Northern Pacific Regional Tournament Most Valuable Player Award that season.

During the 1951 season, Ginny hurled two of the longest games on record during that era — a 23-inning game against the Orange Lionettes, May 25, and a 22-inning 4-0 victory against the Phoenix Ramblers. After the 1958 season, Ginny retired from active play.

In seven ASA national championships, she compiled a 22-11 record. Her 21-year career included four seasons as a manager. In 1968, she coached a newly formed team of Rockets to a third-place finish in the ASA national championship.

Busick, who was born June 28, 1925, was elected to the National Softball Hall of Fame in 1971. She is one of four former Fresno Rockets who has been enshrined. On August 5, 1982, Busick died at age 57 in Fresno. She was employed by the Fresno Housing Authority for 25 years.

Estelle (Ricki) Caito
Inducted 1973

When the Orange Lionettes were winning ASA national tournaments, forming part of their strong inner defense was second baseman Estelle (Ricki) Caito. An intense competitor and clutch hitter, Ricki was one of the most daring baserunners in women's fastpitch and a sure-handed fielder with quick hands. In fact, in her first ASA national championship, she made only one error with 32 assists and 35 putouts.

In all, Ricki participated in 10 ASA national championships and had a batting average of .143 in an era when pitching dominated. Her highest batting average in national championship play was .381 (8 for 21) when she was named first team All-American. She also earned All-American honors in 1956 and 1957.

With the Lionettes (1955-1962), Ricki was a member of three ASA national championship teams: 1955, 1956 and 1962. She also played for Lucky Stores of Alameda, California, from 1940 to 1945; Parichy Bloomer Girls of Chicago, Illinois, 1946-47 and 1950-51; A-1 Queens of Phoenix, Arizona, in 1948; Jax Maids of New Orleans in 1949; Los

RICKI CAITO CONTINUED ...

Angeles Top Hats from 1952 to 1954; and the Phoenix Ramblers from 1963 to 1965.

In 1958, she was one of the leading hitters for the Lionettes with a .292 batting average in the Pacific Coast Women's League. From 1955 to 1965, Ricki made only 57 errors while recording 747 assists and 738 putouts for a fielding percentage of .960.

"I feel my greatest thrill during my career came in beating Louise Mazzuca and Joan Joyce in the same night and winning the 1962 national championship," recalled Ricki. "Softball was the biggest thing in my life. Also it gave me the opportunity of meeting a lot of wonderful people and a chance to see the world. I hope I gave it as much as it gave me."

Ricki, who played from 1940-1965, was elected to the National Softball Hall of Fame in 1973.

Jeanne Contel, Infielder
Inducted 1969

Jeanne Contel was as versatile a player as there was on the roster of the Fresno Rockets — one of the sport's top teams. She could catch, play first and outfield. But it was at third base that earned Jeanne a spot in the National Softball Hall of Fame in 1969.

Contel started her career with Schaffner and Watson of Alameda, California, in 1944 and also played for Dime Taxi Club, Dr. Pepper Girls and Jim Ellis Sports of Oakland before joining the Rockets in 1951 after graduating from college. Jeanne remained with the Rockets for the next 14 years and played in 11 ASA national championships, earning first team All-American honors in 1953, 1956, 1957, 1958 and 1963. In 1956, she was selected to the second team. She also was a member of three national championship teams (1953, 1954 and 1957).

At third base, Contel played the position to near perfection. In fact, in 10 of the 11 national championships, she made 103 putouts and had 122 assists with only nine errors for a fielding percentage of .962. In four of those tournaments, she had a fielding percentage of 1.000. In the 1958 national championship, she had 21 assists playing third base, which is a national championship record. She wasn't too bad as a hitter at the national championship either, batting .286 (47 / 164).

After she retired following the 1964 season, Contel coached Fresno in 1966 and led the Rockets to sixth place in the ASA Women's Major Fast Pitch National Championship. A 1951 graduate of San Francisco State University, Contel did graduate work as she continued to play softball. This eventually prepared her for her career as a high school principal. She retired in 1987 as principal of Fresno Unified School.

Jeanne says her greatest thrill in softball was winning "our first national championship in 1953."

Jeanne feels herself fortunate to have played in the Pacific Coast Women's League, without a doubt the premier women's fastpitch league in the 1950's and 1960's.

Since being retired as a high school principal, Contel has remained active in softball and served as membership chairman of the Fresno State University Booster Club, with membership exceeding 500 people in 1997. A native of Oakland, California, Contel was born April 4, 1928. She was one of 24 Hall of Famers who attended the first ever Olympic softball competition in 1996 in Columbus, Georgia.

Jean Daves, Pitcher
Inducted 1980

Jean Daves didn't have the benefit of individual pitching lessons or clinics to develop as a fastpitch softball pitcher. She taught herself while growing up in Canton, North Carolina. "I used to throw a ball into a blanket strung over a clothesline. My mother never wanted me to play but my dad always did," said Daves. "I taught myself most of the different pitches — I was a finesse pitcher, not an overpowering one."

Daves played for teams in Atlanta, Georgia; Birmingham, Alabama; and Washington, D.C., before joining the Orlando, Florida, Rebels in 1964. She played the last eight years of her 20-year career with the Rebels and earned ASA All-American honors six times in establishing various team records. Among them are most wins in a season, 40 in 1970; most shutouts in a season, 30 in 1966; most strikeouts in a season, 485 in 1967; most consecutive wins, 21 in 1966; most scoreless innings, 95 in 1965; most no-hitters in a season, nine in 1967; and most innings pitched in a season, 344 in 1970.

In eight years with the Rebels, Daves won 255 games and lost 59, with 41 no-hitters and 197 shutouts. She fanned 2,944 batters in 2,370 innings. She was a first team All-American in 1966, 1970 and 1971 and a second team selection in 1967, 1968 and 1969.

Although Jean compiled a 25-15 record in national championship play, the Rebels never won a national championship, although they finished in the top four five times. That was the biggest disappointment in her career, while her greatest thrills were playing in a national tournament and for the Rebels the last eight years of her career. Jean retired from active play in 1971, and in 1980 was elected to the National Softball Hall of Fame. She retired from work in 1986 and was still residing in Orlando, Florida, in 1998. She is one of three former Rebels who have been elected to the National Softball Hall of Fame. The others are Pat Walker and Mickey Davis.

Mickey Davis, Outfielder
Inducted 1984

As if it were yesterday, Mickey Davis remembers her 1984 induction into the National Softball Hall of Fame. She remembers the pomp and ceremony, recalls vividly her flittering introduction and fondly remembers the speeches voiced by the other four inductees. But when Mickey Davis, the six-time All-American, who eclipsed a mountain of team records during her sterling 12-year career, reminisces about her induction, she remembers people — people who helped pave her way into the Hall of Fame. "One of the first things that came to mind when I was being inducted into the Hall of Fame was the memories of all the great people I had become associated with through softball," recalled Davis. Her career began in 1964 with the Atlanta Tomboys and continued through 1978 in the Women's Professional League.

"It was difficult to stand up as a new member of the Hall of Fame and put my career in capsule form. There were just so many people to thank and so many people I owed a debt of gratitude — coaches, teammates, my family and other players," remembered Davis. "I found myself going all the way back to Mr. Crawford hitting us fly balls on an uneven hill, which made it easy when it came to catching flies on a nice,

MICKEY DAVIS CONTINUED ...

level diamond."

As a teenager falling in love with softball in the small town of Ware Shoals, South Carolina, Mickey occasionally read about softball stars and fantasized about becoming one of them. Then she realized her dream during a distinguished career with the Tomboys, Orlando Rebels, and the Orange Lionettes.

Six years in a row, Davis was named an ASA All-American (1967 through 1973) and in the year 1975, she batted .375, her highest in a national championship. In the eight national championships she participated in, she batted .231 and had a fielding percentage of .960, making only two errors. In her first seven national championships, she had a fielding percentage of 1.000.

When the Lionettes won the 1969 ASA national championship and the right to represent the USA in the ISF world championship in Osaka, Japan, Davis batted .375 in the world championship to lead the team in hitting. She was a member of two national championship teams and two runners-up. In 12 years, she compiled a .257 batting average with a fielding percentage of .966.

Dot Dobie, Infielder
Inducted 1995

There are players who are not flashy, however they get the job done. Their teammates count on them in clutch situations, especially in national championships. Dorothy (Dot) Dobie was that kind of player during a fastpitch career that started in 1944 and concluded in 1974.

Growing up in Yakima, Washington, Dot found herself caught up in the game of fastpitch as a teenager. "One day, I just sat down and watched a game," she said. "The coach saw me and asked if I wanted to try out. I didn't see any reason not to."

"She was talented and hard working," recalled Betty Baker, a former coach and pitcher for the Yakima Apple Queens. "She was a natural at it."

Comfortable playing the outfield and infield, Dobie played for some of the top women's teams in the northwest, including the Erv Lind Florists (1958-1965) and the Fresno Rockets (1966). With the Florists, Dot was a member of the national championship team in 1964 and national runners-up in 1959, 1960 and 1963.

Dot batted .333 and captained the Florists when they won the ASA national championship in 1964. Dot was first named an All-American in 1960 and duplicated that achievement in 1965, 1969 and 1970. She played in 15 ASA national championships and two Women's Major Fastpitch All-Star Series (1965 and 1966). Thirteen times she was named all region, either at second base, utility, outfielder or third base.

Lois Williams, one of Dot's coaches, said, "Dottie had a real talent for coming through in the clutch with a key defensive play or a brilliant bit of base running. Her quick reactions at third base often resulted in double plays, nipping potential scoring threats. Always an aggressive, alert, instinctive baserunner, she often put the team in scoring position."

Inducted into the Portland Softball Association Hall of Fame in 1988 and into the Yakima, Washington, Softball Hall of Fame in 1983, Dot and the rest of the members of the 1964 Erv Lind team were inducted into the State of Oregon Sports Hall of Fame in 1993. She also was inducted that year into the Northwest Region ASA Hall of Fame.

Dot holds a master's degree from Oregon State University and the University of Washington. She had a career as an administrator, teacher and coach at high schools and colleges throughout the northwest. She retired from coaching in 1994 after spending nine seasons as a track and field coach at East Valley.

Margaret Dobson, First Base
Inducted 1964   Outfield

Until it was broken in 1975, Dr. Margaret (Mugsy) Dobson held the record for the highest batting average in a women's major fastpitch national championship. She batted .615 in the 1950 ASA national championship held in San Antonio, Texas, collecting eight hits in 13 at bats. Dobson's performance earned her All-American honors for the second year in a row. Three years later, she was named honorable mention All-American, which would be the same as second team All-American today. She participated in nine national championships.

Dobson started her softball career in 1944 with Vancouver, Washington, then joined the Erv Lind Florists of Portland, Oregon, a year later and remained with that team until she retired. She retired in 1959 to devote time to her career as a professional educator. Dobson, who retired from Portland State University in 1992 as Executive Vice President Emeritus, earlier obtained a Bachelor of Science, Master of Science and a Ph.D. from the University of Oregon. She did post-doctoral study in the summer of 1966 at Brigham Young University. She attained full professor status in 1968 at Portland State and served in various capacities during her career there. In 1972, she was named Assistant Dean of the Men's and Women's Physical Education Departments. Four years later, she was named Assistant Vice President for Academic Affairs.

Besides being inducted into the National Softball Hall of Fame, Dobson is a member of the Portland and Northwest ASA Hall of Fame. To recognize her athletic accomplishments, Portland State established the Margaret J. Dobson Award in 1976, which is presented to the outstanding female athlete each year at the institution.

She is listed in various publications including "Who's Who of American Women," "The World's Who's Who of Women," "Who's Who in America," and "Leaders in Education."

Dobson was born June 20, 1931, in Portland, Oregon, and was still residing there in 1998.

Carolyn Fitzwater, Second Base
Inducted 1992   Shortstop

Softball teams have to be strong up the middle and the Erv Lind Florists, one of the top teams in the northwest for years, had one of the best second basemen/shortstops during its era in Carolyn Fitzwater. Fitzwater began with the Florist junior team in 1949 and made it up to the "big" team a year later. From 1950 until the team disbanded in 1965, Fitzwater was an integral part of the Florists. She spent one year with the Fresno Rockets (1966) before returning to Portland to conclude her career from 1969 to 1973. She didn't play softball in 1967, 1968 and 1971 before retiring in 1974.

Retirement did not mean Fitzwater left behind her love of sports. She was a teacher and coach for 32 years, 26 of them at Portland's Grant High School before retiring in 1990. Fitzwater was born October 10, 1935, in Portland.

During her softball career, Fitzwater earned All-American honors four times — 1959, 1962, 1963 and 1964 and participated in 14 ASA national championships. Despite batting only .188 in the 1963 Women's Major Fast Pitch National Championship, Fitzwater starred defensively, handling 36 chances without an error, including 20 assists playing shortstop. The next year, Fitzwater batted .462 in the national championship in leading the Florists to the national title. It was one that Fitzwater fondly recalls.

What stands out about 1964 was the great team effort. "No great stars, just a total team effort," said Fitzwater. It was the late Erv Lind, sponsor-manager of the Florists, who Fitzwater credits with building the team into one of the all time greats. "He was a class man. He gave each of us the opportunity to be someone special, to see and do things we would never have been able to do," stated Carolyn. She also credits former Florist teammate and coach Lois Williams for "putting it together" and bringing home the national championship in 1964 after being runners-up in 1959, 1960 and 1963. Fitzwater is one of six former Florists enshrined in the National Hall of Fame, including Betty Evans Grayson, Chris Pettina Miner, Dot Dobie, Jackie Rice and Margaret Dobson. Fitzwater was inducted in 1992.

Carolyn earned her Bachelor of Science and Master of Science degrees from Oregon State University.

Betty Evans Grayson, Pitcher
Inducted 1959

Although she started her softball career as an outfielder, it would be as a pitcher that Betty Evans Grayson would excel and eventually lead to her selection to the National Softball Hall of Fame in 1959.

Born October 9, 1925, in Portland, Oregon, Betty starred as an outfielder in the Portland City League by the time she was 13. Betty had pitched a little, however, in grade school, and Erv Lind felt she could become a great pitcher. With the help of Betty's father Raymond Evans, and two former pitchers, Eddie Jossi and Archie "Windmill" Hamlin, Betty pitched and pitched. "Dad was fully aware of my aspirations," Betty recalled in later years. "He did everything he could to help me." Ray Evans stressed to his only child the finer points of perfect motion and style, the importance of practice, and studied everyday with her — rain, shine, summer or winter.

Betty played the outfield for the Erv Lind Florists in the summer of 1940. That would be her last year as

BETTY EVANS GRAYSON CONTINUED ...

an outfielder. At the end of the season, Erv Lind told Betty, "from now on you're going to be throwing for us." Betty made all-city as a pitcher in 1941 and 1942. In 1943, she pitched in her first of six ASA national championships. In 1944, she hurled the Florists to the ASA Women's Major Fast Pitch National Championship. She also was named that year as Oregon's Woman Athlete of the Year by the Oregon sportswriters and sportscasters association.

Grayson faced Amy Peralta Shelton, also a National Softball Hall of Famer, in the championship game of the 1944 national championship. Grayson was as determined as Shelton to win the game, which lasted 11 innings before the Florists squeezed out a run to win. "We all have something inside us that we call on in time of real need," stated Betty. "I needed to call on it then and I did."

In 1945 the Florists finished fourth in the ASA national championship, took third place in 1946 and second in 1948. One of the highlights of Betty's career came in 1948, when she struck out five of six Triple A baseball players at Vaughn Street Park. Only Roy Hesler, a Portland Beaver hurler who had played softball, got a hit off Grayson — a dribbler to the infield.

Throughout her career, Betty gave generously of her time in conducting clinics for eager, young softball players and launched many girls on their athletic careers. In 1952, she started the Portland Softball School for Girls. The school was so successful that the Portland Park Bureau took it over and began conducting the school as a city-wide program.

Betty retired from softball in 1955 and worked as a license clerk in the Portland City Hall. She compiled a record of 456 wins and only 99 losses during her career with 51 no-hitters and three perfect games. In 1945, she hurled 115 consecutive scoreless innings.

On July 9, 1979, at the age of 53, Betty died of cancer. On June 21, 1980, the Portland Metro Softball Association dedicated the Betty Evans Grayson Memorial Hall of Fame at Erv Lind Stadium.

Billie Harris, Pitcher
Inducted 1982

Growing up in Tucson, Arizona, Billie Harris didn't play high school softball. "I wasn't allowed."

"They said I was too good." Harris said. "It was maddening for someone who wanted to play and be part of a team." Instead Harris joined a city park and recreation team in 1947 before joining the famed Phoenix Ramblers, one of the dominant women's teams in the 1940's, 50's and 60's. Between 1950 and 1975, Harris played for the Ramblers, the Yakima, Washington, Webcats, and the Sun City Saints of Arizona. In her final season of softball, she was named the Saints' most valuable player. She also won this award in 1971.

Known for her pitching and hitting, Harris participated in more than 15 ASA national championships and won 20 games as a pitcher. Three times she earned ASA All-American honors — twice as a pitcher in 1958 and 1969, and as a utility player in 1959. It is estimated that she hurled 70 no-hitters and four perfect games during her career.

In 1959, Billie compiled a 5-2 pitching record with an earned run average of 0.14 in the national championship. In 1959, she batted .347 in the national tournament. In the 1969 ASA national championship, she showed her pitching and hitting skills, compiling a 4-1 mound record and hitting .400 (8 for 20). This perfor-

BILLIE HARRIS CONTINUED ...

mance earned her the tournament's most valuable player award as her team finished third.

For more than 20 years (1953-1975), she excelled in the Pacific Coast Women's Softball League, compiling a .260 batting average. She had 264 hits in 370 games, scored 123 runs and drove in 59 runs. As a fielder, she made 203 putouts and recorded 851 assists with only 59 errors, for a fielding percentage of .923. She is known for her drag bunting and exceptional speed on the bases.

Harris, whose career covered the period of 1947-1975, was the first African-American inducted into the National Softball Hall of Fame, occurring in 1982. She also is a member of the Arizona Softball Hall of Fame.

Pat Harrison, Outfielder
Inducted 1976

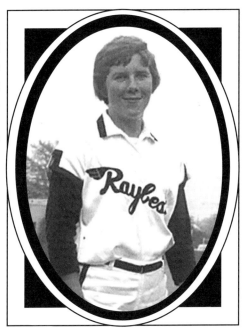

An outstanding defensive player as well as a consistent .300 plus hitter, Pat Harrison played fastpitch softball 20 years. She earned All-American honors four times. She was a first team choice in 1966 (.304 batting average); 1968 (.368); and 1970 (.250 average) and a second team selection in 1963 (.250 batting average).

She played nine years for the Raybestos Brakettes of Stratford, Connecticut, from 1964 to 1972, and was a member of five Brakettes national championship teams. She had an accumulative .303 batting average during this time period with 430 hits in 1,421 at bats. She compiled 66 doubles, 42 triples and 18 home runs. She drove in 189 runs in 482 games and twice she led the Brakettes in batting —1966 (.301 average) and 1971 (.340 average).

The greatest thrill of Harrison's career came in 1972 when she hit a two-run homer in the bottom of the seventh against the Orange Lionettes in the ASA women's fastpitch championship held in Tucson, Arizona. This was the final game of her career. She played in 11 national championships, nine with the Brakettes and two with the Erv Lind Florists team.

Pat also competed in the first ISF world championship in Australia, with the USA finishing second. Harrison batted .087 in the world championship and said "not winning was the greatest disappointment of her career."

A graduate of Southern Connecticut State College, Harrison also played for the South Hills Queens of Vancouver, BC (1957-1961) and Erv Lind Florists. In 1988, Harrison was living in Qualicum Beach, British Columbia, Canada, and was a career counselor/writer and inspirational speaker for Career Center in Parksville, BC. She was born March 31, 1943, in Vancouver, British Columbia.

Caroyln Thome Hart, Outfield
Inducted 1966

If there was one thing that made Carolyn Hart more than just another softball player, it was hustle.

"I learned early from Coach Chuck McCord that if you didn't hustle all the time, you would be just average," said Hart. "He was a great coach, and I learned a great deal from him."

Hart was anything but average. She earned ASA All-American honors five times — 1950, 1951, 1952, 1955 and 1959. She had a lifetime batting average of .301. She retired in 1962 to devote more time to her family.

Carolyn, who was known as Cotton Top or Cotton because of her striking blonde hair, was the youngest player ever to play for the Caterpillar Dieselettes at age 16, and played for them from 1947-1955. After the Dieselettes folded, Hart joined the Pekin-Lettes and played until retiring. She worked at Caterpillar for 30 years, retiring in 1977 from the East Peoria plant.

Hart had some excellent years. In 1950, she batted .305 with 32 RBI's and seven home runs. She was the fourth leading hitter in the ASA national championship that year with a .391 batting average. In 1951, she batted .333 in the ASA national championship to earn All-American honors and finished the year with a .319 average with 16 RBI's and seven homers. She repeated as an All-American in 1952 and finished the season with a .331 batting average with 47 runs batted in and nine home runs. Her batting average in the ASA national championship was .222. Hart was named second team All-American in 1955 and had one of her best years. She batted .333 with 28 RBI's and eight home runs. She followed with a .405 batting average with 28 RBI's and four homers in 1956 followed by .379 batting average (36 RBI's, six homers) in 1957. In 156 games, Carolyn batted 1,873 times, scored 460 runs (leading her team eight times), hit 71 doubles, 31 triples, 68 home runs and stole 160 bases (leading her team six times).

In 1966, Hart was selected to the National Softball Hall of Fame. At the induction, her former coach Chuck McCord said, "She was one of the greatest players I had the privilege to coach. She was a fierce competitor and very fast." In 1983, she was elected to the Greater Peoria Sports Hall of Fame.

In 1982, Carolyn learned she had multiple sclerosis and fought a gallant battle for more than 20 years until her passing March 10, 1996, at the age of 65. Multiple sclerosis crippled her legs but didn't break her spirit during this time.

Nancy Ito, Catcher
Inducted 1982

As a teenager growing up in Denver, Colorado, Nancy Ito played the infield, developing into an outstanding shortstop and third baseman. As fate would have it and because she was such an outstanding athlete, her coach, Andy Hale, asked her to learn catching when the regular catcher left the softball team. She learned the position well enough to earn ASA All-American honors 13 times — five first team and eight second team accolades.

In the beginning of her 25-year softball career, Ito played for teams in the Denver area from 1947 to 1959 before a job transfer in 1960 brought her to California. In California, Ito continued to play top-level softball with the Orange Lionettes. During her 15 years with the Lionettes, Nancy participated in 13 ASA national champi-

NANCY ITO CONTINUED ...

onships and one International Softball Federation world championship in 1970 in Osaka, Japan. She was a member of four ASA national championship teams and four teams that finished runner-up. She participated in 18 ASA national championships during her career.

Known as an outstanding defensive player, Ito made only 10 errors in 1,401 fielding chances in 222 games in the Pacific Coast League from 1967 to 1974 — a fielding percentage of .993. In five seasons, Nancy made only one error each season, and in 1972, she played errorless ball, handling 134 chances. During this eight-year span with the Lionettes, she had an accumulative .242 batting average and a .986 fielding percentage with only 55 errors among 3,609 putouts and 378 assists in 603 games.

Former teammate and Hall of Famer Carol Spanks called Ito "the best catcher I have ever seen. Not only was she strong and secure around the plate, but she had a great arm and was fundamentally sound in every aspect of her defensive play."

Ito was employed as a computer programmer for the Federal Aviation Agency in Westminster, California, before she retired from amateur competition in August, 1974. When the pro women's softball league started in 1975, Nancy came out of retirement. She played for the San Diego Sandpiper team in 1976 and served as head coach of the Santa Ana, California, Lionettes in 1977.

In 1982, Ito was elected to the ASA National Hall of Fame. She was born June 26, 1933, and passed away December 19, 1987.

Joan Joyce, Pitcher
Inducted 1983

If any one individual dominated a team sport, it was Joan Joyce. Joyce started to play softball at age eight because her father played and it was the only team sport available at the time. At 13, Joan tried out for the Raybestos Brakettes and playing sparingly. At the age of 15 or 16, she received the suggestion that started her up the ladder of stardom. Joan was pitching, and a man who was working on a field for a Little League tournament suggested she try pitching slingshot instead of windmill. Joan tried a few pitches and from that day on hurled slingshot. Former Cardinal pitchers Johnny Spring and Howie Weiland showed her how to hold the ball, and she practiced, practiced and practiced.

After graduating from high school, Joyce attended Southern Connecticut State Teachers College. In 1963, she left Connecticut to attend Chapman College. While in California, she played three years for the renowned Orange Lionettes, winning 80 games and losing only six. She hurled 21 no-hitters and compiled an 11-2 record in national championship play.

Joan played eight years for the Brakettes before playing three years for the Orange Lionettes. She then rejoined the Brakettes and played for another nine years. In 17 years with the Brakettes, she compiled a record of 429 wins and 27 losses. She fanned 5,677 batters in 3,397 1/3rd innings and hurled 105 no-hitters and 33 perfect games. She yielded only 102 earned runs in 476 games for an earned run average of 0.21.

Besides her pitching, Joyce was an outstanding hitter, compiling a Brakettes' .327 lifetime average and leading the team six times in batting. Her highest batting average was .406 in 1973. In 1971, she was the leading hitter in the ASA Women's Major Fast Pitch National Championship with a .467 average as well as sharing the most valuable player award with Donna Lopiano.

In 1974, a year before retiring from amateur competition, Joyce added to her legendary career by hurling the USA team (represented by the Brakettes) to the ISF world championship. It was the first time the United States won the gold medal. Joyce was undefeated in five games. She pitched 36 consecutive scoreless innings with two perfect games, one no-hitter and two one-hitters. Her earned run average was 0.00 and she had 76 strikeouts. While she was unbeatable on the mound, Joyce also was among the best offensively, batting .407 and driving in 10 runs.

After completing her amateur career in 1975 with an undefeated season, Joyce turned her efforts toward helping to launch a professional women's league in 1976. The league lasted until 1979. Joyce's team, the Connecticut Falcons, won the championship each year. At the same time, Joyce was pursuing a career on the LPGA tour.

As an amateur player, Joyce was named to the ASA All-American team 18 consecutive years and eight times was named the tournament's most valuable player. She was a member of 12 national championship teams. In national championship play, she won 67 games and lost 10, and had an earned run average of 0.25. She shared or owned outright six Brakette pitching records, including most wins in a season (42 in 1974), most no-hitters in a national tournament (two in 1958, 1961, 1970, 1971 and 1973), most perfect games in a national tournament (one in 1961), most shutouts (38 in 1974) and the longest game (29 innings in 1968).

In May of 1994, Joyce returned to coaching and guided Florida Atlantic University to a 33-18 record. She was named the Trans America Athletic Conference Coach of the Year and the Palm Beach County Coach of the Year. In 1965, she coached the team to a 37-32 record. Joyce also coaches the FAU golf team and in January, 1996, assumed the senior woman administrator duties.

Besides being a member of the National Softball Hall of Fame, Joyce is a member of the Connecticut Fast Pitch Hall of Fame, the Connecticut Women's Basketball Hall of Fame, the Hank O'Donnell Hall of Fame and the International Women's Sports Hall of Fame. In 1976, she was runner-up for the *Women's Sports* magazine athlete of the year award.

In 1996, Joan was one of 24 ASA Hall of Famers to attend the debut of softball as an Olympic sport at Golden Park in Columbus, Georgia.

Diane Kalliam, Outfield
Inducted 1984

Diane Kalliam could run, field, hit and throw — the four ingredients needed to be an outstanding softball player. Diane could do all of these skills well. She probably will be remembered most for her outstanding hitting in ASA national championship play. Appearing in seven ASA national championships between 1961 and 1979, Kalliam had an accumulative .430 batting average (43 hits in 100 at bats). Five times during her career, she earned ASA All-American honors (1961, 1971, 1973, 1974 and 1975), with four first team selections.

In 15 years, Kalliam batted 2,843 times and smashed 1,060 hits for a .427 lifetime batting average. Diane was an outstanding baserunner. She stole 448 bases, including a career high of 55 in 1969. She also

<u>DIANE KALLIAM CONTINUED ...</u>

scored 842 runs, including a career best of 89 in 1966.

In the 1975 ASA Women's Major Fast Pitch National Championship, Kalliam set the all time batting average record for a tournament with 12 hits in 19 at bats, an average of .632. It marked the second year in a row Kalliam led the national championship in hitting after batting .444 in 1974. Kalliam's .632 average broke the former mark of .615 held by Hall of Famer Margaret Dobson in 1950.

Although Kalliam set an individual record in 1975, her team — the Santa Clara Laurels — didn't win the national championship, losing 2-1 to Raybestos Brakettes in the final game. "It was the biggest disappointment of my career," said Kalliam. Setting the batting record and playing in two national championship games were the biggest thrills of her career.

After retiring from amateur softball in 1975, Kalliam played professional softball with the San Jose Sunbirds (1976-77) and San Jose Rainbows (1979). In 1976, she batted .379 to finish second in hitting.

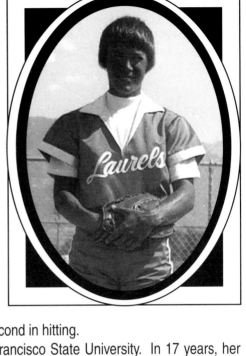

In 1979, Kalliam was named head softball coach at San Francisco State University. In 17 years, her teams compiled a record of 237-474-5. In 1991, she coached the team to a school record of 29 victories. Other highlights included a Western Regional Championship in 1981 and a pair of second-place finishes in the Northern California Athletic Conference (1988 and 1991).

In 1984, Kalliam was elected to the National Softball Hall of Fame. In 1986, she was elected to the California State University, Hayward, Hall of Fame and in 1994 to the San Mateo County Hall of Fame. She has a bachelor's degree from Cal State Hayward (1966) and a master's degree from San Francisco State (1979). Diane was born August 24, 1943, in San Mateo, California, and was residing in San Francisco in 1998.

Peggy Kellers, Catcher
Inducted 1986

Except for one season, Peggy Kellers' amateur softball career was with the Raybestos Brakettes — from 1964 to 1974. During that time, Peggy earned ASA All-American honors six times as a catcher. She was a first team selection in 1968, 1971, 1973 and 1974, and a second team choice in 1969 and 1970.

Kellers played in 11 ASA national championships and was a member of seven ASA national championship teams with the Brakettes. She compiled an aggregate batting average of .238 in national championship play. Her highest average was .267 in a national tournament. During the regular season, her highest batting average was .281. A starter nine of the 11 years for the Brakettes, Kellers compiled a .218 batting average in 529 games with 280 hits/1.287 at bats. This included 29 doubles, 21 triples, seven home runs and 121 RBI's.

Kellers also played in seven ASA Women's Major Fast Pitch

PEGGY KELLERS CONTINUED ...

All-Star Series (1968, '69, '70, '71, '72, '73 and '74), the ISF Third Women's World Fast Pitch Championship in 1974, and the 1967 Pan American Games in Winnipeg, Canada. Peggy batted .238 in the world championship.

Prior to the start of the 1975 season, Peggy was forced to retire from active play after her right arm did not respond to surgery in September of 1974. She had the first surgery in November, 1972.

In 1993, Peggy was named head softball coach at the University of Virginia. In her first season, she coached the team to a 32-12 record and a 19th place national ranking. In 1989, she was named Atlantic Coast Conference Coach of the Year after leading the Cavaliers to a 33-18 record and a national ranking of 25th. Prior to coaching at the University of Virginia, Kellers served four years as Executive Director of the National Association of Girls and Women in Sports in Reston, Virginia.

A native of Stratford, Connecticut, Peggy graduated from Southern Connecticut State in 1970 with a bachelor's degree in physical education. As a senior, she was named SCSU's Female Athlete of the Year. Kellers played basketball, field hockey and volleyball at Southern Connecticut State. She also earned her master's degree in physical education from the University of Bridgeport in 1977 and a doctorate in sports psychology from Virginia in 1989.

After earning her undergraduate degree, Kellers taught and coached at Daniel Hand High School in Madison, Connecticut. Her college coaching experiences included four years of college basketball, 10 years coaching volleyball and eight years softball. She also coached volleyball and softball at Eastern Mennonite College in Harrisonburg, Virginia. With Peggy's leadership, the softball team participated in the AIAW state and regional championships in 1982. The next year, the team was ranked 17th.

In 1984, Kellers coached the United States in the first Athlete in Action International Softball Tournament. The team compiled a 31-1 record and was comprised of Division I players who toured Italy, Finland and Sweden.

For more than 20 years, Peggy has been a clinician and speaker at numerous national, regional and local events. She also works with pitchers and catchers on developing basic fundamentals, and with coaches and athletes on confidence building, performance enhancement and maximizing one's potential.

In 1982, Peggy was elected to the Connecticut ASA Hall of Fame and in 1986, she was named to the National Softball Hall of Fame.

Kathryn (Sis) King, Outfield/
Inducted 1975   Second

When it came to hitting a softball for a high average with power, Kathryn (Sis) King was among the best, playing for teams in Cincinnati, Ohio; Phoenix, Arizona; and Stratford, Connecticut. In three years with the Brakettes, Sis had a .322 batting average after 15 years with teams in Cincinnati and Phoenix.

She played in six ASA national championships and was named a first team All-American four times. She was named as a second baseman in 1959 and as an outfielder in 1963, 1964 and 1965. In 1963, Sis batted .400 in the national championship with averages of .417 in 1964 and .400 in 1965.

In 1965, when the Brakettes were selected to represent the

KATHRYN (SIS) KING CONTINUED ...

USA in the first International Softball Federation (ISF) Women's World Fast Pitch Championship in Melbourne, Australia, King led the team with a .352 batting average and a team high 12 hits, including four triples. She finished the year with a .333 batting average, second best on the team.

In 1967, when softball was a demonstration sport for the Pan American Games, King was a member of the Raybestos Brakettes team of Stratford, Connecticut, that won the gold medal.

During her career, she was the first woman to hit a home run over the scoreboard at Raybestos Memorial Field (1959) and the first woman to hit back-to-back homers in a national championship.

She was selected to the National Softball Hall of Fame in 1975.

Nina Korgan, Pitcher
Inducted 1960

When Nina (Tiger) Korgan joined a local softball team after her high school graduation in Council Bluffs, Iowa, only one position was vacant — pitcher. Nina was confused about the date and almost missed practice. This move turned out to be one of the best of her career — a career that spanned the period of 1934 to 1949 and earmarked her as one of the top pitchers of that era. Korgan won 49 of 50 games her first year and during a 14-year period (1934-1948), she played on six ASA national championship teams.

Five were with the famed New Orleans Jax of New Orleans, Louisiana (1942, 1943, 1945, 1946 and 1947), and one year with the Higgins Midgets of Tulsa, Oklahoma (1941). Nina hurled the Syracuse Northeast Bluebirds to state titles in 1935, 1936, and 1937 before joining the Midgets in 1941.

The 1941 ASA national championship with the Midgets was one of Korgan's best years. She struck out 67 batters in 30 innings, hurling four shutouts, had a perfect game and 20 strikeouts in another game. She allowed only five hits in four games.

"Winning the title in 1941 marked the first time I had been on a national championship team and, along with being inducted into the Hall of Fame, was the biggest thrill of my career," Nina said. Korgan extended her scoreless inning streak to 67 innings in national tournament play the next year before it was ended in the seventh inning of the championship game in Detroit, Michigan. She won four games with three of them one-hitters.

She continued to play for the Jax until retiring in 1949. She worked for Jackson Brewing Company until her retirement in 1978 and was living in San Springs, Oklahoma, in 1998. Korgan was inducted into the Omaha, Nebraska, and National Softball Hall of Fame the same year — 1960.

Majorie Law, Pitcher/Outfielder/Infielder
Inducted 1965

Skilled enough to win All-American honors at three different positions, Marjorie Law played more than two decades for the famed Phoenix Ramblers, Arizona, and was a member of three national championship teams (1940, 1948 and 1949). Starting her softball career in 1935 as an outfielder, Law played first base and

third base before switching back to the outfield and to the mound. She started as a slingshot hurler before becoming a windmill pitcher. She was tutored by her husband, Ken, who showed her how to throw a rise and drop ball.

Margie earned ASA All-American honors no less than eight times during her career, including 1948 when she was named as an outfielder. She repeated All-American honors in 1949 and was again selected in 1951, 1952, 1953, 1954, 1955 and 1957. She played in 22 ASA national championships and hurled three perfect games.

After compiling a 20-10 record in the regular season in 1951, Margie had a 3-2 record with 51 strikeouts in 29 innings in the ASA national championship, leading her team to a fourth-place finish.

In 1952, she had a 47-20 regular-season pitching record followed by a 5-2 record in the national championship with 0.47 earned run average and 58 strikeouts (47 innings) to lead the Ramblers to a second-place finish. In 1954, Margie again split her four games on the mound. One of her wins was a 3-0 perfect game against St. Louis, Missouri, striking out 14.

The Ramblers placed second in the ASA national championship in 1955 with the 5"7" Margie pitching all the games, winning four and losing two with 31 strikeouts and nine walks. During the regular season, Margie won 35 games, lost 20 and fanned 200 batters, walking 102. She also batted .300 during the regular season and .316 in the national championship.

In 1957, her last season before retiring, Law earned All-American utility honors, including winning two of three games in the ASA national championship. During the regular season, she compiled a 38-15 win-loss record, striking out 530 batters.

Donna Lopiano, Pitcher/First
Inducted 1983

Before becoming a nationally known, influential person in women's sports, Donna Lopiano was an outstanding softball player. Although she played only 10 years in the ASA women's major fastpitch program, Lopiano made the most of her decade, earning ASA All-American honors nine times and winning the most valuable player award three times.

A versatile athlete who could play second, first and pitch, Lopiano was an ASA All-American in 1963, 1965, 1966, 1967, 1968, 1969, 1971 and 1972. She was named most valuable player in 1966 and 1972, and shared the honor in 1971 with Joan Joyce in the women's major fastpitch national championship.

She had a .295 batting average, playing for the Raybestos Brakettes with 518 hits in 1,756 at bats. Donna scored 285 runs, driving in 281 runs, hitting 23 home runs, 67 doubles and 54 triples.

DONNA LOPIANO CONTINUED ...

Twice Lopiano led the Brakettes in batting (1970 – .316 and 1972 – .367) and still shares the team record for homers in a season with eight. In 1972, she also was the leading hitter in the ASA Women's Major Fast Pitch National Championship with a .429 average.

As a pitcher, Lopiano had a .910 winning percentage, highest in Brakettes history, winning 183 games and losing only 18. In 10 years, she hurled 817 innings, striking out 1,633 batters and walking only 384 . Donna hurled 16 no-hitters. In national championship play, she won 15 of 17 games and was a member of six national championship teams and four runners-up. When Australia hosted the first ISF world championship in 1965, Raybestos represented the United States and Lopiano was the second leading hitter with a .345 average as the team placed second.

Besides being an outstanding softball player, Lopiano also participated in basketball, volleyball and field hockey. During her career, she had the opportunity to participate in 26 different national championships in those four sports.

An excellent student, Lopiano has a Bachelor of Science degree in health and physical education from Southern Connecticut State College, a Master of Arts degree in physical education from the University of Southern California (1969) and a Doctor of Philosophy in physical education from the University of Southern California (1974).

From 1969-70, Donna was a teaching assistant, women's intramural director and volleyball coach at the University of Southern California. From 1971-75, she was assistant professor of physical education, assistant athletic director and head volleyball, softball and basketball coach at Brooklyn College of the City University of New York. She served as women's athletic director at the University of Texas for more than a decade before taking over as Executive Director of the Women's Sports Foundation in April, 1992.

According to *The Sporting News*, Donna is listed as No. 46 of "The Most Influential People in Sports." The *College Sports* magazine ranked her No. 22 among "The Fifty Most Influential People in College Sports."

Besides being a member of the National Softball Hall of Fame, Lopiano is a member of the National Sports Hall of Fame and the Texas Woman's University Hall of Fame.

Amy Peralta May, Pitcher/First
Inducted 1957

Amy Peralta May not only was a talented pitcher who won a lot of games during her career, but she was also an excellent hitter. Amy often batted cleanup for the renowned Phoenix Ramblers, one of the sport's all time great teams.

In the 1945 ASA national championships, May batted .577. She was a member of three national championship teams — 1940, 1948 and 1949. She posted some impressive pitching stats for the Ramblers, including a 54-10 record in 1947, a 56-10 record in 1949, and hurling 55 of the 85 Rambler wins that same year.

May earned ASA All-American honors six times, and in the 1948 ASA national championships compiled a 5-1 pitching record with 25 strikeouts in 42 innings, allowing only 12 hits. At the plate she batted .304 and drove in five runs. In the 1949 ASA national championships, she was unbeaten (3-0), striking out 14 batters in 20 innings. She was one of four pitchers to win three games. In

AMY PERALTA MAY CONTINUED ...

the 1950 championships, she won three of five games and fanned 20 batters.

May, who also played outfield, played 17 of her 20 years with the Ramblers. She compiled a record of 447-79 with 300 shutouts. Her lifetime record was 670 wins and 150 losses with 20 no-hitters and 80 one-hitters.

From 1952 to 1967, Amy was a beautician before retiring to travel with her husband Charles, a civil engineer. May gave credit to the Ramblers for her success. "I was a good pitcher because I had a good team behind me. Without them and our coach, Ford Hoffman, I would have never been the pitcher that I was," stated Amy.

In 1957, Amy Peralta May was a unanimous selection to the National Softball Hall of Fame.

Gloria May, First Base
Inducted 1973

When it is time to talk about the slickest fielding first baseman in women's major fastpitch, Gloria May is one of the names often mentioned. May was certainly one of the best fielding first basemen during an impressive career, which started in 1940 and ended in 1969.

May, born February 19, 1929, earned ASA first team All-American honors three times (1955, 1957 and 1963) and was a second team choice twice (1956 and 1965). She participated in 15 ASA national championships and in 10 of those had a 1.000 fielding percentage. In 11 national championships, she had 413 putouts and 25 assists with only two errors — a .995 fielding percentage. Her highest batting average in national tournaments was .444 in 1955.

May joined the Fresno Rockets in 1949 and remained with them until she retired after the 1958 season. She was a member of three national championship teams — 1953, 1954 and 1957. Gloria recalled winning her first national championship in 1953 as her "greatest thrill" in softball. Not having a chance to participate in the Olympics was a disappointment.

Retired, Gloria was living in Kerman, California, with her husband Vernon in 1998. They had a trailer in Baja, Mexico, and traveled there two to three times a year. She had been competing in cross country air races since 1987, never finishing below 15th place as of 1998.

Chris (Pettina) Miner, Infielder
Inducted 1986

The youngest player (16 years, 1 month and 29 days) ever named to an ASA All-American team, Chris (Chrissy) Miner started her softball career in 1960 with the Portland Rosebuds, a junior team. In 12 years (she sat out during the 1968 and 1969 seasons), Miner played for the Rosebuds, Erv Lind Florists, Dr. Bernard's, Sun City Saints, Fresno Rockets and the Fullerton Royals.

Miner, born July 2, 1946, played in seven ASA national championships and was a member of the 1964 ASA national championship team — Erv Lind Florists. She was named an ASA All-American in 1962 (.227

CHRIS (PETTINA) MINER CONTINUED ...

batting average), 1963 (.318 batting average), 1965 (centerfielder), 1970 (second team centerfielder and first team shortstop) and 1972 (.462 batting average). In 1972, she was named winner of the Erv Lind Award presented to an outstanding defensive player in the Women's Major Fast Pitch National Championship.

Despite a broken thumb, Chris played errorless ball for the Fresno Rockets at shortstop in five games. "It meant so much to me because it was Erv's," said Miner about the award. Miner credits a number of people who "greatly influenced" her career, starting with Erv Lind. "He was a great influence, a great man and a first class person. I cannot say enough good things about him," stated Miner. Chris also singles out Portland coaches Lois Williams and Hap Piper for praise. "They were two different types of coaches but they would get the best from you," stated Chris. Portland coach Harvey Oberg also was important. "He was like the father I didn't have," stated Chris.

Complications from a knee injury in 1970 forced her retirement in 1973. Despite four knee operations, Chris said, "I'd give up my knee again for those last years. Those seasons meant a lot to me and I wouldn't have traded them," lamented Chris. The knee injury and the death of Erv Lind were the greatest disappointments of Miner's career.

Miner has an Associate of Arts degree from Los Angeles Valley Junior College (1974), a bachelor's degree from California State University, Los Angeles (1978), and a master's degree from the University of Nebraska, Omaha. Chris coached at Glendale Junior College and Pasadena Junior College before starting the program at Long Beach State University in 1980. From 1982 to 1988, Chris was named the head coach at the University of Nebraska, Omaha, compiling a record of 168-126-1. She led the Lady Mavs to one North Central Conference Championship and two trips to the NCAA Division II regional tournament. In 1985, she was named the conference's coach of the year. After UNO, Miner served as head softball coach at Ohio University for five years, compiling a 75-148 record. In 1998, Miner was the director of a fastpitch academy in Fairfield, Ohio, and also was the director/manager of two ASA Junior Olympic 16-18 under teams in Cincinnati.

Lorene Ramsey, Pitcher
Inducted 1987

It didn't matter to Lorene Ramsey, a member of the National Softball Hall of Fame since 1987, if she was playing a game or practicing for one. "I loved to play the game, I even loved practice," stated Lorene. In a career that spanned more than two decades, Lorene established herself as the mainstay for the Chuck McCord Pekin-Lettes. From 1955 to 1972, Ramsey played for the Caterpillar Dieselettes, Sunnyland Lettes and Pekin-Lettes and compiled a win-loss record of 401-90, a winning percentage of .816. Prior to 1955, she had a pitching record of 82-33 for an amateur team in St. Louis. Lorene was 21-1 in 1951, 7-21 in 1952, 20-5 in 1953 and 34-5 in 1954.

Lorene played in her first of 13 ASA national championships in 1954, and compiled a 3-1 record for the fourth place Orange Lionettes. In national championship play, Lorene won 22 games, lost 23, and four times was named an ASA All-American (1959, 1960, 1965 and 1970). She also participated in three ASA Women's Major Fast Pitch All-Star Series.

LORENE RAMSEY CONTINUED ...

In 18 years, Ramsey fanned 3,811 batters in 3,460 innings, allowing 1,793 hits, 277 runs and 616 walks. Lorene's lifetime earned run average was 0.56. In 1955 and 1956, she was named most valuable player of the Houston Warren Paine Tournament, annually one of the nation's top women's major fastpitch tournaments. In 1965, Lorene had a consecutive scoreless inning streak of 93 1/3rd innings, breaking the old Pekin record of 59 held by Hall of Famer Marie Wadlow.

After Lorene's retirement in 1972, she devoted herself to coaching basketball and softball at Illinois Central College where she has had an outstanding career. As a basketball coach, she achieved a 705-255 win-loss record through 1996 and, as a softball coach, 670 wins and 166 losses through 1996. Her softball team won the NJCAA national tournament in 1982, finished second in 1987 and 1989, and in third place six times. Her basketball team won the NJCAA national title three times — in 1992, 1993 and 1998. She is the only NJCAA coach to win championships in two sports and has amassed more wins than any community college coach in the nation.

In 1979 and 1982, Ramsey served as the assistant coach for the USA Women's Pan American Games teams. In 1987, Lorene was listed as an alternate coach for the USA Women's Pan American Games team. In 1988, she was honored by the Women's Sports Foundation as the winner of the "Unsung Heroine Award" at the community college level. In addition to being a member of the National Softball Hall of Fame, Ramsey is a member of six other halls of fames, including the NFCA Hall of Fame, the Peoria Sports Hall of Fame and the Illinois Basketball Coaches Hall of Fame.

Marilyn Rau, Catcher
Inducted 1991

In 1960, Marilyn Rau, then nine, got the first of many softball trophies — Girl's Little League Rookie of the Year. In the years that followed, Rau continued to play softball and collect more trophies. From the little league fields of Phoenix, Arizona, Rau went on to put together one of the finest careers in women's major fastpitch softball starring for two decades with the powerful Sun City Saints.

Named an ASA All-American 11 times, Rau was considered among the finest defensive catchers in the country as well as a power and clutch hitter. She got her start in competitive softball as an eighth grader with the Dudettes, a farm team of the legendary Phoenix Ramblers. When the Ramblers disbanded in 1966, several players formed a team that would eventually be legendary in their own right — the Sun City Saints. With Bev Dryer doing the catching, Rau played shortstop. Eventually Dryer took over the coaching duties and Rau moved behind the plate until her retirement in 1986. She then played for Arizona Scorpions.

With Rau, the Sun City Saints participated in 19 ASA national championships, compiling a record of 59

MARILYN RAU CONTINUED ...

wins and 26 losses — a winning percentage of .694. The Saints finished no lower than fourth place 11 times.

The highlight of Rau's career, without a doubt, was winning the national championship in 1979. The championship was held in Springfield, Missouri. Rau led the Saints with a .500 batting average and was named the tournament's most valuable player. Earlier that year, she helped the USA win the gold medal in the Pan American Games in Puerto Rico. It was the first time softball was an official Pan American sport. Rau capped the year off by being named Arizona's Athlete of the Year.

In 1980, Marilyn led all hitters in the ASA Women's Major Fast Pitch National Championship with a .520 batting average and had 24 total bases. She also tied a national championship record of three triples, which she later duplicated in her career.

Besides being a member of a Pan American team and a ASA national championship team, Rau also was a member of one International Softball Federation (ISF) world championship team. In 1978, she helped the Raybestos Brakettes win the ISF Women's World Fast Pitch Championship, batting .350. That year she also helped the Saints win a gold medal in the National Sports Festival in Colorado Springs, Colorado. The festival, a mini-Olympic involving athletes from USA national governing bodies, was later renamed the United States Olympic Festival.

In 1981 and 1982, the Sun City Saints repeated as Olympic Festival gold medalists. Rau played in her last festival in 1985, helping the Arizona Scorpions win a silver medal. She finished her career with the Scorpions in 1986.

Marilyn earned bachelor's and master's degrees from Arizona State University. In 1991, she earned amateur softball's highest honor with her election into the ASA National Softball Hall of Fame.

Jackie Rice, Pitcher
Inducted 1984

As a pitcher, Jackie Rice didn't allow too many earned runs. In fact, in 203 1/3rd innings of national championship play, she allowed less than half a run per game (0.48 earned run average). Eleven of her 21 wins were shutouts, and she lost only eight games. Jackie's pitching helped teams win three national championships (1964, 1969, and 1970) and she was named an ASA All-American five times (1963, 1964, 1966, 1967 and 1968). She participated in seven ASA Women's Fast Pitch All-Star Series (1964, 1965, 1967, 1968, 1969, 1970 and 1971).

In 1963, Jackie achieved a 4-1 record in the national championship — leading Erv Lind Florists to a runner-up spot. In 1964, led by Rice, the Florists won the national title. Rice was undefeated 4-0 on the mound and was named the tournament's most valuable player. She also was a finalist for the *Oregon Journal's* "Ten Women of Accomplishment Award" and was a finalist for the Oregon Athlete of the Year Award. In 1966, playing for Fresno, Rice compiled a 3-1 record in the national championship with a 0.22 earned run average.

A year later, she joined the Orange Lionettes and helped them win a pair of ASA national championships in 1969 and 1970. Winning the 1969 national tournament entitled the Lionettes to represent the United States in the second ISF Women's World Fast Pitch Championship. Orange finished as runner-up behind Japan as Rice won both of her games. In her first years with the Lionettes, Rice led the Pacific Coast League in earned run average (0.07) as well as compiling a 23-4 record. In 1968, she compiled a 4-2 record and had a 1.16

earned run average for the Lionettes in the national championship.

After the 1974 season, Rice retired as an active player and was an associate professor in the Department of Physical Education, Health and Athletics at Western Oregon State College. She retired in 1984. She was head softball coach at Western Oregon State College for 12 years and had only one losing season. Her last three teams won 64 and lost only 38 games. Her 1989 team compiled a 27-12 record and won a third consecutive NAIA District II Championship. In 1983, her team reached the NAIA World Series, the only Western Oregon squad to reach this event.

Rice, who was still teaching part-time in 1998 at Western Oregon, was inducted into the Oregon Sports Hall of Fame in 1989. Previously she was inducted into the ASA National Softball Hall of Fame in 1984, the Northwest Softball Hall of Fame (1983) and the Portland Metro Association Hall of Fame (1977).

Jackie is a graduate of the University of Oregon, earned a master's degree from Oregon State University in 1969 and received her doctorate from Loma Linda University in 1979.

Kay Rich, Infielder
Inducted 1963

It didn't matter to Kay Rich if the opposing pitchers were hurling from 35 or 38 feet. Kay could get hits off them and obtain a high batting average during her brilliant 21-year career. Kay established herself as one of the greatest all-around players in the history of softball.

Rich starred in an era when high average hitters were rare. This was an exception in Rich who hit over .400 three times in national championships and in 1955 batted an astounding .611. She made her 10 hits count, driving in a record 10 runs.

Between 1949 and 1957, Rich appeared in eight national championships and batted .371 (53-143) and had a fielding percentage of .974 (99 putouts, 87 assists and only 5 errors). When she played in the 1949 national championship, the pitching distance was 35 feet and Rich batted .444, hitting a pair of home runs. When the pitching distance was increased to 38 feet in 1952, Rich had one of her sterling performances, batting .400 with six of eight hits for extra bases. This led the tournament with 17 total bases. Kay also starred at shortstop with a 1.000 fielding percentage (27 assists, 14 putouts and 0 errors).

Rich played every position except pitcher and there wasn't any doubt she would have done well at pitching if she wanted. She had an accurate arm and a smooth easy manner in any position.

Rich, born January 31, 1924, was named an ASA All-American eight times — first team in 1949, 1951, 1952, 1953, 1954 and 1955, and a second team choice in 1956 and 1957. In 1954, Kay was named the tournament's most valuable player, batting .316 and earning a .916 fielding percentage. In all, Kay participated in 12 ASA national championships.

Rich started her career in 1938 with the Colton Cuties before joining the renowned Fresno Rockets in 1946 through 1959. During her nine years in the Pacific Coast Women's League, Kay batted .312 (375 hits in 1.210 at bats). "God only knows what Kay's batting average would be hitting off 43 feet," said former teammate and Hall of Famer Jeanne Contel.

With Fresno, Rich was a member of three national championship teams in 1953, 1954 and 1957. Prior to joining the Rockets, Kay was a member of the Alameda, California, national championship team in 1945.

KAY RICH CONTINUED ...

A graduate of the University of California at Berkeley, Rich had a 34-year career as a physical education teacher, 21 years with the Fresno CYO, and 13 years in the Fresno Unified School District before retiring in 1981. In 1965, she was elected to the Fresno Athletic Hall of Fame. In 1998, Kay was residing in Volcano, California.

Willie Roze, Outfield
Inducted 1985

Playing 10 years for the Raybestos Brakettes, Wiltraud (Willie) Roze earned All-American honors eight times in helping win eight ASA women's major fastpitch national championships. Noted for her base running and clutch hitting, Roze earned first team All-American laurels five times in 1967, 1969, 1971, 1972 and 1974, and was a second team choice in 1968, 1970 and 1973. She was selected as an All-American outfielder each year except for 1974 when she was selected at second base.

Willie participated in 10 ASA national championships and batted .248 (53 / 214). Twice she batted .333 in national championship play — in 1967 and 1972. In 10 years with the Brakettes, she compiled a .281 batting average with 526 hits in 1,869 at bats in 629 games. The best single season batting performance came in 1975 with a .342 average, her last season with the Brakettes.

Roze played on eight ASA national championship teams (1966, 1967, 1968, 1971, 1972, 1973, 1974 and 1975) and the 1974 ISF Women's World Fast Pitch Championship team. The world championship was held in Stratford, Connecticut, and the Brakettes represented the United States, winning the gold medal. Roze batted .455 (10/22) in the world championship, was the fifth leading hitter and drove in seven runs.

Willie earned her bachelor's and master's degrees from Southern Connecticut State College. She played three years of pro softball after retiring from amateur competition in 1975. In the three professional years, Roze had an aggregate .288 batting average and led the Connecticut Falcons in runs scored in 1977 (43 runs). In 1976, she was the ninth leading hitter in the league (.285 average) and was third in runs scored with 62. In 1977, Willie batted .296 and was fourth on the team in hitting.

Born November 8, 1948, in Germany, Roze said her greatest thrill came in 1974 when the Brakettes won the ASA national championship and ISF world championship. Roze said her greatest disappointment was in 1969, when the Brakettes didn't win the ASA national championship and didn't qualify for the ISF championship in Osaka, Japan, in 1970.

In 1998, Roze was a physical education teacher for Madison County, living in Wallingford, Connecticut. She was one of 24 Hall of Famers who, in 1996, attended softball's Olympic debut in Columbus, Georgia.

Freda Savona, Shortstop
Inducted 1998

Freda Savona was considered to be one of the greatest, if not the best, player in women's fastpitch history. Kay Rich, who played for the Fresno Rockets and is a member of the National Softball Hall of Fame, said, "I believe Freda Savona was the absolute best woman softball player in the history of the game and probably the premier woman athlete of her time. She had all the skills — unusual speed, great arm, devastating bat power for average and distance, tremendous fielding range and agility. She was aggressive, daring, highly

FREDA SAVONA CONTINUED ...

competitive and the complete player."

Savona hit consistently around .400 for the New Orleans Jax Brewers of New Orleans, Louisiana, one of the premier teams in the country in the 1940's. Freda led the Jax to five ASA Women's Major Fast Pitch National Championships between 1942 and 1947. The Jax rarely lost and at one time won 89 of 90 games. One of their few losses in ASA tournament play came in 1944 when the Phoenix Ramblers beat them twice by 1-0 scores.

Stories of Freda's feats are still talked about by the pioneers of the game. She was known to have thrown the ball on the fly to home plate while standing with her back against the centerfield fence, and while playing in the National Girls Baseball League (softball was played), to have hit a home run over a 400-foot fence. Dot Wilkinson, a Hall of Famer and All-American catcher for the Phoenix Ramblers, tells of a time when she was cheated out of a hit by Freda, who, while running directly away from home plate, made a fantastic catch of a looping drive.

Awarded posthumously, Freda was a unanimous selection to the Softball Hall of Fame in 1998.

Diane Schumacher, First Base
Inducted 1992

Diane Schumacher played fastpitch from 1976 to 1986 with the Raybestos Brakettes. During that time, she led the team in hitting five times while compiling a .329 lifetime batting average. Schumacher was a member of eight ASA national championship teams (1976, 1977, 1978, 1980, 1982, 1983, 1984 and 1985) and one International Softball Federation world championship team (1978).

In ASA national championship play, Diane earned first team All-American honors four times — at first base in 1976, 1977 and 1978, and as a designated hitter in 1984. She also was selected on the second team at first base twice (1982 and 1983) and third team once (1985). In 1978, she led all hitters in the ASA Women's Major Fast Pitch National Championship with a .400 average. She participated in six U.S. Olympic Festivals and twice was named to

the USA Pan American team. In the Pan American competition, with the United States winning the gold medal in 1979 and a silver medal in 1983, Diane batted .333 and .387.

Recognized for her hitting ability as well as her defensive skills at first base, Schumacher also pitched. She compiled a 55-16 record with a 1.01 earned run average. She retired as an active player in 1986. In 1985, Diane received the Outstanding Alumni Award from Springfield College for outstanding service to softball.

Starting in 1987, she coached the Holland team for four years in international competition, including the 1990 ISF Women's World Fast Pitch Championship in Normal, Illinois. The team also won the European Cup

DIANE SCHUMACHER CONTINUED ...

in 1990. She was one of eight coaches in the USA Softball Coaching pool from which the head coach and assistant coaches were selected for the 1996 USA Olympic team.

A native of West Springfield, Massachusetts, Schumacher has a bachelor's degree in health and physical education from Springfield College. From 1975-1979, she was a member of the Fieldston School in New York City and served as assistant basketball coach at Fordham University. She later was selected as the first full time women's basketball coach at Princeton University. She has a master's degree in sports administration from Temple University (1984).

Since 1984, she has served as both the head women's basketball and softball coach at Augustana College, Rock Island, Illinois. Through 1996, Diane had a softball win/loss record of 184-195 and a basketball record of 221-109 at the college. Including three seasons at Princeton University, Schumacher's overall basketball record is 252-156, a winning percentage of .617. She also is the director of women's athletics at Augustana College and has been a member of the NCAA Division III Midwest Regional selection committee in both softball and basketball. An outstanding softball clinician, Schumacher has been a member of the ASA's Junior Olympic national coaching school staff and has given numerous clinics throughout the United States.

In 1992, Diane was elected to the ASA National Softball Hall of Fame, the Springfield College Hall of Fame and the Connecticut ASA Fast Pitch Hall of Fame. In 1993, she was the first USA player elected to the International Softball Federation (ISF) Hall of Fame.

Ruth Sears, First Base
Inducted 1960

Ruth Sears was one of the best fielding left-handed first basemen in women's fastpitch in the 1930's, 1940's and 1950's. Ruth (Lefty) Sears started her career with Santa Ana, California, in 1936 and ended it in 1955 with the Orange Lionettes.

She earned ASA All-American honors four times (1950, 1951, 1953 and 1954) and participated in seven ASA national championships. In six of those championships, Sears had a .984 fielding percentage with 185 putouts, one assist and only three errors. As a hitter, she had a .363 average in nationals from 1950 through 1955 with 41 hits/149 at bats.

Except for one season (1948), Ruth played for the Orange Lionettes. She was one of the original players when the team started in 1937 and played first base until 1965. Ruth retired with a .425 lifetime batting average. In her first two years of playing fastpitch, she batted .560 (Santa Ana) and .585 (Orange Lionettes).

Ruth's father was responsible for her success, teaching her to throw, bat, bunt and field. Ruth's first All-American selection in 1950 proved to be a memorable one. Not only did she score the winning run in the championship game on a double, but she batted .393. Ruth had 11 hits in 28 times at bat, which was the fourth highest in the tournament. She followed with a .350 batting average in 1951 and a .343 average in 1953.

Winning that first championship in 1950 was Ruth's "greatest thrill in softball." She helped coach the Orange Lionettes from 1947 through 1955 with her husband Leroy "Chub" Sears ... Nicknamed "Lefty," Ruth retired June 1, 1973, after working 22 1/2 years as executive secretary to the Superintendent of the San Joaquin School District. In 1960, Ruth was elected to the ASA National Softball Hall of Fame. Ruth was born August 23, 1917, in Taber, Alberta, Canada.

Carol Spanks, Infielder/Pitcher
Inducted 1981

Carol Spanks once told a reporter, "I'd like to be playing forever rather than doing anything else." That sums up how much Spanks enjoyed playing major fastpitch softball. Spanks played fastpitch softball for more than two decades for the Buena Park Kittens (1951-1953), Buena Park Lynx (1953-1957) and the renowned Orange Lionettes (1958-1975) before retiring.

Spanks pitched, played third base and shortstop during her career. She earned ASA All-American honors in 13 of the 19 ASA national championships in which she was a participant. Ten times she was a first team selection and three times a second team selection. She starred on four national championship teams (1962, 1965, 1969, 1970).

The Lionettes were members of the Pacific Coast Women's League, and 16 times Spanks was named to the Pacific Coast Women's League All-Star team. Five times she led the league in hitting with averages of .328 (1954), .400 (1969), .321 (1970), .327 (1971), and .400 (1972), and six times she led the Lionettes in hitting. Three times Spanks batted .400 or higher in national championship play with a .438 average in 1967, .417 in 1972 and a .429 average in 1973. Two years later, in her last national championship, she batted .545. Her batting average in 15 of the ASA national championships was .300 (91/303). From 1967-1975, Spanks had an overall .322 batting average for the Lionettes with 700 hits out of 2,176 at bats in 686 games.

Besides excelling at bat, Carol also starred on defense and won the Erv Lind Award as the outstanding defensive player at the national championships three times (1968, 1969 and 1970). In the 1968 national championship, she had 27 assists, 26 putouts and only one error at shortstop.

After winning the ASA national title in 1969, the Lionettes represented the USA in the second International Softball Federation Women's World Fast Pitch Championship held in 1970 in Osaka, Japan. As a pitcher, Spanks compiled a win-loss record of 122-28 with an earned run average of 0.72. She allowed 112 earned runs, walked 162 and fanned 480.

After her amateur career, Spanks played one season, 1976, in the newly formed Women's Professional League and earned All League Western Division honors. With an outstanding career concluded, Spanks turned to coaching women's college softball and was named head coach at California Polytechnical Institute, Pomona, in 1978. Again the results were outstanding as she and former Orange Lionettes' coach Shirley Topley coached Cal Poly Pomona for 15 years.

During that span, the Lady Broncos won 577 games, lost 310 and tied 5 for a winning percentage of .650. The team made 11 postseason appearances (three AIAW and eight NCAA). Five times her teams advanced to the NCAA Women's College World Series, with the 1979 and 1988 squads finishing third in the nation. Nine times a Bronco player was named an All-American and 16 times was named first team All Big West. From 1989-1990, Cal Poly was a member of the Big West Conference and the Broncos won the inaugural Big West Championship in 1985. In 1985 and 1989, Spanks was named Big West Conference Coach of the Year and twice the Broncos won 50 or more games. Sue Enquist, head coach at UCLA, said that "along with Topley, Carol established a reputation as the coach who was able to get the full potential out of her athletes. They believed they could beat anyone and often did."

CAROL SPANKS CONTINUED ...

Involved with the ASA/USA softball program during the summer, Spanks coached ASA teams for 17 years with the 1987 team, Orange County Majestics, winning the ASA women's major fastpitch national title and being one of the highest-finishing ASA teams during this period. Six times the Majestics played in the United State Olympic Festival and twice won a bronze medal.

In 1987, Carol was the head coach of the USA Pan American team that won a gold medal at the Pan American Games in Indianapolis, Indiana. A year later she was inducted into the Orange County Sports Hall of Fame. In 1994, she was one of the assistant coaches for the USA softball national team that won a gold medal in the ISF Women's World Fast Pitch Championship in St. John's Newfoundland, Canada. She also was one of the eight coaches named to the USA National Coaches pool from which the Olympic coach was selected.

In 1995, Carol was named associate head coach at the University of Nevada, Las Vegas, and in the fall of that year was inducted into the National Softball Coaches Association Hall of Fame (now the National Fastpitch Coaches Association). A native of Whittier, California, Spanks is a 1958 graduate of UCLA with a bachelor's degree in physical education with a special secondary teaching credential. She went on to receive her secondary administrative credential while doing graduate work at Whittier College.

Looking back on her career, Spanks was really happy about the era she played. "The players today may have more conveniences, but I played with people who really had to love the game to play. I think I was pretty lucky."

In 1981, Carol was inducted into the National Softball Hall of Fame and is one of 11 former Lionettes who have received this honor.

Mickey Stratton, Catcher
Inducted 1969

Catcher Rosemary (Mickey) Stratton played all but two of her 12 years of major women's fastpitch with the Raybestos Brakettes. She led the team in hitting three times — .320 batting average in 1959, .324 in 1961 and a personal high of .370 in 1965. In 10 national championships, she batted .272 (61/224) with her highest average of .348 in 1965.

Mickey spent the first two years of her career, 1954-1955, with the Wallingford Owlettes before joining the Brakettes in 1956. She played in 10 ASA national championships and was a member of four national championship teams.

In addition to catching, Stratton also played first base and outfield. Defensively, she rarely made an error behind the plate and, from 1958-1961, Mickey had a fielding percentage of 1.000 in national championship play.

Seven times Mickey earned ASA All-American honors, including first team selections in 1958, 1959, 1961, 1964 and 1965, and second team honors in 1956 and 1963. In 1965, she played in the first International Softball Federation World Championship in Melbourne, Australia. She had a batting average of .348 as a Brakette, representing the United States, which finished second. Stratton was named to the world all-star first team.

Mickey says the greatest thrill of her career was "winning the 1958 ASA national championship. Every event, winning or losing, was a learning experience. I've traveled places and met wonderful people that I would not have done if I hadn't played softball."

Mickey was born July 12, 1938, in Middlefield, Connecticut, and in 1998, was a nurse/drug counselor. Stratton was inducted into the Softball Hall of Fame in 1969 and was the first Brakette to receive the honor.

Marlys Taber, Shortstop
Inducted 1991

Marlys Taber's major fastpitch career started at 14 in 1958 for the Earlville Victorians of Earlville, Illinois. Her career concluded in 1983 when she was forced to retire because of acute tendonitis resulting from a shoulder injury.

Taber earned ASA All-American honors five times — first team selections in 1978 and 1980, and second team honors in 1965 (.385 batting average), 1966 (.260 BA) and 1976 (.238 BA). Taber played for some of the top teams in the Midwest, including the Pekin-Lettes, the Greater Milwaukee Bankettes and the West Allis State Bankettes, Wisconsin. With Pekin, Taber had a 10-year fielding average of .961 and a .345 batting average (384/1,116). For the Bankettes, she had a .260 batting average with 350 hits out of 1,350 at bats. Her accumulative average in 20 years was .298 (734 hits out of 2,466 at bats).

Besides being named an All-American, Taber participated in three ASA Women's Major Fast Pitch All Star Series in 1966, 1968 and 1977. Her .389 batting average in 1966 led all hitters. In 1979, she was one of the players invited to the Pan American softball tryouts in Colorado Springs, Colorado.

After playing softball, she turned to coaching and for three years taught physical education in Peoria, Illinois. For more than 20 years, she taught physical education at Golf Middle School in Morton Grove, Illinois. She also coached basketball and softball at Niles North High School and soccer, basketball and volleyball at Golf Middle School. She took early retirement in 1995, and in 1998, found herself extremely busy golfing, making craft projects and participating in community activities in Dows, Iowa.

"I always loved to play and was fortunate to be associated with first class coaches and players — it was the best of times," stated Taber.

In 1982, Taber was inducted into the Illinois State University Hall of Fame. She is a 1966 graduate of Illinois State, where she played field hockey, basketball, volleyball and softball. In 1989, she was selected to the Greater Peoria Sports Hall of Fame and, in 1991, to the ASA National Softball Hall of Fame. Taber called it "the greatest thrill of her career."

Bertha Tickey, Pitcher
Inducted 1972

A true test of greatness is consistency over a period of time and pitcher Bertha Ragan Tickey certainly met that criteria. Tickey's legendary career covered more than two decades. The only girl in a family of seven children, Bertha played her first softball game in 1939 for Alta Chevrolet in Dinuba, California. She was a shortstop first and switched to pitching at the age of 16. Bertha played her last game in 1968 for the renowned Raybestos Brakettes. Actually, Bertha had retired in 1967, compiling a 17-1 record for the Brakettes. When Bertha walked off the field following the national championship that year, there were three pitchers — Joan

BERTHA TICKEY CONTINUED ...

Joyce, Donna Lopiano and Donna Hebert. Little did she know she would be back in 1968. Tickey came out of retirement to bolster a staff that was depleted by Lopiano going to graduate school and Hebert undergoing shoulder surgery.

In typical Tickey style, Bertha came through, winning 25 of 26 games as the Brakettes repeated as national champions. In her final three games in the national championship, Bertha hurled a no-hitter against Redwood City in 1967, and in 1968, finished her career with a perfect game against Houston, Texas, and a 13 inning no-hitter against Fresno. "Everyone respected Bertha for her skills," stated former Brakette Brenda Reily. "She was kind of like a Lou Gehrig, a lot of class but not flashy."

From 1956 through 1968, Bertha pitched for Raybestos and won 285 games, losing only 26. In 2,402 2/3rds innings, she struck out 3,529 batters and never lost more than five games per season. Bertha's lifetime record was 757 wins and 88 losses, including 162 no-hitters. Eighteen times she was named an ASA All-American and eight times most valuable player in the ASA Women's Major Fast Pitch National Championships. Each year since 1967, the Bertha Tickey Award is given to the outstanding pitcher in the Women's Major Fast Pitch National Championship.

Eleven times Bertha was a member of a national championship team, winning a record 74 games and losing 18 in national play. Bertha said that winning the ASA national championship in 1950 was her greatest thrill in softball because it was the first time she was on a national championship team. That year Bertha won 65 of 72 games, fanned 795 batters in 513 innings, yielding only 143 hits and walking 58. She also had a scoreless inning streak of 143 innings that year, hurling 53 shutouts and nine no-hitters. In 1949, Tickey struck out 756 batters in 60 games and had a scoreless inning streak of 120.

In the 1950 national championship, Tickey was nothing less than amazing. She hurled four consecutive shutouts before losing her first game — a heartbreaking 1-0 decision in 11 innings to the Phoenix Ramblers. With only 20 minutes between games, Tickey hurled the next game, beating the Phoenix Ramblers 3-1 in 15 innings.

The greatest disappointment in Bertha's career came in 1962 when softball wasn't accepted as an Olympic sport. In 1991, however, softball was finally accepted, and when the sport made its debut in 1996, Tickey was one of 24 Hall of Famers who attended the softball competition in Columbus, Georgia.

In 1965, Bertha compiled a 4-1 record and batted .286 in the first ISF Women's World Fast Pitch Championship for the Brakettes, who finished second. Bertha had an earned run average of 0.19 and allowed only 10 hits in 36 innings. Bertha was one of five Brakettes named to the world all-star first team.

In addition to being a member of the Connecticut ASA Hall of Fame, Bertha was inducted into the Orange County Sports Hall of Fame in 1991. Bertha was married to Edward Tickey and has a daughter. Ed, who is now deceased, caught for the Brooklyn Dodgers and the Raybestos Cardinals, a fastpitch team. Bertha is one of four softball players profiled in the book, *The Twentieth Century: Great Athletes.*

Shirley Topley, First Base
Inducted 1981

Growing up in Hondo, Alberta, Canada, Shirley Topley excelled in a variety of sports, including basket-

ball, field hockey, track and field, curling, ice hockey and softball. But it would be softball in which Topley would establish herself as one of the greatest players of all time. Shirley was inducted into the ASA National Softball Hall of Fame in 1981.

Topley played softball for several Canadian teams, including the South Hill Queens of Vancouver, British Columbia. Topley, born April 14, 1934, played in her first ASA national championship in 1960 for South Hill and earned second team All-American honors. This earned her a spot on the 1961 Women's Major Fast Pitch All-Star team where Ricki Caito, Orange Lionettes' second baseman and owner, was impressed with her ability. Ricki asked Shirley to play for the Lionettes and she joined the team in 1962. That year, Shirley helped the Lionettes capture the ASA Women's Major Fast Pitch National Championship, earning first team All-American honors as a first baseman. She played in 1963 and 1964 with the Raybestos Brakettes before rejoining the Lionettes in 1965. With the Brakettes, she led the team in hitting twice with averages of .372 in 1963 and .340 in 1964.

In 1967, she took over as Lionettes head coach and in the next seven years guided the team to 389 wins, 67 losses and 3 ties — a winning percentage of .853. During Topley's reign, the Lionettes won the Pacific Coast Women's Softball League title from 1967-1972, two ASA national titles (1969 and 1970) and represented the United States in the ISF Women's World Fast Pitch Championship in Osaka, Japan, in 1970.

Shirley participated in 16 ASA national championships, and was a member of five national championship teams and five runners-up. The championship teams included the Orange Lionettes in 1962, 1965, 1969, 1970, and Raybestos Brakettes in 1963. Eleven times she was named an ASA All-American.

As a member of the Pacific Coast League, Shirley was a league all-star 11 times and led the league in hitting twice — in 1966 and 1974. Six times she led the Lionettes in hitting and six times in runs batted in (RBI). During her nine-year span with the Lionettes, she batted .298 (613 hits/2,055 at bats), scored 322 runs and smashed 16 home runs.

Shirley also excelled defensively. She led the Lionettes in fielding percentage three times and was runner-up six times. She had a fielding percentage of .987 from 1967-1975 — 5,460 putouts, 234 assists and only 75 errors.

After retiring as an active player, Shirley served as assistant coach for Cal Poly Pomona from 1979-1990. She also was head coach of various ASA summer teams, including the Orange County Desperadoes, Orange County Majestics and the Newport Beach Activities A's. In 1987, the Majestics captured the ASA Women's Major Fast Pitch National Championship and placed second in 1988. In 1988, she led the Majestics to a gold medal in the Tri-Nation Friendship Series against Japan and China in Oklahoma City. Topley also coached the team to a silver medal and three bronze medals in the United States Olympic Festival.

In 1991, Shirley was head coach of the USA Women's Pan American team and led the team to a gold medal in the Pan American Games in Cuba. In 1990, she served as one of the assistant coaches for the USA national team in the ISF Women's World Fast Pitch Championship in Normal, Illinois, which won the gold medal. In 1995, she was one of the assistant coaches for the USA Women's Pan American team that won the gold medal in Argentina.

One of the most respected and dedicated people in softball, Topley also is a member of the Orange County Sports Hall of Fame. She has had a career as a coach and player that would be difficult to match.

Gina Vecchione, Outfielder
Inducted 1996

Teams that consistently win have a clutch player — someone who delivers a key hit or comes up with an outstanding defensive play with the outcome hanging in the balance. More often than not, that is what Gina Vecchione did during her 12-year career with the Raybestos Brakettes — a career that ended in 1989.

A sociology graduate of UCLA, where she starred for three years after transferring from Southern Connecticut State College in New Haven, Gina was inducted into the ASA National Hall of Fame in 1997. Gina is the 15th former Brakette to earn the sport's ultimate honor.

Originally, Vecchione, a native of New Rochelle, New York, didn't start out playing fastpitch. She played slow pitch (left-handed shortstop and outfield) from age 13-17 and didn't get acquainted with fastpitch until she was a freshman attending Southern Connecticut State College on a basketball scholarship.

Also a member of the basketball team was Joan VanNess, who played third base for the Brakettes in the summer. Joan suggested to Gina that she try out that summer. It so happened that Memorial Field, home of the Brakettes, hosted the eastern regional and after it was completed, Gina tried out for the team. John Stratton, then assistant coach for the Brakettes, was interested in Gina playing for the team. The rest, as they say, is history. Vecchione made the team, batting .299 in 1978, and went on to become one of the top clutch players in Raybestos history.

She earned All-American honors seven times and twice (1980 and 1988) she led the Women's Major Fast Pitch National Tournament in batting. She was a member of six national championship teams, four ISF world championship teams and a member of the 1983 USA Pan American team.

"She was a true blue Brakette," stated coach Ralph Raymond. "She was a fierce competitor, a pleasure to have on the team. It was great to work with a super clutch player — she certainly did the job for us."

Gina is now an assistant coach at Oregon State University. Gina continues to do the job, coaching the outfielders and working with the hitters. She is hoping that they will have the same love and passion for fastpitch as when she played. "Sure I miss playing. I was a competitive player, but I enjoy coaching, working with kids and seeing them do well," said Vecchione.

Vecchione, who was a team player with a capital "T," had a .322 batting average in the 12 years with the Brakettes and an average of .242 in national championship play. After hitting .444 to win her second ASA batting title in 1988, she announced that she was retiring at the end of the season. She had a .328 season average.

Gina then decided to return and play one more season after her best friend, Allyson Rioux, passed away in February, 1989. It was an emotional time for Gina as well as for the entire Brakette team. Anyone who knew Rioux well had to be upset. The game's finest second baseman had battled long and hard to overcome a brain tumor and just when it seemed that the battle had been won, the disease came back again to take away a player who touched you not only as a player but as a human being. "I don't know anyone who ever said anything negative about Allyson," said Gina, who returned that summer. "I felt I wanted to go through that difficult summer with the Brakettes....my family." Playing that season helped Gina get through the passing of Rioux. "I'm sure that my stats, for that season, are probably my lowest, but in this case, there was something way more important that the game itself," stated Gina.

M. Marie Wadlow, Pitcher
Inducted 1957

Little did M. Marie Wadlow realize when she started playing softball on the sandlots of St. Louis in 1929 for Tabernacle Baptist Church, that in 1957 she would be the first women inducted into the ASA National Softball Hall of Fame. Between 1929 and when she retired in 1950, Wadlow compiled an impressive pitching record of 341 wins, 51 defeats and 42 no-hitters. Seven of those years she played for the Caterpillar Dieselettes of Peoria, Illinois, winning 107 games and losing only 18. Former Dieselette manager Chuck McCord said, "Marie was one of the greatest competitors I've seen anywhere."

Although Wadlow had numerous thrills in her outstanding career, a game she lost in 1950 in her last ASA national championship, was her "greatest thrill." She compiled a 2-2 record in the championship, striking out 26 batters. "We had a 17 inning, 1-0 loss to the Phoenix Ramblers, giving us third place in the national tournament in San Antonio," said Wadlow. "The thrill was watching the Ramblers come back in the evening after a more than three-hour struggle in the intense heat of the afternoon. We had about two hours rest, then beat the undefeated Orange Lionettes 1-0 in 11 innings, took a half-hour rest and lost a heartbreaking 15-inning game to Orange, 3-1, for the championship. We played 43 innings in about 11 hours. Bertha Tickey pitched 26 innings in the last two games. She was knocked to the ground by a vicious line drive to the stomach, only to get up and finish the game and the tournament."

Wadlow, who was retirement plans accountant for Caterpillar Tractor Company, retired from the company in February, 1977. Besides being elected to the National Softball Hall of Fame, she also was selected to the St. Louis Metro Hall of Fame in 1969, the Illinois ASA Hall of Fame in 1971 and the Greater Peoria Sports Hall of Fame in 1994. Marie Wadlow passed away April 6, 1979, at the age of 61.

Pat Walker, Outfield
Inducted 1976

Pat Walker was double-trouble for the opposition during her 25-year fastpitch career. She was not only a good hitter, with a lifetime batting average of .314, but she was a base-stealing threat every time she was on base. During her career with the Rebels, she stole 172 bases and led the team in most steals eight times. Seven times she was the team's leading hitter, and had a personal best of .431 in 1955.

Pat started playing softball at the age of 13 in Orlando, and by the time she was 16, she had appeared in her first of eight ASA Women's Major Fast Pitch National Championships. She earned All-American honors three times — first team honors in 1966 and 1968, and second team laurels in 1961. In those championships, she made only one error with her highest average .417 in 1967.

At the regional level, she was named all-region in 11 out of

PAT WALKER CONTINUED ...

12 regional appearances. She hit .350, had only two errors with 69 putouts and four assists. Pat, however, was more than just an outstanding hitter and base runner. She was team captain and occasionally even pitched. In eight years, she compiled a 47-24 pitching record and hurled three no-hitters and 13 shutouts. She allowed less than two runs a game in 536 innings. Marge Ricker, former Orlando manager, said that no better defensive player than Pat played for her or had she seen a better one.

Although the Rebels were among the top finishing teams in the national championship during Pat's career, they never won the title. That unfortunately was the biggest disappointment of Walker's career. The biggest thrill was an extra inning game in the 1961 national championship against New Jersey in Portland, Oregon.

Born March 19, 1933, in Orlando, Pat retired in 1987 from Southern Bell. She graduated from high school in 1951. Pat still resided in Orlando in 1998. In 1969, she was elected to the ASA National Hall of Fame and is one of three former Rebels who have received this honor. The others are Mickey Davis and Jean Daves.

Nancy Welborn, Pitcher
Inducted 1982

When Nancy's parents moved to Montana and she opted to stay in Eugene, Oregon, it turned out to be one of the most important decisions in her softball career. By staying in Eugene, Jack Moore, manager of the McCulloch Chain Saws was able to work with Nancy, who was pitching using a figure-eight style. Due to Nancy's height (5'11") and coordination, Moore figured Nancy would make a better windmill pitcher. As history has documented, Moore's assessment was correct as Welborn developed into a pitcher who ultimately would enter the Hall of Fame in 1962. However, before that happened, there was a lot of work. They worked all winter, three times a week on speed, then control. The first games she pitched for the Chain Saws were a bit wild.

Ultimately Nancy's determination and effort paid off. In 1965, she nipped Yakima 1-0 in a 20-inning regional final and earned her team a berth into the ASA Women's Major Fast Pitch National Championship. The Chain Saws finished eighth. In 1966, Yakima turned the tables on the Chain Saws and whipped them in the regional semifinals to put them into the loser's bracket. Led by Welborn, the Chain Saws battled back and whipped the Yakima team twice for the regional crown and another berth to the championships. Eugene improved on its 1965 finish, placing fifth. Welborn was named second team All-American for the second year in a row.

By this time, the renowned Orange Lionettes, who won the national title in 1965, were in need of pitching after Joan Joyce moved to Stratford and Lou Albrecht retired. Nancy was asked by the Lionettes to try out but turned them down to stay with the Chain Saws. In 1967 and 1968, the Chain Saws didn't make it to the nationals and Welborn, who wanted to compete on a national level, had a change of heart and decided to play for the Lionettes. "It was then that I seriously thought about coming to Orange," stated Welborn, who wrote a letter asking for a tryout. It was a decision that neither Welborn or the Lionettes would regret.

From 1969-1975, Welborn compiled a record of 306 wins and 68 losses, which included 27 no-hitters and 46 one-hitters. With the Lionettes, Welborn was a first team All-American in 1969, 1970, 1971, 1972 and 1973. She also was a winner of the most valuable player award and the Bertha Tickey outstanding pitcher

NANCY WELBORN CONTINUED ...

award in 1970. She was bestowed the Bertha Tickey award also in 1969, 1971 and 1972.

After pitching the Lionettes to the national championship in 1969, they earned a berth in the second ISF Women's World Fast Pitch Championship in Osaka, Japan, where they finished second behind host Japan. Welborn set two pitching records at that event — most wins (6-0) and most innings pitched (50).

In eight national championships, two with the Chain Saws and six with the Lionettes, Welborn compiled a 34-11 record, an earned run average of 0.39. She struck out 288 batters in 338 innings and allowed 169 hits and 37 walks. She was a member of the Orange Lionettes championship teams in 1969 and 1970. In 1971 and 1972, the Lionettes were runners-up, fourth place in 1973 and eighth place in 1975 — Nancy's last year as an active player.

Although she did not hit for a high average, Welborn was runner-up in RBI's in1971 and led the team in assists in 1973. In seven years, she made only 51 errors in 411 games — a fielding percentage of .945. At the regional level, Nancy had a 10-2 win-loss record and an ERA of 0.21 in 98 innings.

Nancy was elected to the ASA National Softball Hall of Fame in 1982.

Dorothy (Dot) Wilkinson, Catcher
Inducted 1970

Dorothy (Dot) Wilkinson excelled not only in softball, being named an ASA All-American a record 19 times, but she also is a member of the Women's International Bowling Congress Hall of Fame. She was inducted into the WIBC Hall of Fame in 1990 — 20 years after having been inducted into the ASA Hall of Fame.

Wilkinson retired from softball in 1965. She started her career in 1933, and during that time led the Phoenix Ramblers to ASA national championships in 1940, 1948 and 1949. Wilkinson had some impressive seasons. In 1953, she batted .363 during the regular season; in 1952, she had a .374 season batting average and in 1957, Dot had a .387 batting average in national championships. In 1955, she had a .450 batting average in the national championship, committing no errors in 36 chances, and in 1954, a .455 batting average with a 1.000 fielding percentage on 84 chances.

Dot said that one of her greatest thrills was winning the ASA national championship in 1940 in Detroit, Michigan. Another thrill came in 1970 when she was presented her Hall of Fame plaque at Orange, California — receiving a standing ovation. "If there was a disappointment, it was not winning the national tournament in 1964 in Florida," Dot said.

Dot, who used a five-fingered glove rather than a catcher's mitt, was the first woman inducted into the Arizona Sports Hall of Fame in 1976. She is also a charter member of the Arizona Softball Hall of Fame.

Retired from the real estate business since 1985, Wilkinson was living in Phoenix, Arizona, in 1998. Dot was born October 9, 1921.

NATIONAL CHAMPIONSHIP TEAMS

1947 A-1 Queens, Phoenix, AZ	1951 A-1 Queens, Phoenix, AZ
1948 Jax Brewers, New Orleans, LA	1952 A-1 Queens, Phoenix, AZ
1949 A-1 Queens, Phoenix, AZ	1953 Erv Lind Florists, Portland, OR
1950 Funk Gems, Phoenix, AZ	1954 A-1 Queens, Phoenix, AZ

INDIVIDUAL RECORD HOLDERS

OUTSTANDING PITCHERS
1947 Charlotte Armstrong, Phoenix, AZ
1948 Lottie Jackson, New Orleans, LA
1949 Carolyn Morris, Phoenix, AZ
1950 Carolyn Morris, Phoenix, AZ
1951 Charlotte Armstrong, Phoenix, AZ
1952 Charlotte Armstrong, Phoenix, AZ
1953 Betty Evans Grayson, Portland, OR
1954 Alma Wilson, Phoenix, AZ

MOST VALUABLE PLAYERS
1947 Margie Yetman, Oklahoma City, OK
1948 Dodie Nelson, Phoenix, AZ
1949 Alma Wilson, Oklahoma City, OK
1950 Lois Williams, Phoenix, AZ
1951 Dodie Nelson, Phoenix, AZ
1952 Elizabeth Loche, Portland, OR
1953 Bonnie Martin, Salt Lake City, UT
1954 Beverly Cox, Phoenix, AZ

LEADING HITTERS
1947 Margie Yetman, Oklahoma City, OK
1948 Alma Wilson, Oklahoma City, OK
1949 Alice Jorgenson, Seattle, WA
1950 Alma Wilson, Oklahoma City, OK
1951 Dodie Nelson, Phoenix, AZ
1952 Marie Jull, Seattle, WA
1953 Nancy VanDeVenter, Phoenix, AZ
1954 Dodie Nelson, Phoenix, AZ

MISS SOFTBALL HONORS
1947 Carolyn Morris, Phoenix, AZ
1948 Lois Williams, Phoenix, AZ
1949 Dianne Holder, Los Angeles, CA
1950 Dodie Nelson, Phoenix, AZ
1951 Betty Luna, Phoenix, AZ
1952 Margaret Dobson, Portland, OR
1953 Dixie McCarty, Phoenix, AZ
1954 Jan Newman, Phoenix, AZ

NATIONAL SOFTBALL CONGRESS ALL-AMERICANS (1947-1954)

NAME	YEARS	TEAM	POSITION
— A —			
Anderson, Eleanor	1947	A1 Queens-AZ	INF
Anderson, Jackie	1947	Chevrolet Queens-OK	OF
Armstrong, Charlotte	1947, 48, 49, 1950, 51, 52	A-1 Queens-AZ	P
— B —			
Ballard, Flossie	1949, 51	A-1 Queens-AZ	INF
Barrett, Doris	1951	Erv Lind Florists-OR	P
Burris, Marie	1951	A-1 Queens-AZ	OF
— C —			
Caito, Ricki	1948	A-1 Queens-AZ	INF
Cox, Beverly	1953, 54	A-1 Queens-AZ	INF
Curtis, Louise	1947	Holsum Bakery-AZ	UT

NAME	YEARS	TEAM	POSITION
— D —			
Darby, Goldie	1954	Peaches-GA	C
Dean, Dorothy	1954	Peaches-GA	P
Deckard, Jamie	1952	Mesa Premiums-AZ	INF
Dixon, Mildred	1947	Holsum Bakery-AZ	INF
	1950	Funk Gems-AZ	INF
Dobson, Margaret	1952, 53	Erv Lind Florists-OR	INF
Doyle, Snookie	1951	A-1 Queens-AZ	INF
— E —			
Eden, Jane	1949	Erin Brews-OH	OF
— F —			
Freston, Wilma	1953	Shamrocks-UT	P
— G —			
Gebron, Jody	1953	Bell Comets-TX	C

NSC ALL-AMERICANS CONTINUED ...

NAME	YEARS	TEAM	POSITION
Giertz, Betty	1949	A-1 Queens-AZ	INF
Gill, Hazel	1948, 49	Jax Brewers-LA	INF
Grayson, Betty Evans	1952, 53	Erv Lind Florists-OR	P

— H —

Hamrick, Louise	1954	Peaches-GA	INF
Hernandez,Jeanna	1954	Tempe Debs-AZ	OF
Hicks, Mary	1947	Bell Comets-TX	P
Hoehn, Nonie	1947	Ramblers-CA	UT

— I —

Ito, Nancy	1950	Industrial Bank-CO	INF

— J —

Jackson, Lottie	1948, 49	Jax Brewers-LA	P
	1952	Premiums-AZ	
Jorgensen, Alice	1949, 50, 51	Epicures-WA	C/UT
	1953	Nash Airflytes-WA	P

— K —

Keagle, Merle	1947	A-1 Queens-AZ	OF
	1950	Funk Gems-AZ	OF
King, Sis	1948	Holsum Bakery-AZ	OF
Korgan, Nina	1948	Jax Brewers-LA	P

— L —

Locke, Elizabeth	1952, 53	Erv Lind Florists-OR	OF
Lopez, Stretch	1954	Ramblers-OK	UT
Luna, Betty	1951	A-1 Queens-AZ	INF

— M —

Maas, Irene	1951	Erv Lind Florists-OF	INF
McCarty, Dixie	1954	A-1 Queens-AZ	OF
Marshall, Theda	1950	Funk Gems-AZ	INF
Martin, Bonnie	1953	Shamrocks-UT	INF
Martin, Jo	1951	Chevrolet Queens-OK	C
Massa, Babe	1947	Rival Dog Food-IL	INF
Moore, Dottie	1952	Erv Lind Florists-OR	C
Morris, Carolyn	1947, 49, 50	A-1 Queens-AZ	P
Mulkey, Robbie	1951, 52, 53	Erv Lind Florists-OR	INF/OF
Munoz, Lucy	1954	Tempe Debs-AZ	P
Myers, Dorothy	1948	Chevrolet Queens-OK	OF
	1949	A-1 Queens-AZ	
	1950	Funk Gems -AZ	

—N —

Nelson, Dodie	1947	Ramblers-CA	OF
	1948, 49, 50, 51		
	1952, 53, 54	Queens-AZ	OF
Newman, Jan	1953	A-1 Queens-AZ	INF

— P —

Parrish, Thelma	1952	Erv Lind Florists-OR	OF
Pembo, Mary	1948	Jax Brewers-LA	INF
Pomeroy, Gerry	1954	Ramblers-OK	INF

NAME	YEARS	TEAM	POSITION

— R —

Rochelle,Catherine	1954	Peaches-GA	INF
Rohrer, Kay	1948	A-1 Queens-AZ	UT
	1949	Jax Brewers-LA	INF
	1950	Funk Gems-AZ	C
	1952	Mesa Premiums-AZ	UT

— S —

Savona, Freda	1948	Jax Brewers-LA	INF
Savona, Olympia	1948	Jax Brewers-LA	C
Sharpe, Sue	1953	Slick Chicks-CA	INF
Sheever, Jo	1951	Chevrolet Queens-OK	OF
Sipe, Betty	1954	Rancherettes-AZ	UT

— T —

Topley, Shirley	1952	Epicures-WA	UT
	1953	Crowhurst Motors-BC	INF

— W —

Wadsworth,Beverly	1953	Erv Lind Florists-OR	C
Walker, Annabelle	1950	Industrial Bank-CO	P
Whitmore, Pat	1953	Shamrocks-UT	C
Williams, Lois	1947, 48, 49, 50		
	1951, 52	A-1 Queens-AZ	C
Wilson, Alma	1948, 49,		
	1950, 51,	Chevrolet Queens-OK	UT
	1954	A-1 Queens-AZ	P
Woodard, Charlene	1954	A-1 Queens-AZ	C

— Y —

Yetman, Margie	1947, 49, 50	Chevrolet Queens-OK	INF
	1952	A-1 Queens-AZ	INF

Alice Jorgensen, a member of the Seattle Epicures team, earned All-American honors as both a catcher and pitcher.

Margie Yetman was the leading hitter and MVP in 1947.

Charlotte Armstrong, a pitcher for the A-1 Queens, was a six-time All-American.

Lois Williams, catcher and captain of the A-1 Queens, was selected All-American six consecutive years, from 1947-1952.

Dodie Nelson, an outfielder for the A-1 Queens, was the only player in the league to earn All-American honors eight consecutive years.

Source: Connie Claussen, Nebraska-Omaha

NATIONAL TOURNAMENT CHAMPIONS 1969-1972 (NAGWS & ASA)

YEAR	CHAMPION	COACH	RUNNER-UP
1969	John F. Kennedy	Coach Don Joe	Illinois State
1970	John F. Kennedy	Coach Ken Christensen	Southwest Missouri State
1971	John F. Kennedy	Coach Ken Christensen	Iowa State
1972	Arizona State	Coach Mary Littlewood	University of Tokyo

ASSOCIATION OF INTERCOLLEGIATE ATHLETICS FOR WOMEN (AIAW) NATIONAL CHAMPIONS (1973-1981)

1973-1979 — ALL DIVISIONS

YEAR	CHAMPION	COACH	RUNNER-UP
1973	Arizona State	Coach Mary Littlewood	Illinois State
1974	Southwest Missouri State	Coach Kay Hunter	Northern Colorado
1975	Nebraska-Omaha	Coach Connie Claussen	Northern Iowa
1976	Michigan State	Coach Dianne Ulibarri	Northern Colorado
1977	Northern Iowa	Coach Jane Mertesdorf	Arizona
1978	UCLA	Coach Sharron Backus	Northern Colorado
1979	Texas Woman's	Coach Donna Terry	UCLA

1980-1881 — DIVISION I

1980	Utah State	Coach Kelly Phipps	Indiana
1981	Utah State	Coach Kelly Phipps	Cal State Fullerton

1980-1881 — DIVISION II

1980	Emporia State	Coach Betty Walters	Chapman
1981	Cal State Sacramento	Coach E. J. McConkie	C.W. Post

WOMEN'S COLLEGE WORLD SERIES INDIVIDUAL HONORS (1969-1979)

1969	Judy Lloyd	John F. Kennedy	Most Valuable Player
	Carmen Imel	Illinois State	Outstanding Coach
1970	Kay Camp	John F. Kennedy	Most Valuable Player
	Reba Sue Sim	Southwest Missouri State	Outstanding Coach
1971	Paula Miller	Arizona State	Most Valuable Player
	Pat Noe	Iowa State	Outstanding Coach
1972	Jean Hulzkamp	South Dakota State	Leading Hitter — .500
	Valerie Lindbloom	Western Illinois	Outstanding Coach
1973	Kris Meyer	Northern Iowa	Leading Hitter — .417
1974	Gail Gault	Arizona	Leading Hitter — .615
1975	Chris Thornock	Weber State	Leading Hitter — .900
1976	Diane Spoelstra	Michigan State	Leading Hitter — .467
1977	Gayle Barrons	Michigan State	Leading Hitter — .450
	Pat Stockman	Northern Iowa	Leading Pitcher — Best ERA — 0.00

WCWS INDIVIDUAL HONORS CONTINUED ...

	Lou Piel	Northern Colorado	Leading Pitcher — Best ERA — 0.00
	Gloria Graves	Kansas	Leading Pitcher — Best ERA — 0.00
1978	Sue Enquist	UCLA	Leading Hitter — .421
	Kathy Arendsen	Texas Woman's	Leading Pitcher — Most K's — 67
	Jan Jeffers	UCLA	Leading Pitcher — Best ERA — 0.00
	Lisa Richardson	UCLA	Leading Pitcher — Best ERA — 0.00
1979	Sue Reinders	Nebraska-Omaha	Leading Hitter — .545

Cal State Sacramento won the AIAW Division II Women's Softball Championship in 1981. Members of the team pictured here are back row, left to right, manager Sue Smoot, Sherri Uffelman, Linda Nielsen, Joanne English, Michelle Malsam, Stefanie Fontana, Paulla Hyatte, Janelle Johnson, Sandee Denmark, Coach E.J. McConkie, Cliff Strickland. Front row, left to right, Fawn Spradlin, Tricia Guntly, Joyce Johnson, Dawn Puhr, Denise Orocchi, Sue Sears, Tonya Moore, Diane Anderson.

NATIONAL COLLEGIATE AHTLETIC ASSOCIATION
NATIONAL CHAMPIONS (1982-1997)

DIVISION I

YEAR	CHAMPION	COACH	RUNNER-UP
1982	UCLA	Coach Sharron Backus	Fresno State
1983	Texas A&M	Coach Bob Brock	Cal State Fullerton
1984	UCLA	Coach Sharron Backus	Texas A&M
1985	UCLA	Coach Sharron Backus	Nebraska
1986	Cal State Fullerton	Coach Judi Garman	Texas A&M
1987	Texas A&M	Coach Bob Brock	UCLA
1988	UCLA	Coach Sharron Backus	Fresno State
1989	UCLA	Coach Sharron Backus	Fresno State
1990	UCLA	Coach Sharron Backus	Fresno State
1991	Arizona	Coach Mike Candrea	UCLA
1992	UCLA	Coach Sharron Backus	Arizona
1993	Arizona	Coach Mike Candrea	UCLA
1994	Arizona	Coach Mike Candrea	Cal State Northridge
1995	VACATED due to NCAA violations		Arizona
1996	Arizona	Coach Mike Candrea	Washington
1997	Arizona	Coach Mike Candrea	UCLA

DIVISION II

YEAR	CHAMPION	COACH	RUNNER-UP
1982	Sam Houston State	Coach Wayne Dagle	Cal State Northridge
1983	Cal State Northridge	Coach Gary Torgeson	Sam Houston State
1984	Cal State Northridge	Coach Gary Torgeson	Akron
1985	Cal State Northridge	Coach Gary Torgeson	Akron
1986	Stephen F. Austin State	Coach Dianne Baker	Cal State Northridge
1987	Cal State Northridge	Coach Gary Torgeson	Florida Southern
1988	Cal State Bakersfield	Coach Kathy Welter	Lock Haven
1989	Cal State Bakersfield	Coach Kathy Welter	Cal State Sacramento
1990	Cal State Bakersfield	Coach Kathy Welter	Cal State Northridge
1991	Augustana (SD)	Coach Sandy Jerstad	Bloomsburg
1992	Missouri Southern State	Coach Pat Lipira	Cal State Hayward
1993	Florida Southern	Coach Chris Bellotto	Augustana
1994	Merrimack	Coach Michele Myslinski	Humboldt State
1995	Kennesaw State	Coach Scott Whitlock	Bloomsburg
1996	Kennesaw State	Coach Scott Whitlock	Nebraska-Omaha
1997	California (PA)	Coach Rick Bertagnolli	Wisconsin-Parkside

DIVISION III

YEAR	CHAMPION	COACH	RUNNER-UP
1982	Eastern Connecticut State	Coach Clyde Washburne	Trenton State

NCAA NATIONAL CHAMPIONSHIP TEAMS CONTINUED ...

1983	Trenton State	Coach June Walker	Buena Vista
1984	Buena Vista	Coach Marge Willadsen	Trenton State
1985	Eastern Connecticut State	Coach Clyde Washburne	Trenton State
1986	Eastern Connecticut State	Coach Clyde Washburne	Central (Iowa)
1987	Trenton State	Coach June Walker	Wisconsin-Whitewater
1988	Central (Iowa)	Coach George Wares	Allegheny
1989	Trenton State	Coach June Walker	Eastern Connecticut State
1990	Eastern Connecticut State	Coach Jeff Anderson	Trenton State
1991	Central (Iowa)	Coach George Wares	Eastern Connecticut State
1992	Trenton State	Coach June Walker	Buena Vista
1993	Central (Iowa)	Coach George Wares	Trenton State
1994	Trenton State	Coach June Walker	Bridgewater (Mass.)
1995	Chapman	Coach Lisle Lloyd	Trenton State
1996	Trenton State	Coach Sally Miller	Chapman
1997	Simpson	Coach Henry Christowski	Montclair State

NCAA NATIONAL CHAMPIONSHIP TEAM RECORDS (1982-1997)

DIVISION I
FIELDING

Highest Fielding Percentage, Series — 1.000; UCLA, 1988 (six games); Texas A&M, 1988 (three games); Louisiana Tech, 1986 (two games); UCLA, 1982 (five games).

Most Putouts, Game — 75; Texas A&M (1) vs. Cal Poly Pomona (0) (25 inn.), May 24, 1984.

Most Putouts, Both Teams, Game — 148; Texas A&M (1) vs. Cal Poly Pomona (0) (25 inn.), May 24, 1984 (75-73).

Most Assists, Game — 37; Cal Poly Pomona (0) vs. Texas A&M (1) (25 inn.), May 24, 1984.

Most Assists, Both Teams, Game — 68; Texas A&M (1) vs. Cal Poly Pomona (0) (25 inn.), May 24, 1984 (31-37).

Most Errors, Game — 7; Cal Poly Pomona (0) vs. UCLA (9), May 26, 1989; Fresno State (1) vs. UCLA (6), May 27, 1988; Iowa (9) vs. Michigan (7) (14 inn.), May 27, 1995.

Most Errors, Series — 14; Cal State Fullerton, 1983 (five games); Iowa, 1995 (four games).

Most Errors, Both Teams, Game — 11; Iowa (9) vs. Michigan (7) (14 inn.), May 27, 1995 (7-4).

Most Double Plays, Game — 3; Nebraska (0) vs. UCLA (3), May 22, 1987; Cal State Fullerton (1) vs. Texas A&M (2) (13 inn.), May 22, 1987.

Most Double Plays, Series — 4; Cal State Fullerton, 1987 (four games).

Most Double Plays, Both Teams, Game — 4; Nebraska (0) vs. UCLA (3), May 22, 1987 (3-1); Cal State Fullerton (1) vs. Texas A&M (2) (13 inn.), May 22, 1987 (1-3); UCLA (2) vs. South Carolina (1) (17 inn.), May 28, 1983 (2-2).

BATTING

Highest Batting Average, Series — .394; Arizona, 1995 (four games: 41 hits, 104 at bats).

Most At Bats, Game — 88; Texas A&M (1) vs. Cal Poly Pomona (0) (25 inn.), May 24, 1984.

Most At Bats, Series — 254; Texas A&M, 1984 (six games).

Most At Bats, Both Teams, Game — 174; Texas A&M (1) vs. Cal Poly Pomona (0) (25 inn.), May 24, 1984 (88-86).

Most Runs Scored, Game — 12; Arizona vs. Fresno State (0) (five inn.), May 25, 1989.

Most Runs Scored, Series — 31; UCLA, 1992 (five games).

Most Runs Scored, Both Teams, Game — 16; Iowa

NCAA DIVISION I TEAM RECORDS CONTINUED ...

(9) vs. Michigan (7) (14 inn.), May 27, 1995; Washington (9) vs. California (7), May 24, 1996.

Most Runs Scored, One Inning — 9; UCLA (11) vs. Massachusetts (1) (five inn.), May 24, 1992 (fifth inning).

Most Hits, Game — 17; Iowa (9) vs. Michigan (7) (14 inn.), May 27, 1995.

Most Hits, Series — 47; Washington, 1996 (four games).

Most Hits, Both Teams, Game — 31; Iowa (9) vs. Michigan (7) (14 inn.), May 27, 1995 (17-14).

Most Runs Batted In, Game — 11; Arizona (12) vs. Fresno State (0) (5 inn.), May 25, 1989.

Most Runs Batted In, Both Teams, Game — 12; Iowa (9) vs. Michigan (7) (14 inn.), May 27, 1995 (6-6).

Most Bases on Balls, Game — 8; Creighton (4) vs. Louisiana Tech (3) (13 inn.), May 22, 1986.

Most Bases on Balls, Both Teams, Game — 13; Fresno State (1) vs. Cal Poly Pomona (0) (12 inn.), May 26, 1984 (6-7).

Most Strikeouts, Game — 20; Oklahoma State (1) vs. UCLA (2), May 27, 1982.

Most Strikeouts Both Teams, Game — 28; UCLA (1) vs. Northwestern (0) (9 inn.), May 26, 1984 (11-17); Texas A&M (1) vs. UCLA (0) (14 inn.), May 29, 1983 (11-17).

Most Doubles, Game — 4; Cal State Fullerton (5) vs. Iowa (6) (nine inn.), May 27, 1995.

Most Doubles, Both Teams, Game — 5; Iowa (9) vs. Michigan (7) (14 inn.), May 27, 1995 (2-3).

Most Triples, Game — 2; Florida State (4) vs. UNLV (1), May 26, 1990; Cal State Fullerton (3) vs. Indiana (1) (8 inn.), May 24, 1986.

Most Triples, Both Teams, Game — 2; Florida State (4) vs. UNLV (1), May 26, 1990 (2-0); Cal State Fullerton (3) vs. Indiana (1) (eight inn.), May 24, 1986 (2-0).

Most Home Runs, Game — 2; by several teams (most recent: UCLA [2] vs. Arizona [10], May 26, 1997; Fresno State [3] vs. Arizona [0], May 25, 1997; Arizona [6] vs. Fresno State [3], May 25, 1997; UCLA [4] vs. Washington [3], May 25, 1997; Iowa [6] vs. Fresno State [7], May 24, '97).

Most Home Runs, Both Teams, Game — 3; UCLA (11) vs. Massachusetts (1) (five inn.), May 24, 1992 (2-1); UCLA (6) vs. Fresno State (1), May 27, 1988 (2-1); *UCLA (2) vs. Iowa (1), May 26, 1995 (2-1); Arizona (6) vs. Fresno State (3), May 25, 1997. *Vacated

Most Stolen Bases, Game — 4; Pacific (Cal.) (1) vs. Missouri (0) (12 inn.), May 26, 1983; Arizona (8) vs. UNLV (0) (six inn.), May 28, 1995; Washington (9) vs. California (7), May 24, 1996 (4-2).

Most Stolen Bases, Both Teams, Game — 6; Washington (9) vs. California (7), May 24, 1996.

Most Total Bases, Game — 20; UCLA (11) vs. Massachusetts (1) (five Inn.), May 24, 1992; Arizona (10) vs. Iowa (2) (six inn.), May 26, 1996.

Most Total Bases, Both Teams, Game — 39; Iowa (9) vs. Michigan (7) (14 inn.), May 27, 1995.

Most Sacrifice Hits, Game — 5; UCLA (2) vs. South Carolina (1) (17 inn.), May 23, 1983.

Most Sacrifice Hits, Both Teams, Game — 8; Arizona (1) vs. Oklahoma State (0) (nine inn.), May 30, 1993 (3-5); Arizona (1) vs. UNLV (0) (13 inn.), May 23, 1991 (4-4).

Most Sacrifice Flies, Game — 2; Cal State Northridge (5) vs. Utah (1), May 27, 1994; Oklahoma State (5) vs. Florida State (2), May 27, 1993; Arizona (4) vs. Cal Poly Pomona (1), May 27, 1988; UCLA (7) vs. Michigan (3), May 24, 1997.

Most Sacrifice Flies, Both Teams, Game — 2; by several teams (most recent: UCLA [7] vs. Michigan [3], May 24, 1997 [2-0]).

PITCHING

Most Innings Pitched, Series — 72.2; Texas A&M, 1984 (six games).

Most Runs Allowed, Series — 19; Iowa, 1995 (four games).

Most Earned Runs Allowed, Series — 16; UCLA, 1997 (six games).

Lowest Earned Run Average, Series — 0.00; Arizona, 1994 (four games); Utah State, 1984 (two games).

DIVISION II
FIELDING
Most Errors, Game — 7; Truman State (1) vs. Stephen F. Austin (6), May 10, 1985.

Most Errors, Both Teams, Game — 10; Sacred Heart (6) vs. New Haven (5), May 12, 1995 (4-6).

Most Double Plays, Game — 3; Bloomsburg (3) vs. Merrimack (2), May 15, 1993; UC Davis (6) vs. Humboldt State (0), May 9, 1997.

Most Double Plays, Both Teams, Game — 3; Missouri Southern State (1) vs. Cal State Hayward (0), May 17, 1992 (2-1); Bloomsburg (3) vs. Merrimack (2), May 15, 1993 (3-0); Kutztown (2) vs. California (PA) (0), May 12, 1995 (1-2); UC Davis (6) vs. Humboldt State (0), May 9, 1997.

BATTING
Most At Bats, Game — 69; Sacred Heart (1) vs. Bloomsburg (0), May 11, 1984.

Most At Bats, Both Teams, Game — 129; Sacred Heart (1) vs. Bloomsburg (0), May 11, 1984 (69-60).

Most Runs, Game — 14; Augustana (SD) vs. Valdosta State (0), May 16, 1993.

Most Runs, Both Teams, Game — 17; American International (9) vs. Sacred Heart (8), May 15, 1993.

Most Runs, One Inning, Game — 9; Augustana (SD) (14) vs. Valdosta State (0), fourth inning, May 16, 1993.

Most Hits, Game — 20; Florida Southern (11) vs. Augustana (SD) (5), May 23, 1993.

Most Hits, Both Teams — 32; Kennesaw State (3) vs. Columbus State (1), May 9, 1997.

Most Doubles, Game — 5; Bloomsburg (3) vs. Merrimack (2), May 15, 1993; New Haven (5) vs. Merrimack (2), May 10, 1996; Kennesaw State (8) vs. Columbus (3), May 10, 1996.

Most Triples, Game — 2; Cal State Northridge (1) vs. Sam Houston State (0), May 20, 1983; Wayne State (Mich.) (4) vs. Cal State Chico (1), May 11, 1984; SIU-Edwardsville (2) vs. Augustana (SD) (5), May 12, 1990; Kennesaw

State (7) vs. Carson-Newman (0), May 11, 1996; American International (4) vs. LIU-C.W. Post (1), May 9, 1997; Nebraska-Omaha (3) vs. Augustana (SD) (1), May 10, 1997.

Most Home Runs, Game — 4; Augustana (SD) (8) vs. Mankato State (6), May 9, 1997.

Most Total Bases, Game — 27; Augustana (SD) (14) vs. Valdosta State (0), May 16, 1993.

Most Total Bases, Both Teams — 39; Florida Southern (11) vs. Augustana (SD) (5), May 23, 1993 (25-14).

Most Stolen Bases, Game — 5; Florida Southern (2) vs. Barry (0), May 10, 1996.

DIVISION III
FIELDING
Most Errors, Game — 7; by five teams (most recent: North Adams State [4] vs. Rowan [5] [nine inn.], May 13, 1995).

Most Errors, Both Teams, Game — 11; Wisconsin-Whitewater (8) vs. Concordia (Ill.) (5), May 11, 1984 (5-6); Ithaca (4) vs. Cortland State (6), May 10, 1985 (6-5); Christopher Newport (6) vs. William Patterson (11), May 14, 1993 (7-4).

Most Double Plays, Game — 3; Montclair State (3) vs. Rowan (9), May 13, 1994; Wisconsin-River Falls (2) vs. Simpson (0), May 13, 1994; Buena Vista (3) vs. Simpson (2) (13 inn.), May 14, 1995.

Most Double Plays, Both Teams, Game — 3; by several teams (most recent: Buena Vista [3] vs. Simpson [2] [13 inn.], May 14, 1995 [3-0]).

BATTING
Most At Bats, Game — 56; Buena Vista (4) vs. Sonoma State (1), May 13, 1983.

Most At Bats, Both Teams, Game — 110; Buena Vista (4) vs. Sonoma State (1), May 13, 1983.

Most Runs, Game — 18; College of New Jersey vs. Kean (1) (five inn.), May 12, 1995.

Most Runs, Both Teams, Game — 19; Eastern Connecticut State (15) vs. Queens (NY) (4), May 15, 1982; Montclair State (13) vs. Cortland State (6), May 12, 1984; Trenton State (18) vs. Kean (1) (five inn.), May 12, 1995;

NCAA DIVISION III RECORDS CONTINUED ...

Salisbury State (10) vs. Montclair State (9), May 10, 1997.

Most Runs, One Inning, Game — 11; Eastern Connecticut State (15) vs. Queens (NY) (4), third inning, May 15, 1982; Aurora (11) vs. Simpson (5), fifth inning, May 11, 1990.

Most Hits, Game — 18; Adrian (9) vs. Aurora (8), May 14, 1993; Trenton State (14) vs. Allegheny (4), May 14, 1994; Trenton State (18) vs. Kean (1) (five innings), May 12, 1995.

Most Hits, Both Teams, Games — 30; Adrian (9) vs. Aurora (8), May 14, 1993 (18-12).

Most Doubles, Game — 6; Salisbury State (11) vs. Rowan (0), May 9, 1997.

Most Triples, Game — 3; Trenton State (10) vs. Wilkes (2), May 14, 1982; Wisconsin-Whitewater (5) vs. Aurora (2), May 11, 1985; Illinois-Benedictine (5) vs. Rowan (4), May 22, 1993.

Most Home Runs, Game — 5; Trenton State (18) vs. Kean (1) (five inn.), May 12, 1995.

NCAA NATIONAL CHAMPIONSHIP INDIVIDUAL RECORDS (1982-1997)

DIVISION I

FIELDING

Most Putouts, Game — 35; Laura Myers, Cal Poly Pomona (0) vs. Texas A&M (1) (25 inn.), May 24, 1984.

Most Assists, Game — 13; Rhonda Wheatley, Cal Poly Pomona (0) vs. Texas A&M (1) (25 inn.), May 24, 1984.

Most Errors, Game — 4; Rhonda Wheatley, Cal Poly Pomona (6) vs. Northwestern (3), May 23, 1985.

BATTING

(Minimum 10 at bats for series records)

Highest Batting Average, Series — .750; Leah O'Brien, Arizona, 1994 (9 hits, 12 at bats.).

Most At Bats, Game — 11; Laura Myers, Cal Poly Pomona (0) vs. Texas A&M (1) (25 inn.), May 24, 1984; Cindy Foster, Texas A&M (1) vs. Cal Poly Pomona (0), May 24, 1984; Shawn Andaya, Texas A&M (1) vs. Cal Poly Pomona (0), May 24, 1984.

Most At Bats, Series — 31; Judy Trussell, Texas A&M, 1984.

Most Runs Scored, Game — 4; Lorraine Maynez, UCLA (9) vs. Cal Poly Pomona (0), May 26, 1989.

Most Runs Scored, Series — 6; Lisa Fernandez, UCLA, 1992; Yvonne Gutierrez, UCLA, 1992; Lorraine Maynez, UCLA, 1989; Alison Johnsen,

Arizona, 1997.

Most Hits, Game — 5; Kellyn Tate, Michigan (7) vs. Iowa (9) (14 inn.), May 27, 1995; Brandi Macias, Iowa (9) vs. Michigan (7) (14 inn.), May 27, 1995.

Most Hits, Series — 10; Lorraine Maynez, UCLA, 1989.

Most Runs Batted In, Game — 4; Tammy Utley, Iowa (6) vs. Fresno St. (7), May 24, 1997; *Tanya Harding, UCLA (5) vs. Iowa (0), May 25, 1995; Yvonne Gutierrez, UCLA (11) vs. Massachusetts (1) (five inn.), May 24, 1992; Nicki Dennis, Arizona (12) vs. Fresno St. (0) (five inn.), May 25, 1989; Jennifer Simm, UCLA (6) vs. Utah St. (0), May 23, 1984. *Vacated.

Most Runs Batted In, Series — 8; Yvonne Gutierrez, UCLA, 1992.

Most Bases on Balls, Game*— 3; Jenny Dalton, Arizona (5) vs. Iowa (2), May 23, 1996; Leanne Rosser, Washington (5) vs. Iowa (1), May 23, 1997.

Most Strikeouts, Game* — 4; Chris Dimer, South Carolina (1) vs. UCLA (2) (17 inn.), May 28, 1983; Gay McNutt, Texas A&M (1) vs. UCLA (0) (14 inn.), May 29, 1983; Mary Schwind, Texas A&M (1) vs. UCLA (0) (14 inn.), May 29, 1983; Kim Kirk, Cal State Fullerton (0) vs. Texas A&M (2) (12 inn.), May 29, 1983.

*Statistics from the 1982 and 1984 finals do not include number of bases on balls and strikeouts

NCAA DIVISION I RECORDS CONTINUED ...

per individual; therefore, statistics from those years are not included in these categories.

Most Doubles, Game — 2; by several players (most recent: Alison Johnsen, Arizona [2] vs. Massachusetts [1], May, 22, 1997).

Most Doubles, Series — 3; Shauna Wattenberg, UCLA, 1987; Jennifer Simm, UCLA, 1985.

Most Triples, Game — 1; by several players (most recent: Julie Marshall, UCLA [7] vs. Michigan [3], May 24, 1997; Christy Hebert, Iowa [1] vs. Washington [5], May 23, 1997; Leanne Rosser, Washington [6] vs. South Caro. [0], May 22, 1997).

Most Triples, Series — 2; Rina Foster, Cal State Fullerton, 1986; Patti Holthaus, Texas A&M, 1983.

Most Home Runs, Game — 2; Yvonne Gutierrez, UCLA (11) vs. Massachusetts (1) (five inns.), May 24, 1992.

Most Home Runs, Series — 3; Yvonne Gutierrez, UCLA, 1992; Kerry Dienelt, UCLA, 1989.

Most Stolen Bases, Game — 3; Leslie Barton, Florida State (2) vs. Massachusetts (4), May 23, 1992.

Most Stolen Bases, Series — 4; Judy Trussell, Texas A&M, 1984; Alison Johnsen, Arizona, 1996.

Most Total Bases, Game — 8; Yvonne Gutierrez, UCLA (11) vs. Massachusetts (1) (five inn.), May 24, 1982.

Most Sacrifice Hits, Game — 2; by several players (most recent: Katie Swan, Arizona [2] vs. Massachusetts [1], May 22, 1997; Debbie Bilbao, Iowa [3] vs. Michigan [2], May 22, 1997).

Most Sacrifice Flies, Game — 1; by several players (most recent: five plays in 1997).

PITCHING

(Series records minimum 10.0 innings pitched)

Lowest Earned Run Average, Series — 0.00; by several players (most recent: Jenny McMahon, Iowa, 1995).

Most Wins, Series — 5; Shawn Andaya, Texas A&M, 1987; Debbie Doom, UCLA, 1982.

Most Complete Games, Series — 6; Lisa Fernandez, UCLA, 1993 (4-2); Shawn Andaya, Texas A&M, 1987 (5-1).

Most Innings Pitched, Game — 25; Shawn Andaya, Texas A&M (1) vs. Cal Poly Pomona (0) (25 inn.), May 24, 1984.

Most Innings Pitched, Series — 52.0; Shawn Andaya, Texas A&M, 1984.

Most Hits Allowed, Game — 13; Maureen Brady, Fresno St. (0) vs. Arizona (3), May 27, 1994.

Most Hits Allowed, Series — 37; Christa Williams, UCLA, 1997.

Fewest Hits Allowed, Game — 0; by several players (most recent: Cheryl Longeway, USL [5] vs. Michigan [0], May 26, 1995; *Tanya Harding, UCLA [3] vs. USL [0], May 26, 1995). *(Minimum 7.0 Innings Pitched) *Vacated.*

Fewest Hits Allowed, Series — 0; Tracy Compton, UCLA, 1984.

Most Runs Allowed, Game — 10; Robyn Burgess, California (0) vs. UCLA (10) (five inn.), May 23, 1992; Christa Williams, UCLA (2) vs. Arizona (10) (five inn.), May 26, 1997.

Most Runs Allowed, Series — 18; Debbie Bilbao, Iowa, 1995.

Fewest Runs Allowed, Game — 0; by many players (six times in 1997). *(Minimum 7.0 innings pitched)*

Fewest Runs Allowed, Series — 0; by several players (most recent: Lisa Fernandez, UCLA, 1992; Susie Parra, Arizona, 1992).

Most Earned Runs Allowed, Game — 8; Christa Williams, UCLA (2) vs. Arizona (10), May 26, 1997.

Most Earned Runs Allowed, Series — 15; Christa Williams, UCLA, 1997 (45 inn.)

Fewest Earned Runs Allowed, Game — 0; by many players (seven times in 1997). *(Minimum 7.0 innings pitched)*

Fewest Earned Runs Allowed, Series — 0; by several players (most recent: Jenny McMahon, Iowa, 1995).

<u>NCAA DIVISION I RECORDS CONTINUED ...</u>

Most Bases on Balls, Game — 7; Stacey Johnson, Louisiana Tech (3) vs. Creighton (4) (13 inn.), May 22, 1986.

Most Bases on Balls, Series — 15; Christa Williams, UCLA, 1997.

Fewest Bases on Balls Allowed, Game — 0; by many players (four times in 1997). (Minimum *7.0 innings pitched*)

Fewest Bases on Balls Allowed, Series — 0; by several players (most recent: Susie Parra, Arizona, 1992; Mary Letourneau, Long Beach State, 1992).

Most Strikeouts, Game — 20; Debbie Doom, UCLA (2) vs. Oklahoma State (1) (13 inn.), May 27, 1982.

Most Strikeouts, Series — 62, Debbie Doom, UCLA, 1982.

DIVISION II
FIELDING

Most Putouts, Game — 30; Tracy Gelsinger, Sacred Heart (1) vs. Bloomsburg (0), May 11, 1984.

Most Assists, Game — 16; Kathy Behan, Bloomsburg (0) vs. Sacred Heart (1), May 11, 1984.

Most Errors, Game — 4; Kathy Kopacz, Sacred Heart (0) vs. Cal State Northridge (1), April 28, 1982.

BATTING

Most At Bats, Game — 10; Elizabeth Luckie, Sacred Heart (1) vs. Bloomsburg (0), May 11, 1984.

Most Runs, Game — 4; Jessie Johnson, Wisconsin-Parkside (12) vs. Wayne State (Mich.) (3), May 10, 1996.

Most Hits, Game — 5; Caren Napolitano, Columbus State (1) vs. Kennesaw State (3), May 9, 1997.

Most Doubles, Game — 2; by many players.

Most Triples, Game — 1; by several players.

Most Home Runs, Game — 2; Janelle Tieken,

Augustana (SD) (14) vs. Valdosta State (0), May 16, 1993; Apple Gomez, Humboldt State (9) vs. UC Davis (2), May 13, 1995; Allison Temple, Emporia State (7) vs. Nebraska-Kearney (8), May 10, 1996; Becky Mancuso, Augustana (SD) (8) vs. Mankato State (6), May 9, 1997; Jamie Sortino, Shippensburg (4) vs. California (Pa.) (2), May 9, 1997.

Most Runs Batted In, Game — 5; Apple Gomez, Humboldt State (9) vs. UC Davis (2), May 13, 1995.

Most Total Bases — 8; Jana Baringer, Wayne State (Mich.) (4) vs. Cal State Chico (1), May 11, 1984; Raffaella Paparo, Merrimack (8) vs. American Int'l (0), May 15, 1993; Janelle Tieken, Augustana (SD) (14) vs. Valdosta State (0), May 16, 1993; Apple Gomez, Humboldt State (9) vs. UC Davis (2), May 13, 1995; Becky Mancuso, Augustana (SD) (8) vs. Mankato State (6), May 9, 1997; Jamie Sortino, Shippensburg (4) vs. California (Pa.) (2), May 9, 1997.

Most Stolen Bases, Game — 2; by many players.

PITCHING

Most Innings Pitched, Game — 23; Debbie Tidy, Sacred Heart (1) vs. Bloomsburg (0), May 11, 1984.

Most Strikeouts, Game — 23; Kathy Slaten, Cal State Northridge (1) vs. Cal State Chico (0), May 14, 1983.

Most Bases on Balls — 7; Kathy Slaten, Cal State Northridge (0) vs. Stephen F. Austin (2), May 16, 1986; Mindi Prince, Morningside (2) vs. Nebraska-Omaha (4), May 12, 1995.

Most No-Hit Games, Championship — 2; Kathy Slaten, Cal State Northridge (4) vs. Cal State Chico (0), May 13, 1983, and Cal State Northridge (4) vs. Stephen F. Austin (0), May 21, 1983.

DIVISION III
FIELDING

Most Putouts, Game — 26; Holly Stevens, Simpson (2) vs. Buena Vista (3) (13 inn.), May

NCAA DIVISION III RECORDS CONTINUED ...

14, 1995.

Most Assists, Game — 11; Jodie Hemmingsen, Luther (0) vs. Buena Vista (2), May 8, 1992; Laurie Machuga, Allegheny (2) vs. Muskingum (1), May 12, 1995.

Most Errors, Game — 4; Kathy Wagner, Buffalo (2) vs. Ithaca (12), May 10, 1985.

BATTING

Most At Bats, Game — 7; by several players.

Most Runs, Game — 4; Paige Cosgrove, Simpson (5) vs. Cal Lutheran (4), May 14, 1995; Michelle Carlson, Trenton State (18) vs. Kean (1) (five inn.), May 12, 1995.

Most Hits, Game — 6; Holly Stevens, Simpson (2) vs. Buena Vista (3) (13 inn.), May 14, 1995.

Most Doubles, Game — 3; Tara Dickert, Allegheny (10) vs. Muskingum (3), May 15, 1993; Jen Dodson, Salisbury State (11) vs. Rowan (0) May 9, 1997.

Most Triples, Game — 2; Barb Arnold, UC San Diego (6) vs. Calvin (1), May 10, 1985; Amy Trench, Benedictine (Ill.) (5) vs. Rowan (4), May 22, 1993; Megan Coe, Buena Vista (6) vs. Wartburg (4), May 15, 1994.

Most Home Runs — 3; Michelle Carlson, Trenton State (18) vs. Kean (1) (five inn.) May 12, 1995; Anita DeFeo, Trenton State (9) vs. Brockport State (5), May 9, 1997.

Most Runs Batted In, Game — 6; Lynn Rocheleau, Eastern Conn. State (12) vs. Montclair State (1), May 21, 1988.

Most Total Bases, Game — 13; Michelle Carlson, Trenton State (18) vs. Kean (1) (five inn.), May 21, 1995.

Most Stolen Bases, Game — 3; by five players (most recent: Robin Selbst, Col. of New Jersey [10] vs. Kean [1] [five inn.], May 13, 1995; Jennifer Hoselton, Ithaca [2] vs. North Adams State [0], May 12, 1995).

PITCHING

Most Innings Pitched, Game — 16; Julie Hoffman, Alma (3) vs. Central (Iowa) (4), May 19, 1994.

Most Strikeouts, Game — 20; Christy Guidorizzi, Chapman (5) vs. Allegheny (0), May 19, 1995.

Most Bases on Balls, Game — 11; Patti Russell, Benedictine (Ill.) (4) vs. Concordia (Ill.) (2), May 11, 1984; Robyn Baron, Montclair St. (5) vs. Trenton State (4), May 12, 1985.

Most No-Hit Games, Championship — 1; Lisa Kirk, Eastern Conn. State (1) vs. Allegheny (0), May 21, 1983; Christia Mohan, Eastern Conn. State (4) vs. Wisconsin-Whitewater (0), May 16, 1987; Jona Tolomeo, Montclair State (3) vs. William Paterson (0), May 11, 1990; Christy Guidorizzi, Chapman (6) vs. Calvin (0), May 11, 1996; Kelly Schade, Simpson (6) vs. Cal Lutheran (0), May 11, 1996.

NAIA TEAM CHAMPIONS (1981-1997)

YEAR	CHAMPION	COACH	RUNNER-UP
1981	Sam Houston State	Coach Wayne Daigle	Emporia State
1982	Missouri Western	Coach Rhesa Sumrell	St. Francis (IL)
1983	Emporia State (KS)	Coach Betty Walters	Kearney State (NE)
1984	Emporia State (KS)	Coach Betty Walters	Quincy State (IL)
1985	Quincy State (IL)	Coach Sharlene Peter	Washburn (KS)
1986	St. Mary's (IL)	Coach Jim Zeleznak	Oklahoma City
1987	Kearney State (NE)	Coach Brad Horky	Francis Marion (SC)
1988	Pacific Lutheran (WA)	Coach Ralph Weekly	Minnesota-Duluth
1989	Saginaw Valley State (MI)	Coach Art Tolfree	Kearney State (NE)
1990	Kearney State (NE)	Coach Dan Simmons	Pacific Lutheran (WA)
1991	Hawaii Loa	Coach Howard Okita	Puget Sound (WA)
1992	Pacific Lutheran (WA)	Coach Ralph Weekly	Kennesaw State (GA)
1993	West Florida	Coaches Doug Palmer/Tami Cyr	Oklahoma City
1994	Oklahoma City	Coach Phil McSpadden	Athens State (AL)
1995	Oklahoma City	Coach Phil McSpadden	Puget Sound (WA)
1996	Oklahoma City	Coach Phil McSpadden	Shawnee State (OH)
1997	Oklahoma City	Coach Phil McSpadden	Athens State (AL)

NAIA NATIONAL CHAMPIONSHIP TEAM RECORDS (1981-1997)

BATTING

Most At Bats, Game — 56; Southern Utah vs. Mesa (CO) (14 inn.), 1981.

Most At Bats, Tournament — 245; Francis Marion (SC), 1987.

Most Runs Scored, Game — 18; Winthrop (SC) vs. Beaver (PA), 1985.

Most Runs Scored, Tournament — 45; Oklahoma City, 1997.

Most Hits, Game — 20; Winthrop (SC) vs. Wayne State (NE), 1983.

Most Hits, Tournament — 81; Oklahoma City, 1993.

Most RBI's, Game — 14; Erskine (SC) vs. Wiley (TX), 1981.

Most RBI's, Tournament — 35; Oklahoma City, 1993; Oklahoma City, 1996.

Most Walks, Game — 15; Sam Houston State (TX) vs. Lincoln Memorial (TN), 1981.

Most Walks, Tournament — 28; Erskine (SC), 1981.

Most Stolen Bases, Game — 8; Tarkio (MO) vs. Georgian Court (NJ), 1988.

Most Stolen Bases, Tournament — 15; Saginaw Valley (MI), 1988.

Most Singles, Game — 16; IUPU-Indianapolis vs. Kearney State (NE), 1985.

Most Singles, Tournament — 71; Oklahoma City, 1993.

Most Doubles, Game — 5; Winthrop (SC) vs. Winona State (MN), 1983.

Most Doubles — 12; Shawnee State (OH), 1996.

Most Triples, Game — 4; Winthrop (SC) vs. Beaver (PA), 1985.

Most Triples — 6; Winthrop (SC), 1985.

Most Home Runs, Game — 3; Oklahoma City vs. Mobile (AL), 1997.

Most Home Runs, Tournament — 6; Oklahoma City, 1996; Athens State (AL), 1994.

Most Total Bases, Game — 31; Tusculum (TN) vs. St. Rose (NY), 1991.

Most Total Bases, Tournament — 97; Oklahoma City, 1993.

Highest Batting Average, Tournament — .359;

NAIA TEAM RECORDS CONTINUED ...

Mobile (AL), 1995 (28 of 78).

Lowest Batting Average, Tournament — .029; Beaver (PA), 1995 (1 of 34).

PITCHING

Most Hits Allowed, Game — 20; Wayne State (NE), vs. Winthrop (SC), 1983.

Most Hits Allowed, Tournament — 55; Quincy (IL), 1984 (8 games).

Most Earned Runs Allowed, Game — 14; Wiley (TX) vs. Erskine (SC), 1981.

Most Earned Runs Allowed, Tournament — 27; Francis Marion (SC), 1987 (8 games).

Most Strikeouts, Game — 19; Oklahoma City vs. Davis & Elkins (WV), 1989.

Most Strikeouts, Tournament — 65; St. Mary's (TX), 1986 (8 games).

Most Walks, Game — 15; Lincoln Memorial (TN) vs. Sam Houston State (TX), 1981.

Most Walks, Tournament — 22; St. Mary's (TX), 1986 (8 games).

Lowest Earned Run Average — 0.00; Emporia State (KS), 1984; 0.00, Kearney State (NE), 1987.

Fewest Hits Allowed, Tournament — 22; St. Mary's (TX), 1986 (8 games).

Fewest Walks, Tournament — 1; Quincy (IL), 1984.

Fewest Earned Runs Allowed, Tournament — 4; St. Mary's (TX), 1986 (8 games).

Fewest Strikeouts, Tournament — 59; Quincy (IL), 1984 (8 games).

Most Shutouts, Tournament — 5; Emporia State (KS), 1984.

Most Consecutive Scoreless Innings — 38; Emporia State (KS), 1984.

NAIA NATIONAL CHAMPIONSHIP INDIVIDUAL RECORDS (1981-1997)

BATTING

Most At Bats, Game —7; by several individuals.

Most At Bats, Tournament — 34; Dawn Beard, Athens State (AL), 1997.

Most Runs, Game — 4; Chris Razmie, Southern Utah vs. Concordia (NY), 1984; Laura Laurenzi, Wisconsin-Parkside vs. Lincoln Memorial (TN), 1981.

Most Runs, Tournament — 11; Tracey Mosley, Oklahoma City, 1993.

Most Hits, Game — 4; by several individuals.

Most Hits, Tournament — 15;Tracey Mosley, Oklahoma City, 1993.

Most RBIs, Game — 7; Jennifer Smith, Southern Utah vs. Concordia (NY), 1994.

Most RBIs, Tournament — 10; Tracey Mosley, Oklahoma City, 1993.

Most Stolen Bases, Game — 4; Dana Dawson, Tarkio (MO) vs. Georgian Court (NJ), 1988.

Most Stolen Bases, Tournament — 5; Shannon Tigner, St. Mary's (TX), 1989; Kari Meyer, Saginaw Valley (MI), 1989; Dana Dawson, Tarkio (MO),1988; Milyse Larkin, St. Mary's (TX), 1986.

Most Walks — 6; Freda Franklin, Puget Sound (WA), 1995.

Most Singles, Tournament — 12; Tracey Mosley, Oklahoma City, 1993.

Most Doubles, Game — 2; by several individuals.

Most Doubles, Tournament — 4; Jessica Balsavich, Athens State (AL), 1997; Tiffany Shanks, Shawnee (OH), 1996; Kristi Anderson, Francis Marion (SC), 1987; Renee Livell, Missouri Southern, 1986; Vicki Levensky, IUPU-Indianapolis, 1986

Most Triples, Game — 2; Kathy Higgins, Emporia State (KS) vs. Pacific (OR), 1984; Teresa Ryans, Tusculum (TN) vs. Missouri Western, 1984.

Most Triples, Tournament— 3; Sherrie Mattlews, Quincy (IL), 1985.

Most Home Runs, Game — 2; Bobbi Towers, Oklahoma City, vs. Mobile (AL), 1997.

Most Home Runs, Tournament — 3; Kim White, Shawnee State (OH), 1996.

Most Total Bases, Game — 8; Bobbi Towers, Oklahoma City, 1997.

NAIA INDIVIDUAL RECORDS CONTINUED ...

Most Total Bases, Tournament — 20; Tracey Mosley, Oklahoma City, 1993.
Highest Batting Average, Tournament —.692; Stacy Araki, Hawaii-Loa, 1991.

PITCHING
Fewest Hits Allowed, Game — 0; by several individuals.
Fewest Hits Allowed, Tournament — 5; Cheryl Shelby, Missouri Southern, 1986 (22 innings).
Most Hits Allowed, Game — 16; Phyllis DeBuhr, Kearney State (NE) vs. IUPU-Indianapolis, 1985.
Most Earned Runs Allowed, Game — 12; Phyllis DeBuhr, Kearney State (NE) vs. IUPU-Indianapolis, 1985.
Fewest Earned Runs Allowed, Tournament — 0; by several individuals (minimum of 10 innings).
Most Walks, Game — 12; Ann Franklin, Beaver (PA) vs. Winthrop (SC), 1985.
Most Walks — 16; Ann Franklin, Beaver (PA), 1985.
Most Strikeouts, Game —19; Andrea Drake, Oklahoma City vs. Davis & Elkins (WV), 1989.
Most Strikeouts, Tournament — 65; Leticia Morales, St. Mary's (TX), 1986.
Most Innings Pitched, Tournament — 64; Melissa Moyers, Francis Marion (SC), 1987.

Most Appearances, Tournament — 8; Melissa Moyers, Francis Marion (SC), 1987; Leticia Morales, St. Mary's (TX), 1986; Amy Miller, Quincy (IL), 1984.
Most Wins, Tournament — 7; Leticia Morales, St. Mary's (TX), 1986.
Most Complete Games, Tournament — 8; Melissa Moyers, Francis Marion (SC), 1987; Leticia Morales, St. Mary's (TX), 1986; Amy Miller, Quincy (IL), 1984.
Most Shutouts, Tournament — 5; Rhonda Clarke, Emporia State (KS), 1984.
Most Consecutive Scoreless Innings — 38; Rhonda Clarke, Emporia State (KS), 1984.

FIELDING
Most Putouts, Game — 20, Missy Donnelly, St. Mary's (CA) vs. Concordia (MN), 1987.
Most Putouts, Tournament — 96, Cindy Alford, Francis Marion (SC), 1987.
Most Assists, Game — 12; Leann Buneta, West Florida vs. Puget Sound (WA), 1985; Sandy O'Rourke, St. Francis (IL) vs. Moorhead State (MN), 1993.
Most Assists — 38; Laura Klamm, Washburn (KS), 1985.
Most Chances, Tournament — 102, Cindy Alford, Francis Marion (SC), 1987.
Most Errors, Tournament — 9; Allyson Volzke, Hastings (NE), 1995.

NAIA FIRST TEAM ALL-AMERICANS (1983-1997)

— A —

Abramic, Janet	1997	St. Francis (IL)	INF
Akau, Shannon	1991, 94	Hawaii Loa/ Hawaii Pacific	P
Alexander, Lori	1997	Southeastern OK	INF
Allen, Keri	1992	Pacific Lutheran	INF
Alton, Chrissy	1989	Pacific Lutheran	OF
Anderson, Kristi	1987, 88, 89	Francis Marion	C

— B —

Baas, Sue	1983	IUPU-Indianapolis	UT
Bayless, Lori	1991	St. Francis IL	OF
Baysinger, Leta	1991, 92	Pacific Lutheran	OF
Becker, Patty	1990	Minnesota-Duluth	2B
Booker, Kim	1986, 87, 88	Francis Marion	OF

Bradburn, Samantha	1988	Findlay	DP
Braithwaite, Tammy	1994, 95	Oklahoma City	P
Britt, Tracey	1994	Kennesaw State	OF
Brummett, Jeri	1991	Emporia State	P
Burbach, Tracy	1988, 90	Wisconsin-Parkside	OF
Burken, Jennifer	1989	Missouri Southern	OF
Burris, Sheryl	1988	IUPU-Indianapolis	P

— C —

Case, Angie	1997	St. Mary (NE)	INF
Castor, Wendy	1991	IUPUI-Indianapolis	OF
Chaney, Carole	1985	Pittsburg State	LF
Clark, Shelly	1995, 96	Athens State	OF
Clarke, Rhonda	1983, 84	Emporia State	P
Cline, Ronda	1983	Winthrop	LF

NAIA ALL-AMERICANS CONTINUED ...

Connell, Cindy	1996	Houston Baptist	OF
Crawford, Leah	1992	Kennesaw State	INF
Cromer, Missy	1989, 90	West Florida	C
Cuddeford, Michelle	1988	Kearney State	INF
Cummings, Judy	1983, 84	IUPUI-Indianapolis	OF

— D —

Daeschler, Sue	1990	St. Xavier	OF
Daily, Chris	1995	William Woods	OF
Dashkin, Ivy	1992	Mobile AL	P
DeBuhr, Phyllis	1987, 88	Kearney State	P
Deskin, Sheree	1997	Pacific Lutheran	OF
Dickerson, Tanya	1992, 95	Siena Heights	INF
Dobbelaar, Brenda	1990, 91	Pacific Lutheran	SS
Dowlen, Melissa	1994, 95	Athens State	2B
Downey, Nan	1983, 84	William Woods	INF
Drake, Andrea	1990	Oklahoma City	P
Duffek, Debbie	1985	Mesa State	INF
Duffin, Tammy	1993	William Woods	P
Durbala, Teresa	1985, 86	Wayne State	C

— E —

Ebinger, Ann	1993	West Florida	P
Eckert, Donna	1987	St. Mary's	OF
Eddins, Robyn	1991	West Florida	INF

— F —

Faircloth, April	1995	Belmont	P
Fairhust, Sue	1994	Oklahoma City	UT
Farquhar, Andrea	1993, 95	Pacific Lutheran	1B
Ferin, Elaine	1989	Peru State	INF
Fluellen, Monique	1992, 93, 94	St. Mary's (TX)	UT
Fondersmith, Kami	1995	Athens State	INF
Fownes, Nicole	1996	Faulkner	P
Frey, Kisha	1995	Athens State	P

— G —

Gailey, Tina	1986, 87	Oklahoma City	P
Gardner, Jeanine	1990	Pacific Lutheran	DP
Giblin, Cheryl	1987	Emporia State	DH
Gonnerman, Brenda	1984	Kearney State	INF
Green, Christy	1994, 95, 96	Webber	P
Griffin, Gladys	1985, 86, 88	Central State	P
Gunter, Janelle	1996	Pacific Lutheran	P

— H —

Hansen, Heather	1990	West Florida	P
Harbin, Ann	1992	Lander	INF
Harper, Kim	1985, 86, 87	Lander	OF
Harris, Jennifer	1988	Pittsburg State	OF
Harris, Patty	1985	Quincy	OF
Hatcher, Samantha	1992, 93	Carson-Newman	INF
Hauck, Adrienne	1992	West Florida	INF
Hayes, Cathy	1991	Oklahoma City	OF
Haynes, Misty	1993, 94	West Florida	OF
Hilliard, Jennifer	1993	Mobile	P
Hoddevik, Becky	1993	Pacific Lutheran	P

Hoffman, Tammy	1983, 84	Emporia State	C
Holmes, Tina	1996	Oklahoma City	DP
Horney, Teresa	1996	Limestone	C
Hosp, Pam	1989	Wisconsin-Parkside	INF
House, Kim	1987	Missouri Southern	INF
Huff, Angie	1991	Tusculum	INF
Huinker, Ann	1983	Loras	OF
Hutchins, Kim	1990, 91	Mount Mercy	C

— J —

Jansen, Sheila	1984, 85	Mesa State	OF
Johnson, Dolly	1996, 1997	Oklahoma City	P
Johnson, Lynne	1987	Spring Arbor	INF
Johnson, Susan	1989, 90	Kearney State	P
Jonietz, Adrian	1989	St. Mary's	INF
Junck, Zena	1983	Morningside	C

— K —

Kalinel, Mary	1986	St. Mary's	OF
Kempf, Cheri	1983, 84	Missouri Western	OF
Ketchem, Gina	1991	Western New Mexico	OF
Klamm, Laura	1984, 86	Washburn	UT
Koehn, Kari	1997	Shawnee State	C
Kuhlman, Dana	1992	Tiffin	OF

— L —

Lagrimas, Tracie	1992	Hawaii-Hilo	P
Lammers, Ann	1985	Mount Mercy	INF
Lammers, Jill	1993	Mount Mercy	C
Lawson, Missy	1997	Shawnee State	INF
Lawson, Rhonda	1985	Central State	C
Leary, Renee	1992	Wilmington	UT
Levensky, Vicki	1988	IUPU-Indianapolis	INF
Liu, Christie	1997	Oklahoma City	INF
Livell, Renee	1986	Missouri Southern	INF
Loos, Dot	1983	Westmar	OF

— M —

McCormick, Terri	1997	Mobile	OF
McDuffie, Kelly	1993	Kennesaw State	OF
McGuire, Georgia	1987, 88	St. Xavier	INF
McKellar, Kelly	1995	Oklahoma City	OF
McKenzie, Ena	1988	West Florida	OF
Maly, Rochelle	1990, 91	St. Xavier	UT
Mason, Melanie	1996, 97	Northwestern (IA)	UT
Miller, Amy	1983, 84	Quincy	P
Montooth, Audrey	1991	Columbia	INF
Moore, Lucretia	1992	Athens State	OF
Morales, Leticia	1985	St. Mary's (TX)	P
Mosley, Tracey	1993, 94, 95	Oklahoma City	3B
Munson, Laura	1992, 93	Kennesaw State	OF
Murphy, Deena	1984, 85	Missouri Western	INF

— N —

Nelson, Kathy	1983	Kearney State	INF
Nichols, Chris	1983	IUPU-Indianapolis	INF
Nichols, Paige	1984, 85	Winthrop	OF

NAIA ALL-AMERICANS CONTINUED ...

— O —

O'Rourke, Sandy	1993	St. Francis	1B
Otis, Kathy	1987	IUPU-Indianapolis	
Owens, Coby	1996	Mobile	OF

— P —

Palmer, Kim	1985	Missouri Western	OF
Pascua, Felisa	1996	Hawaii Pacific	INF
Paulsen, Heather	1995, 96, 97	Puget Sound	INF
Perkins, Kim	1984	Pittsburg State	C
Phillippi, Torrie	1997	Oregon Tech	INF
Pikington, DeeAndra	1989	California Lutheran	UT
Ponder, Suzi	1992	North Florida	OF
Powell, Peri Ann	1986	Wheeling	DH
Pratt, Lisa	1992, 94, 95	Southern Wesleyan	C
Prinster, Cindy	1986	William Woods	INF

— R —

Recic, Dee Dee	1983	Wayne State	C
Reese, Cindy	1987, 88	IUPU-Indianapolis	INF
Rindal, Carrie	1991	Concordia (MN)	C
Ringor, Michele	1996, 97	Hawaii Pacific	OF
Robinson, Lisa	1987, 88	West Florida	INF
Rose, Brandi	1996	Shawnee State	OF
Ruiz, Hope	1996	Mary	INF
Rushing, Bonita	1989, 90	West Florida	OF
Rutledge, Lana	1991	St. Mary's (TX)	INF
Ryan, Lori	1986	Oklahoma City	INF

— S —

Sackman, Wendy	1986	Wisconsin-Parkside	INF
Schoales, Susie	1997	Hawaii Pacific	P
Seamons, Kelly	1995	Athens State	INF
Sederburg, DeAnne	1985	Tarkio	P
Shandy, Lisa	1993, 95	Hawaii Pacific	P
Sheehan, Ivy	1989	Wilmington	INF
Sherwood, Julie	1983	Missouri Western	INF
Silva, Aimee	1993, 94	St. Mary's	OF
Sisley, Diane	1984, 85	Winthrop	INF
Slavens, Stacey	1991	Emporia State	P
Sloan, Cicely	1996	Southern Wesleyan	OF
Sonnenberg, Debbie	1992, 93, 94	Huntingdon	P
Spratt, Wendy	1990	Columbia	SS
Stanley, Laurie	1992	National-Louis	C

Stanley, Melody	1992	Puget Sound	UT
Stary, April	1993, 94	Culver-Stockton	OF
Stout, Karen	1988	Pacific Lutheran	C
Swanson, Jennifer	1994	Pacific Lutheran	2B

— T —

Tang, Heather	1997	William Woods	OF
Teehee, Stephanie	1987	Oklahoma City	P
Thorburn, Colleen	1994	Kennesaw State	C
Tobin, Joann	1989	West Florida	P
Tomaszkiewicz, Shelle	1986	Wayne State	OF
Towers, Bobbi	1997	Oklahoma City	C

— V —

Vaandering, Johanna	1986, 87	Pacific	C
Vanderbush, Kim	1990	Wisconsin-Parkside	1B
Vaughn, Charleste	1993	Mobile	SS
Von Gonten, Jennifer	1997	Schreiner	DP
Vogel, Jamie	1991	IUPU-Indianapolis	DP
Vrba, Sheryl	1983	Loras	P

— W —

Walls, Renee	1995	Shawnee State	OF
Warner, Kim	1993	Pacific	C
Weber, Ann	1994	William Woods	OF
Weed, Kristie	1990, 91	Lander	OF
Weibert, Cindy	1992	West Florida	P
Wells, Jenifer	1994, 95, 96	Oklahoma City	C
White, Kim	1994, 95, 1996, 97	Shawnee State	UT
Williams, Lynette	1996	Hawaii Pacific	INF
Williams, Toni	1987	Oklahoma City	OF
Wilson, Kim	1994	Oklahoma City	SS
Wilson, Nikki	1997	Mobile	P
Witherspoon, Melodye	1983	Winthrop	IF
Wright, Laurie	1984	Fort Hays State	OF
Wright, Tammy	1991	Wisconsin-Parkside	UT

— Y —

Yan, Cindy	1997	Oklahoma City	INF
Yarnell, Latisha	1987	Washburn	INF
Yates, Rendy	1988	Francis Marion	UT

— Z —

Zachary, Carol	1989, 91	Carson-Newman	DP
Zapalac, Jennifer	1989	St. Mary's	OF

National Junior College Athletic Association
Source: NJCAA

NJCAA TEAM CHAMPIONS (1977-1997)

YEAR	CHAMPION	COACH	RUNNER-UP
1977	Ellworth CC	Unknown	Jackson CC
1978	Golden West CC	Coach Judi Garman	St. Louis CC/Meramec
1979	Phoenix	Coach Mary Swiess	Lansing CC
1980	Erie CC	Coach Santo DeSain	Pima CC
1981	Erie CC	Coach Santo DeSain	Lake Michigan
1982	Illinois Central	Coach Lorene Ramsey	Central Arizona
1983	Arizona Western	Coach Charlie Dine	Kirkwood CC
1984	Central Arizona	Coach Mike Candrea	Crowder
1985	Central Arizona	Coach Mike Candrea	St. Louis CC/Meramec
1986	Crowder	Coach Annie Westfall	Arizona Western
1987	Arizona Western	Coach Charlie Dine	Illinois Central
1988	Central Arizona	Coach Clint Myers	Ranger
1989	Central Arizona	Coach Clint Myers	Illinois Central
1990	Central Arizona	Coach Clint Myers	Northeastern Oklahoma
1991	Central Arizona	Coach Clint Myers	Crowder
1992	Central Arizona	Coach Clint Myers	Crowder
1993	Lake Michigan	Coach Kathy Leitke	Glendale CC
1994	Glendale CC	Coach Rick Gamez	Ranger
1995	Central Arizona	Coach Clint Myers	Northeastern Oklahoma
1996	Palm Beach CC	Coach JoAnn Ferrieri	Central Arizona
1997 DI	Central Arizona	Coach Craig Nicholson	Lake City CC
1997 DIII	Corning (NY)	Coach Marc Prutsman	DuPage

NJCAA SEASON RECORD HOLDERS (1989-1997)

INDIVIDUAL PITCHING
Lowest ERA — 0.10; Stacey Cowen, Onondaga, (NY), 1990; Dani Fowler, Chattanooga (NJ), 1996.
Strikeouts Per Inning — 1.89; Chelsey Sakizzle, Central Arizona, 1995.
INDIVIDUAL HITTING
Highest Batting Average — .716, Jessica Balsavich

Becker College (MA), 1995.
Most RBIs — 102; Michelle Clampitt, South Mountain (AZ), 1994.
TEAM
Highest Batting Average — .466; Cazenovia (NY), 1993.
Best Team Record — 56-1; Central Arizona, 1995.

NJCAA FIRST TEAM ALL-AMERICANS (1983-1997)

— A —

Alberts, Kelli	1983	Kirkwood, IA
Alcorn, Kristen (D3)	1997	Massasoit CC, MA
Alexander, Lori	1995	Eastern Oklahoma, OK
Alexander, Tara	1993	Glendale, AZ
Amborski, Andrea	1981	Lake Michigan, MI
Ambrose, Cindy	1992, 93	Central Arizona, AZ

Anderson, Autumn	1997	Eastern Arizona
Ashburn, Shirley	1979	Harford, MD
Atkins, Amber	1994	Kirkwood, IA

— B —

Baetsle, Deb	1992	Indian Hills, IA
Banks, Val	1982	Erie, NY
Barrus, Laurie	1990	Snow, UT

NJCAA ALL-AMERICANS CONTINUED ...

Barry, Barb	1985	Ulster County, NY
Barton, Melinda	1985, 86	Wabash Valley, IL
Becher, Kelle	1992	Johnson County, KS
Bell, Patricia	1980	St. Louis, Flo Valley, MO
Bench, Allison	1987	Utah Technical, UT
Benford, Andrea	1995	Glendale, AZ
Bollin, Shelly	1984	Crowder, MO
Boutin, Patricia Lynn	1988	Central Arizona, AZ
Boyd, Melissa	1993	Waldorf, IA
Bradley, Jennifer	1989	Wabash Valley, IL
Briley, Christy	1995	N'Eastern Oklahoma A&M
Brodle, Melissa	1991	Illinois Central, IL
Brotherton, (D3) Alison	1997	Alred State, NY
Brown, Rachel	1989	Arizona Western, AZ
Brown, Diane	1980	Pima, AZ
Brummett, Jeri Ann	1988	Allen County CC, KS
Burrows, Kelly	1990	Ranger, TX
Bustos, Crystl	1996, 97	Palm Beach, FL

— C —

Campbell, Luann	1985	Kirkwood, IA
Carroch, Wendy	1987	Mercer County, NJ
Castro, Chrissi	1992, 93	Hutchinson, KS
Chla, Michele	1986	Crowder, MO
Clark, Connie	1984, 85	Central Arizona, AZ
Clifford, Sheryl	1982	Becker College, MA
Clinchy, Lisa	1980	Mesa, AZ
Contreraz, Sophia	1996	Palm Beach, FL
Cook, Dee	1990	Illinois Central, IL
Cowell, Maymie	1996	Rend Lake, IL
Cowen, Julie	1982	Lake Michigan, MI
Criswell, Amy	1996	Central Arizona, AZ
Cross, Shawnee	1987	Barton County CC, KS
Curry, L. Kristi	1997	Johnson County CC

— D —

Dall, Robin	1982	Arizona Western, AZ
Daly, Missy	1990	Onondaga, NY
Davison, Judy	1984	Central Arizona, AZ
DeArmon, Ricki	1997	John A. Logan, IL
Deitrick, Mary	1997	Lakeland CC
DeLuca, Anne (D3)	1997	College of DuPage, IL
Dodrill, Laura	1985	Central Arizona, AZ
Downey, Carolyn	1987	Snow, UT
Duer, Jennifer	1985	Prince George, MD

— E —

Erickson, Terri	1990	Utah Valley, UT
Ernst, Pam	1986	Illinois Central, IL
Espinoza, Rene	1994	Central Arizona, AZ
Estes, Keesha	1991	Louisburg, NC
Estes, Kym	1990	Utah Valley, UT
Exter, Debbie	1980	Essex, MD

— F —

Fish, Cheri	1993, 94	N'Eastern Oklahoma A&M
Flores, Anna	1991	Pima, AZ
Fluke, Natasha	1992	N'Eastern Oklahoma A&M
Foll, Diane	1984	Lincoln, IL
Fowler, Dani	1996, 97	Chattonooga State CC, TN
Fritz, Maureen	1985	St. Louis, Meramec, MO

— G —

Garcia, Kristine	1997	Central Arizona, AZ
George, Millie	1992	Crowder, MO
Geyer, Dana	1987	Crowder, MO
Gilles, Tonya	1979	Illinois Central, IL
Gilles, Brenda	1986	Illinois Central, IL
Gomez, Raina	1997	Phoenix, AZ
Gonzales, Stephanie	1992	Central Arizona, AZ
Goree, Trish	1994	Ranger, TX
Goree, Patricia	1995	Ranger, TX
Granteed, Michelle	1992	Onondaga, NY

— H —

Hacker, Deanna	1982, 83	Illinois Central, IL
Hansen, Lorry	1984, 85	Lake Michigan, MI
Hartzler, Kim	1995	Illinois Central, IL
Hatfield, Dejah	1997	Central Arizona, AZ
Hatfield, Tara	1997	Wabash Valley, IL
Hazen, Holly	1983	Onondaga, NY
Headrick, Halle	1991	Crowder, MO
Hebenstriet, Pat	1979	Johnson County, KS
Hedler, Christine	1988	Oakland, MI
Held, Theresa	1980	Anoka-Ramsey CC, MN
Herberger, Vanessa	1996	Daytona Beach, FL
Hokal, Venita	1985	Central Arizona, AZ
Houle, Sarah (D3)	1997	Central Lakes, MN
Huerta, Rosa	1993, 94	Pima, AZ
Huggins, Tina	1989	Lake Michigan, MI
Hurley, Monika	1997	Ricks, ID
Hust, Brandi	1987, 88	Arizona Western, AZ
Hyde, Tammy	1981	Mattatuck, CT

— I —

Irvine, Kimberly	1993	N'Eastern Oklahoma A&M

— J —

Jackson, Bridget	1995	Central Arizona, AZ
Jackson, Jenn	1987	St. Louis, Meramec, MO
Jackson, Nancy	1992	Central Arizona, AZ
Jacobs, Wera	1979	Pima, AZ
Jacobson, Laura	1984	CC of Morris, NJ
James, Karey	1989	Arizona Western, AZ
Janowski, Joann	1989	Erie, NY
Jenkins, Minday	1991, 93	St. Louis, Meramec, MO
Jirdtano, Diane	1982	Erie, NY
Johnson, Pam	1985	Barton County CC, KS
Jones, Denise	1981	Westchester, NY
Justin, Jennifer	1989	Moraine Valley, IL

NJCAA ALL-AMERICANS CONTINUED ...

— K —

Kennett, Dana (D3)	1997	Brookdale, CC, NJ
Kent, Debbie	1979	Lansing, MI
Kerr, Suzanne	1997	Cowley County CC, KS
Kivlor, Joan	1978	Becker College, MA
Klintz, Jennifer	1995	Daytona Beach, FL
Koehl, Crhis	1990	Illinois Central, IL
Kress, Ellen	1989	Ellsworth, IA
Kroemer, Joy	1993	Lake Michigan, MI
Krummel, LeeAnn	1979	Johnson County, KS

— L —

Lamar, Sherri	1986	Eastern Arizona, AZ
Launer, Linda	1979	Illinois Central, IL
Leinen, Lisa	1987	Crowder College, MO
Leitke, Kathy	1981, 82	Lake Michigan, MI
Lelia, Laura	1980	CC of Morris, NJ
Lindous, Donna	1979	Prince George, MD
Long, Sandy	1986	Lake Michigan, MI
Looper, Marla	1991, 92	Crowder, MO
Lotre, Sherri	1979	Lansing, MI
Loucks, Jennifer	1994	Spartanburg Methodist, SC
Lundien, Shally	1992, 93	Crowder, MO
Lyon, Sue	1988	Utah Valley, UT

— M —

McDougal, Amekea	1997	Louisburg, NC
McKinney, Tammy	1986	Central Arizona, AZ
McLane, Michelle	1982	Ulster County, NY
McNamara-Jones, Mary	1993	Lake Michigan, MI
McNeely, Lisa	1995	Lake City, FL
Marshall, Katrina	1991	N'Eastern Oklahoma A&M
Martinez, Barbara	1995	Pima, AZ
Martinez, Kim	1984	St. Louis, Meramec, MO
Mausteller, (D3) Michelle	1997	Corning CC, NY
Medina, Dina	1996	Phoenix, AZ
Melfi, Dawn	1990	Onondaga, NY
Miller, Jill	1994	Johnson County, KS
Mitchell, Holly	1996	St. Louis, Meramec, MO
Mitchell, Shawna	1996	Rock Valley, IL
Mix, Julie	1990	Lake Michigan, MI
Moehring, Caryl	1982	Illinois Central, IL
Monroe, Shelly	1983, 84	Crowder, MO
Moore, Heather	1995	N'Eastern Oklahoma A&M
Moore, Jamie	1996	Palm Beach, FL
Morris, Kim	1986	Eastern Utah, UT
Morrisroe, Maureen	1980	Macomb, MI
Mortimer, Nicole	1993	Indian Hills, IA
Mullins, Dena	1990, 91	Central Arizona, AZ
Murray, Melanie	1994	Spartanburg Methodist, SC
Mygind, Debbie	1983	Arizona Western, AZ

— N —

Napora, Chris (D3)	1997	Anne Arundel CC, MD
Natividad, norma	1986	Pima, AZ
Neuman, Christi	1981	St. Louis, Meramec, MO
Nevil, Kelly	1989	Ranger, TX

— O —

O'Callaghan, Sue	1981	Erie, NY
Olcheski, Arlene	1979	Bergen CC, NJ
Olsen, Jessica	1980	Mitchell, CT
Otten, Jodi	1996	Central Arizona, AZ

— P —

Pace, Kim	1992	Central Arizona, AZ
Panzer, Missy	1994	Central Arizona, AZ
Paris, Christine	1988, 89	Crowder, MO
Parish, Tammy	1987	Hutchinson, KS
Piccoli, Sandy	1981	Illinois Central, IL
Pollard, Cami	1986	Snow, UT
Preece, Danielle	1996	Palm Beach, FL
Pump, Marty	1982	Waldorf, IA

— R —

Rader, Sheree	1991	N'Eastern Oklahoma A&M
Reinhardt, Cyndi	1988	Lincoln, IL
Reviere, Kris	1987	Illinois Central, IL
Roach, Cindy	1980	Johnson County, KS
Rogers, Luann	1980	Glendale, AZ
Romanovsky, Jill (D3)	1997	Middlesex CC, NJ
Rudanovich, Andrea	1990	St. Louis, Meramec, MO

— S —

Sakizzie, Chelsey	1995, 96	Central Arizona, AZ
Sandstede, Nicole	1988	Central Arizona, AZ
Scharnhorst, Angie	1995	St. Louis, Meramec, MO
Schrader, Brenda	1992	Illinois Central, IL
Schwebach, Rhonda	1991	Central Arizona, AZ
Sherwood, Dieotra	1994, 95	Ranger, TX
Sibla, Kathy	1983	Becker, MA
Sievers, Jodi (D3)	1997	Joliet JC, IL
Skowronski, Monica	1983	Triton, IL
Smith, Cindy	1994	Central Arizona, AZ
Snow, Rhonda	1983, 84	Cleveland State CC, TN
Sokol, Janice	1982	Prince George, MD
Stevens, Stacey	1989	Cloud County CC, KS
Stevens, Shelly	1989, 90	Cloud County CC, KS
Strasser, Renee	1985	Moraine Valley, IL
Sutton, Patty	1979, 80	St. Louis, Meramec, MO
Swiderski, Janis	1994	St. Louis, Meramec, MO

— T —

Taylor, Rashunda	1993	Spartanburg Methodist, SC
Tharp, Stephanie	1994	Indian Hills, IA
Thompson, Terri	1981	Johnson County, KS
Thompson, Lynn	1981	Lincoln, IL
Tipton, Cassie	1996	Connors State College, OK
Tobin, Joann	1987	Oakland, MI
Trease, Julie	1993	N'Eastern Oklahoma A&M

NJCAA ALL-AMERICANS CONTINUED ...

Triplett, Tracy	1982	Central Arizona, AZ
Turley, Genice	1993	Glendale, AZ
Turner, Bekki	1986	Crowder, MO
Turner, Tammy	1987	Arizona Western, AZ
Tyler, Leanne	1995	N'Eastern Oklahoma A&M

— U —

Uhde, Kelly	1995, 96	Indian Hills, IA

— V —

Vallejo, Shawnte	1997	Lake City CC
Varoz, Leslie	1988	Utah Valley, UT
Vassor, Missy	1983	Arizona Western, AZ
Verr, Vicki	1985	DuPage, IL
Vineyard, Vicki	1992	Lake Michigan, MI

— W —

Wagner, Jean	1981	Kirkwood, IA
Walter, Jen	1983	Golden Valley Lutheran, MN
Warner, Pam	1983	Lake Michigan, MI

Weatherford, Andrea	1992	N'Eastern Oklahoma A&M
Webster, Joanne	1986	Onondaga, NY
Weed, Nicole	1996, 97	Daytona Beach, FL
Wheeler, Kim	1984	Lake Michigan, MI
Wilkes, Karen	1980	Bergen CC, NJ
Wilkins, Lisa	1991	Central Arizona, AZ
Williams, April	1991, 92	Crowder, MO
Wilson, Sheri	1988	Barton County CC, KS
Wooden, Julie Lynn	1988	Anne Arundel CC, MD
Woods, Bridget	1994	Eastern Oklahoma, OK
Wright, Melanie	1983	Highland, KS

— Y —

Young, Julie	1984	Mesa, AZ
Young, Lori	1983	Kirkwood, IA

— Z —

Zinks, Hope (D3)	1997	DuPage, IL
Zinkula, Lynette	1988, 89	Kirkwood, IA
Zuspann, Angie	1994	Illinois Central, IL

California Community College — 1978-1997

Source: Judi Garman

CALIFORNIA COMMUNITY COLLEGE TEAM CHAMPIONS (1978-1997)

YEAR	CHAMPION	COACH	RUNNER-UP
1978	Cerritos	Coach Nancy Kelly	
1979	Golden West	Coach Judi Garman	Los Angeles Valley
1980	Fullerton	Coach Margo Davis	West Valley
1981	Golden West	Coach Mickey Davis	Orange Coast
1982	Santa Rosa	Coach Marv Mays	
1983	Golden West	Coach Mickey Davis	Sacramento City
1984	Golden West	Coach Jan Dunlap	
1985	Santa Ana	Coach Jim Reach	
1986	Rancho Santiago	Coach Jim Reach	
1987	Saddleback	Coach Pete Morris	
1988	Sacramento City	Coach Tim Kiernan	
1989	Palomar	Coach Mark Eldridge	Fullerton
1990	West Valley	Coach Les Hearn	Palomar
1991	Cypress	Coach Brad Pickler	Chabot
1992	Sacramento City	Coach Tim Kiernan	Palomar
1993	Palomar	Coach Mark Eldridge	Cypress
1994	College of the Sequoias	Coach Ken Tokunaga	Long Beach City
1995	Long Beach City	Coach Patty Gasso	Palomar
1996	Sacramento City	Coach Tim Kiernan	Fullerton
1997	Cypress	Coach Brad Pickler	Sacramento City

NATIONAL GIRLS BASEBALL LEAGUE* CHAMPIONSHIP RECORDS**
(1944 - 1952)

YEAR	CHAMPION	YEAR	CHAMPION
1944	Queens (Brachs Kandy Kids)	1948	Bloomer Girls
1945	Music Maids	1950	Queens
1946	Bluebirds	1951	Queens
1947	Bloomer Girls	1952	Queens

NGBL INDIVIDUAL RECORD HOLDERS

OUTSTANDING PITCHERS

1944	Lonnie Stark
1945	Information Not Available
1946	Wilda Mae Turner
1947	Wilda Mae Turner

Other Outstanding Pitchers Were:
Ann Kmezich
Betty Evans
Ginny Busick

LEADING HITTERS

1944	Marge Smith
1945	Dottie Hane-Music Maids
1946	Information Not Available
1947	Pat Carson-Queens
1948	Pat Carson-Queens
1949	Betty Wanless-Bluebirds
1950	Freda Savona-Queens
1951	Freda Savona-Queens
1952	Freda Savona-Queens

Even though the league was called baseball, the game of softball was played.

*** Records were incomplete.*

Outstanding Hitters

Freda Savona

Pat Carson

Betty Wanless

Outstanding Pitchers

Outstanding pitchers in the National Girls Baseball League included Ginny Busick, top left; Ann Kmezich, top right; Lonnie Stark, far left; and Betty Evans, left.

NATIONAL FASTPITCH COACHES ASSOCIATION HISTORY
(1982 to Present)

The idea for a softball coaching association first developed from discussions at the National Collegiate Women's Softball Championships in 1982, with Judy Martino of the University of North Carolina credited with the initial thought. Collegiate coaches wanted awards programs, a forum to discuss issues affecting their sport, a means to better educate coaches and update them on softball-related actions, and representation of the group's views in organizations such as the NCAA and the ASA.

Shortly thereafter in April of 1983, the National Softball Coaches Association (NSCA) was founded. It was organized by Martino, with Susan Craig, Connie Claussen, June Walker, Hank Dicke, Bonnie Koch and Lorene Ramsey serving as the first officers.

The first meeting of the NSCA directors was held in Durham, North Carolina, in December of that year. The first set of bylaws was adopted, Susan Craig was elected as the first president and Martino was confirmed as the executive director of the NSCA, a position she held for five years. Martino and NSCA lawyer Roger Bernholtz had written the first set of bylaws, based largely on those of other coaches associations.

It was determined that the purpose of the National Softball Coaches Association was "to educate softball coaches and the public in the game of softball, including coordinating the relationship between softball team membership and other educational endeavors through the development of softball in all its aspects as an amateur sport, including maintaining communication of new ideas and discussion of issues involving softball and education." The NSCA planned to achieve these goals by initiating softball clinics, hosting national softball conventions, conducting regional meetings, and by providing official publications to all members. The major sources of income were expected to come from membership dues, corporate sponsors and clinics.

At that time, dues were $35 a year, and the 1984 budget showed income of $17,375 and expenses of $14,529.

Since then, the organization's college coaches have welcomed high school coaches, travel ball coaches (associate members), and affiliate members, which consist of umpires, foreign coaches, professional coaches, former coaches and those persons generally interested in softball. Other milestones in the Association's history are:

- Approval as an affiliate member of the NCAA in 1984.
- Approval as an allied member of the Amateur Softball Association in April, 1988.
- Hiring of first full-time executive director — Rayla Allison — in 1991.

In December of 1995, attendees at the NSCA National Convention voted to change the name of the Association to the National Fastpitch Coaches Association (NFCA). It went into effect September 1, 1996.

Today, the NFCA has grown from 40 members in 1983, to over 2,600 members in March of 1998. Revenues exceed $500,000 a year, and the NFCA has a full-time staff of four and one part-time position. Major programs run by the NFCA are awards programs (All-American, coach of the year, victory club, scholar-athlete and top 10 academic teams), a national convention, recruiting camps, Leadoff Classic NCAA Division I national tournament, USA Today coaches polls for NCAA Division I and high school, a national NCAA Division III poll, and an umpire satellite clinic.

The NFCA's newspaper, Fastpitch Delivery, has become one of the nation's best softball publications.

NFCA FIRST TEAM ALL-AMERICANS (1986-1997)

NCAA DIVISION I

NAME	YEARS	SCHOOL	POSITION
— A —			
Alcin, Joanne	1992	UCLA	1B
Allard, Jenny	1989	Michigan	UT/DP
Andaya, Shawn	1987	Texas A&M	P
— B —			
Benedict, Patti	1993	Michigan	OF
Berg, Laura	1995, 97	Fresno State	OF
Bilbao, Debbie	1997	Iowa	UT
Boxx, Gillian	1993, 95	California	C
Braatz-Cochrane,	1994, 97	Arizona	C
Leah	1995	Arizona	At-Large/C
Brewer, Dee	1988	Oklahoma State	OF
Brown, Rachel	1992	Arizona	OF
Brundage, Jennifer	1994, 95	UCLA	3B
Bunge, Tracy	1986	Kansas	UT/DH
Burns, B'Ann	1996	UCLA	P
— C —			
Calcante, Beth	1993	Cal State Northridge	OF
Carpenter, Terry	1989, 91	Fresno State	P
Cavanaugh, Julie	1991	Oregon	1B
Chellevold, Amy	1994, 95	Arizona	1B
Church, Michelle	1996	Washington	1B
Clark, Connie	1987	Cal State Fullerton	P
Compton, Heather	1991	UCLA	P
Connolly, Shelia	1987	Kansas	OF
Conrad, Traci	1997	Michigan	At-Large/1B
Coombes, Missy	1989	Cal State Fullerton	1B
Cooper, Cindy	1986	Texas A&M	3B
— D —			
Dacquisto, Lisa	1996, 97	Arizona State	DP
Dalton, Jenny	1994, 95, 96	Arizona	2B
Davidson, Lisa	1993	Florida State	2B
Dawson, Sarah	1997	Northeast Louisiana	P
Day, Debbie	1992	Arizona	P
DeFeo, Stephanie	1994	USL	DP
Delloso, Michelle	1989	South Carolina	2B
	1990	S. Carolina	At Large/2B
Dolan, Carrie	1995	Arizona	P
Dyer, Kathy	1986	New Mexico	1B
— E —			
Escarcega, Kathy	1986	Arizona State	OF
Espinoza, Laura	1994, 95	Arizona	SS
Evans, Nancy	1997	Arizona	P
— F —			
Fernandez, Lisa	1990, 91, 92		
	1993	UCLA	UT/DP
Fredstrom, Sarah	1997	Colorado St.	At Large/SS
Frohnheiser, Cathy	1993	Furman	3B

NAME	YEARS	SCHOOL	POSITION
— G —			
Granger, Michelle	1990, 91, 92		
	1993	California	P
Green, Charmelle	1990	Utah	OF
Griffin, Sara	1995, 96	Michigan	UT
Gutierrez, Yvonne	1990, 91, 92	UCLA	OF
— H —			
Hall, Kyla	1993	USL	P
	1994	USL	At-Large/P
Harvey, Lisa	1989	Oklahoma State	C
Heggen, Jamie	1993	Arizona	OF
Hess, Carey	1989	Cal State Fullerton	OF
Holm, Vivian	1990	Arizona	OF
— J —			
Johnsen, Alison	1996, 97	Arizona	OF
Johnson, Shari	1989	Oklahoma State	SS
Johnson, Stacey	1986	Louisiana Tech	P
Johnson, Trinity	1997	South Carolina	P
Justin, Jill	1987, 88, 89	Northern Illinois	OF
— K —			
Kanter, Leslie	1986	South Florida	SS
King-Randolph,	1990	Toledo	1B
Rhonda			
Kovach, Kelly	1995	Michigan	At-Large/P
Kubin, Christine	1996	North Carolina	3B
— L —			
LeFebvre, Susan	1986	Cal State Fullerton	P
Lindenberg, Nina	1996	Fresno State	At-Large/2B
Longaker, Lisa	1987, 88, 90	UCLA	P
Longeway, Cheryl	1995, 96	USL	P
— M —			
McFalls, Jennifer	1993	Texas A&M	SS
Maumausolo, Scia	1993	Cal State Northridge	DP
	1996	CS Northridge	At-Large/C
Maynez, Lorraine	1988	UCLA	OF
Melfi, Dawn	1992	Florida	2B
Meyer, Heather	1996	Washington	P
Miller-Pruitt, Jody	1992	Arizona	C
Mizera, Liz	1987, 88	Texas A&M	SS
Moore, Karleen	1986	Indiana	OF
Morton, Kathy	1994, 95	USL	OF/DP
— N —			
Nelson, Rachel	1996	Minnesota	OF
Nichols, Debbie	1988	Louisiana Tech	P
Noffsinger, Martha	1990	Fresno State	SS
Nowak, Missy	1995	DePaul	At-Large/2B
Nuveman, Stacey	1997	UCLA	At-Large/C
— O —			
O'Brien, Leah	1994, 95, 97	Arizona	OF/1B

DIVISION I ALL-AMERICANS CONTINUED

NAME	YEARS	SCHOOL	POSITION
— P —			
Parker, Lindsay	1996	Fresno State	At-Large/P
Parks, Janice	1987, 88, 89	UCLA	3B
Parra, Susie	1993, 94	Arizona	P
Parrent, Melanie	1988	Fresno State	P
Parus, Cyndi	1993	UNLV	1B
	1995	UNLV	At-Large/1B
Pickering, Sara	1996	Washington	At-Large/2B
	1997	Washington	2B
Pineda, Leticia	1996, 97	Arizona	C/3B
Pohl, Diane	1990, 91	Iowa	C
Popowski, Tricia	1989, 91	South Carolina	OF
— R —			
Rhea, Sandy	1997	Utah	OF
Richards, Kendall	1996	Texas A&M	At Large/SS
Roche, Melanie	1992, 93	Oklahoma State	P
Rogers, Chenita	1986, 87	Cal State Fullerton	OF
Rondina, Kim	1995	UNLV	At-Large/SS
— S —			
Sanchelli, Karen	1987, 88	South Carolina	C
Schwartz, Jody	1988	Creighton	1B
Scott, Amanda	1997	Fresno State	At-Large/UT
Seegert, Alicia	1986	Michigan	C
Skoglund, Kristie	1987	Utah State	UT/DH
Smith, Julie	1987	Texas A&M	2B
	1990, 91	Fresno State	2B
Smith, Michele	1988, 89	Oklahoma State	UT/P
Spitaleri, Camille	1990, 91, 92	Kansas	3B
Standering, Julie	1991	Arizona	SS
Stanley, Pam	1991	Central Michigan	OF
Steamer, Dorsey	1992	USL	OF
Strang, Gena	1987	Fresno State	1B
Stowell, Alison	1986, 88	Cal Poly Pomona	2B
— T —			
Tootle, Tiffany	1992	South Carolina	SS
— U —			
Unterbrink, Amy	1986	Indiana	P
— V —			
Viola, Ali	1996	Nebraska	SS
— W —			
Ward, Kim	1994	Oklahoma State	UT
Weiman, DeeDee	1994	UCLA	P
Whitton, Stefni	1990	USL	P
Wiese, Katie	1989	Oregon	P
Wilkins, Brooke	1995	Hawaii	P
Williams, Laura	1997	Georgia Tech	SS
Windmiller, Amy	1994	CS Northridge	At-Large
Wilson, Shamalene	1996	Florida State	OF
Wright, Barb	1997	Missouri	At-Large/P

NAME	YEARS	SCHOOL	POSITION
— Y —			
Yorke, Robyn	1994, 95	Fresno State	OF

NCAA DIVISION II

NAME	YEARS	SCHOOL	POSITION
— A —			
Aiken, Jackie	1995,	Wisconsin-Parkside	C
	1996, 97	Wisconsin-Parkside	3B
Albright, Staci	1996	Coker	C
Alcorn, Traci	1986	Akron	3B
Allen, Robin	1988	Florida Southern	OF
Arscott, Ramona	1996	Columbus	2B
Avis, Lorie	1988	Cal State Sacramento	3B
— B —			
Bachleda, Michaelene	1989	Wayne State (MI)	OF
	1990	Wayne State	At-Large
Baetsle, Deb	1993, 94	Nebraska-Omaha	1B
Barnabei, Lisa	1989	American International	3B
Bartals, Liz	1997	Rollins	UT
Bartolo, Elisa	1995	Florida Tech	OF
Blake, Jacki	1991	Chapman	P
Boyd, Jennifer	1994	Barry	OF
Brown, Cynthia	1992	Cal State Bakersfield	P
Buckheit, Janet	1991	Bloomsburg	OF
Buskirk, Jean	1992, 93	Bloomsburg	1B/UT
— C —			
Carey, Tracy	1994	Nebraska-Omaha	UT/DP
Carlisle, Tonya	1995	Kennesaw State	3B
Carlson, Jeree	1996	Morningside	P
Castro, Stellis	1986	S.F. Austin State	OF
Circo, Amy	1992	Cal State Hayward	UT/DP
Clay, Pam	1986	S.F. Austin State	P
Clift, Katie	1993	Barry	P
Craft, Lee Ann	1992	Barry	3B
Cunningham, Sharlie	1997	UC Davis	DP
— D —			
Davis, Shelly	1994, 96	Florida Southern	SS
Dickman, Debbie	1987, 88, 1989, 90	Cal State Northridge	P
Doffing, Lori	1986	Mankato State	OF
Dornstauder, Cara	1995	Kennesaw State	DP
— E —			
Eagleston, Terri	1989	Cal State Sacramento	OF
Erickson, Lisa	1990	Cal State Northridge	OF
— F —			
Foster, Lisa	1989	Southeast Missouri	SS
— G —			
Garcia, Julie	1997	Columbus State	OF
Gass, Kathy	1987	Nebraska-Omaha	OF
Gomez, Apple	1995	Humboldt State	SS
Graham, Joanne	1986	Sam Houston St.	UT/DH

DIVISION II ALL-AMERICANS CONTINUED

NAME	YEARS	SCHOOL	POSITION
Graham, Wanda	1993	Florida Southern	OF
Greig, Beth	1987	Florida Southern	OF
Grund, Ferris	1991	Augustana (SD)	1B

— H —

NAME	YEARS	SCHOOL	POSITION
Hansen, Laura	1997	Humboldt State	C
Hillstrom, Heather	1996	Mankato State	C
Hopkins, Angie	1993	Augustana (SD)	SS
	1994	Augustana	At-Large/SS
Horton, Chasidy	1997	Central Oklahoma	SS
Houska, Lisa	1991	Missouri Southern	OF
Howell, Sherry	1992	Eckerd	At-Large/OF
Hughes, Michelle	1990	Portland State	UT/DP
Hunsinger, Megan	1997	UC Davis	C
Huse, Amber	1994	Southern Indiana	OF

— J —

NAME	YEARS	SCHOOL	POSITION
Jacobs, Kristin	1991	Portland State	P
Jordan, Barbara	1986, 87	Cal State Northridge	OF

— K —

NAME	YEARS	SCHOOL	POSITION
Kapla, Bobbi	1996	Wisconsin-Parkside	DP
Karr, Kristine	1993, 94	Cal State Bakersfield	P
Kinasz, Kathy	1992	Saginaw Valley	P
Kouri, Kim	1988, 90	Augustana (SD)	SS
Kovach, Theresa	1993	Lock Haven	3B
Krauth, Julie	1991, 94	Augustana (SD)	P

— L —

NAME	YEARS	SCHOOL	POSITION
Laudato, Marty	1990, 91, 92	Bloomsburg	C
LeFebvre, Michelle	1995	Merrimack	OF
Lefever, Jen	1995	Bloomsburg	SS
Levine, Stephanie	1988	Cal State Sacramento	OF
Lewis, Penni	1986	S.F. Austin State	C
Lindenmuth, Gina	1990	Bloomsburg	P
Litteral, Sunny	1996, 97	Ashland	OF
Longquist, Stacie	1993	Humboldt State	OF
Lundien, Shally	1995	Missouri Southern	1B
Lutes, Cheryl	1991	Cal Poly	2B

— M —

NAME	YEARS	SCHOOL	POSITION
Mader, Sandy	1986	Sam Houston State	SS
Maguire, Kim	1993, 94	Bloomsburg	P
Martin, Lisa	1988	Cal State Northridge	UT
Meaden, Cathleen	1993	Bridgeport	2B
Millen, Jean	1986, 87	Bloomsburg	1B

— N —

NAME	YEARS	SCHOOL	POSITION
Nelson, Kim	1994	UC Davis	OF
Novak, Toni	1997	Nebraska-Omaha	2B

— O —

NAME	YEARS	SCHOOL	POSITION
Olivas, Sandra	1990, 91	Chapman	3B
Onestinghel, Beth	1988	Cal State Northridge	OF

— P —

NAME	YEARS	SCHOOL	POSITION
Palmer, Chris	1987	Florida Southern	2B
Palmer, Michelle	1992, 93	Sacred Heart	OF
Paoli, April	1995	Bloomsburg	P

NAME	YEARS	SCHOOL	POSITION
Paparo, Daniela	1995	Merrimack	2B
Paparo, Raffaella	1993, 96	Merrimack	OF
Penner, Danielle	1997	California (PA)	P
Peterson, Jamie	1997	Humboldt State	OF
Piorek, Maryann	1987	Sacred Heart	3B
Prince, Mindi	1996	Morningside	UT

— R —

NAME	YEARS	SCHOOL	POSITION
Rafter, Kelly	1995	Kennesaw State	P
Reifel, Terri	1988	Cal State Bakersfield	C
Reinhardt, Trisha	1997	UC Davis	1B
Robinson, Kellie	1989, 91, 92	Florida Southern	1B/SS
Rouse, Priscilla	1987	Cal State Northridge	UT

— S —

NAME	YEARS	SCHOOL	POSITION
Sago, Patsy	1988	Florida Southern	2B
Sandstede, Nycki	1989, 90	Florida Southern	P
Santa Cruz, Barb	1989, 90	Cal State Bakersfield	2B
Saunders, Dawn	1994	Merrimack	3B
Schmidt, Kim	1987	Sacred Heart	C
Shelly, Lori	1987, 89	Cal State Northridge	UT/DP
	1991	Bloomsburg	UT/DP
Sielaf, Rachel	1993	Wisconsin-Parkside	C
Slaten, Kathy	1986	Cal State Northridge	P
Slocum, Cindy	1990	Bloomsburg	OF
Stankewitz, Dori	1987, 88	Florida Southern	P

— T —

NAME	YEARS	SCHOOL	POSITION
Teresi, Chrissy	1991, 92	Florida Southern	2B
Thomas, Julie	1986	Sam Houston State	2B
Tidy, Debbie	1986, 87	Scared Heart	P
Toth, Sharon	1988	Kutztown	1B
Tschida, Carrie	1989	Mankato State	P

— U —

NAME	YEARS	SCHOOL	POSITION
U'Ren, Paula	1994, 95	Augustana (SD)	C
Upenieks, Jenni	1997	Nebraska-Omaha	OF

— V —

NAME	YEARS	SCHOOL	POSITION
Van Allen, Amy	1990, 91, 92	Cal State Bakersfield	OF

— W —

NAME	YEARS	SCHOOL	POSITION
Wagner, Angie	1993	Mankato State	C
Wagner, Jen	1996	California (PA)	1B
Wallace, Pam	1990	Sacred Heart	1B
Webb, Lith	1995, 96,	California (PA)	3B
	1997	California	At-Large/3B
Weber, Gena	1995, 96, 97	UC Davis	P
Weidemann, Dianne	1989	Florida Southern	C
Weno, Deb	1988	Northeast Missouri St.	P
Wiley, Charlotte	1992	Cal State Hayward	SS
Wolff, Wendy	1996, 97	Wisconsin-Parkside	P
Wood, Traci	1995, 96	Florida Southern	OF

— Y —

NAME	YEARS	SCHOOL	POSITION
Young, Heather	1992	Bloomsburg	P

DIVISION III

NAME	YEARS	SCHOOL	POSITION
— A —			
Acevedo, Jerrilyn	1997	Montclair State	C
Acker, Margie	1992	Trenton State	OF
Adler, Ginny	1988	E. Connecticut State	OF
Allen, Missey	1995	Central (IA)	P
Allocco, Stephanie	1997	Rowan	SS
— B —			
Backof, Julie	1997	Western Maryland	2B
Baird, Karen	1993	Adrian	SS
Barnett, Kerry	1994	Ohio Northern	SS
Baudouin, Amy	1986	Aurora	UT/DH
Boyer, Michele	1988	Augsburg	UT/DP
Brooks, Donna	1986, 89, 90	Montclair State	OF
Brown, Shelly	1988, 89	Allegheny	P
Buckheit, Carol	1986	Ithaca	SS
Butler, Rachel	1994	Alma	OF
— C —			
Camuso, Keri	1996	Springfield	At-Large/SS
Cancilla, Lisa	1995	Chapman	SS
Carine, Randi	1997	Wheaton (MA)	3B
Carlson, Michelle	1992, 94, 95	Trenton State	3B
Carpenter, Karen	1996	Plymouth State	2B
Celularo, Gia	1986, 87, 88	Allegheny	2B
Citarella, Jennifer	1996, 97	Montclair State	OF
Cohen, Ilene	1988	Trenton State	OF
Constantine, Angela	1994	Bridgewater State	1B
Costa, Andrea	1988	E. Connecticut State	OF
Curran, Marie	1993	Trenton State	C
Cwinski, Beth	1997	Aurora	OF
— D —			
Davidson, Laurie	1995	Aurora	C
DeAquino, Dina	1988, 87	Montclair State	P
DeFeo, Anita	1996	Trenton State	At-Large/1B
Dockz, Kelly	1990	Montclair State	OF
Domino, Janet	1991, 92	Trenton State	SS
Donovan, Kathy	1995, 96	Chapman	C
Doyle, Darsi	1986	Luther College	P
DuPuis, Margaret	1993	William Patterson	3B
Durocher, Kim	1986	E. Connecticut State	P
— E —			
Eaton, Paula	1992	Westfield State	OF
Enochs, Katie	1996	Illinois Benedictine	P
Ericson, Karyn	1995	Aurora	3B
— F —			
Fata, Mary Ellen	1990	Kean	SS
Feo, Crystal	1996	Rowan	OF
Fisher, Sandy	1986	Kean	1B
Flinn, Jennifer	1993, 94, 95	Montclair State	2B
Fyfe, Lois	1992	Montclair State	P
— G —			
Garin, Jenny	1997	St. Mary's (MN)	DP

NAME	YEARS	SCHOOL	POSITION
Giarrusso, Linda	1989	Montclair State	2B
Gilligan, Kara	1994	Rowan	C
Goodwin, Jen	1996	Bridgewater St.	UT/DP
Grimes, Emily	1992, 93	Central (IA)	P
Grower, Jenny	1991	Mt. Union	3B
Guidorizzi, Christy	1995, 96	Chapman	P
— H —			
Haeder, Amy	1992, 94	Buena Vista	P
Haight, Andrea	1991	Augsburg	C
Heckethorn, JoAnne	1993, 94	Trenton State	OF
Hengemuhle, Jeanne	1991, 92	Trenton State	1B
Herman, Jill	1989, 90	Trenton State	1B
Holloman, Carla	1990	Allegheny	2B
Horn, Kim	1995	Aurora	OF
Hudak, Rachel	1993, 94, 95	Trenton State	OF
Hunt, Deanna	1996	Buffalo State	At-Large/UT
— K —			
King, Kelly	1997	St. Mary's (MN)	At-Large
Kinghorn, Patti	1991	Trenton State	OF
Kittelson, Danielle	1989, 90	Luther	P/UT/DP
Klueg, Diane	1986, 87,	Trenton State	UT/DP
	1988, 89	Trenton State	3B
Koolhaus, Shauna	1997	Calvin	At-Large
— L —			
LaFleur, Marnie	1991	Cal St. San Bernardino	UP
LoPresti, Jennifer	1991	Trenton State	P
Lorber, Sharon	1990	Coe	P
— M —			
McCreesh, Pam	1988, 89	Trenton State	SS
Machuga, Laurie	1993, 94, 95	Allegheny	P
Madden, Jenny	1993	Illinois Benedictine	1B
Mahnke, Jamie	1991	Central (IA)	P
Maiben, Jessamine	1995, 96	Chapman	OF
Marghella, Jill	1988	Trenton State	At-Large
Mays, Stacey	1993	LaVerne	At-Large
Mohan, Christia	1989, 90	E. Connecticut State	P
Montas, Sunny	1995, 96	Trenton State	DP/C
Moore, Wendy	1996	Hope	3B
Mullen, Lynette	1995	Central Iowa	1B
Musey, Jami	1996, 97	Rowan	1B
— N —			
Naegele, Kris	1992	Muskingum	OF
— O —			
O'Connell, Donna	1987	Trenton State	P
Ormsbee, Sharon	1997	Montclair State	P
— P —			
Periman, Amy	1993	Aurora	OF
Phillips, Michelle	1993	Redlands	DP/UT
Pittner, Joy	1996	Rowan	SS
Psconda, Johana	1992	Hope	2B

DIVISION III ALL-AMERICANS CONTINUED ...

NAME	YEARS	SCHOOL	POSITION
— Q —			
Quirin, Julie	1987	Buena Vista	OF
— R —			
Rocheleau, Lynn	1989	E. Connecticut St.	UP/DH
— S —			
Sanchez, Alicia	1997	College of New Jersey	OF
Schade, Kelly	1997	Simpson	P
Seeger, Danielle	1991	Cortland State	OF
Selbst, Robin	1994, 95	Trenton State	UT/DP/2B
Sheaffer, Chris	1992	Muskingum	UT/DH
Shoop, Leanne	1989, 90	E. Connecticut State	OF
Shumbo, Mariann	1988	E. Connecticut State	1B
Sparks, Stacey	1990	Milliken	OF
Spirko, Lynn	1991	Trenton State	2B
Sutten, Laurie	1987	Central Iowa	P
— T —			
Theobald, Marge	1986, 87, 88	Montclair State	C
Thompson, Kris	1987	Central Iowa	1B
Titus, Kate	1990	Muskingum	C
Trecroce, Janetta	1997	Ursinus	UT
— V —			
Van Werden, Christi	1991	Central Iowa	2B
Vashaw, Deb	1992	Hope	C
Vogel, Missy	1986, 87	Allegheny	OF
— W —			
Warren, Tracy	1986, 87	Trenton State	3B
Westerkamp, Anne	1987	Illinois Benedictine	SS
White, Heather	1994	Buena Vista	P
Whiteman, Penny	1989, 91	Allegheny	OF
Wilson, Kim	1990	Montclair State	3B
Wischmeier, Dee	1997	Simpson	C
Wodatch, Trish	1986	E. Connecticut State	OF
Workman, Sandy	1987	Illinois Benedictine	OF

NAIA

NAME	YEAR	SCHOOL	POSITION
— A —			
Alexander, Lori	1997	Southeastern Okla. St.	1B
Allen, Keri	1992	Pacific Lutheran	2B
Aplin, Candy	1989	Tri State	C
Asbury, Jenny	1991, 93	Wilmington	2B
— B —			
Barnett, Brandy	1996	Trevecca Nazarene	IF
Baysinger, Leta	1992	Pacific Lutheran	OF
Becker, Patty	1991	Minnesota-Duluth	
Booker, Kim	1986	Francis Marion	OF
Braithwaite, Tammy	1994, 95	Oklahoma City	P
Britt, Tracy	1994	Kennesaw State	OF
Brown, Lori	1994	Mt. Vernon Nazarene	IF
Brummett, Jeri	1991	Emporia State	
Burbach, Tracy	1989, 90	Wisconsin-Parkside	OF

NAME	YEARS	SCHOOL	POSITION
— C —			
Capogreco, Lynde	1997	Union	UT
Carlisle, Tonya	1993	Kennesaw State	3B
Castaneda, Dawn	1997	Azusa Pacific	3B
Castor, Wendy	1990, 91	IUPUI	OF
Chavis, Terri	1994	Mobile	OF
Chen, Sharon	1990	Oklahoma City	P
Clark, Shelly	1995, 96	Athens State	OF/IF
Clem, Kerry	1991	Tri State	
Connell, Cindy	1996, 97	Houston Baptist	OF
Crawford, Leah	1992	Kennesaw State	SS
Cromer, Missy	1989	West Florida	C
— D —			
Daily, Chris	1995	William Woods	OF
Dashkin, Ivy	1992	Mobile	P
DiGrazia, Lynne	1993	St. Xavier (IL)	OF
Dobbelaar, Brenda	1991	Pacific Lutheran	
Dockz, Kelley	1989	Bloomfield	OF
Dowlen, Melinda	1994, 95	Athens State	IF/C
Durbala, Teresa	1986	Wayne State (NE)	C
— E —			
Eddins, Robyn	1990	West Florida	IF
Everhart, Heather	1994	Grace	P
— F —			
Faircloth, April	1995	Belmont	P
Fairhurst, Sue	1994	Oklahoma City	UT
Farquhar, Andrea	1993	Pacific Lutheran	1B
Faubion, Shelly	1990	Oklahoma City	IF
Fondersmith, Kamie	1995, 96	Athens State	IF/C
Fownes, Nicole	1996	Faulkner	P
Frey, Kisha	1995	Athens State	P
— G —			
Gailey, Tina	1986	Oklahoma City	P
Griffin, Gladys	1986	Central State (OK)	P
Groves, Mitzi	1996	Oklahoma City	P
Gunter, Janell	1996	Pacific Lutheran	P
— H —			
Hansen, Heather	1990	West Florida	P
Harbin, Ann	1992	Lander	P
Harding, Sharon	1994	Wilmington	OF
Harper, Kim	1986	Lander	OF
Harvey, Danelle	1993	West Florida	OF/UT
Haug, Megan	1995	Pacific (OR)	OF
Haulk, Adrianna	1992, 93	West Florida	3B/SS
Hayes, Cathy	1991	Oklahoma City	
Haynes, Misty	1993	West Florida	OF
Henke, Marni	1990	Winona	C
Hilliard, Jennifer	1993	Mobile	P
Hoddevik, Becky	1991, 92, 93	Pacific Lutheran	P
Holmes, Tina	1996	Oklahoma City	DP
Hosp, Pam	1989	Wisconsin-Parkside	IF
Howell, Jennifer	1996	Bethel	IF

NAIA ALL-AMERICANS CONTINUED

NAME	YEARS	SCHOOL	POSITION
Hudson, Leslie	1996	Oklahoma City	IF

— J —

NAME	YEARS	SCHOOL	POSITION
Jeannette, Dana	1997	Georgian Court	2B
Johnson, Dolly	1996	Oklahoma City	P

— K —

Kalinel, Mary	1986	St. Mary's (TX)	OF
Klamm, Diana	1986	Washburn	UT
Klamm, Laura	1986	Washburn	P
Knox, Karen	1989	IUPU-Indianapolis	P

— L —

Lagrimas, Tracey	1992	Hawaii-Hilo	P
Lammers, Jill	1993	Mount Mercy	C
Leary, Renee	1992, 93	Wilmington	UT/DP
Livell, Renee	1986	Missouri Southern	IF

— M —

McCormick, Terri	1997	Mobile	OF
McDuffie, Kelly	1992, 93	Kennesaw State	OF
McKellar, Kelly	1995	Oklahoma City	OF
Maly, Rochelle	1991	St. Xavier	
Martin, Kerry	1997	Azusa Pacific	P
Matcuk, Stacey	1993	Georgian Court	P
Michelle, Missy	1989	IUPU-Indianapolis	IF
Mosley, Tracey	1993, 94, 95	Oklahoma City	3B/IF
Munson, Laura	1992, 93	Kennesaw State	OF
Murphy, Patti	1989, 90	Bloomfield	IF
Murray, Lisa	1990	Bloomfield	P

— O —

O'Rourke, Sandy	1993	St. Francis (IL)	1B
Owens, Coby	1996	Mobile	OF

— P —

Pascua, Felisa	1995, 96	Hawaii-Pacific	IF
Paulsen, Heather	1997	Puget Sound	SS
Powell, Peri Ann	1986	Wheeling	DH
Prinster, Cindy	1986	William Woods	IF

— R —

Rafter, Kelly	1994	Kennesaw State	P
Ringor, Michele	1996	Hawaii-Pacific	OF
Rushing, Bonita	1989, 90	West Florida	OF
Ryan, Lori	1986	Oklahoma City	IF

— S —

Sackman, Wendy	1986, 89	Wisconsin-Parkside	IF
Seamons, Kelly	1994, 95	Athens State	OF
Shandy, Lisa	1995	Hawaii-Pacific	UT
Slavens, Stacey	1991	Emporia State	
Smith, Eva	1989	Tri-State	OF
Solana, Jodi	1995	Georgian Court	UT
Stanfill, Kim	1995, 97	Belmont	C
Stanley, Laurie	1992	National Louis	C
Starkey, Malveena	1993	Hawaii-Hilo	UP
Swanson, Jennifer	1994	Pacific Lutheran	IF

NAME	YEARS	SCHOOL	POSITION

— T —

Tang, Heather	1997	William Woods	OF
Tebbe, Kris	1994	Lindenwood	IF
Thomas, Melissa	1996	Mobile	IF
Thorburn, Colleen	1994	Kennesaw State	C
Tobin, Joann	1989	West Florida	P
Tomaszkiewicz, Shelle	1986	Wayne State (NE)	OF
Tyler, Moose	1995	Oklahoma City	IF

— V —

Vaandering, Johanna	1986	Pacific (OR)	IF
Vanderbush, Kim	1990	Wisconsin-Parkside	IF
Vaughn, Charleste	1993	Mobile	SS
Vogel, Jamie	1991	IUPU-Indianapolis	

— W —

Warner, Kim	1993	Pacific	C
Weed, Kristie	1990, 91	Lander	OF
Wells, Jennifer	1994, 95, 96	Oklahoma City	C
Westmoreland, Leslie	1996	Athens State	IF
Williams, Lynette	1996	Hawaii-Pacific	IF
Wilson, Kim	1994	Oklahoma City	IF
Wilson, Nikki	1997	Mobile	P
Wright, Sherri	1993, 94	Belmont	P

— Y —

Yarnell, Latisha	1986	Washburn	IF

NJCAA

NAME	YEAR	SCHOOL	POSITION

— A —

Ambrose, Cindy	1993	Central Arizona, AZ	C
Anderson, Amber	1991	Lake Michigan, MI	IF
Antcliff, Margaret	1993	Lake Michigan, MI	P
Aquilar, Marci	1989	Pima CC, AZ	

— B —

Balch, Shelli	1996	Crowder, MO	C
Balsavich, Jessica	1996	Lake City CC, FL	DP/UT
Barton, Melinda	1986	Wabash Valley, IL	P
Blasko, Mary Ann	1994, 95	Lake Michigan, MI	C
Bond, Donita	1987	Rock Valley, IL	1B
Botkin, Kim	1992	Arizona Western, AZ	IF
Brant, Diane	1990	Central Arizona, AZ	IF
Britton, Brandie	1991	Central Arizona, AZ	Battery
Brodie, Melissa	1991	Illinois Central, IL	IF
Bustos, Crystl	1996	Palm Beach CC, FL	IF

— C —

Caswell, Meshia	1992	Lake Michigan, MI	IF
Cather, Joan	1989	St. Louis/Meramec, MO	
Chia, Michele	1986	Crowder, MO	P
Conn, Crystal	1996	Ranger, TX	IF
Contreraz, Sophia	1996	Palm Beach CC, FL	P

NJCAA ALL-AMERICANS CONTINUED ...

NAME	YEARS	SCHOOL	POSITION
Cornish, Brigit	1994, 95	Illinois Central, IL	OF
Cosby, Stacy	1994	Ranger, TX	OF
Contryman, Karla	1996	Phoenix, AZ	IF
Crosby, Kim	1996	Tallahassee CC, FL	OF
Crotts, Amy	1995	Johnson County, KS	OF

— D —

Davis, Jill	1995	Crowder, MO	IF
DeMarie, Donna	1987	Erie CC, NY	C

— E —

Ernst, Pam	1986	Illinois Central, IL	OF

— F —

Fiebig, Kris	1994	Illinois Central, IL	IF
Flannery, Stacy	1994	St. Louis/Meramec, IL	IF
Flowers, Melanie	1993	St. Louis/Meramec, IL	OF
Fluke, Natasha	1992	Northeastern Okla A&M	OF
Frate, Stacey	1990	Central Arizona, AZ	Battery
Friese, Kim	1990	Wabash Valley, IL	OF

— G —

Gilles, Brenda	1986	Illinois Central, IL	IF
Gonzales, Stephanie	1991, 92	Central Arizona, AZ	OF

— H —

Hanley, Dawn	1993	Illinois Central, IL	IF
Hanover, Ellie	1995	Erie CC, NY	IF
Hare, Annie Marie	1994	Johnson County, KS	P
Hartzler, Kim	1995	Illinois Central, IL	IF
Head, Lori	1994	Spartanburg Methodist	P
Herberger, Vanessa	1996	Daytona Beach CC, FL	P
Hugins, Tina	1989	Lake Michigan, MI	
Hunter, Allison	1995	Johnson Cnty, KS	DP/UT

— I —

Irvin, Karrie	1991	Illinois Central, IL	OF

— J —

Jackson, Analisa	1992, 93	Central Arizona, AZ	IF
Jackson, Jenn	1987	St. Louis/Meramec, MO	UT
Jackson, Nancy	1991, 92	Central Arizona, AZ	P
Jenkins, Mindy	1993	St. Louis/Meramec, MO	OF
Jose, Karen	1995	Daytona Beach CC	P

— K —

Kintz, Jenny	1995	Daytona Beach CC	OF
Koehl, Chris	1990	Illinois Central, IL	Battery
Kroemer, Joy	1993	Lake Michigan, MI	IF

— L —

Lamar, Sherri	1986	Eastern Arizona, AZ	C
Long, Sandy	1986	Lake Michigan, MI	OF
Looper, Marla	1991, 92	Crowder, MO	P
Loucks, Jennifer	1994	Spartanburg Methodist	C
Lundien, Shally	1993	Crowder, MO	IF

— M —

McCall, Marnie	1990	Central Arizona, AZ	OF
McKinney, Tammy	1986	Central Arizona, AZ	IF

NAME	YEARS	SCHOOL	POSITION
McNamara-Jones, Mary	1993	Lake Michigan, MI	C
McNeley, Lisa	1995	Lake City CC, FL	P
Marcott, Gloria	1990	Wabash Valley, IL	IF
Marzetta, Angie	1992	Central Arizona, AZ	OF
Mealman, Nicole	1995	Johnson County, KS	P
Mendoza, Linda	1991	Ranger, TX	IF
Merchant, Sadie	1994	Illinois Central, IL	DH
Miller, Dawn	1994	Phoenix, AZ	OF
Miller, Jill	1994	Johnson County, KS	OF
Mitchell, Holly	1996	St. Louis/Meramec, MO	OF
Mix-Lake, Julie	1990	Lake Michigan, MI	OF
Miyahara, Janet	1992, 93	Central Arizona, AZ	P
Moore, Jamie	1996	Palm Beach CC, FL	C
Morris, Kori	1986	Eastern Utah, UT	OF
Motyke, Andrea	1987	Erie CC, NY	2B
Murray, Melanie	1994	Spartanburg Methodist	IF
Muller, Rachel	1990	Illinois Central, IL	Battery
Mullins, Dena	1990, 91	Central Arizona, AZ	Battery

— N —

Natividad, Norma	1986	Pima CC, AZ	IF
Nevil, Kelly	1989	Ranger, TX	
Newbern, Kim	1992	Hutchinson, KS	IF
Nickell, Brandi	1996	Johnson County, KS	P

— P —

Pace, Kim	1992	Central Arizona, AZ	C
Panzer, Missy	1993	Central Arizona, AZ	DP
Pardo, Mary	1996	Ranger, TX	OF
Paul, Lauren	1990	St. Louis/Meramec, MO	OF
Pollard, Cami	1986	Snow, UT	P
Pond, Danita	1987	Rock Valley, IL	IF
Poste, Tracey	1992	Johnson County, KS	IF
Preece, Danielle	1996	Palm Beach CC, FL	IF

— R —

Reinhardt, Cyndi	1989	Lincoln, IL	
Riggs, Keri	1993	Central Arizona, AZ	OF
Riviere, Kris	1987	Illinois Central , IL	OF
Rudanovich, Andrea	1990	St. Louis/Meramec, MO	IF

— S —

Schrader, Brenda	1992	Illinios Central, IL	OF
Schultz, Donna	1987	Lake Michigan, MI	P
Schwebach, Rhonda	1991	Central Arizona, AZ	OF
Simmons, Pam	1990	Central Arizona, AZ	DP
Stout, Ericka	1995	Crowder, MO	C
Sturgeon, Kathleen	1993	Louisburg, NC	C
Swiderski, Janis	1994	St. Louis/Meramec, MO	IF
Szczechowski, Kelly	1993	Lake Michigan, MI	IF

— T —

Toeneboehn, Kristi	1993	Johnson County, KS	OF
Turner, Bekki	1995, 96	Crowder, MO	OF

— U —

Uhde, Kelly	1995, 96	Indian Hills CC, IA	IF

NJCAA ALL-AMERICANS CONTINUED ...

NAME	YEARS	SCHOOL	POSITION
— V —			
Vineyard, Vicky	1992	Lake Michigan, MI	OF
VunKannon, Tracy	1989	St. Louis/Meramec, MO	
— W —			
Ward, Chris	1989	Illinois Central, IL	
Washington, Sara	1995	Lake Michigan, MI	OF
Webster, Joanne	1986	Onondaga CC, NY	IF
Weed, Nicole	1996	Daytona Beach CC,FL	OF
Wilkens, Lisa	1990, 91	Central Arizona, AZ	IF
Williams, April	1992	Crowder, MO	IF
Wyatt, Lisa	1995	Daytona Beach CC, FL	IF
— Y —			
Yanire, Isabelle	1994	Ranger, TX	IF
— Z —			
Zuspann, Angie	1994	Illinois Central, IL	P

CalJC

NAME	YEARS	SCHOOL	POSITION
— A —			
Adams, Carrin	1987	Palomar	OF
Ahumada, Nece	1995	Allan Hancock	P
Allen, Cami	1989	Palomar	
Anderson, Cheryl	1996	Rancho Santiago	P
Andrews, Kristina	1996	Chabot	OF
— B —			
Belford, Augrista	1995, 96	Palomar	IF
Benyak, Chris	1995	Long Beach City	IF
Bolle, Kristi	1996	Rancho Santiago	IF
— C —			
Caldwell, Julie	1987	San Joaquin Delta	SS
Catalano, Angie	1997	San Jose City	C
Clark, Kim	1996	Delta	C
— D —			
Deleon, Veronica	1997	College of the Sequoias	IF
Dennis, Nicki	1987	Sacramento City	IF
Dow, De	1989	Moorpark	IF
— E —			
Escobedo, Cindy	1993, 95	Fullerton	IF
Ewertz, Nikki	1989	Palomar	
— F —			
Fale, Tracey	1997	Palomar	UT
Field, Erin	1994	Sacramento City	P
Flores, Lisa	1996	Palomar	OF
Fode, Candice	1995	Palomar	C
— G —			
Gilley, Shannon	1994	Sacramento City	OF
Graham, Melissa	1994	Fullerton	OF
Gwinner, Autumn	1997	Cypress	IF
— H —			
Haag, Danielle	1997	Sacramento City	P
Hargrave, Deborah	1997	Fullerton	OF

NAME	YEARS	SCHOOL	POSITION
— J —			
Johnson, C.J.	1997	Allan Hancock	OF
— K —			
Kayleffler, Kenda	1989	Palomar	
Kephart, Nicki	1993	Long Beach City	P
Klein, Lyndsey	1997	Sacramento City	IF
— L —			
Lopez, Jenny	1995	Cypress	OF
Luna, Monica	1995	Delta	OF
Lyman, Joyce	1987	Rancho Santiago	P
— M —			
Manley, Christa	1994	Sacramento City	IF
Marrone, Alicia	1993	Palomar	IF
Martinez, Christina	1995	Pasadena	DP
Mazurie, Christina	1994, 95	Rancho	IF
McDonnell, Tiel	1996	West Valley	At-Large/IF
Mendoza, Stephanie	1995	Fullerton	UT
Murano, Renee	1994	Delta CC	C
— O —			
Olive, Audra	1989	Moorpark	
Ontiveros, Kacie	1995	Chabot	P
Osborne, Kristy	1996	Fullerton	UT
Ouzts, Malia	1987	Moorpark	OF
— P —			
Paoli, April	1994	Delta	P
— R —			
Ray, Lyndon	1996	Sacramento City	OF
Redding, Laura	1996	Sacramento City	IF
Reed, Tracy	1994	Delta	OF
Robles, Alicia	1993, 94	Fullerton	P/UT
— S —			
Saindon, Christa	1995, 96	Cypress	IF
Schott, Karrie	1987	Palomar CC	P
Schreiner, Carol	1994	Pasadena CC	DP
Shinn, Cheri	1996	Sacramento City	P
Sickles, Shadie	1997	Long Beach City	OF
Strohman, Jackie	1994	Sacramento City	OF
Sullivan, Shannon	1997	West Valley	IF
Sweeney, Nikki	1995	Long Beach City	OF
— T —			
Taylor, Renee	1995	Rancho	OF
Thomas, Tracy	1996	Long Beach City	DP
Torres, Chris	1994	Hartnell CC	IF
Tracey, Fale	1997	Palomar CC	UT
— V —			
Vandiver, Rachelle	1997	Cypress	OF
Velazquez, Lynette	1997	Fullerton	IF
— W —			
Ward, Kim	1993	Palomar	P
Ward, Shandy	1996	Delta	OF
Wedekind, Tricia	1994	Fullerton	IF

CAL JC ALL-AMERICANS CONTINUED ...

NAME	YEARS	SCHOOL	POSITION
Wilkerson, Kelly	1997	Fullerton	DP
Wilkes, Jaime	1997	Cypress	P
Woods, Raja	1996	Solano	IF

— Z —

NAME	YEARS	SCHOOL	POSITION
Zboril, Chris	1994	Pasadena	IF

HIGH SCHOOL

— B —

NAME	YEARS	SCHOOL	POSITION
Barth, Lindy	1994, 97	Brighton HS, MI	3B
Bauer, Lauren	1995, 97	Foothill HS, CA	OF
Beach, Erica	1997	Chaparral HS, AZ	P
Beard, Lisa	1995	Chelsea HS, MI	UT
Beeler, Shannon	1995	Shelton HS, WA	At-Large
Benet, Jennifer	1993	North Rockland HS, NY	OF
Berggren, Ashley	1994	Barrington HS, IL	1B
Birmingham, Brooke	1997	West Islip HS, NY	UP

— C —

NAME	YEARS	SCHOOL	POSITION
Carey, Lisa	1996	Washburn Rural, KS	At-Large/P
Cassell, Nicole	1994	Brighton HS, MI	OF
Clark, Tiffany	1996	Cajon HS, CA	2B
Cook, Barb	1997	Susquehanna Valley, NY	P
Cooper, Bridget	1997	New Trier HS, IL	2B
Crowell, Clarisa	1997	McDonough HS, MD	At-Large/P

— D —

NAME	YEARS	SCHOOL	POSITION
Dale, Courtney	1994, 95, 96	Bullard HS, CA	P
Darbonne, Candice	1994	Sacred Heart HS, LA	P
Dinger, Laura	1997	Jenison HS, MI	OF
DiPaola, Maria	1995	Eastchester HS, NY	1B

— F —

NAME	YEARS	SCHOOL	POSITION
Fournie, Bridget	1997	Belleville East HS, IL	OF
Franks, Amy	1993	Regina HS, MI	UP
Freed, Amanda	1997	Pacifica HS, CA	P

— G —

NAME	YEARS	SCHOOL	POSITION
Garrett, Amanda	1997	Grapevine HS, TX	C
Grey, Laurie	1993	Charter Oak HS, CA	SS
Gonzales, Janelle	1994	The Linfield School, CA	UT

— H —

NAME	YEARS	SCHOOL	POSITION
Hashimoto, Lisa	1996	Box Elder HS, UT	OF
Hershman, Sarah	1995	Mt. Carmel, CA	2B
Horton, Kim	1997	Clinton HS, MI	At-Large/P
Huske, Danelle	1996	Silver Lake HS, KS	1B

— I —

NAME	YEARS	SCHOOL	POSITION
Iancin, Lisa	1996	Charter Oak HS, CA	SS

NAME	YEARS	SCHOOL	POSITION

— K —

NAME	YEARS	SCHOOL	POSITION
Kennedy, Kelly	1993	Light&Life Christian, MI	1B
	1994	Light&Life Christian	UT
Klier, Korrie	1994	Alleman HS, IL	P
Koehne, Kyree	1996	Brenham HS, TX	OF

— L —

| Lukowski, Amy | 1995 | Lake Fenton HS, MI | P |

— M —

McAllister, Leslie	1997	South Florence HS, SC	1B
McMullen, Julie	1997	San Marcos HS, TX	SS
Martinez, Heather	1996	J. Frank Dobie HS, TX	3B
Meinecke, Rachel	1996	Rochester Adams	OF
Mitchell, Tara	1994	Richlands HS, VA	OF
Mohler, Kathy	1994, 95,	Silver Lake HS, KS	UT
	1996	Silver Lake	At-Large/UT
Moran, Lana	1994, 95, 96	Cajon HS, CA	P
Mortrud, Jennifer	1993	Bethany Christian, IN	1B

— N —

| Navarrete, Angela | 1995 | Cajon HS, CA | OF |
| Norris, Allie | 1993 | Pelham HS, AL | OF |

— P —

| Pasquerella, Jackie | 1995, 96 | Bay Shore HS, NY | 3B |
| Price, Natalie | 1996 | Bishop O'Connell, VA | P |

— R —

| Robison, Lacey | 1994 | Silver Lake HS, KS | UT |

— S —

| Scott, Amanda | 1996 | Clovis HS, CA | P |
| Shipman, Kelly | 1995 | Northern HS, MD | At-Large/UT |

— T —

| Tucker, Christy | 1993 | Charter Oak HS, CA | P |

— V —

Venissat, Erin	1995	Sulphur HS, LA	OF
Vitale, Christina	1994	Regina HS, MI	2B
Vinson, Robyn	1997	Hawley HS, TX	UP

— W —

Ward, Trisha	1993, 94, 95	Sacred Heart HS, LA	SS
White, Jennifer	1997	Tuttle HS, OK	P
Wiginton, Kellie	1994, 95, 96	Bullard HS, CA	C
Williams, Christa	1995, 96	J. Frank Dobie HS, TX	P
Womack, Debbie	1994	Silver Lake HS, KS	OF

— Y —

| Young, Susan | 1993 | North Shore HS, TX | OF |

NFCA HALL OF FAMERS (1986-1997)

Sharron Backus, University of California, Los Angeles
Inducted 1991

During her 21 years as head coach of UCLA, Sharron Backus compiled a record of 847-167-3. She led the Bruins to eight national team championships, while compiling a postseason record of 118-32. Since the NCAA began staging women's championships during the 1981-82 school year, UCLA reached the Women's College World Series 14 of 15 seasons and won seven NCAA crowns, including three straight (1988-90).

She also coached five players who won the Honda Broderick Award, presented to the sport's top player, a total of eight times in 12 seasons. No less than 29 of her players earned All-American acclaim a total of 53 times. Backus has been selected to the NFCA Hall of Fame, Amateur Softball Association Hall of Fame and the Women's Sports Foundation Hall of Fame. She also coached Olympic gold medalists Dot Richardson, Lisa Fernandez and Sheila Cornell.

Mike Candrea, University of Arizona
Inducted 1996

At the end of the 1997 softball season, Arizona head coach Mike Candrea had won his fifth NCAA Women's College World Series title. He was honored in 1996 and 1997 as the Speedline/NFCA Division I National Coach of the Year as his Wildcat team claimed the Women's College World Series crowns both those years.

Under Candrea's direction, Arizona had made the NCAA regional tournament 11 consecutive times and had been in the Women's College World Series 10 straight years by 1997. That season was his sixth 50th-win season in seven years. After going 61-5 in '97, Candrea improved his record at Arizona to 627-139 and his 12-year overall record to 795-205. He had been named the Pacific Region Coach of the Year three consecutive years and had been named the Pacific-10 Conference Coach of the Year four times as his teams won conference titles in four of six seasons (1992, 1994, 1995 and 1997).

Candrea had trememdous success at Central Arizona College for five seasons. While at the junior college, Candrea won a pair of National Junior College Athletic Association (NJCAA) championships in 1984 and 1985.

Connie Claussen, University of Nebraska, Omaha

Inducted 1996 — Pioneer Category

Nebraska-Omaha Associate Athletic Director Connie Claussen has nurtured the growth of women's athletics at UNO since its inception. A graduate of the institution, formerly known as Omaha University, she was chairing the department in two years. During that time, she began laying the groundwork for what has become one of the top programs in NCAA Division II. She has served on several NCAA Division II national committees, including the NCAA Executive Committee and as chair of the NCAA Division II Championships Committee. She was a member of the UNO Alumni Board and was given the Chancellor's Medal in 1981.

Claussen is the first woman member of the UNO Athletic Hall of Fame and has been inducted into the Omaha Benson High School Hall of Fame. In 1969, Claussen started a women's athletic program at the school. She became the school's softball coach in 1970, compiling a record of 98-57 from 1970 to 1977. During the course of her softball coaching tenure, Claussen won the national championship in 1975.

Connie spent 12 years as the chair for the Women's College World Series/Omaha Softball Association Committee. Claussen and her committee started the collegiate women's softball championship in 1969.

Linda Draft, University of Wisconsin, Parkside

Inducted 1991

In 15 seasons as the head softball coach at Wisconsin-Parkside, Linda Draft compiled a record of 357-229-2. During her time as head coach at the Kenosha, Wisconsin, school, Draft led her squad to the NAIA national tournament eight times.

In 1990, her team finished fourth at the national tournament and Draft was honored by being inducted into the National Softball Coaches Association Hall of Fame. In 1997, Draft was an associate athletic director at Wisconsin-Parkside, and she had served on the Great Lakes Valley Conference's Executive Committee and as the GLVC's Softball Coaches Committee Chair. She also served as an ASA Council Representative from 1986-1991.

Sharon Drysdale, Northwestern University

Inducted 1994

After completing 19 seasons at Northwestern in 1997, Sharon Drysdale had guided her Wildcats to five Big 10 League titles, more than any other Big 10 school. Drysdale's career record in 19 years was 590-428-3. Named the Big 10 Coach of the Year three times (1984, 87 and 95), Drysdale reached a personal milestone in 1996 when she recorded her 500th victory as NU's head coach on April 10 with a 4-0 victory over Loyola-Chicago. The Wildcats made three consecutive Women's College World Series appearances during her tenure from 1984 to 1986 and reached the NCAA regional tournament in 1987. Northwestern took third place at the 1984 WCWS, fifth in 1985 and seventh in 1986. Under her tutelage, the Wildcats have put together 10 30-win seasons, including six in a row from 1982 to 1987. Drysdale came to NU from Kansas, where she compiled a 64-17 mark and directed the Jayhawks to a top 10 finish in the AIAW softball championship in each season of her four-year tenure. At Kansas, she also served as field hockey coach for two years, basketball coach for one year and director of women's athletics for two years.

Judi Garman, California State University, Fullerton

Inducted 1993

After completing her 26th year of coaching in 1997, Judi Garman was the winningest all-time coach in the history of the National Fastpitch Coaches Association. Her career record, including her years at Golden West College, was an amazing 1,056-358. Garman reached her 1,000th career win on March 7, 1996, with a 1-0 win over Long Beach State. The first 211 victories came at Golden West from 1972 through 1979.

Her inaugural Cal State Fullerton team finished third in the West Coast Athletic Association and ninth at the AIAW national championship. Since then, Garman's teams have won or shared eight conference titles and seven regional championships, while finishing second in the Women's College World Series in 1981, 1983 and 1985; third in 1982 and 1987; fifth in 1995 and first in the 1986 NCAA championship. Very involved professionally, Garman served as president of the National Softball Coaches Association from 1990 to 1991. Garman graduating from the University of Saskatchewan in 1966, and then went to California where she earned her master's degree from the University of California, Santa Barbara.

At Golden West, she also coached basketball and cross country. She led the Rustlers to a junior college national championship in 1978 and California JC title in 1979.

Betty Hoff, Luther College
Inducted 1992

In 1997, Betty Hoff had coached 29 years at NCAA Division III institution Luther College in Decorah, Iowa. In her 29 seasons at the controls of the Luther College softball program, Hoff ranked 23rd among active Division III coaches with a .623 winning percentage. She ranked first in career victories with a career record of 458-265.

She coached Luther to the Iowa Intercollegiate Athletic Conference championship four times, and made it to the NCAA Division III Women's Softball Championship final six three times. Her best finish was fourth place in 1985.

In both 1990 and 1991, the Norse finished fifth at the NCAA tournament. Luther College softball has participated in postseason regional play eight times since 1985. Hoff is also a professor of health and physical education and head of the Luther College athletic training program.

Mary Littlewood, Arizona State University
Inducted 1995 — Pioneer Category

During 19 years at the Arizona State helm, Mary Littlewood amassed a 468-202-1 (.699 winning percentage) win-loss record. In addition, she saw her teams qualify for nine Women's College World Series, including national championships in 1972 and 1973. Arizona State finished fourth on four occasions (1971, 1976, 1977 and 1982), seventh once (1987) and ninth twice (1978 and 1979). She coached the Sun Devils in five NCAA regionals, including four in five seasons (1984-87).

The Sun Devils won three conference championships during Littlewood's tenure and she was named the 1986 Pacific West Conference co-coach of the year. Coach Littlewood coached six All-Americans and more than 30 all-conference players. Littlewood went to Arizona State in 1965 and taught physical education, coaching several sports until 1976 when she was appointed to the dual position of softball and volleyball coach. Three years later, in 1979, she relinquished her volleyball duties and concentrated on softball. A standout athlete during her collegiate career, Littlewood lettered in five sports at Miami (Ohio) University in Oxford, Ohio.

Judy Martino,
University of North Carolina
Inducted 1993 — Founder's Award

Judy Martino began her coaching career in 1978 as head coach at South Carolina. Nearly 20 years later, Martino is a pioneer once again as she is the head coach of the Carolina Diamonds in the Women's Professional Fastpitch league that had its inaugural season in 1997. Martino played ASA women's major fastpitch starting at age 14 and began coaching even before she was out of high school. After graduating from college in 1971, she coached high school ball in Florida while playing for the Orlando Rebels. From there she took her talents to South Carolina. Although she was only at the school for three years, she directed the Lady Gamecocks to top 10 finishes each season and made the AIAW national tournament. Martino left South Carolina after the 1981 season to go to graduate school at North

Carolina, where she was also an assistant coach in both softball and volleyball for two years. It was at this time that Martino decided to stop coaching collegiate softball and work on forming the National Fastpitch Coaches Association. She served as the executive director from 1982 to 1986. Martino played in the first pro-softball league as a catcher for the league champion Connecticut Falcons.

Mary Nutter,
National Sports Clinics
Inducted 1997 — Pioneer Category

After a successful eight-year career as head coach at Pittsburg State (KS), where she posted an overall record of 204-125, Nutter became the executive director of National Sports Clinics. Her clinics are among the top softball clinics in the country and feature some of the nation's most notable clinicians.

Nutter was an outstanding player for the Lansing Laurels, an ASA women's major fastpitch team, and she spent one year (1976) as a player/coach for the Michigan Travelers of the Women's Professional Softball League. Nutter was twice named women's major first team All-American, in 1974 and 1975.

She began teaching in 1970 in Elsie, Michigan. She taught there until 1977 when she began her collegiate coaching career as a graduate assistant at Michigan State. She spent three seasons there before moving to Pittsburg State.

In 1981, she claimed her first of three NAIA District 10 championships and District 10 Coach of the Year awards. She was named District 10 Coach of the Year in 1981, 1982 and 1985. Her 1981 Pittsburg team finished fourth at the NAIA national championship. She also served as an assistant coach for the 1983 Pan American Tri-Nations team and as a member of the 1984 U.S. Pan American selection committee. She was honored in 1988 as an inductee of the NAIA Hall of Fame.

Gerry Pinkston, University of Central Oklahoma

Inducted 1995

Dr. Gerry Pinkston ended her 22-year coaching career at Central Oklahoma with a 418-271-1 record, resigning at the conclusion of the 1997 season. Pinkston has led UCO to 20-win seasons in five of the past six years, with the Lady Bronchos averaging 22 wins a season in the 1990's. The Lady Bronchos flourished under Pinkston while members of the NAIA and averaged nearly 25 wins in a season in the decade of the 1980's (245-150). UCO was regularly ranked in the NAIA top 20, rising as high as fifth in the country in 1988. Central Oklahoma joined NCAA Division II in 1990 and struggled to a 17-19 mark that first year before reeling off four-consecutive 20-win seasons, capped by a 30-15 mark in 1994 when the Lady Bronchos broke into the NCAA Division II top 20 rankings for the first time.

Pinkston started her coaching career at Chickasha High School, serving as tennis coach for two years before coming to UCO in 1975 as the softball, tennis and volleyball coach. She directed the tennis team for one year and was the volleyball coach for seven seasons, compiling a 131-109 record. In 1998, she was still teaching at Central Oklahoma.

Lorene Ramsey, Illinois Central College

Inducted 1992

By 1997, Lorene Ramsey, women's softball coach at Illinois Central College in East Peoria, Illinois, finished her 28th year coaching the Lady Cougars with a cumulative record of 783 wins and 239 losses. Ramsey, honored in both the NFCA Hall of Fame and the Illinois Softball Association Hall of Fame, was selected to coach four United States Pan American softball teams. She was an alternate coach for the 1996 USA Olympic Softball Team. She is a member of the Illinois High School Girls Association Hall of Fame, Illinois State University Hall of Fame and the National Amateur Softball Association Hall of Fame.

She also earned outstanding records pitching for the Pekin-Lettes Softball team. The Lettes' game record during her pitching reign was 401 wins and 90 losses with 3,800 strikeouts. She pitched 12 national tournaments, was a four-time ASA All-American selection and was a member of the Hummers Professional Women's Softball League coaching staff.

Ramsey also coaches basketball at Illinois Central and has won three NJCAA national championships in the sport.

Judy Sherman, Pacific University
Inducted 1992

In her career, former Pacific University head coach Judy Sherman had a softball coaching record of 418-146, which was good enough for a career winning percentage of .741 and is one of the highest winning percentages in the history of collegiate softball. Currently, Sherman is the athletic director and chair of the exercise science division at Pacific University. She has held that position since 1991. She is also still heavily involved with softball as she is a member of the ASA National Team Selection Committee, which will ultimately be responsible for the selection of the 2,000 United States Olympic Softball Team. Sherman was inducted into the NAIA National Hall of Fame in 1988.

As a softball coach at the Forest Grove, Oregon, school, Sherman directed her team to seven NAIA national softball tournaments in which they finished ninth once, seventh four times, fourth once and third once. Her squads competed in district softball tournaments 10 years and were in nine bi-district softball championships. Like other NFCA Hall of Fame members, Sherman not only produced great players, but also great students. Her teams produced five Academic All-Americans as well as five NAIA All-Americans. In one season, Sherman won conference championships in both volleyball and softball. Her teams competed in three AIAW national tournaments.

Carol Spanks, University of Nevada, Las Vegas
Inducted 1994

UNLV Associate Head Coach Carol Spanks had spent 18 years as a collegiate coach and had compiled a career record of 688-375-5 by 1997. Spanks spent 15 seasons as the head coach at Cal Poly Pomona. She posted a record of 577-310-5 (.650 winning percentage) with the Broncos while leading her teams to 11 postseason appearances (three AIAW and eight NCAA). Her teams advanced to the Women's College World Series five times with the 1979 and 1988 squads finishing third in the nation. While serving as head coach at Cal Poly Pomona, nine Bronco players were named to the All-American team and 16 were selected as first team All-Big West.

Spanks also has an extensive international coaching career. Besides her stint as assistant at the 1985 world championships, Spanks served as the head coach of the USA team at the 1995 South Pacific Classic in Australia where her team captured the gold medal and was the head coach of the Pan American Games squad that also captured the gold medal in 1987. She was an assistant for the 1987 Tri-Nations and the 1994 world championships, all of which won gold medals. Before coaching internationally, Spanks was a player on the 1970 USA world championship team.

June Walker, Trenton State College
Inducted 1992

In 22 years as head coach at Trenton State (now College of New Jersey), June Walker compiled an amazing record of 721-154 (.825 winning percentage). Her 721 victories ranked her No. 1 all time in NCAA Division III and No. 3 all time for all NCAA softball coaches. Her .825 winning percentage is also No. 1 among all NCAA softball coaches, as of 1997.

Some of Dr. Walker's career highlights include: 65 All-Americans (more than any other coach, Division I, II or III); 48 first team All-Americans, more than any other coach; 16 consecutive national tournament berths, including 16 national semifinal berths. Under Walker's reign at Trenton State, the Lions also produced 13 GTE Academic All-Americans and seven Division III National Player of the Year Awards. Currently, six of her former players are now collegiate softball head coaches. Walker molded Trenton State into the most powerful Division III softball program during her tenure with a total of five NCAA Division III national championships (1983, 1987, 1989, 1992 and 1994). She also coached a pair of U.S. national team members and two GTE Academic All-Americans of the Year.

Linda Wells, Arizona State University
Inducted 1991

Arizona State's tradition of softball excellence has flourished under the tutelage of eight-year head coach Linda Wells, one of the winningest active coaches in the NCAA. She has led the Sun Devils to four NCAA regional appearances in eight seasons, compiling a record of 263-210 (.546 winning percentage).

A native of Pacific, Missouri, Wells was a three-sport athlete in high school and played five sports — softball, volleyball, basketball, tennis and field hockey — at Southeast Missouri State. An all-around athlete, she competed at the national level in volleyball (USVBA), basketball (AAU), field hockey (USFHA) and softball (ASA). Wells played 18 years of women's major fastpitch, first as a shortstop and then as a pitcher and catcher at the end of her career. She began her coaching career in 1973 at Minnesota, where she led three different sports to national championship competition.

Wells served as head volleyball coach (1974-81). During her softball-coaching tenure, Wells led the Golden Gophers to three Big 10 softball crowns and compiled a 362-176-1 record. Her career coaching record is 619-486 (.560 winning percentage/23 seasons), as of 1997, and she is a past president of the NSCA.

Marge Willadsen, Buena Vista University

Inducted 1997

Marge Willadsen, head coach at Buena Vista University for 17 years, has led her team to the NCAA Division III championship five times, winning the national championship in 1984.

By the close of the 1997 season, Willadsen had amassed a 398-226 record and had earned two NFCA coach of the year titles, in 1984 and in 1996. In both 1983 and 1992, her squads finished second at the NCAA championship. In addition, Buena Vista placed third in 1989 and fifth in 1994.

Willadsen was named West Region coach of the year in 1992, 1993, 1994 and 1996. She also has been honored as her conference's coach of the year in 1983, 1984, 1992 and 1995. She was given the Buena Vista University Presidential Citation in 1984 and is one of only two recipients to ever receive this award at her school.

Willadsen has produced 19 All-Americans, seven GTE All-Americans and 31 academic All-Americans. She has served on the NCAA Division III Women's Softball Committee, as well as on the West Region ranking subcommittee. Willadsen has been a member of the NFCA since its inception.

1887
George Hancock created the game of indoor baseball, played for the first time in the gymnasium of the Farragut Boat Club in Chicago. Because of the shorter base and pitching distances, it is felt that this game was the origin of modern day softball.

1895
The first women's indoor baseball team was organized at Chicago's West Division High School.

1900
Lewis Rober Sr., a lieutenant in the Minneapolis fire department, took the game outdoors so that his men would have something to do during their leisure time. It was named "kitten ball" after his team, the Kittens.

1908
The first Playground Ball Rulebook was published. The rules were unique in that the first batter in each inning determined in which direction to run after hitting the ball — to first base or to third base. All other batters that inning followed suit.

1922
The name of the outdoor game was changed to diamond ball. Indoor baseball was still being played by men and women.

1933
The first world championships were held in conjunction with the Century of Progress Exposition in Chicago. A total of 70,000 spectators watched the men's and women's competitions.

1934
The first national rules committee met at the Hotel Sherman in Chicago. The major outcomes of the meeting were the writing of the first universal set of rules, the decision to call the game softball, and the formation of the Amateur Softball Association of America. This first set of rules allowed for 10 players on a team and disallowed bunting.

1937
The Fiedler Field League and the San Gabriel Valley Girls Niteball League were strong in the Los Angeles area. A total of 88 teams participated in the ASA world championships held at Soldier Field in Chicago. The first national radio broadcast did a play-by-play of the important games.

1939
The Phoenix Cantaloupe Queens (later the A-1 Queens) played before 18,000 and 21,000 fans in two nights of games in Madison Square Garden.

1940
The ASA claimed that more than five million people played the game of softball. The New Orleans Jax, with Freda and Olympia Savona, Nina Korgan and Lottie Jackson, and the PBSW Ramblers, with Dot Wilkinson, Margie Law and Amy Peralta, dominated national play during the 1940's.

1942	The ASA started "Miss Softball of America" contests in conjunction with the world championships.
1943	The All-American Girls Professional Baseball League was started in the Midwest by P.K. Wrigley and some of his associates. During the first two years, the game played resembled softball with underhand pitching, but, by 1946, the pitching was overhand and the game was baseball.
1944	The National Girls Baseball League was started in Chicago by Charley Bidwill, owner of the Chicago Cardinals football team, and Emery Parichy. The game played was softball.
1947	Larry Walker, manager of the Phoenix A-1 Queens and unhappy with the ASA, started his own organization, the National Softball Congress.
1948	Billie Harris, the first African-American woman to be inducted into the ASA Hall of Fame, started her playing career with the Tucson Sunshine Girls. A total 279,000 fans saw the Phoenix A-1 Queens play a 153-game schedule.
1949	For the first time, the men's and women's championships were held separately.
1950	Bertha Ragan, pitcher for the Orange Lionettes, was emerging as one of the most successful and durable players ever to play women's fastpitch softball. The Orange Lionettes, with Bertha Ragan and Ruth Sears, and the Fresno Rockets, with Kay Rich, Ginny Busick, Gloria May and Jeanne Contel, won the title eight times during this decade.
1951	Madeline Lorton, 25, of the Bronx, New York, became the first registered female umpire with the ASA. She umped 35 games that first season. There were, at that time, a total of 5,000 male umpires. It wasn't until 1967 that the second female umpire appeared.
1952	The International Softball Federation held its first meeting. This organization would govern all international play. It wasn't until 1965, however, that the ISF became very active.
1954	The All-American Girls Profrressional Baseball League, the National Girls Baseball League and the National Softball Congress were discontinued.
1955	Bertha Ragan pitched 69 games for the Orange Lionettes and led them to a world championship title.

1956
Bertha Ragan joined the Raybestos Brakettes.

1957
The National Joint Committee for Extramural Sports for College Women began its work.

1958
Bertha Ragan and rookie Joan Joyce teamed up to pitch the Brakettes to their first world championship title. This was the beginning of a dynasty unequaled in sports history.

1960
The Division for Girls and Women's Sport (DGWS) was a powerful organization in the growth of women's athletics in the 1960's and 1970's.

1961
Television cameras appeared for the first time at the 1961 ASA World Championships as ABC taped coverage of the crucial games.

1962
Women's fastpitch softball continued to be one of the most popular sports to watch in the country. The Pekin-Lettes in Illinois drew a total of 20,000 fans to watch a two-game series they played against a team from Japan.

1965
The first ISF world championships were held in Melbourne, Australia. The Raybestos Brakettes, representing the United States, were defeated in the final game, 1-0, by Australia. The PBSW Ramblers from Phoenix, Arizona, disbanded after having been a national contender for three decades. Several other major teams that were founded in the 1930's and '40's followed suit.

1967
The Commission on Intercollegiate Athletics for Women (CIAW) — the direct foremother of AIAW — began to function.

1968
Bertha Ragan Tickey, one of the all-time greats, retired from the game.

1969
First Women's College World Series, co-sponsored by DGWS and ASA, was held in Omaha, Nebraska.

1970
Over 15 million Americans were playing some form of softball regularly.

1971
The Commission on Intercollegiate Athletics for Women (CIAW) became the Association of Intercollegiate Athletics for Women (AIAW).

1972
Title IX, a federal legislation that has affected the future of female athletes in the United States more than any other in history, was passed on June 23, 1972. Title IX of the Education Amendments to the Civil Rights Act of 1964 is a federal law that states: No person . . . shall, on the basis of sex, be excluded from

1972 participation in, be denied the benefits of, or be subjected to discrimination under any educational programs or activities receiving federal financial assistance. The AIAW took over complete control of women's intercollegiate athletics.

1973 The Amateur Softball Association (ASA) opened its Hall of Fame in Oklahoma City.

1974 The ASA started its youth program — a program designed to provide quality instruction and playing experiences for the youth of the country. In 1974, there were 6,207 registered teams in the ASA's youth program.

1975 Many of the strongest players in the country retired from amateur softball in order to join the International Women's Professional Softball Association that was scheduled to start in 1976. Among these players was Joan Joyce, one of the most dominating players in the history of women's fastpitch softball. The National Junior College Athletic Association approved a women's division.

1976 The International Women's Professional Softball Association (IWPSA) was founded and made its debut on May 28. The Connecticut Falcons, led by Joan Joyce and the Raybestos Brakettes team, dominated the league and won the title. The number of colleges having women's fastpitch teams increased from 120 in 1971-72, to 342 in 1975-76.

1977 Ellsworth Community College from Iowa Falls, Iowa, won the first NJCAA National Softball Championships. The number of high schools having girls fastpitch teams increased from 373 (9,813 athletes) in 1970-71 to 6,496 (133,458 athletes) in 1976-77.

1979 For the first time in its history, softball was played at the Pan American Games. The U.S. women's team won the gold medal. AIAW severed its relationship with the NAGWS.

1980 The IWPSA folded after struggling financially for four years. The Women's College World Series became the national championship for AIAW with AIAW as the sole sponsor.

1981 The National Association of Intercollegiate Athletics (NAIA) conducted national championships for women.

1982 UCLA won the first women's NCAA Division I Women's Softball Championship. AIAW conducted 39 national championships in 19 sports. This was the last year of operation for the AIAW.

1983 The total number of women's teams registered with the ASA was 37,651, a stunning rise from the 5,361 teams 10 years earlier (1973).

1984	The dominance in ASA women's softball moved from the East Coast (Raybestos Brakettes) to the West Coast. California teams began to dominate the national scene because of the quality of their ASA Junior Olympic teams and the strength of the collegiate programs.
1991	On June 13, the International Olympic Committee added softball to its list of medal sports for the 1996 Olympic Games.
1992	More than 250,000 teams were registered with the ASA.
1995	There were 2,806 women's fastpitch teams, and 71,036 girls youth teams registered with the ASA. Of all participants in fastpitch softball, 62 percent were female; 39 percent were between the ages of 12 & 17; and 69 percent were from metropolitan areas with a population in excess of 500,000. Fastpitch softball ranked as the fourth most popular program for girls in high school athletic programs with a total of 11,452 schools and 305,217 girls participating.
1996	For the first time in the history of the Olympic Games, women's fastpitch softball was played as a medal sport. The United States women's fastpitch softball team won the gold medal in Columbus, Georgia.
1997	The number of NCAA collegiate programs increased from a total of 441 in 1983 to 767 in 1997.

Lisa Fernandez presented First Lady Hillary Rodham Clinton with a Louisville Slugger fastpitch bat during a 1995 visit to the White House in honor of National Women and Girls in Sports Day. The event was sponsored by the Women's Sports Foundation.

Softball Organizations in 1998

Source: NFCA, 1997

American Fastpitch Association (AFA)
2536 Greenacre Avenue
Anaheim, CA 92801
714/952-9311

The American Fastpitch Association began in Anaheim, California, in 1980 and has grown to over 14,000 teams participating in three countries and 46 states. The AFA ranges from 12-under all the way to 18-under and offers tournaments at the local, state, national and international level for those age groups. There is also an open league for ages 18 and above.

Amateur Softball Association (ASA)
2801 NE 50th Street
Oklahoma City, OK 73111
405/424-5266
405/424-3855 fax

The ASA is the national governing body of amateur softball in the United States, including regulating ASA competition to assure fairness and equal opportunity to the thousands of teams, umpires and sponsors who play the sport. There are more than 73,000 Junior Olympic (youth) teams, including slowpitch, and ASA sponsors national championships in six different age groups, ranging from 10-under through 18-Gold.

ASA also offers national championships in both women's and men's major fastpitch leagues. There are approximately 2,300 women's fastpitch teams and around the same number for men.

Bobby Sox
P.O. Box 5880
Buena Park, CA 90622
714/522-1234

While remaining regional, only played in five states, Bobby Sox Softball has over 40,000 players. Bobby Sox Softball, in its 34th season, is played in Arizona, California, Hawaii, Nevada and Utah. The league is based around local league play with an all-star team selected from each league to participate in district tournaments and a National Tournament of Champions.

Bobby Sox also offers a winter league in which local leagues can put together a team in an all-star format. In 1995, Bobby Sox saw 276 teams participate in its winter league. Bobby Sox age groups are: 5-8; 8-9; 9-11; 12-13; 12-15; 15-18.

Dixie Softball, Inc.
P.O. Box 109
Adamsville, AL 35005
205/785-2255

Dixie Softball is comprised of approximately 70,000 girls playing both slowpitch and fastpitch. Dixie is played in 11 states, all in the south. There are no travel teams involved in Dixie. League seasons run from 15 to no more than 25 league games. At the end of the season, leagues choose an all-star team that advances to sub-district play. From there, teams can advance to district and state tournaments all the way to the Dixie World Series.

There are six different age groups in Dixie Softball, ranging from the SweeTees (6-under, T-Ball) to the Debs (18-under). The three youngest age groups do not play a World Series, but Dixie does offer a World Series in its three oldest age groups, both fastpitch and slowpitch.

National Fastpitch Coaches Association (NFCA)
409 Vandiver Drive, Suite 5-202
Columbia, MO 65202
573/875-3033 • 573/875-2924 fax • http://www.nfca.org

Founded in 1983, the NFCA is the professional growth organization for fastpitch softball coaches at all levels of play. In addition, it invites non-coaching members to join as affiliate members. Benefits include 16 issues of the NFCA's own newspaper, *Fastpitch Delivery*; annual copies of the NFCA Directory and Calendar; discounts on softball coaching videos and books; a national convention; awards programs, and more. To find out more information, contact the NFCA at 573/875-3033.

National Softball Association (NSA)
P.O. Box 23403
Lexington, KY 40523
606/887-4114

The NSA holds its championships for its five age groups for girls fastpitch at one site at the same time. In 1995, in Jupiter, Florida, there were 358 teams all playing at one site. The NSA offers both recreational play and competitive play. It is in 40 states, and to qualify for the World Series, a team must win a qualifying tournament, compete in the state tournament or win a direct berth through various invitational tournaments. The NSA also offers national championships in women's and men's fastpitch as well.

The age groups involved in the NSA's youth fastpitch program range from 12-under to 18-under, with all five age groups having a World Series.

Pony Softball
412/225-9852 Fax

PONY Softball began in 1982 and while it is divided into four sections of the country — Northeast, South, West and East — it is growing by leaps and bounds. PONY offers both fastpitch and slowpitch for its participants. The organization has tournaments at the local and national level. It has seven different age groups ranging from the Shetland Girls (6-under), through the Palomino Girls (18-under). In between these two age groups are the Pinto Girls (8-under), Mustang Girls (10-under), Bronco Girls (12-under), Pony Girls (14-under) and Colt Girls (16-under).

USSSA
3935 S. Crater Road
Petersburg, Virginia 23805
804/732-4099

The United States Specialty Sports Association was founded in 1968 primarily as a slow pitch organization. With high schools and colleges emphasizing fastpitch, the USSSA started its Girl's fastpitch program in 1994 and by 1997 had grown to over 3,000 teams. In 1997, the USSSA offered seven national invitational tournaments with the season highlighted by world tournaments for 12, 14, 16, and 18-under age groups.

BIBIOGRAPHY

BOOKS
1. Bealle, Morris A. *The Softball Story*. Columbia Publishing Co., P.O. Box 1623, Washington D. C., 1957.
2. Carruth, Gorton. *What Happened When — A Chronology of Life & Events in America*. Harper & Row Publishers, Inc., 1991.
3. Claflin, Edward. *The Irresistible American Softball Book*. Doubleday & Co., Inc., Garden City, N. Y., 1978.
4. Dickson, Paul. *The Worth Book of Softball*. Facts on File, New York, N. Y., 1994.
5. Eastman Kodak Co., & Thomasson —Grant. *At the Rim — A Celebration of Women's Collegiate Basketball, 1991*.
6. Fischer, Leo H. *How To Play Winning Softball*. Prentice - Hall, Inc., N. Y.,1940.
7. Gerber, Ellen. *The American Woman in Sport*. Addison — Wesley Publishing Co., Phillipines, 1974.
8. Gorn, Elliott and Warren Goldstein. *A Brief History of American Sports*. Hill & Wang — A Division of Farrar, Straus & Giroux, 1993.
9. Guttman, Allen. *Women's Sports — A History*. Columbia University Press, N. Y., 1991.
10. Hult, Joan & Marianna Trekell (Edited By). *A Century of Women's Basketball — From Frailty to Final Four*. American Alliance for Health, Physical Education, Recreation & Dance, 1991.
11. Lipsyte, Robert and Peter Levine. *Idols of the Game — A Sporting History of the American Century*. Turner Publishing, Inc., Atlanta, 1995.
12. Meyer, Gladys C. *Softball for Girls and Women*. Charles Scribner's Sons, New York, 1982.
13. Palmer, Gladys. *Baseball for Girls and Women*. A.S. Barnes and Company, New York, 1929.
14. Reeder, Amy L. and John R. Fuller. *Women in Sport — Sociological and Historical Perspectives*. Darby Printing Co., Atlanta, Georgia, 1985.
15. Remley, Mary Lou. *Women in Sport: A Guide to Information Sources*. Gale Research Company, Detroit, Michigan, 1980.
16. Shoebridge, Michele. *Women in Sport — A Select Bibliography*. Mansell Publishing Limited, London and New York, 1987.
17. Wetterau, Bruce. *Book of Chronologies*. Prentice — Hall Press, N. Y., 1990.

THESES
18. Dillahunt, Betty Jane. *The History and Organization of Softball for Girls and Women in the United States*. The Ohio State University, 1953.
19. Garman, Judith Fay. *A Study of Attitudes Toward Softball Competition for Women*. University of California, Santa Barbara, June 1969.

NEWSPAPERS/MAGAZINES
20. *Arizona Highways*, August, 1949.
21. *The Arizona Republic*, January, 1997.
22. *The New York Times Magazine*, June 23, 1996.
23. *Reader's Digest*, June, 1939.
24. *ASA Balls and Strikes*, March, 1957.
25. *Women's Fastpitch World*, August, 1989.
26. *History of the Fresno Rockets*. Sandy Taylor.

PHOTOS AND ILLUSTRATIONS

WARNING — DISCLAIMER

Every effort has been made to make this book as complete and accurate as possible. However, there may be mistakes, both typographical and in content. If you find an error, please write the NFCA at 409 Vandiver Drive, Suite 5-202, Columbia, MO 65202, so that the material can be corrected in a future reprint.

The purpose of this book is to educate and entertain. The author and the National Fastpitch Coaches Association shall have neither liability nor responsibility to any person or entity with respect to any loss or damage caused, or alleged to be caused, directly or indirectly by the information contained within.

If you do not wish to be bound by the above, you may return this book, if undamaged, to the publisher for a refund.

INDEX